CONTENTS AT A GLA

TABLE OF CONTENTS

iPad® and iPhone®
Tips and Tricks

Jason R. Rich

que®

800 East 96th Street
Indianapolis, Indiana 46240 USA

iPAD® AND iPHONE® TIPS AND TRICKS
SECOND EDITION

ISBN-13: 978-0-7897-5096-9
ISBN-10: 0-7897-5096-1

The Library of Congress cataloging-in-publication data is on file.

Printed in the United States of America

First Printing: December 2012

BULK SALES

Que Publishing offers excellent discounts on this book when ordered in quantity for bulk purchases or special sales. For more information, please contact

U.S. Corporate and Government Sales
1-800-382-3419
corpsales@pearsontechgroup.com

For sales outside the United States, please contact

International Sales
international@pearson.com

EDITOR-IN-CHIEF
Greg Wiegand

ACQUISITIONS EDITOR
Laura Norman

DEVELOPMENT EDITOR
Jennifer Ackerman-Kettell

MANAGING EDITOR
Kristy Hart

PROJECT EDITOR
Jovana Shirley

INDEXER
Lisa Stumpf

PROOFREADER
Sheri Replin

TECHNICAL EDITOR
Greg Kettell

PUBLISHING COORDINATOR
Cindy Teeters

BOOK DESIGNER
Anne Jones

COMPOSITOR
Bumpy Design

ONLINE CONTENT

The following online-only content can be downloaded from
www.quepublishing.com/title/9780789750969.

ABOUT THE AUTHOR

Jason R. Rich (www.JasonRich.com) is the bestselling author of more than 55 books, as well as a frequent contributor to a handful of major daily newspapers, national magazines, and popular websites. He's also an accomplished photographer, and an avid Apple iPhone 5, iPad, Apple TV, and Mac user.

Jason R. Rich is the author of the book *Your iPad at Work: 3rd Edition*, as well *OS X Mountain Lion Tips and Tricks*, both published by Que Publishing. He's also written *How To Do Everything MacBook Air* and *How To Do Everything iPhone 5* for McGraw-Hill.

More than 100 feature-length how-to articles by Jason R. Rich, covering the Apple iPhone and iPad, can be read free online at the Que Publishing website. Visit www.iOSArticles.com and click on the Articles tab. You can also follow Jason R. Rich on Twitter (@JasonRich7).

DEDICATION

I am honored to dedicate this book to Steve Jobs (1955–2011), a true visionary, entrepreneur, and pioneer, and who forever changed the world. My condolences to his family, friends, and coworkers at Apple, and to those whose lives he touched. Thank you, Mr. Jobs…For everything.

ACKNOWLEDGMENTS

Thanks to Laura Norman at Que Publishing for inviting me to work on this book, and for all of her guidance as I've worked on this project. My gratitude also goes out to Greg Wiegand, Jovana Shirley, Cindy Teeters, Jennifer Ackerman-Kettell, Greg Kettell, and Paul Boger, as well as everyone else at Que Publishing/Pearson who contributed their expertise, hard work, and creativity to the creation of this all-new edition of *iPad and iPhone Tips and Tricks*.

Thanks also to my friends and family for their ongoing support. Finally, thanks to you, the reader. I hope this book helps you fully utilize your iOS device in every aspect of your life, and take full advantage of the power and functionality your iPhone and/or iPad offers.

WE WANT TO HEAR FROM YOU!

As the reader of this book, *you* are our most important critic and commentator. We value your opinion and want to know what we're doing right, what we could do better, what areas you'd like to see us publish in, and any other words of wisdom you're willing to pass our way.

We welcome your comments. You can email or write to let us know what you did or didn't like about this book—as well as what we can do to make our books better.

Please note that we cannot help you with technical problems related to the topic of this book.

When you write, please be sure to include this book's title and author as well as your name and email address. We will carefully review your comments and share them with the author and editors who worked on the book.

Email: feedback@quepublishing.com

Mail: Que Publishing
ATTN: Reader Feedback
800 East 96th Street
Indianapolis, IN 46240 USA

READER SERVICES

Visit our website and register this book at quepublishing.com/register for convenient access to any updates, downloads, or errata that might be available for this book.

Introduction

Whether you're a new iPhone, iPad or iPad mini user who just purchased an Apple mobile device that runs iOS 6, or you're a veteran iPhone and/or iPad user who has witnessed firsthand the evolution of the iOS operating system and have recently upgraded your device to run the latest and greatest of Apple's device operating systems (or you're about to), you're in for an amazing experience.

> **TIP** To determine what model iPhone or iPad you're using, and what version of the iOS operating system it's currently running, launch Settings from the Home Screen. When the main Settings menu appears, tap on the General option. From the General menu, tap on the About option. Scroll down on the About screen to determine the iOS version number and the model number of your device. The model number will be displayed as an Apple code, such as MD634LL or MC775LL. You can then visit the

online-based Apple Store (http://store.apple.com) and enter the model number into the Search field to determine which model and configuration iPhone or iPad you're holding in your hands.

Released in September 2012, Apple's iOS 6 operating system not only enables your iPhone, iPad, iPad mini or iPod touch to be a powerful mobile device that's capable of handling a wide range of tasks simultaneously, it also enables you to utilize an incredibly fast-growing library of apps. In fact, there are more than 700,00 iPhone apps (some of which have been enhanced for the iPhone 5) that also run on the iPad, and more than 275,000 iPad-specific apps currently available from the App Store.

Between the customizability of iOS 6 and your ability to utilize your mobile device with preinstalled and optional apps, you can personalize your phone or tablet so that it's perfectly suited to meet your unique personal or work-related needs.

Like other operating systems, such as Microsoft Windows for PC-based computers, or Apple's OS X Mountain Lion for the Mac, for example, iOS is an operating system created by Apple that works with its mobile devices, including the various iPhone, iPad, or iPod touch models. Just like any operating system, iOS manages and controls the device's hardware and software resources, and handles every task it ultimately carries out.

Apple introduced the world to the original Apple iPhone in early 2007. Since then, the phone hardware, as well as the iOS operating system, have quickly evolved. Each updated version of Apple's iOS has introduced users to new features and functionality, ultimately making the iPhone, and later the iPod touch, iPad, and most recently the iPad mini, among the bestselling and most versatile mobile devices on the planet—not to mention that they're among the most technologically advanced in terms of what's available to consumers.

[⌇ **NOTE** Throughout this book, anything that's discussed relating specifically to the iPad, refers to the iPad 2, the 3rd or 4th generation iPad, and the iPad mini.

WHY YOU NEED iOS 6 ON YOUR DEVICE

The introduction of iOS 6 for the iPhone, iPad, and iPod touch marks a significant advancement and improvement, not just in the operating system itself, but in how we can utilize and interact with Apple's mobile devices. If these advancements and innovations could be summarized in a single world, the term used to describe all that's new in iOS 6 would be "integration."

> **! CAUTION** iOS 6 refers to the version of the operating system, and should not be confused with the model number of your device, such as the iPhone 5. The Apple iPhone 3GS, iPhone 4, iPhone 4S, iPod touch (4th generation), iPod touch (5th generation), iPad 2, 3rd/4th generation iPad, and the iPad mini are among the devices that have the capability to run the iOS 6 operating system.

As soon as you begin using iOS 6 on your device, you'll discover that your favorite apps, as well as many of the features and functions built in to the operating system, now nicely integrate with each other, making it easier for you to fully utilize, access, manipulate, and share all sorts of data, files and content, not just on the device you're using, but across multiple devices and your computer(s).

NEW AND MODIFIED APPS AND FEATURES

Using the familiar Photos app (the focus of Chapter 11, "Shoot, Edit, and Share Photos and Videos"), not only can you view the digital images stored on your iPhone or iPad, you also can now crop, rotate, enhance, and edit them, and then share them via email, Twitter, Facebook or iCloud. You'll also soon discover how to fully utilize the new Panoramic option for taking photos using the improved Camera app, and how to share the images stored on your iOS mobile device with others using iCloud's new Shared Photo Stream feature.

Likewise, when using Safari to surf the Web (which is covered within Chapter 13, "Use New Safari Features to Surf More Efficiently"), you can now save entire webpages within your Reading List (to refer back to later, even if your device doesn't have access to the Internet), read webpages without on-screen clutter using the Reader feature, plus from your iOS mobile device, access iCloud Tabs (which are browser windows that are open on your other computers and/or iOS mobile devices).

Other popular apps, such as Mail, Calendar, Music, and iTunes, also offer new features that you'll soon be wondering how you ever lived without. Plus, the Maps app has been redesigned from scratch, while the new Passbook app has been added to the iPhone. Even Siri has been given improved functionality, and is now capable of responding to a broader range of questions, commands and requests. Siri also works in conjunction with more apps, like Facebook and Twitter.

> **NOTE** On October 23, 2012, during the same press conference in which Apple announced the 4th generation iPad and the iPad mini, a new version of the iBooks app was released that adds new functionality to this already popular eBook reading app. For example, you can now highlight a quote from a book you're reading and share it with other people via email, Facebook or Twitter using the Share functionality that's now incorporated into iBooks. The app also offers a new Continuous Scrolling reading mode, so instead of swiping your finger horizontally to turn a page, you can scroll up or down on the screen.

WHICH DEVICES USE iOS 6?

To fully utilize all the features and functionality of iOS 6, you'll need to use it with an iPhone 5, a 3rd or 4th generation iPad, or the iPad mini. However, many (but not all) of the functionalities of this newly revised operating system also work fine with the iPhone 3Gs, iPhone 4, iPhone 4S, the iPad 2, as well as the iPod touch (4th or 5th generation).

You'll soon discover how to use many of the more than 200 new features built in to iOS 6, plus learn how to quickly and easily share data and content between apps and various devices, and with other people. Not only will this book help you get the most out of your Apple mobile device, it also will help you stay connected and more easily manage the data stored on your phone or tablet.

> **NOTE** If you're active on Facebook or Twitter, iOS 6 now fully integrates with both of these popular online social networking services. Thus, you can compose and send tweets (to your Twitter followers), and/or compose and publish Facebook Status Updates from within many of the apps that come preinstalled with iOS 6, as well as directly from the Notification Center screen.
>
> The official Facebook and Twitter apps allow you to fully manage all aspects of your accounts from your iOS mobile device. In addition, data from your Facebook or Twitter account can be synced with the Contacts and Calendar apps. You'll learn how to fully utilize Facebook and Twitter's integration with iOS 6 from Chapter 10, "Make the Most of Social Networking Apps."

NEW AND IMPROVED INTERACTIVITY

One of the many things that set the iPhone 5 apart from its competition, and later made the 3rd and now 4th generation iPads the world's most sought-after tablets, are the multi-touch Retina touchscreens built in to these devices. Using a series of onscreen taps, swipes, and finger movements, it's possible to interact with all of your device's apps and handle a wide range of tasks—without needing a traditional keyboard or even a stylus.

NEW AND IMPROVED TOUCHSCREEN TECHNIQUES

From the moment you turn on your iPhone or iPad (or take it out of Sleep mode), aside from pressing the Home button to return to the Home screen at any time, virtually all of your interaction with the tablet is done through the following finger movements and taps on the device's highly sensitive multi-touch touchscreen:

- **Tap:** Tapping an icon, button or a link that's displayed on your device's screen serves the same purpose as clicking the mouse when you use your main computer. And, just as when you use a computer, you can single-tap or double-tap, which is equivalent to a single or double click of the mouse.

- **Hold:** Instead of a quick tap, in some cases, it is necessary to press and hold your finger on an icon or onscreen command option. When a hold action is required, place your finger on the appropriate icon or command option and hold it there. There's never a need to press down hard on the tablet's screen.

- **Swipe:** A swipe refers to quickly moving a finger along the screen from right to left, left to right, top to bottom, or bottom to top, to scroll to the left, right, down, or up, respectively, depending on which app you're using.

- **Pinch:** Using your thumb and index finger (the finger next to your thumb), perform a pinch motion on the touchscreen to zoom out when using certain apps. Or "unpinch" (by moving your fingers apart quickly) to zoom in on what you're looking at on the screen when using many apps.

> **TIP** Another way to zoom in or out when looking at the device's screen is to double-tap the area of the screen you want to zoom in on. This works when you're surfing the Web in Safari or looking at photos using the Photos app, as well as within most other apps that support the zoom in/out feature.

- **Pull-Down:** Using your index finger, swipe it from the very top of the iPhone or iPad quickly downward onto the screen. This will cause the Notification Center window to appear, alerting you of incoming email messages, text messages, alarms, or other time-sensitive actions that need to be dealt with. You can be holding the device in portrait or landscape mode for this to work.

- **Five Finger Pinch (iPad Only):** To exit any app and return to the Home Screen, place all five fingertips of one hand on the screen so that they're spread out, and then draw your fingers together, as if you're grabbing something. Be sure, however, that the new multitasking features are turned on from within the Settings app (found under the General heading).

■ **Swipe-Up (iPad Only):** Make the multitasking bar appear at the bottom of the screen by using several of your fingers and swiping them upward, from the very bottom of the screen toward the top. (Or press the Home button twice in quick succession to access the multitasking bar.) On the iPhone or iPad, you can also access the multitasking bar by pressing the Home button twice.

■ **Multi-Finger Horizontal Swipe (iPad Only):** When multiple apps are simultaneously running, swipe several fingers from left to right or from right to left on the screen to switch between active apps.

You can also use several of your fingers together and swipe left or right when looking at the multitasking bar to switch between active apps.

> **TIP** To wake up your iPhone when it is in Sleep mode, press the Home button or Power button once.
>
> When viewing the Lock Screen on the iPhone, when you double-tap on the Home button, Music app control icons are revealed. Use these music controls to play, pause, fast forward, or rewind music from an active playlist.
>
> Also from the iPhone's Lock Screen, swipe your finger upwards on the Camera icon to launch the Camera app, and then use the Volume Up (+) button on the side of the iPhone to quickly snap a photo.
>
> On the iPad, when you double-tap on the Home button when the tablet is in Sleep mode (or when viewing the Lock Screen), the Music app's controls appear at the top of the Lock Screen.

HOW TO MAKE THE BEST USE OF THE VIRTUAL KEYBOARD

Whenever you need to enter data into your iPhone or iPad, you almost always use the virtual keyboard that pops up on the bottom portion of the screen when it's needed. The virtual keyboard typically resembles a typewriter or computer keyboard; however, certain onscreen keys have different purposes, depending on which app you're using.

For example, when you access the iPhone or iPad's main Spotlight Search screen, notice the large Search key on the right side of the keyboard. However, when you use the Pages word processor app, the Search key becomes the Return key (shown in Figure I.1). When you surf the Web using the Safari web browser app, the Search key becomes the Go key in certain situations.

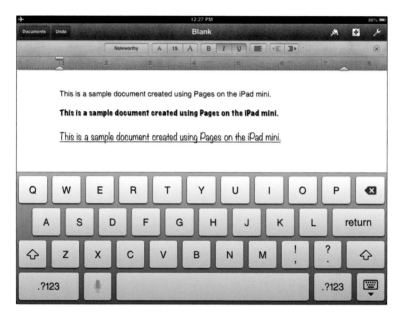

FIGURE I.1

Shown here is the optional Pages app running on the iPad mini with the standard virtual keyboard displayed.

When you're using an app that involves numeric data entry, such as Numbers, the layout and design of the virtual keyboard can change dramatically (shown in Figure I.2).

On the iPad, using your index fingers on your right and left hand simultaneously, place them in the center of the virtual keyboard, and move them apart quickly to divide the onscreen keyboard into two sections, as shown in Figure I.3. Some people find this virtual keyboard format more convenient for typing while they're holding their device. When the virtual keyboard appears, use your fingers to tap the keys and type.

> **TIP** When looking at the keyboard on the iPad, place and hold down your finger on the Hide Keyboard key (displayed in the lower-right corner of the keyboard). You'll be given the opportunity to split or merge the keyboard, as well as undock the virtual keyboard. Undocking the keyboard allows you to drag it up or down on the screen, away from its fixed location near the bottom of the screen.

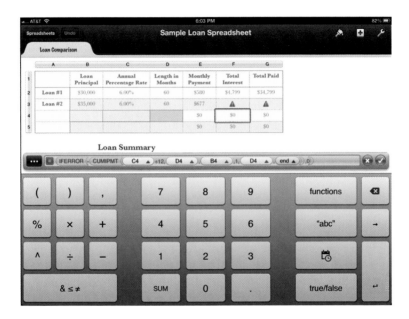

FIGURE I.2

When using the Numbers app (shown here on the new iPad), the app can alter the virtual keyboard's layout dramatically.

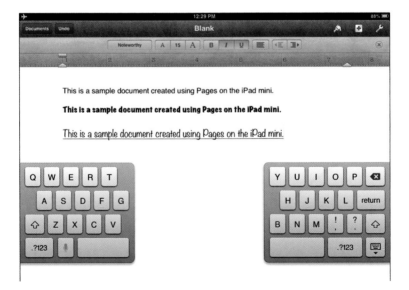

FIGURE I.3

Splitting the virtual keyboard in half makes it easier to type with your thumbs when holding the iPad (or iPad mini, shown here) with two hands. To adjust the keyboard, press and hold down the Hide Keyboard key.

> **TIP** From the Settings app, you can turn off the keyboard click noise that's otherwise heard when you're tapping the virtual keyboard keys. You also can turn on or off the Auto-Capitalization, Auto-Correction, Check Spelling, and Enable Caps Lock features that, when turned on, automatically fix what you're typing when the iOS deems the change appropriate.

To make the keyboard disappear, you can often tap anywhere on the screen except on the virtual keyboard itself, or you can tap the Hide Keyboard key, which is always located in the lower-right corner of the virtual keyboard.

Often, when data entry is required when you're using an app, the virtual keyboard automatically displays as it's needed. However, if you need to fill in a data field when using a particular app, for example, and the virtual keyboard is not visible, simply tap the blank onscreen field where data needs to be entered, and the appropriately formatted virtual keyboard will appear.

> **MORE INFO** If you expect to do a lot of data entry or word processing on your iPhone or iPad, instead of using the virtual keyboard, you can purchase an optional external keyboard, which connects to the phone or tablet either using the device's 30-pin Dock Connector port (or Lightning port), or via a wireless Bluetooth connection, depending on which model of keyboard you'll be using.
>
> The iPhone 5, 4th generation iPad and iPad mini all have a Lighting Connector port located on the bottom of the unit, as opposed to a 30-pin Dock Connector found on Apple's older iOS mobile devices.
>
> A variety of external keyboards are available from Apple, as well as from companies such as Logitech (www.logitech.com), Zagg (www.zagg.com), and Brookstone (www.brookstone.com). For example, the Brookstone Virtual Keyboard ($99.99, www.brookstone.com/laser-projection-virtual-keyboard) is one of the "coolest" and most cutting-edge optional keyboards available for your iPhone or iPad.

In terms of the iPad's hardware (the device itself), from the Settings app, you can decide how the tablet's side switch (located above the volume control buttons) will work. Your options include Lock Rotation and Mute button. Chapter 2, "Tips and Tricks for Customizing Settings," explains how to personalize this feature. Otherwise, the power button, Home button, and volume buttons on your iPhone or iPad continue to serve the same purposes as they did in the past.

WHAT THIS BOOK OFFERS

This all-new second edition of *iPad and iPhone Tips and Tricks* will help you quickly discover all of the important new features and functions of iOS 6, easily update your mobile device, and discover how to fully utilize this operating system so that you can transform your iPhone, iPad, or iPod touch into the most versatile, useful, and fun-to-use tool possible.

This book also teaches you how to utilize the new features built into iOS 6 as you find, purchase (if applicable), download, install, and use a wide range of optional apps on your mobile device, and ultimately use your iPhone and/or iPad as a powerful personal productivity, organizational, or communications tool; state-of-the-art entertainment system; gaming system; and/or as a web surfing and email management device.

Each chapter of this book focuses on one or more iOS 6 preinstalled apps, or on specific features and functions of iOS 6. The book begins by explaining how to upgrade your device, while also getting you up-to-speed when it comes to fully utilizing all of the new features incorporated into Apple's online-based iCloud service.

> **TIP** Most of this book focuses on using iOS 6 with an iPhone, iPad, or iPad mini; however, some of the content also relates directly to using this operating system with an iPod touch (4th or 5th generation), especially if it's connected to the Web via a Wi-Fi connection.

You will soon discover how to fully personalize your iPhone or iPad by adjusting the various options within Settings. You also learn strategies for protecting your privacy and maximizing the capabilities of your device's security options.

> **WHAT'S NEW** Many of the apps designed to run using iOS 6, including but not limited to the latest versions of Maps, Twitter, Safari, Camera, Passbook (on the iPhone) and Reminders, now make even greater use of the device's GPS (Location Services) capabilities. Thus, your iPhone or iPad has the capability to pinpoint and continuously share your exact location with others.
>
> To control your privacy and limit this capability, be sure to personalize the Location Services features of iOS 6 (found within Settings) to manage when your iPhone or iPad will have the capability to track and share your location.

Later, we explore how to utilize the online-based App Store to find, purchase (if applicable), download, install, and use the optional apps that best address your unique needs.

As of late-2012, the App Store offered more than 700,000 iPhone-specific apps, in addition to more than 275,000 iPad-specific apps. A growing number of apps are being designed specially for the iPhone 5 or the 3rd/4th generation iPad, while others are "hybrid," and work flawlessly on most iOS mobile devices. Chapter 3, "Strategies for Finding, Buying, and Using Third-Party Apps," will help you quickly find the very best apps that are of direct interest to you, and that will enhance your overall experience using your phone or tablet.

Most apps created for the iPhone will work flawlessly on the iPad. However, iPhone-specific apps that are not hybrid iPhone/iPad apps will not fully utilize the iPad's larger display. iPad-specific apps will not work on an iPhone, but they will work on the iPad mini.

Much of this book focuses on the core apps that come preinstalled with iOS 6. The chapters that cover these apps are chock-full of tips and strategies for getting the most out of the new features and functionality that these apps offer.

First and foremost, your iPhone is a smartphone that's capable of making and receiving phone calls. iOS 6 introduces a handful of new calling features, while improving on functionality your iPhone was already capable of. Later in this book, you discover how to do things like choose customized ringtones, manage incoming calls, access voicemail, and initiate conference calls using the phone functionality built in to iOS 6.

Using Apple's iCloud service, transferring data between your Apple mobile device(s) and other computers can now be done wirelessly via the Web. However, in conjunction with iOS 6, Apple has introduced a handful of new and useful features related to iCloud that allow you to sync and share more types of app-specific information between your iPhone, iPad, iPad mini, iPod touch and/or your computers (both Macs and PCs).

Although you can still use the iTunes Sync process and connect your iPhone or iPad to your PC or Mac using a USB cable to transfer and/or back up data, iCloud enables you to wirelessly move files between devices and computers from anywhere via the Web. Plus, you can sync (back up) your iPhone or iPad data with a wireless version of iTunes sync, which will store your data on your primary computer, assuming that a Wi-Fi Internet connection is available.

If you thought your ability to surf the Web using your iPhone or iPad was impressive before, wait until you experience the enhancements made to the Safari Web browser with iOS 6.

iOS 6 **WHAT'S NEW**   The latest model iPhone 5, the 3rd/4th generation iPad and the iPad mini enable users to connect to and surf the Web using a 4G (LTE) Internet connection (as opposed to a significantly slower 3G connection, which is used by all older models). However, it's up to the various wireless data service providers as to whether a 4G (LTE) connection can be used instead of a Wi-Fi connection to utilize certain iCloud features, such as iCloud Backup, Photo Stream, Shared Photo Stream, or the capability to download TV show episodes or movies from iTunes.

Because Apple's online-based iCloud service is now fully integrated with iOS 6, from this book you discover how to set up a free iCloud account and use the iCloud service to back up your iPhone and/or iPad, plus wirelessly transfer or sync app-specific data whenever your mobile device is connected to the Web.

The iPhone and iPad have always been useful tools for surfing the Web, managing email, and streaming web-based content. iOS 6, however, offers many improvements to this functionality. This latest operating system, along with revised versions of Apple-created apps, including Pages, Numbers, and Keynote, now enable you to handle more complex tasks that you previously would have relied on a full-featured desktop, laptop, or netbook computer to handle.

Your ability to do word processing, perform spreadsheet management, and work with digital slide presentations on your iPhone or iPad has been greatly improved, as has your ability to edit photos and video, and/or work with Microsoft Office (Word, Excel or PowerPoint) files created on your primary computer.

Now, transferring files between your iPhone or iPad and your primary computer (or with another user) is easier than ever, thanks to iCloud and the other functionality built in to iOS and the latest versions of Pages, Numbers, and Keynote (each sold separately from the App Store). In no time, you will learn how to use these three optional apps to create, view, edit, manage, print, and share Microsoft Office–compatible documents using your iPhone or iPad.

Although your iPhone is, of course, a smartphone that enables you to make and receive calls, both the iPhone and the iPad can be used for real-time videoconferencing using Apple's FaceTime, which comes bundled with iOS 6. However, you can also use the Skype app (along with a wireless Internet connection) to make and receive voice-over-IP or videoconferencing calls using either the iPhone or iPad.

NOTE The iPad-specific version of Skype enables you to engage in real-time videoconferencing with any other Skype users, whether they're using a PC that's running Windows, a Mac, or any other tablet or mobile device.

As an entertainment device, your iPhone or iPad can play music and enable you to watch TV show episodes and high-definition movies. It also can be used as an eBook reader, or enable you to experience thousands of different fun and interactive games. When connected to an HDTV, for example, what you'd typically see on your iPhone or iPad's screen can also be displayed on any high-definition TV or monitor with an HDMI port.

Or when your device is used with an Apple TV device (sold separately) and a Wi-Fi Internet connection, you can begin viewing a TV show, a movie, or your favorite digital photos on your iPhone or iPad's screen, and then instantly switch to watching that same content on your home television screen using iOS 6's enhanced AirPlay functionality.

WHAT'S NEW Many of the core apps that come preinstalled with iOS now offer an enhanced Share button (or icon) which gives you the ability to share app-specific information via email, text/instant message, Facebook or Twitter, or send that content to a wireless printer using AirPrint. The options available from the Share menu within apps varies.

ATTENTION, PLEASE...

Throughout this book, look for Tip, Note, Caution, What's New, and More Info boxes that convey useful tidbits of information relevant to the chapter you're reading.

The What's New boxes, for example, highlight new features or functionality introduced in iOS 6, while the More Info boxes provide website URLs or list additional resources you can use to obtain more information about a particular topic.

1

UPGRADING TO iOS 6

If you've had your iPhone or iPad for a while and it's currently running an older version of the iOS operating system, such as iOS 5.1, now that Apple has made the iOS 6 operating system available, you'll definitely want to upgrade your device. Keep in mind that some of the very early iPhone, iPad and iPod touch models cannot be upgraded to iOS 6.

> **NOTE** iOS 6 will run on the iPhone 3GS, iPhone 4, iPhone 4S, iPhone 5, iPod touch (4th and 5th generations), iPad 2, 3rd generation and 4th generation iPad, and on the iPad mini, as well as any other iPhone, iPad or iPod touch models released after October 2012.

Whether you're using an iPhone or iPad, making the transition from iOS 4.3.4 (or earlier) to iOS 6 will require you to use the iTunes sync process. However, if you're upgrading from iOS 5.1 to iOS 6, the upgrade can be done wirelessly (which is an easier and more convenient process).

This chapter helps you install iOS 6 onto your Apple mobile device or, if it's already installed, teaches you how to keep the iOS up to date with the latest version, plus ensure that you're running the most current versions of your favorite apps.

> **NOTE** *iPad and iPhone Tips and Tricks* applies to the iOS 6 operating system running on a compatible iPhone, iPad, iPad mini or iPod touch. Throughout this book, these iPhone, iPad, and iPod touch models are often referred to often as "iOS devices" or "Apple mobile devices."

Also in this chapter, you discover what iCloud is all about and learn how to set up a free Apple iCloud account. You also learn how Apple has further integrated wireless data backup and file-transfer capabilities using iCloud (via the Web) into iOS 6. Later, you learn more about how to utilize iCloud for file transfers, data backup, and file sharing.

> **NOTE** If you purchased your new iPhone or iPad after September 2012 (or an iPad mini after November 2, 2012), it came with iOS 6 preinstalled. However, it may be necessary to update the iOS using the wireless update feature that's described within this chapter. For example, about a month after Apple released iOS 6, a minor update to the operating system (iOS 6.01) was released, and a more significant update (iOS 6.1) was already in the works. Even if your iPhone, iPad, or iPad mini is running iOS 6, you'll definitely want to download and install the latest version of the operating system that's available.

HOW TO UPGRADE FROM iOS 4.3.4 (OR EARLIER) TO iOS 6

If you have an iPhone or iPad that currently has iOS 4.3.4 (or an earlier version) installed, follow the directions in this section to download and install the latest version of the iOS 6 operating system onto your device.

HOW TO FIND OUT WHICH VERSION OF iOS YOUR DEVICE USES

To determine which version of the iOS operating system your device currently has installed, from the Home Screen, tap on the Settings app, and then tap on the General option. Next, tap on the About option, found under the General heading, and look at the Version information. Figure 1.1 shows this on an iPhone 4 that is currently running iOS 4.3.4.

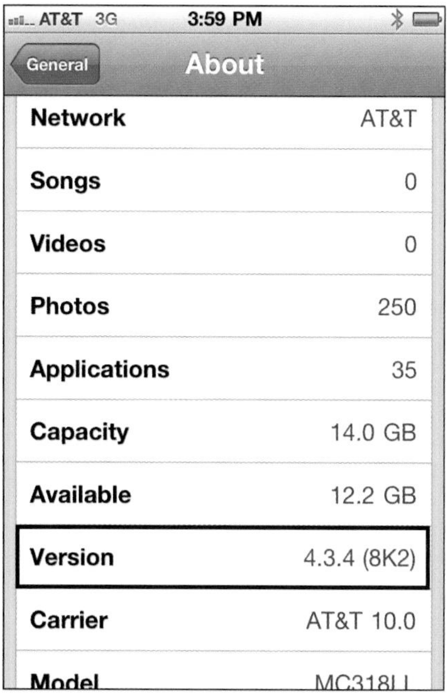

.ıll. AT&T 3G	3:59 PM	⁕ ▭
General	**About**	
Network		AT&T
Songs		0
Videos		0
Photos		250
Applications		35
Capacity		14.0 GB
Available		12.2 GB
Version		4.3.4 (8K2)
Carrier		AT&T 10.0
Model		MC318LL

FIGURE 1.1

From Settings on your device, you can easily determine which version of iOS it's running.

Here's an even easier method: When your iPhone or iPad is connected to your primary computer via a USB cable, and iTunes is running on your PC or Mac, on the left side of the iTunes screen, click the device name for your iPhone or iPad, which is listed under the Devices heading. When the main iTunes Device Summary screen appears on the right side of the main iTunes screen (on your computer), look near the top of the screen in the iPhone or iPad information box that lists the device's name, its capacity, and the iOS software version it's currently running, along with its serial number and phone number (if applicable).

> ☑ **TIP** To upgrade from iOS 4.3.4 (or earlier) to iOS 6, your primary computer must be running the most current version of iTunes (version 11 or later). From the iTunes pull-down menu that's displayed in the upper-left corner of the screen when iTunes is running, click the Check for Updates option to ensure you're running the latest version of this software on your Mac or PC. If you're informed that a more up-to-date version of the iTunes software is available, download and install it before upgrading your mobile device to iOS 6.
>
> If you need to download and install iTunes for the first time on your PC or Mac, visit www.apple.com/itunes/download.

AVOIDING iTUNES CONFUSION

Don't confuse the different versions of iTunes as you begin using iOS 6 on your iPhone, iPad, or iPod touch. The iTunes software on your PC or Mac is, among many other things, used to initiate the iTunes sync process between your primary computer and your iOS device. Using either the wired or the wireless connection capabilities of this feature, you can back up your iPhone or iPad data to the hard drive of your primary computer, or transfer data or files between devices.

From your primary computer, you can also use iTunes to manage your digital music and eBook library, purchase and watch TV show episodes and movies on your Mac or PC, purchase and listen to audiobooks, and access the iTunes Store, the App Store, Apple's iBookstore or Newsstand.

However, the iTunes app on your iPhone or iPad is used exclusively for accessing the iTunes Store to find, purchase, and download music, movies, TV shows, ringtones, podcasts, audiobooks, and other content. Other apps are then used to watch or listen to the content purchased (if applicable) and downloaded using the iTunes app. For example, you'll use the Music app to manage and listen to your digital music library on your iPhone or iPad, and you'll use the Videos app to watch TV show episodes and movies you download from the iTunes Store.

HOW TO UPGRADE WITH iTUNES

After the latest version of iTunes (version 11 or later) is running on your PC or Mac, use the iTunes sync procedure to create a current backup for your iPhone or iPad before starting the iOS 6 download and install process. To do this, iTunes must be running on your primary computer, and your mobile device should be connected to your computer via the white USB cable that came with your iOS device. If you're using an optional dock, your iPhone or iPad should be inserted into the dock, and the dock should be connected to your primary computer (or a USB hub that's connected to your primary computer) via the supplied USB cable.

> **NOTE** If you're using an iPhone 5, 4th generation iPad, or an iPad mini, it came with iOS 6 already installed. However, you will need to download and install the latest version of the iOS. When doing this using iTunes Sync, use the Lightning Port to USB cable that came with the iPhone 5, 4th generation iPad, or iPad mini to connect the device to your computer. However, you can also install the update directly to your device via Wi-Fi. To do this, launch Settings, tap on the General option, select the Software Update option, and follow the on-screen prompts.

From this point forward, your primary computer must be connected to the Internet to continue with the iOS 6 upgrade procedure. After completing the backup process, click the Summary tab for your iPhone, iPad, or iPod touch that's displayed at the top of the iTunes screen (on your primary computer). In the Version box that displays about halfway down the screen, click the Check for Update icon.

iTunes will determine what the most recent version of iOS 6 is. If your iOS device is running an older version of the operating system, a message appears stating that you should download and install the latest version of the iOS operating system, which will be iOS 6 or later.

Follow the onscreen prompts on your primary computer to begin downloading iOS 6. During this procedure, do not touch your iPhone, iPad, or iPod touch; simply leave it connected to your primary computer. Depending on the speed of your Internet connection, the iOS 6 download process could take a while, so be patient.

When iOS 6 has been downloaded, it will automatically be transferred to your iPhone or iPad and installed. Again, this process could take up to 30 minutes, so be patient and do not disconnect your iOS device from the primary computer during this process or attempt to use the device.

After iOS 6 is installed on your Apple mobile device, it will reset. At this point, it will be necessary to configure iOS 6 on your device, and then restore your saved apps and data.

> **NOTE** Unless otherwise indicated, the tips, strategies, and how-to information throughout this book also apply to the iPod touch (4th and 5th generation models), even if it's not specifically listed.

WIRELESS UPGRADE FROM iOS 5 TO iOS 6 (OR LATER)

If you're upgrading from iOS 5 (or later) to iOS 6 (or later), the process can be done wirelessly, as long as the iPhone or iPad can connect to a wireless network or Wi-Fi hotspot. To do this, launch Setting, tap on the General option, and then tap on Software Update. Be sure your device's battery is fully charged or perform this upgrade process with the iPhone or iPad connected to an external power source.

Your iPhone or iPad will connect via the Internet with Apple and determine whether your iOS need to be updated. If so, the update will download and automatically install. This process will take between 15 and 30 minutes. Once the installation is complete, all of your old phone or tablet settings, apps and data should be intact, but the device itself will be running iOS 6.

> **☑ TIP** Before initiating the iOS 5 to iOS 6 upgrade using the wireless method, it's a good idea to back up your device via the iTunes Sync or iCloud Backup process, although the upgrade process should not delete any apps or data stored on your device.

HOW TO CONFIGURE iOS 6 ON YOUR NEW iPHONE OR iPAD

After iOS 6 is installed on your iPhone or iPad, or the newly purchased device is turned on for the first time, you'll see the initial Set-Up screen (shown in Figure 1.2) when the device is turned on. Plan on spending 5 to 10 minutes configuring the new operating system, or if applicable, restoring your previously backed up data, personal settings, and apps.

FIGURE 1.2

After iOS 6 is installed on your iPhone or iPad, a initial Set Up screen appears. (It's shown here in the iPhone 5.) The word "iPad" appears if you're installing iOS 6 on an iPad.

This part of the process can be done with your device connected to your primary computer using the iTunes sync process, or it can be done wirelessly. Configuring iOS 6 wirelessly on your iPhone or iPad requires that the device have access to the Web.

From the initial iOS 6 setup screen (which boldly says "iPhone" or "iPad"), move the slider from left to right to proceed to the next Welcome screen, which is animated. From this screen, select a language. English is the default, but Spanish and many other options are available. Tap on your selection so that a check mark appears on the screen next to it, and then tap on the blue-and-white Next or right-pointing icon that's displayed in the upper-right corner of the screen.

Next, from the Country or Region screen, select where you'll be primarily using your iOS device. As shown in Figure 1.3, the default option is United States, but the pull-down menu lists every other country on the planet. Tap on your selection so that a check mark appears next to it, and then tap on the Next icon.

FIGURE 1.3
Select the country or region where you'll primarily be using your iPhone or iPad. This is shown on an iPhone 5.

When the Wi-Fi Networks screen appears (shown in Figure 1.4), under the Choose a Network heading, all available Wi-Fi hotspots will be listed.

> **TIP** If no Wi-Fi hotspots appear, your device may give you the option to connect to the Internet using a 3G/4G wireless connection (look for the Use Cellular Connection button). If not, to continue, you'll need to keep your iPhone or iPad connected to your primary computer via the supplied USB cable, and select the Connect to iTunes option by tapping it.

FIGURE 1.4

From the Wi-Fi Networks screen, determine how your iPhone or iPad will connect to the Internet to continue the iOS 6 setup process.

The Location Services screen appears next. Your iPhone or iPad has the capability to pinpoint and track its exact location using the device's Location Services and GPS capabilities, crowd-sourced Wi-Fi hotspots, and cell-tower locations. From this screen, you can turn on this feature or disable it. However, after iOS 6 is operational, you can customize this feature from the Settings app.

For now, tap on either the Enable Location Services or the Disable Location Services option that's displayed near the bottom center of the screen. When a check mark appears next to your selection, tap on the Next icon.

> **TIP** The Maps, Camera and Reminders apps, as well as Siri, for example, reply heavily on Location Services. Using this feature, however, does drain the iPhone or iPad's battery faster.

You'll see the Set Up iPhone or Set Up iPad screen displayed next. From this screen, you can choose one of three options:

- Set Up As New iPhone (or iPad)
- Restore from iCloud Backup
- Restore from iTunes Backup

If you're setting up a brand-new iPhone or iPad, tap on the Set Up As New iPhone/iPad option. However, if you're upgrading your existing iPhone or iPad, tap and select the Restore from iTunes option to continue. This will allow you to restore your data, personalized preferences, cellular phone number, and Internet account data (if applicable), as well as your apps.

If you're already an iOS 5 user with an active iCloud account, or after you have set up iOS 6 and an iCloud account, you'll be able to restore your device wirelessly from backup data stored on iCloud by selecting the Restore from iCloud Backup option. Or, if your backup data is stored on your primary computer, you'll be able to restore data wirelessly (or using the supplied USB cable) from your primary computer using iTunes sync. For now, however, depending on your situation, tap on the Set Up As New iPad (iPhone) or Restore from iTunes option, and then tap on the Next icon to continue.

HOW TO SET UP A NEW iPHONE OR iPAD

If you opted to continue the iOS 6 setup procedure by selecting the Set Up As New iPhone or Set Up As New iPad option, the next screen enables you to create an Apple ID account or continue the process using your existing Apple ID and password.

From the Apple ID screen (as shown in Figure 1.5), tap either the Sign In with an Apple ID or Create a Free Apple ID option. Or you can tap on the Skip This Step option and complete this step later.

> **TIP** If you already own any Apple equipment, such as a Mac, an iPhone, an iPad, or an iPod, chances are you have already created a free Apple ID account. Enter this existing Apple ID account username and password when prompted. This information will ultimately allow you to use the App Store, iBookstore, Newsstand, and the iTunes Store to make purchases and to set up a free iCloud account. This same Apple ID can be used to set up your free Game Center, iMessage and FaceTime accounts as well. (The iMessage service is used in conjunction with the Messages app.)

> **NOTE** Keep in mind, you can utilize different Apple ID accounts. For example, one can be used for your iTunes Store, App Store, iBookstore and Newsstand purchases, and the other can be used for your iMessage/FaceTime accounts, if you choose to keep this separate. Although most people use just one Apple ID account, there are reasons for using two or more Apple ID account, which will be explained later.

Assuming that you have an Apple ID account and password, select the Sign In with an Apple ID option by tapping it. When prompted, use the virtual keyboard to enter your Apple ID and corresponding password. Tap on the Next icon to continue.

FIGURE 1.5

Sign in using an existing Apple ID or create a new Apple ID account in order to proceed.

Next, if your iOS mobile device is Siri-compatible (some older model iPhones and iPads are not), the Siri screen will appear. Your options here include Use Siri or Don't Use Siri. This is a master switch for this feature. For now, tap on the Use Siri feature. You can later customize this feature from within Settings.

When the Terms and Conditions screen appears, tap on the blue-and-white Agree icon that's displayed in the bottom-right corner of the screen to continue. You will be prompted to confirm this decision when a pop-up Terms and Conditions window appears. Once again, tap on the Agree icon.

You'll also be given the opportunity to set up an iCloud account using your Apple ID and password. As you'll learn later in this chapter, iCloud is an online-based file-sharing service that has been designed to be used with iOS 6 and your favorite apps. Thus, you can use this free service to wirelessly transfer and synchronize files, contacts, calendars, to-do lists, notes, photos, music, eBooks, documents, and other content.

Near the bottom center of the Set Up iCloud screen, you'll see a virtual switch that allows you to turn on or off the iCloud functionality within your iPhone or iPad. If you turn on this switch and then tap on the Next icon, your free iCloud account will be set up, and your device will configure itself to begin using the iCloud service. You can fully customize how your iPhone or iPad interacts with iCloud later.

Assuming that you have access to a Wi-Fi connection on an ongoing basis, you can configure your iPhone or iPad to automatically and wirelessly back itself up once per day and store the backup data on iCloud. During this setup procedure, when the iCloud Backup screen appears, you can choose to maintain a wireless backup of your mobile device using iCloud, or choose to maintain a backup of your device on your primary computer (using the iTunes sync process).

> **✓ TIP**   Should you store your backup files on iCloud or your hard drive? Each option offers benefits:
>
> ▪ The benefit to storing your iPhone or iPad's backup data files on iCloud is that as long as a Wi-Fi Internet connection is available to your mobile device, you can wirelessly create a backup file or, if necessary, restore data from that backup from virtually anywhere. However, a Wi-Fi Internet connection must be present to create or restore from a backup that's stored on iCloud, and during the backup (or restore) process, your iOS device must be connected to an external power source. Your device will automatically be backed up once per day. However, from within Settings, you can also initiate the backup process manually whenever you wish.
>
> ▪ The benefit to storing your iPhone or iPad's backup data files on your primary computer's hard drive via iTunes Sync is that its always available to you, regardless of whether a Wi-Fi Internet connection is available. However, to create or restore from the backup, your iPhone or iPad must be connected to your primary computer via the supplied USB cable, or you must be able to establish a wireless connection within a Wi-Fi network between your computer and your mobile device. Whenever the iTunes sync connection is made between your primary computer and your iOS device, a new backup will be created. You can manually initiate this connection as often as you wish.

The Thank You screen will appear next. To begin using your iPhone or iPad, simply tap on the Start Using iPhone or Start Using iPad button that appears near the bottom center of this screen.

The Home Screen will now be displayed on your iPhone or iPad (see Figure 1.6). It will be operating using iOS 6 and be ready to use. Displayed on the Home Screen are icons for all the preinstalled (core) apps, some of which include: Messages, Calendar, Notes, Reminders, Maps, Videos, Contacts, Game Center, iTunes, App Store, Newsstand, FaceTime, Camera, Clock, Settings, Safari, Mail, Photos, and Music. If you're using an iPhone, the Phone and Passbook apps will also be displayed on the Home Screen.

FIGURE 1.6
The iOS 6 Home Screen on an iPhone 5.

HOW TO RESTORE FROM iTUNES

If you're upgrading your iPhone or iPad from iOS 4.3.4 (or earlier) to iOS 6, and previously created a backup with your device before starting the iOS 6 installation procedure, you can continue the iOS 6 installation process and restore all your data, personal settings, cellphone number/Internet account information, and apps by selecting the Restore from iTunes option during the iOS 6 setup procedure.

With your iPhone or iPad still connected to your primary computer via the USB cable, iOS 6 automatically installs on your device, and your backup data, apps, and preferences are restored. When the process is completed, you'll be ready to use your iPhone or iPad, which will now be running iOS 6.

Depending on how much data, how many apps, and what content needs to be restored to your iPhone or iPad from a previously stored backup, the process of finalizing the iOS 6 install and then restoring your content could take up to 30 minutes, so be patient.

> **NOTE** If you've upgraded from iOS 5 to iOS 6 using the wireless upgrade method, all of your preexisting data, apps and system preferences will remain intact.

WHERE'S MY DEVICE? HOW TO USE THE FIND MY iPHONE OR FIND MY iPAD FEATURE

If turned on, the Find My iPhone (or Find My iPad) feature is now fully integrated into the iOS 6 operating system. To turn on or modify the settings related to this feature at anytime, launch Settings, tap the iCloud option, and then select the Find My iPad (iPhone) option.

This feature enables you to access the Web from any device, have Apple locate the exact location of your iPhone or iPad, and then display its whereabouts on a detailed map. You can then perform certain tasks that will protect your data or help you recover the lost or stolen device.

Even when Find My iPhone/iPad is set up and active, the device must be turned on (or in Sleep mode, but not turned off) and must have a connection to the Internet via 3G/4G or Wi-Fi for the feature to work. There is an option, however, that will notify you when the device gets turned back on, if it's turned off when you initially attempt to locate it.

After Find My iPhone/iPad is activated, if you misplace the device or it gets stolen, from any computer or wireless Internet device, visit www.icloud.com/#find and have Apple quickly pinpoint the location of your device and display its location on a map. You can also use the Find My iPhone app on your other iOS mobile devices. For example, you can pinpoint the location of your iPhone using your iPad, or vice versa.

From this website, you can also type a message that will instantly appear on your missing device's screen (asking for it to be returned, for example), or you can force the device to emit a sound (so that you can find it easier if it's lost in your office, for example).

It's also possible to lock the device using a password or wipe out and delete the contents of your iPhone/iPad remotely, which ensures that your sensitive data doesn't fall into the wrong hands. You can always restore your data using your iCloud or iTunes sync backup files after the unit has been retrieved.

Find My iPhone/iPad isn't a perfect solution for finding a lost or stolen device, but it can be useful in certain situations. However, if someone knows your Apple ID and password, he or she can easily track your exact whereabouts anytime using the www.icloud.com/#find website. Later, we focus more on security measures you can implement on your iPhone or iPad to help protect your privacy.

TIP In addition to the Find My iPhone/iPad feature, Apple offers the Find My Friends app. When given permission, this optional app (which is available from the App Store) enables others to track your whereabouts in real time. Although this feature has many practical real-world applications, to ensure your privacy, it can be turned on or off quickly and at your discretion. Plus, you can choose exactly who has the ability to "follow" you.

You can also set up the ability for others to follow you for only a specific period of time. Using the enhanced Restrictions features of iOS 6, parents can keep tabs on their kids who use an iPhone or iPad, for example, but prevent them from being able to turn off the Find My Friends feature. Again, for the Find My Friends feature to work, the iOS device must have access to the Web via a Wi-Fi or 3G/4G connection.

There's also an optional Find My iPhone app that allows you to track the whereabouts of your Mac(s), iPhone, iPad and/or iPod touch from your iOS mobile device, as long as those devices are linked to the same Apple ID and/or iCloud account.

INTEGRATE YOUR DATA, APPS, AND MORE WITH APPLE'S iCLOUD

In the past, if you wanted to send a file or data between your primary computer and your iPhone or iPad, it needed to be done via email or using the iTunes sync process (which involves connecting the devices using the supplied USB cable). However, some types of data and files could also be transferred using a compatible online-based file-sharing service, such as Dropbox or WebDAV. This capability was limited to certain types of data and could be used with only a handful of apps.

iOS 6, however, fully integrates with Apple's iCloud service. iCloud is an online-based file-sharing service. If you opt to turn on and use this initially free service, you'll quickly discover that it makes synchronizing data, transferring files and content, and sharing information between your iPhone, iPad, Mac, and/or PC a simple process, plus it allows you to maintain a wireless backup of your iOS device, and easily share photos with others.

TIP Using iOS 6 on your iPhone or iPad, you can decide whether you want to back up your device whenever you manually connect it to your primary computer using the iTunes sync process, or whether you want your device to automatically create a backup of its contents wirelessly and store the data on iCloud. If you opt for the once-daily wireless backups to be created, you must keep this feature turned on, and your device needs to be within a Wi-Fi hotspot to connect to iCloud and also be plugged into an external power source. To use the automatic wireless backup feature, a 3G/4G connection will not work. However, you can initiate a manual wireless backup to iCloud using a 3G/4G Internet connection while the device is running on battery.

Initially, when used with your iPhone or iPad, iCloud automatically handles a handful of tasks because it's fully compatible with many of the core apps that come preinstalled on your device, as well as other popular apps, such as Pages, Numbers, Keynote, iPhoto, iMovie and GarageBand. Many third-party app developers have also implemented iCloud compatibility into their apps (or will soon be doing so).

So what's iCloud anyway? Basically, it's a glorified online-based file-sharing service that's operated by Apple. Because your iPhone or iPad has access to the Internet, it can access information from or send information to iCloud, which in its simplest form serves as a remote (online-based) external hard drive for storing data or files.

When you set up a free iCloud account using your existing Apple ID and password (which can also be established for free), you're immediately given 5GB of free online storage space, plus an unlimited amount of additional online storage space to store the content you purchase from the iTunes Store, the App Store, and Apple's iBookstore (including music, movies, TV show episodes, apps, and eBooks) and Newsstand.

TIP   For an additional annual fee, you can purchase extra online storage space for your iCloud account. Plus, you can upgrade to Apple's premium iTunes Match service for $24.99 per year. (See the later section, "Upgrade to the Premium iTunes Match Service," for details.)

Especially when you use a Wi-Fi Internet connection, content, files, and data can quickly be transferred between your iPhone or iPad and iCloud. The process takes a bit longer if you're using a 3G/4G connection (and excludes the capability to transfer very large files).

iCloud really becomes useful when you consider that it can be used as a hub in cyberspace for wirelessly and quickly sharing data, files, and content between your iPhone, iPad and your computer(s) that are linked to the same iCloud account. So, using iCloud, you can transfer a Microsoft Office file from your computer to iCloud, for example, and then retrieve it from iCloud and store it on your iPhone or iPad.

Depending on the type of file, you can then use it with Pages, Keynote, Numbers, or another app installed on your device.

Pages is a full-featured word processor for the iPhone and iPad that is compatible with Microsoft Word. Numbers is a spreadsheet management program for the iPhone and iPad that is compatible with Microsoft Excel, and Keynote is a digital slide presentation tool compatible with Microsoft PowerPoint.

These three apps, sold separately for $9.99 each, are also fully compatible with iCloud. This allows you to load a Microsoft Word file directly into Pages from iCloud, for example, and then view, edit, print, and/or share that file. Or you can create a Word-compatible document on your iPhone or iPad using Pages, and then easily send it to your primary computer via iCloud. Using these apps, you can also create PDF files from your documents, spreadsheets, or presentations, which are more readily compatible and viewable with other devices and computers.

When you begin using iCloud, you'll quickly discover that it is more than just a remote hard drive in cyberspace that allows you to wirelessly share content and data among multiple computers and devices. iCloud also provides an easy way to instantly and wirelessly synchronize photos, music, emails, contacts, scheduling data, to-do lists, Safari bookmarks (and data), eBooks, and other information between your primary computer and your iPhone and/or iPad.

SYNCHRONIZE YOUR DIGITAL PHOTOS

You've probably discovered how much fun it is to take digital photos using the cameras built in to your iPhone or iPad, or even with your standalone digital camera. Using iOS 6, not only can you now edit and then share these images via email or quickly post them on Twitter, Facebook, Google+ or Instagram, for example, you also can keep your digital images wirelessly synchronized between your iOS mobile device(s) and your primary computer using iCloud.

> **NOTE** You'll learn all about how to shoot, edit and share your digital photos and videos, plus how to use iCloud's Photo Stream and new Shared Photo Stream feature from Chapter 11, "Shoot, Edit, and Share Photos and Videos."

After it's set up, iOS 6 enables you to create a My Photo Stream. Thus, when you snap a new photo on your iPhone or iPad, for example, it will automatically be transferred (uploaded) to iCloud, and then downloaded to your other computer(s) or other iOS devices. There's no longer a need to manually sync your devices to share your favorite digital images on all of your devices and computers (both Macs and PCs).

Any photo that's shot using an iPhone or iPad (or imported into your iOS device from another source) can be shared with iCloud and made available on your other iOS devices and computers. You can later edit your Photo Stream.

NOTE As with some of the other file-sharing features offered using iCloud, to create and manage My Photo Stream and keep large numbers of digital images synchronized among your devices, your iPhone and/or iPad must have access to a Wi-Fi web connection as opposed to a 3G/4G Internet connection.

After setting up the My Photo Stream feature once, you'll discover that it can also be used to automatically transfer your favorite digital images to your Apple TV device. My Photo Stream can include up to 1,000 of your most recent digital images. iCloud stores all new images for 30 days, during which time you can arrange to download them to any or all of your computers and/or devices and store them in Albums.

TIP Beyond the 30-day period during which a photo is automatically saved on iCloud, you can transfer your favorite images from the Photo Stream to a specific Photo Album, where it will be stored indefinitely. However, you never need to worry about images being erased accidentally. An archival copy of every digital image added to your Photo Stream (and temporarily stored on iCloud) is also automatically stored indefinitely on your primary computer's hard drive until you delete it manually.

WHAT'S NEW Thanks to iOS 6, you can also create and share separate Shared Photo Streams—not just with your other computers and iOS mobile devices, but with other people as well. Shared Photo Streams provide an easy way to share multiple digital photos with specific people via the Internet.

TRANSFER FILES AND DOCUMENTS

iCloud is fully compatible with the optional Pages, Numbers, and Keynote apps, allowing you to easily transfer Microsoft Office–compatible files between your iPhone, iPad, and primary computer (Mac or PC). It also works with PDF files, photos, and other types of data files that can be utilized on both your primary computer and your mobile device.

> **iOS 6** **WHAT'S NEW** Not only will iCloud enable you to wirelessly transfer data files and documents between devices, but it also will ensure that your documents are kept up to date on each device and computer; so as long as you have access to the Web, you will also always have access to the most current version of your files or data as changes are made to them.

If set up to do this, all of your files are automatically uploaded to iCloud, so you never have to worry about manually transferring documents or figure out which version of which document you saved in a particular location. This same capability is also being incorporated into other apps and software packages offered by third-party developers.

SYNC YOUR APPS, EBOOKS, BOOKMARKS, AND OTHER CONTENT

In addition to automatically keeping track of and making important documents available to you via iCloud, when they work together (which they were designed to do), iOS 6 and iCloud also keep track of your apps, eBooks, and other content, and makes them available on any of your devices at any time (as long as an Internet connection is present).

For smaller files, this feature works with both a 3G/4G and a Wi-Fi Internet connection. So if you purchase and begin reading an eBook on your iPad, you can also download that eBook file (and your current digital eBook bookmarks) to your iPhone or primary computer, and continue reading on another device.

You'll also discover that iCloud can be used to automatically and wirelessly sync your web browser bookmark data. Thus, as you're surfing the Web on your primary computer, you can store a bookmark using your browser, and that bookmark will almost instantly appear when you use Safari to surf the Web on your iPhone or iPad. Or you can save a Safari bookmark on your iOS mobile device and have it transferred to the web browser on your primary computer. Using the iCloud Tabs feature, open browser windows on your Mac or iPad, for example, can be accessed from your iPhone (or vice versa).

> **iOS 6** **WHAT'S NEW** When you set up an iCloud account, Apple offers you a free [username]@me.com or [username]@icloud.com email account as well. The benefit to using this optional email account is that it automatically remains synchronized on all your devices via iCloud. (If you have a [username]@mac.com account from Apple, this too will work with iCloud.)

SYNC YOUR APP-SPECIFIC DATA WITH iCLOUD

When iCloud is used with the Contacts, Calendar, Reminders, Notes and/or Safari apps on your iPhone and/or iPad, all of your contacts and scheduling data, as well as your to-do lists and Safari Bookmarks (as well as open browser windows and Reading List information) can automatically be synchronized in real time, between your mobile device(s) and primary computer, as long as a web connection is available to each device.

As a result, if you're out and about and add an important appointment to the Calendar app on your iPhone, that new appointment will also appear on your compatible calendar program on your Mac or PC, your compatible online-based scheduling application, and/or the Calendar app on your iPad.

NOTE It's also possible to maintain a real-time sync between the Contacts and Calendar apps and online-based applications operated by Google, Yahoo!, or that are Microsoft Exchange compatible.

TIP As you'll discover, setting up iOS 6 on your iPhone or iPad to work with iCloud to wirelessly keep your app-specific data (and/or other compatible files or data) synchronized takes just seconds, and after it's set up once, the synchronization process happens automatically, continuously, and in the background.

To set up this feature, launch Settings, tap on the iCloud option, and then turn On the virtual switch associated with each app that you want to be able to sync with iCloud automatically. This needs to be done on each of your iOS mobile devices and your computer(s) that are linked to the same iCloud (Apple ID) account.

MAINTAIN A RELIABLE REMOTE BACKUP OF YOUR iPHONE OR iPAD

Both the iPhone and the iPad are technologically advanced and extremely reliable devices, but they're not flawless. Occasionally, problems can occur that could result in the loss or corruption of data. Thus, it's an extremely smart strategy to maintain a reliable backup of the complete contents of your iPhone or iPad. Prior to the release of iOS 5, the iTunes Sync process was used to create a backup of your iOS mobile device, allowing the data, apps, and files to be archived on your primary computer.

This backup method is still available to you using the iTunes sync process. However, with iOS 6, if you have access to Wi-Fi in your home or office, you can avoid connecting your primary computer and mobile device via the supplied USB cable, and opt to use a wireless iTunes sync process to back up your iPhone or iPad.

A third option is to use your iPhone or iPad running iOS 6 with iCloud and maintain an automatic daily backup via iCloud. This feature can be initially set up from Settings. (Launch Settings, select the iCloud option, and then tap on Storage & Backup. Turn on the iCloud Backup option using the virtual on/off switch associated with this feature.) When it's activated, a Wi-Fi connection is required for your iPhone or iPad to access the Web and maintain a daily backup of the device. The data, files, and pertinent information stored on your iPhone or iPad will be saved on the iCloud service in a secure format.

> **NOTE** When you create a backup of your iPhone or iPad that's stored on iCloud, it's accessible only via your secure Apple ID account and password. More information about using iCloud's various services and features, including iCloud Backup is offered within Chapter 6, "Sync and Share Files Using iCloud."

> **TIP** Once you set up the iCloud Backup feature, you can initiate a manual wireless backup of your device anytime. To do this, launch Settings, tap on iCloud, tap on the Storage & Backup option, and then tap on the Back Up Now button that's displayed on the Storage & Backup menu screen.
>
> Updates to an existing backup will typically take between one and three minutes to complete, since only new or updated information and data is added to the online-based backup file.

SHARE iTUNES PURCHASES WITH ALL YOUR DEVICES

After your iCloud account is set up, whenever you purchase a new song on iTunes, for example, that song can instantly be made available to you on your primary computer, as well as on all of your iOS mobile devices (including your iPhone, iPad, and/or iPod with Internet compatibility). Plus, all of your past iTunes purchases become accessible on any device from which you can access iCloud because those purchases automatically get stored on iCloud.

> **NOTE** You can connect to iCloud from your iPhone or iPad using a 3G/4G or Wi-Fi connection to transfer music or eBook files. A Wi-Fi connection is required to transfer TV show episodes, movies, or large files.

UPGRADE TO THE PREMIUM iTUNES MATCH SERVICE

Whenever you make a music purchase on iTunes, that purchase automatically gets stored in your iCloud account, but the storage space required for this does not count against your free 5GB of iCloud online storage space.

However, beyond the music you've purchased from the iTunes Store, perhaps you've built up your digital music library by ripping music from your personal audio CD collection, or you've downloaded music from other online sources, such as Amazon.com. If you want to make your entire digital music collection available to all of your computers and devices via iCloud, you'll need to upgrade your iCloud account and sign up for the iTunes Match service for $24.99 per year. To turn on this optional service, launch Settings, tap on the iTunes & App Stores option, and then turn on the virtual switch associated with the iTunes Match feature.

This service analyzes your entire digital music collection and compares it to the entire music library available from iTunes (which encompasses well over 20 million songs). All matches immediately become available from your iCloud account and can be accessed by all of your compatible devices, anytime and from anywhere your iPhone, iPad, iPod (with Internet connectivity), or primary computer has an Internet connection.

Any songs from your personal digital music library that can't automatically be matched up by iTunes Match need to be uploaded to iCloud only once, regardless of where they were purchased, and those songs will also become available wirelessly on all of your iCloud-compatible devices.

Using this service, all your music, as well as your personal playlists, will be automatically synced between devices. So a playlist you create on your iPhone can be listened to on your iPad or on your primary computer at any time.

HOW TO UPDATE YOUR APPS WIRELESSLY

After you've upgraded to iOS 6, you'll probably discover that the developers of your favorite apps have also released updated versions. If you want to check whether you're running the most current versions of the apps already installed on your iPhone or iPad, you can do so wirelessly using a 3G/4G or Wi-Fi connection.

From the Home Screen, tap on the App Store app, and then tap on the Updates icon, which is displayed near the bottom of the screen on the right. If the message All Apps Are Up to Date is displayed, you're in good shape; otherwise, you'll be given the option to upgrade any out-of-date apps.

> ☑ TIP After tapping on the Updates button, if one or more apps require an update, listings for them will be displayed on the Updates screen. You can update each app separately by tapping on the Update button associated with each app listed, or update all of the listed apps by tapping on the Update All button that's displayed near the upper-right corner of the screen. The new versions of the apps will begin downloading to your iPhone (shown in Figure 1.7) or iPad.
>
> During this process, you'll see a progress bar displayed within each app icon. When each app is downloaded and installed, the Installing message will transform into an Open button to the right of each app listing. You can then launch the app by tapping on the Open button, or launch the app from the Home Screen.

FIGURE 1.7

Shown here on the iPhone 5 are two apps being updated at once after tapping the Updates icon, followed by the Update All button within the App Store.

After you initially acquire an app from the App Store, virtually all subsequent updates to that app are free of charge. Plus, now that you're running iOS 6 on your device, you'll be able to easily share your app purchases among multiple iOS devices that you own. For example, if you own an iPhone and an iPad, you'll be able to purchase an iPhone or hybrid iPhone/iPad app once and then install and use it on both devices.

A hybrid app is one that is designed for use on both an iPhone and an iPad. Some apps are iPad-specific, for example, and will run only on the iPad, iPad 2, or 3rd/4th generation iPads (and/or iPad mini). Meanwhile, apps designed specifically for the iPhone will run on iPads, but these apps will not take advantage of the tablet's larger display or advanced capabilities. There are also some iPhone-specific apps being designed exclusively for the iPhone 5.

Although it's often easier to update apps directly from the device itself, you can also download app updates using your primary computer and iTunes, and then use the iTunes sync process to transfer the updated app(s) to your iPhone and/or iPad.

> **☑ TIP** When you create an iCloud account and begin using iCloud with your iPhone or iPad, all your app purchases (and free app downloads) will be stored on iCloud. If you delete an app from your phone or tablet, you can reinstall it anytime, for free, from iCloud.
>
> To do this, when you return to the App Store, tap on the Updates icon that's displayed at the bottom of the screen, and then tap on the Purchased tap that's displayed at the top of the screen. All the apps you've purchased in the past (and the free apps you've downloaded) will be displayed. Tap on the cloud icon displayed along with each app's listing or description to reinstall it on your phone or tablet.

KEEP iOS UP TO DATE WIRELESSLY

Now that iOS 6 is installed on your device, you can opt to upgrade the iOS wirelessly in the future if you have access to a Wi-Fi Internet connection (a 3G/4G Internet connection will not work for this purpose).

Periodically, Apple releases upgrades to the iOS operating system that need to be downloaded and installed on your phone or tablet. To wirelessly check for upgrades and then download and install these iOS upgrades as they become available, from the Home Screen, launch Settings. Tap on the General option under the Settings heading. Then, under the General heading, tap on the Software Update option.

Your device automatically accesses the Web and determines whether an updated version of the iOS is available. During this process, the message Checking for Updates will be displayed. If an update is available, it can now be downloaded and installed via the Web, without your having to connect your iPhone or iPad to your primary computer.

> **NOTE** If you don't have access to a Wi-Fi Internet connection, you can still check for iOS updates and then download and install them as necessary using your primary computer and the iTunes sync process.

IN THIS CHAPTER

- How to personalize your iPhone or iPad by adjusting the options available from within Settings
- How to protect your privacy by adjusting the Location Services and Passcode options from within Settings
- How to move app icons around on the Home Screen and create Folder

2

TIPS AND TRICKS FOR CUSTOMIZING SETTINGS

As you begin using iOS 6 on your iPhone or iPad, one of the first things you'll notice is that many of the core, preinstalled apps now offer functionality that allows them to work seamlessly together. For example, if you're active on Twitter or Facebook, you can create and send tweets or Facebook Status Updates from within several different apps, including Photos and Safari (as well as from the Notification Center screen), without having to launch the official Twitter or Facebook app. Or you can send app-specific data or a file via email or instant/text message from within many different apps without first launching the Mail or Messages app.

Meanwhile, Notification Center keeps track of all alarms, alerts, notifications, incoming (missed) calls, incoming text messages, incoming (missed) FaceTime calls, incoming email messages, and other events or tasks that require your attention, and displays them in one location for easy reference and one-tap access.

Many apps on your iPhone or iPad also utilize the device's built-in GPS and Location Services capabilities, which allow the device to pinpoint its exact location and then utilize and sometimes share that information. For example, the Maps app uses the Location Services capabilities of your device to figure out where you are, and provide turn-by-turn directions to your intended destination. Photos uses the Location Services capabilities to add geo-tagging information to the digital photos (and videos) you shoot so that you can determine later exactly where they were shot. Or, when composing a tweet or Facebook update, you can share your exact location with your online followers and friends.

When you receive attachments within incoming email messages, with a few taps on the screen, you can open specific types of files within compatible apps, which will launch by themselves to display the incoming content.

(iOS 6) WHAT'S NEW   You can communicate with and control your iPhone or iPad using your voice, thanks to Siri. One way to activate this feature is to press and hold down the Home button on your iOS device for several seconds (or hold down the button on your wireless Bluetooth headset), and then speak to the iPhone or iPad using normal sentences.

As required, your compatible iPhone or iPad (or iPad mini) will automatically access apps and whatever data is stored on the device accessible from the Web that's needed to fulfill your verbal requests or commands. See Chapter 5, "Using Siri and Dictation to Interact with Your iOS Device," for tips and tricks for using Siri effectively.

Before using Siri for the first time, you'll need to activate this feature in two places within the Settings app. How to do this is covered within Chapter 5.

To make your iPhone or iPad handle so many tasks and integrate functionality between apps, a lot automatically happens behind the scenes that's controlled by iOS 6. From within Settings, however, you can personalize and customize many different options that give you more control than ever over how your iPhone or iPad responds to you, while managing your apps, files, content, and data.

This chapter focuses on how to use many of the new features offered in the Settings app to personalize your experience using an iOS device. After iOS 6 is installed and fully operational on your iPhone or iPad, you'll definitely want to manually adjust some of these settings, as opposed to relying entirely on their default settings.

TIP   As you install additional apps onto your iPhone or iPad, if those apps allow you to customize specific features within the app, those customization options will often be available to you from within Settings.

USING THE SETTINGS APP

To access Settings, from the Home Screen tap on the Settings icon. On your iPhone, the main Settings menu will appear (shown in Figure 2.1). You can then use your finger to scroll downward, and view all the options and submenus available from within Settings.

FIGURE 2.1

The main Settings menu displayed on an iPhone 5 running iOS 6.

On your iPad, the main Settings menu appears on the left side of the screen (shown in Figure 2.2). When you tap on an option from the Settings menu on the left, the initial submenu that is associated with the selected menu option is displayed on the right side of the screen.

> **(iOS 6) WHAT'S NEW** Although the main layout and interface of Settings is the same as in older versions of the iOS, you'll discover many new Settings options, as well as submenus in the iOS 6 version of Settings, many of which offer you controls over your device's operation that were not previously available. The user-customizable options available from the Settings app will also vary based on what model iOS device you're using.

FIGURE 2.2

The main Settings menu displayed on the iPad running iOS 6.

After you launch Settings, the menus and submenus are displayed in a hierarchi-
cal structure. Under the main Settings heading, you'll see a handful of main menu
options relating to various apps and functions offered by your iPhone or iPad.
By tapping on many of these options on the iOS device, a submenu is displayed.
From that submenu, additional but related options, some of which have submenus
themselves, become accessible.

For example, if you launch the Settings app and then from under the main Settings
menu you tap on the Brightness and Wallpaper option, the submenus associated
with controlling the screen brightness and personalizing the Lock Screen and
Home Screen wallpaper are displayed.

By tapping on the wallpaper thumbnails displayed under the Wallpaper submenu,
additional submenu options are displayed.

> **NOTE** How to customize the particular Settings options related to
> screen brightness and customizing your device's wallpapers is explained shortly.
> Right now, you should simply become acquainted with the menu and submenu
> structure used by Settings, and become comfortable navigating your way around
> this app.

As you work your way deeper into each submenu, a left-pointing icon appears in the upper-left corner of each submenu screen that allows you to exit out of each Settings submenu, and move a step back toward the main Settings menu.

At any time, you can tap on this left-pointing arrow icon to exit out of the submenu you're in (before or after you've made adjustments to the various option settings). If you opt to make adjustments, those changes will automatically be saved when you exit out of the menu or submenu within Settings. Or if you exit out of a menu or submenu without making any changes, nothing will be altered.

> **✓ TIP**   From anywhere within Settings, to instantly return to the Home Screen press the Home button on your iPhone or iPad. On the iPad, you can also use the hand-grab motion that involves placing all five fingers from one hand on the screen simultaneously, such that your fingers are spread out slightly, and then moving your fingers together (dragging them quickly on the screen) as if you're grabbing something.
>
> Or you can access the multitasking bar and switch to another app by pressing the Home button twice in quick succession, or on the iPad also by dragging four fingers (held closely together) from the very bottom of the screen in an upward direction toward the top of the screen.

MAIN OPTIONS AVAILABLE FROM THE SETTINGS APP

When you launch Settings, the first thing you see is the main Settings menu. The following is a comprehensive summary of the main options available from this menu, which varies slightly based on whether you're using an iPhone, an iPad, or another iOS device.

> **✐ NOTE**   As each Settings option is described, reference to its iPhone or iPad compatibility refers to specific models of the iPhone (4, 4S or 5) or models of the iPad (including the iPad 2 or 3rd/4th generation iPad). In most cases, anything having to do with an iPhone also applies to the iPod touch and anything having to do with the iPad also applies to the iPad mini.

AIRPLANE MODE (IPHONE/iPAD WI-FI + 3G/4G MODELS)

This Settings option has no submenu but offers a virtual on/off switch. It's used to switch your device into Airplane Mode. Ideal for when you're on an airplane or traveling overseas, putting your device in Airplane Mode shuts down its capability to access the 3G/4G wireless web and keeps the unit from sending or receiving wireless transmissions. However, all its other features and functions remain fully operational.

In Airplane Mode, a small airplane icon appears in the upper-left corner of the iPhone or iPad's screen, as shown in Figure 2.3.

FIGURE 2.3

In Airplane Mode, a small airplane icon appears in the upper-left corner of your iPhone or iPad's screen. (Shown here on the iPhone 5.)

Even while your device is in Airplane Mode, you can still turn on Wi-Fi mode and/or Bluetooth, allowing the iOS device to access the Web via a Wi-Fi hotspot (to utilize the wireless web access available on some commercial aircrafts, for example), and also communicate with a Bluetooth-enabled wireless keyboard or headset.

> **TIP** When you turn on Airplane mode, the Wi-Fi and Bluetooth features of your iPhone or iPad get turned off automatically. You can, however, turn them back on manually while still in Airplane mode. This is done from within Settings.

If you refer to Figure 2.3, you'll see that the iPhone 5 is in Airplane Mode (the airplane icon is displayed in the upper-left corner of the screen). However, the phone is also connected to a Wi-Fi network. You can see the Wi-Fi signal strength icon displayed in the upper-left corner of the screen, near the Airplane Mode icon. In addition, this iPhone has Bluetooth turned on and a Bluetooth-compatible headset connected. You can tell this from the Bluetooth icons displayed in the upper-right corner of the screen, next to the battery indicator icon and percentage meter.

WI-FI (iPHONE/iPAD)

Located directly below the Airplane Mode option is the Wi-Fi option. On the iPhone, when you tap onto this option, a submenu containing a virtual on/off switch is displayed. When it's turned on, a listing of available Wi-Fi networks is displayed directly below the Choose a Network heading. Tap on the Wi-Fi network you want to connect to.

On an iPad, when you tap on the Wi-Fi option in the left column of the main Settings screen, the right side of the screen immediately displays the various options available to you for choosing and connecting to a Wi-Fi hotspot.

On the right side of the screen are the Wi-Fi Networks options. At the top, the first user-selectable option is labeled Wi-Fi. It's accompanied by a virtual on/off switch to its right.

When this option is turned on, your device immediately begins looking for any and all Wi-Fi hotspots in the vicinity. These networks are displayed under the Choose a Network heading, below the Wi-Fi option, on the right side of the screen.

If one or more Wi-Fi hotspots are available, they are listed in a few seconds under the Choose a Network heading.

> **☑ TIP**   On an iPhone or iPad, when you're reviewing a list of available Wi-Fi networks to connect to, look to the right side of each listing to determine whether a lock icon also appears. This indicates that the Wi-Fi hotspot is password protected. Also on the right side of each listing is the signal strength of each Wi-Fi hotspot in your immediate area.
>
> Tap on a public hotspot that does not display a lock icon unless you possess the password for a locked network.

If you select a Wi-Fi network that is password protected, when you tap on it, an Enter Password window appears on your screen. Using the iPhone or iPad's virtual keyboard, enter the correct password to connect to the Wi-Fi network you selected. You will often have to do this when connecting to a Wi-Fi hotspot offered in a hotel, for example.

To choose any Wi-Fi hotspot listed, simply tap on it. In a few seconds, a check mark appears to the left of your selected Wi-Fi hotspot, and a Wi-Fi signal indicator appears in the upper-left corner of your device's screen, indicating that a Wi-Fi connection has been established.

BENEFITS OF CONNECTING TO A WI-FI HOTSPOT TO ACCESS THE WEB

There are several benefits to connecting to the Internet using a Wi-Fi connection, as opposed to a 3G/4G connection (if you're using an iPhone or iPad Wi-Fi + 3G model), including the following:

- A Wi-Fi connection is typically much faster than a 3G/4G connection. (Although if you're within a 4G LTE coverage area, you may experience faster connectivity using it as opposed to Wi-Fi.)

- When connected to the Internet via Wi-Fi, you can send and receive as much data as you'd like, stream content from the Web, and/or upload or download large files, and not worry about using up your monthly wireless data allocation that's associated with your 3G/4G wireless data plan through your wireless service provider.

- Using a Wi-Fi connection, you can use the FaceTime app for video conferencing, plus download movies and TV show episodes from the iTunes Store directly onto your device. You can also create wireless backups of your iPhone or iPad that are stored on iCloud. (Thanks to iOS 6, some wireless service providers now allow FaceTime to be used with a 3G/4G connection, but only with certain service plans.)

> **NOTE** The main drawback to using a Wi-Fi connection to connect to the Internet from your iPhone or iPad is that a Wi-Fi hotspot must be present, and you must stay within the radius of that Wi-Fi hotspot to remain connected to the Internet. The signal of most Wi-Fi hotspots extends for only several hundred feet from the wireless Internet router. When you go beyond this signal radius, your Internet connection will be lost.

If you leave the Wi-Fi option turned on, your iPhone or iPad can automatically find and connect to an available Wi-Fi hotspot, with or without your approval, based on whether you have the Ask to Join Networks option turned on or off. When the Ask To Join Networks features is turned off, your iPhone or iPad will still re-connect automatically to wireless networks and Wi-Fi hotspots that you have connected to previously, such as each time you return to your home or office.

BLUETOOTH (iPHONE/iPAD)

Turn on Bluetooth functionality on your iPhone or iPad and then "pair" compatible Bluetooth devices for use with your iOS mobile device. A wireless headset, external keyboard or wireless speakers are among the popular Bluetooth devices you might want to use with your iOS mobile device. Be sure to turn on the virtual switch associated with this feature, and then under the Devices heading, make sure each device you want to use is paired. Multiple Bluetooth devices can be used simultaneously with your iPhone or iPad. (Some Bluetooth 4.0 devices do not need to be manually paired with your iPhone or iPad. The pairing process happens automatically.)

> **NOTE**　Once an optional device has been paired once, as long as it's turned on an in close proximity to your iOS device, and the iOS device has the Bluetooth feature is turned on, the two devices will automatically establish a wireless connection and work together.

> **TIP**　If you're using your iPhone or iPad without having a Bluetooth device connected, turn off the Bluetooth feature altogether. This helps extend the battery life of your iOS device. When you turn on this feature, your iPhone or iPad automatically seeks out any Bluetooth-compatible devices in the vicinity. The first time you use a particular Bluetooth device with your iOS mobile device, you will probably need to pair it. Follow the directions that came with the device or accessory for performing this initial setup task. (The pairing process should take only about a minute or two.)

CELLULAR DATA (iPAD WITH WI-FI +3G/4G)

This feature applies to iPad models that have Wi-Fi + 3G/4G. When the Cellular Data option is turned on, your tablet is able to access the wireless data network from the wireless service provider that you're subscribed to. When this option is turned off, your device is able to access the Internet only via a Wi-Fi connection, assuming that a Wi-Fi hotspot is present.

The Data Roaming option appears below the Cellular Data option. When turned on, Data Roaming allows your iPad to connect to a 3G/4G network outside the one you subscribe to through your wireless service provider. The capability to tap in to another wireless data network might be useful if you must connect to the Internet, there's no Wi-Fi hotspot present, and you're outside your own service provider's coverage area (such as when traveling abroad).

> **!CAUTION**　When your iPhone or iPad is permitted to roam and tap in to another 3G/4G wireless data network, you will incur hefty roaming charges, often as high as $20 per megabyte (MB). Refrain from using this feature unless you've

pre-purchased a 3G/4G data roaming plan through your service provider, or be prepared to pay a fortune to access the Web.

When your device can't find a compatible 3G/4G network, it will seek out an older 2G network, which is much slower. For example, when your AT&T Wireless iPhone or iPad (with 3G/4G capabilities) is connected to the Edge network, the letter "E" appears instead of the "3G" or "4G/LTE" label in the upper-left corner of the screen.

Based on the 3G/4G wireless data plan you subscribe to, you can view or modify your account details by tapping on the View Account option. Once you log in using the username and password you created when the account with your service provider was set up, you can change your credit card billing information, or modify your monthly data plan, for example.

TIP Unless specifically instructed by a technical support person representing Apple or your wireless data service provider, avoid changing the SIM PIN option that's displayed at the bottom of the Cellular Data screen. Simply leave this option on its default setting and ignore it.

DO NOT DISTURB (iPHONE/iPAD)

Use the virtual switch associated with this option to turn on or off the Do Not Disturb feature. When turned on, all incoming calls are forwarded directly to voice-mail (iPhone), and incoming FaceTime calls are rejected. You will not be bothered by them until you turn off this feature.

TIP To customize the Do Not Disturb feature, launch Settings and tap on the Notifications option, then select the Do Not Disturb option. For example, you can pre-set this feature to automatically engage and disengage at pre-determined times each day (like if you want to be left alone daily, between 11:00pm and 7:00am the following morning). You can also determine if certain voice (iPhone) or FaceTime callers are able to override the Do Not Disturb feature and get through to you.

NOTIFICATIONS (iPHONE/iPAD)

This Settings option (shown in Figure 2.4) enables you to determine which apps function with Notification Center, plus it allows you to determine other ways that apps that generate alerts, alarms, or notifications notify you. You can also customize the Do Not Disturb feature.

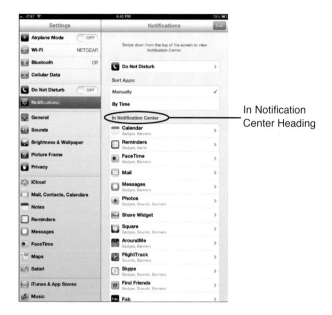

In Notification Center Heading

FIGURE 2.4

Apps that are set to exchange data with Notification Center are listed under the heading In Notification Center when you select the Notifications option from within the Settings app (shown here on the iPad).

> **NOTE** Notification Center is one of the powerful features that comes preinstalled on your iPhone or iPad. From within Settings, determine which apps Notification Center will continuously monitor.
>
> To avoid getting bombarded by excessive alarms, alerts, and notifications from apps that aren't too important to you, manually turn on or off the capability of Notification Center to work with specific apps.

When you tap on the Notifications option, a submenu under the heading In Notification Center will list apps currently installed on your iPhone or iPad that are compatible with Notification Center, and that are set to automatically share data with Notification Center.

These apps include Phone (iPhone only), Passbook (iPhone only), Calendar, Reminders, Game Center, FaceTime, Messages, and Mail, which all come preinstalled with iOS 6. However, additional apps that you install later might also be compatible with Notification Center, and will ultimately be listed here as well. On your iPhone, additional listings found on this menu are for the Weather and Stock Widgets, which can be turned on or off. The Share Widget can also be turned on/off. This allows you to send tweets (via Twitter) or Facebook Status updates from the Notification Center screen (iPhone) or window (iPad).

Below the In Notification Center heading is another heading, labeled Not in Notification Center. Here, other apps that are capable of generating alerts, alarms, badges, or notifications are listed. However, the apps listed here are not currently set to exchange data with the Notification Center app.

As you review each app listed under the In Notification Center or the Not in Notification Center heading, you can tap on it to reveal a secondary submenu pertaining specifically to that app.

For example, when you tap on Calendar, displayed under the In Notification Center heading, the submenu that's revealed offers a handful of additional options for customizing how alerts, alarms, badges, and notifications that are generated by the Calendar app will be handled.

At the top of the Calendar submenu (shown in Figure 2.5), which you can access after selecting Notifications from the Settings app, is the Notification Center option that's accompanied by a virtual on/off switch. When turned on, it allows the Notification Center app to alert you when alerts, alarms, badges, or notifications are generated by the Calendar app. The second option, labeled Show, allows you to determine how many related alerts, alarms, or notifications generated by the Calendar app are listed at any given time in the Notification Center app. Your options include 1, 5, 10, or 20 recent items. As you're first starting to use this iOS 6 feature, keep the number of alerts manageable by selecting just five per app. You can always add more for specific apps that are more important to you.

In addition to determining whether the Notification Center app pays attention to and exchanges data with a particular app, in this case Calendar, you can also select an additional Alert Style by tapping on one of the three Alert Style options, which include None, Banners, and Alerts.

If you select None but have the Notification Center virtual switch for the app turned on, alerts, alarms, and notifications generated by that particular app only appear in the window that's displayed by the Notification Center app, for example, when you swipe your finger downward from the very top of your iPhone or iPad's display.

If you tap on the Banners option, in addition to alerts, alarms, and notifications generated by the app appearing in the Notification Center, a separate banner is displayed at the top of the iPhone or iPad screen to alert you. However, the banner disappears automatically after several seconds.

FIGURE 2.5

You can determine how any app that is capable of generating alerts, alarms, notifications, or badges will act from within the Settings app (shown here on the iPad).

If you tap on the Alerts icon, an alert window will appear on your iPhone or iPad's screen whenever the app you're customizing from within Settings generates an alarm, an alert, or a notification. To make this alert window disappear, you need to tap on a specific icon in the window to confirm receipt of each alert. This feature is useful for getting your attention if the alert or notification is extremely important to you, such as an appointment in the Calendars app.

Some apps also utilize Home Screen badges. If you turn on the Badge App Icon feature for a specific app, when that app has something to alert you of, a special graphic badge, such as a number, appears in the upper-right corner of the app's icon that's displayed on your iPhone or iPad's Home Screen.

NOTE A Home Screen badge (as shown in Figure 2.6) is a small red-and-white circular graphic that can appear in the upper-right corner of an app icon that's displayed on your iPhone or iPad's Home Screen. The Home Screen badge often contains a number. These badges are used to graphically show you that something relating to a specific app has changed and needs your attention. For example, a number will appear as a Home Screen badge on your Mail app icon if you've received new incoming email messages. Likewise, a number will appear as a Home Screen badge on the App Store icon if any of your apps require you to download updates for them.

FIGURE 2.6

On this iPhone 5 Home Screen, the Facebook, Phone, Mail and Messages app icons are all displaying Badges.

Finally, you can determine whether alarms, alerts, or notifications generated by a particular app are displayed on the Lock Screen when your device is otherwise in Sleep Mode, plus adjust audible alarm settings.

GENERAL (iPHONE/iPAD)

The General option is found about halfway down on the main Settings option screen. When you tap this General option, various sub-options become available. Unless otherwise noted, each option is available using an iPhone or iPad. The General options found within Settings include the following:

■ **About**—Tap on the About option to access information about your iPhone or iPad, including its serial number, which version of the iOS it's running, its memory capacity, and how much memory is currently available on the device. This is purely an informative screen with no options to customize or adjust. You can also change the device name by taping on the Name option near the top of the About screen.

■ **Software Update**—Use this option to update the iOS operating system wirelessly, without having to connect your iPhone or iPad to your primary computer and use the iTunes sync procedure. To do this, however, a Wi-Fi Internet connection is required.

- **Usage**—Tap on this option to see how the storage capacity of your iPhone or iPad is being utilized, as well as how your available online-based iCloud storage is being utilized. From the Battery Usage option displayed on this screen, you can decide whether to display your device's battery life as a numeric percentage (for example, 73%), as opposed to just as a battery icon graphic.

  Also, from this screen you can see how much data the iPhone or iPad has sent or received using the wireless data network it's connected to.

  Tap on the Reset Statistics option to reset the Sent and Received settings. When you add the Sent and Received figures together, you'll be able to determine your total data usage since you last tapped the Reset Statistics icon. This feature is particularly useful if you're overseas and roaming, to determine how much you'll be billed, or for making sure you don't go beyond your monthly allocated data usage based on the wireless data plan you've signed up for.

- **Siri**—Turn on or off Siri functionality on compatible devices, and adjust specific settings related to this feature. One of the important options to set from the Siri menu within Settings is related to My Info. When you tap on this menu feature, select your personal contact entry from the All Contacts listing. Ensure your personal contact entry contains properly labeled details about your addresses (home, work, and so on), phone numbers, email addresses, and so on. This is information Siri refers to often. See Chapter 5 for more information about using Siri.

- **Cellular (iPhone)**—Adjust settings related to how and when your iPhone will use its 3G/4G wireless data connection to access the Internet. Depending on which cellular service provider you use, you may also be able to transform your iPhone into a Personal Wi-Fi Hotspot, so other Wi-Fi enabled devices can access the Internet using your iPhone's 3G/4G connection.

- **VPN**—Use this option to turn on and/or establish a connection with a Virtual Private Network.

- **iTunes Wi-Fi Sync**—iOS 6 is capable of wirelessly syncing and backing up your iPhone or iPad so that the backup data is stored on your primary computer's hard drive. This feature works just like the familiar iTunes sync process that involves connecting your iOS device to your computer via the supplied USB cable; however, with this feature, the connection can be established wirelessly if both devices have access to the same Wi-Fi network.

- **Spotlight Search**—Upon tapping this option, you can determine which portions of your iPhone or iPad are searched when you use the Spotlight Search feature built into the device. From the main Home Screen, if you scroll to the left (swipe your finger from left to right), the Spotlight Search screen appears. Search fields also appear in some other apps.

- **Auto-Lock**—Anytime your iPhone or iPad is turned on, if you don't do anything for a predetermined about of time, it can be set to automatically switch into Sleep Mode to conserve battery life.

  From the Auto-Lock option, you can determine whether Sleep Mode is activated after 2, 5, 10 or 15 minutes of non-use. Or you can choose the Never option so that the iPhone or iPad never automatically switches into Sleep Mode, even if it's left unattended for an extended period.

- **Passcode Lock**—Use this feature to set and then turn on or off the Passcode option built in to iOS 6. This is just one level of security you can use to keep unauthorized people from using your phone or tablet.

- **iPad Cover Lock/Unlock (iPad Only)**—This feature places the tablet into Sleep Mode when an optional Apple Smart Cover or Apple Smart Case is placed over the screen, and then wakes up the device when the Smart Cover or Smart Case is removed.

- **Restrictions**—Upon tapping the Restrictions option, you will have the ability to Enable Restrictions, and then manually set those restrictions. For example, you can block certain apps from being used, keep the user from deleting or adding apps to the device, keep someone from making in-app purchases, or keep someone from accessing certain types of iTunes or app content (including TV shows, movies, music, and podcasts). Basically, this is a way to "child-proof" your iPhone or iPad, by allowing a user to gain access to only specific apps or content. If you choose to utilize this feature, make sure you don't forget the password you associate with it. Once a password is set and activated, if you forget it, it might be necessary erase your entire iOS device and reload everything from scratch.

- **Use Side Switch To (iPad)**—Located on the right side of your iPad is a tiny switch. Find it just above the volume up/down button. From the General Settings screen, you can determine what the primary function of this switch will be. You can use it as either a Lock Rotation switch or a Mute switch.

  When it's used as a Lock Rotation switch, when it's turned on, you can physically rotate your iPad but the screen will not automatically switch between landscape and portrait mode.

  Or when it's used as a Mute switch, this turns off the iPad's built-in speaker so that no sounds are heard, such as alarms. This is useful when using your iPad in a meeting, or in a quiet area (such as a library), for example.

> **TIP**   On the iPhone, the Ring/Silent switch silences call-related ringers and many alert sound that your iPhone is capable of generating. It is located on the left side of the handset, above the Volume Up and Volume Down buttons.

■ **Multitasking Gestures (iPad)**—There are several iPad-exclusive finger gestures for interacting with the multi-touch display. You can opt to turn on or off recognition of these gestures by adjusting the virtual on/off switch that's associated with the Multitasking Gestures option.

■ **Date & Time**—These settings allow you to switch between a 12- and a 24-hour clock, and determine whether you want your iPhone or iPad to automatically set the time or date (when it's connected to the Internet). To ensure that the time and date remain correct, based on whatever time zone you travel to, leave the Set Automatically option under the Date & Time screen turned on.

■ **Keyboard**—You can make certain customizations from the Setting screen that impact how your virtual keyboard responds as you're typing. Tap on the Keyboard option when using the Settings app, and you'll discover several customizable settings, such as whether Auto-Capitalization, Auto-Correction, and Check Spelling are turned on.

■ **International**—By default, if you purchased your iPhone or iPad in the United States, the default Language and keyboard options are for English; however, you can adjust these settings by tapping on the International option.

■ **Accessibility**—Designed to make the iPhone or iPad easier to use by people with various sight or hearing difficulties, as well as physical limitations, you can personalize various settings found under the Accessibility option to take advantage of certain features, like Voice Over or Large Text on the screen. Unless you need to utilize any of these options, simply leave them at their default settings.

■ **Reset**—Every so often, you might run in to a problem with your iPhone or iPad such that the system crashes or you need to reset specific settings. For example, to restore your iPhone or iPad to its factory default settings and erase everything stored on it, tap on the Reset option, and then tap on the Erase All Content and Settings option. In general, you should refrain from using any of these settings unless you're instructed to do so by an Apple Genius or a technical support person.

! CAUTION Before using any of the options found under the Settings Reset option, which could potentially erase important data from your iPhone or iPad, be sure to perform an iTunes sync or back up your device wirelessly to iCloud and create a reliable backup of your device's contents. See Chapter 6, "Sync and Share Files Using iCloud," for step-by-step directions for how to do this.

Several of the options found under the General heading you'll probably never need to tinker with or adjust. Leave them at their default settings. Others you'll need to utilize often as you use your iPhone or iPad for different tasks.

SOUNDS (iPHONE/iPAD)

Tap on this option to adjust the overall volume of the iPhone or iPad's built-in speaker (or the volume of the audio you hear through headsets), as well as to turn on or off various audible tones and alarms your phone or tablet generates.

From this menu, you can also assign specific audio tones, sounds, or ringtones to specific types of app-specific alerts and alarms, plus turn on or off the click noise associated with pressing keys on the iPad's virtual keyboard.

When it's in Silent mode, for example, you can turn on the Vibrate mode so that the iPhone handset shakes, instead of playing a ringtone. You can also control the Ringer Volume using an onscreen slider, and adjust the custom ringtones and audio alerts associated with various features and functions of your iPhone. Your iPhone has a library of different audio alarms and alerts, as well as ringtones built in, plus you can download additional ringtones from iTunes.

> **TIP** On your iPhone, you can manually adjust the ringer and speaker volume using the Volume Up and Volume Down buttons located on the left side of your handset. You can also control the vibration of the phone and choose different vibration patterns to alert you of different things. This can be customized from the Sounds menu within Settings.

BRIGHTNESS & WALLPAPER (iPHONE/iPAD)

The Brightness and Wallpaper options (shown in Figure 2.7 on the iPad) allow you to control the brightness of your iPhone or iPad's screen, and also customize the wallpaper of your device's Lock Screen and Home Screen.

When you tap on this option, the Brightness & Wallpaper submenu appears. At the top of this submenu is a brightness slider. Place your finger on the white dot that appears in the slider, and drag it to the right to make the screen brighter, or to the left to make the screen darker. This sets the screen brightness for the current lighting conditions.

The Auto-Brightness option displayed under the brightness slider has a virtual on/off switch associated with it. When it's turned on, your device takes into account the surrounding lighting where you're using your Phone or iPad, and then adjusts the screen's brightness accordingly.

FIGURE 2.7

Use the brightness slider to control how light or dark your iPhone or iPad's screen appears. Shown here is the Brightness & Wallpaper submenu found in the Settings app of the iPad.

The default setting for the Auto-Brightness feature is the On position. Leave it there, unless you consistently have difficulty seeing what's displayed on your iPhone or iPad's screen based on its brightness setting.

Customize Your Lock Screen and Home Screen Wallpaper

One of the ways you can customize the appearance of your iPhone or iPad is to change the wallpaper displayed on the device's Lock Screen and behind your app icons on the Home Screen.

From the Brightness & Wallpaper option available from within Settings, you can quickly change the wallpapers that are displayed on your device. As you'll discover, your iPhone or iPad has more than two dozen preinstalled wallpaper designs built in, plus you can use any digital images stored on your device (in the Photos app) as your Lock Screen or Home Screen wallpaper.

When you tap on the Brightness & Wallpaper option, the Brightness & Wallpaper submenu options appear. Below the brightness slider is the Wallpaper option. Here, you see a thumbnail graphic of your iPhone or iPad's Lock Screen (left) and its Home Screen (right).

Tap on either of these thumbnail images to change its appearance. When you do this, the Settings screen changes, and two options are listed. On top is the Wallpaper option. Below it is the Camera Roll and Photos app Albums options (where photos shot with your iPhone or iPad or that are being stored on your device are stored).

Tap on the Wallpaper option to display thumbnails for the preinstalled wallpaper graphics you can choose from (as shown in Figure 2.8), and then tap on your selection.

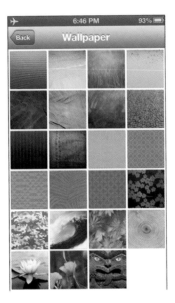

FIGURE 2.8

When looking at the collection of wallpaper graphics, tap on the one you'd like to use. (Shown here on the iPhone 5.)

Next, on the iPad's screen, the graphic you select is displayed in full-screen mode. In the upper-right corner of the screen are three command icons, labeled Set Lock Screen, Set Home Screen, and Set Both. Tap on one of these buttons to continue.

On the iPhone, after tapping on your wallpaper selection and then tapping on the Set button, the Set Lock Screen, Set Home Screen, Set Both and Cancel buttons are displayed near the bottom of the screen (shown in Figure 2.9). Tap on your selection to continue.

Choose one of these options by tapping on its icon:

- Tap on the Set Lock Screen button to change just the wallpaper graphic of your iPhone or iPad's Lock Screen. As a reminder, this is the screen you see when you first turn on your phone or tablet, or wake it up from Sleep Mode. From the Lock Screen, you must swipe your finger along the Slide to Unlock slider to unlock the tablet and access the Home Screen.

- Tap on the Set Home Screen button to change just the wallpaper graphic of your iPhone or iPad's Home Screen. This is the graphic that appears behind your app icons on each of your Home Screen pages.

- Tap on the Set Both button to use the same wallpaper graphic as both your Lock Screen and your Home Screen wallpaper.

- Tap on the Cancel button to return to the wallpaper selection screen.

FIGURE 2.9

After selecting a wallpaper graphic to use, and then tapping on the Set button, tap on one of the four buttons to determine where the graphic is displayed—on your Lock Screen, Home Screen, or on both of these screens.

After making your selection, when you return to the iPhone or iPad's Lock Screen or Home Screen, you see your newly selected wallpaper graphic displayed.

Instead of choosing one of the preinstalled wallpaper graphics, you also have the option to use any of your own digital images, including photos you've transferred to your iOS device and have stored within the Photos app, or photos you've shot using the Camera app.

> **TIP** Using any search engine, enter the keyword "iPhone wallpaper" or "iPad wallpaper" to find free wallpaper graphics you can download.

To select one of your own photos to use as your Lock Screen or Home Screen wallpaper, tap on the Brightness & Wallpaper option within Settings, and then tap on the thumbnails that appear showcasing your iPhone or iPad's Lock Screen and Home Screen.

This time, located below the Wallpaper option, tap on the folder that contains the image you want to use as your wallpaper. This might include a photo you've shot using your iPhone or iPad (found in the Camera Roll folder), or a photo you've imported into the Photos app.

Tap on the folder name that contains the image you want to use. When all the image thumbnails appear, tap on the image thumbnail you want to use as your wallpaper for your Lock Screen and/or Home Screen. When the photo you selected appears in full-screen mode, you may need to crop or reposition the image within the on-screen frame and then tap on the Set button. Next, tap on one of the three command icons that appear. Again, your options include Set Lock Screen, Set Home Screen, and Set Both.

After you've made your selection, your newly selected wallpaper graphic appears on your Lock Screen and/or Home Screen, as you can see in Figure 2.10 and Figure 2.11.

FIGURE 2.10

A newly selected Lock Screen graphic, chosen from a photo stored on the iPhone 5 in the Photos app, is shown.

FIGURE 2.11

The image selected from within Settings is now displayed as your Home Screen wallpaper, behind your app icons (shown here on the iPad).

PICTURE FRAME (iPAD)

When your iPad isn't in use or on the go with you, perhaps it sits idly on your desk. If this is the case, instead of looking at a dark screen while the unit is in Sleep Mode awaiting its next use, you can transform the tablet into a digital picture frame and have it display an animated slideshow of your favorite images.

Every time you turn on your iPad, or awaken it from Sleep Mode, the Lock Screen appears. In the lower-right corner of this screen is a picture frame icon. It's used to transform your tablet into a digital picture frame.

However, to personalize the settings of this Picture Frame app, you'll need to access the Picture Frame options from Settings. When you tap on the Picture Frame option within Settings, the Picture Frame options are displayed.

From the Picture Frame menu in Settings, you can adjust the animated transition shown in between images. Your choices are Dissolve or Origami.

Moving down on this menu screen, determine how long each image is displayed (your choices are 2, 3, 5, 10, or 20 seconds) and whether you want the app to automatically zoom in on each person's face as your images are displayed.

The Zoom In on Faces option and the Shuffle option (which determines whether the images are displayed in order or randomly) both have virtual on/off switches associated with them. Tap on each switch to move it from on to off, or vice versa.

From the bottom area of the Picture Frame menu screen within Settings, choose which images are displayed as part of your slideshow. Choose either All Photos, or a specific Album or Event folder.

When you launch the Picture Frame app from the Lock Screen, how the slideshow is presented is based on the settings you've selected and/or personalized using the Settings app.

! CAUTION If you use the Picture frame feature, plug your iOS device into an external power source. Otherwise, you'll run down the battery faster.

PRIVACY (iPHONE/iPAD)

This newly enhanced menu option within Settings gives you much greater privacy control in terms of how information is shared between apps, as well as shared with other people. From this menu screen, you can control specifically which apps have access to the iOS device's Location Services feature, for example, plus which other apps certain pre-installed apps (including Contacts, Calendar, Reminders and Photos) will be able to share data with.

It's important to customize the Location Services options if you're concerned that certain apps will be able to pinpoint your exact location at any given time and potentially share this information.

Certain apps and services, such as Maps or Find My iPhone (or Find My iPad), for example, utilize the capability to pinpoint your exact location.

TIP If you utilize the Find My Friends app, which allows authorized people to track your whereabouts in real time, customize the Location Services options related to Find My Friends, and from within the app, to determine who can "follow" you and when. You can turn on or off this functionally quickly and whenever you like, but you must remember to turn it off when you want your privacy.

When the master virtual switch for Location Services option is turned on, your iPhone or iPad can fully utilize its GPS capabilities, in addition to crowd-sourced Wi-Fi hotspots and cell towers, to determine your exact location. When it's turned off, your device cannot determine (or broadcast) your location. However, some of your apps will not function properly.

> **TIP** When the Location Services option is turned on and you snap a photo or shoot video using the Camera app, the exact location where that photo or video was shot will be recorded and saved. This feature is deactivated if you turn off the Location Services option. You can also leave the master Location Services feature for your device turned on, but turn off this feature in conjunction with specific apps, such as the Camera app.

iCLOUD (iPHONE/iPAD)

You'll learn all about using iCloud in conjunction with your iPhone or iPad from Chapter 6.

MAIL, CONTACTS, CALENDARS (iPHONE/iPAD)

If you use your iPhone or iPad on the job, three apps you probably rely on heavily are Mail, Contacts, and Calendars. From the Settings app, you can customize a handful of options pertaining to each of these apps, and you can actually set up your existing email accounts to work with your iPhone or tablet.

For information about how to use the Settings app to customize the Mail app-related settings, see Chapter 14, "Manage Your Email Efficiently." You can find details about customizing the settings of the Contacts and Calendar apps in Chapter 15, "Calendar and Contact Management Strategies."

> **TIP** Under the Calendars heading of the Mail, Contacts, Calendars option, one feature that's available is Default Alert Time. Tapping on this option within Settings reveals the Default Alert Times menu screen, from which you can automatically set advance alarms for birthdays, events, and all-day events stored in your Calendar app.
>
> If you fill in the Birthday field as you create contact entries in the Contacts app, these dates can automatically be displayed in the Calendars app to remind you of birthdays. By setting the Default Alert Times feature within Settings once, you will automatically be reminded of each upcoming birthday, event, or all-day event at 9:00 on the morning of the event, one day before the event, two days before the event, or one week before the event, based on your preference.
>
> The advance warning of a birthday, for example, gives you ample time to send a card (using the optional Cards app, for example) or send a gift.

MORE APP-SPECIFIC OPTIONS WITHIN SETTINGS

As you scroll down on the main Settings menu on your iPhone or iPad, you'll see specific apps listed, including some of the core preinstalled apps (such as Notes, Reminders, Messages, FaceTime, Maps, Safari, iTunes, App Store, Music, Newsstand and Videos), as well as optional Apple-created apps if they're installed on your device (such as iBooks).

As you continue scrolling down, you'll see listings for Twitter and Facebook, which lead to sub-menus that offer the ability to fully customize Twitter and Facebook integration within iOS 6 and many of the apps you'll soon be using.

Towards the bottom of this app listing within the main Settings screen will be third-party apps that have features or functions that can be customized from within Settings. Among these app listings will be Pages, Numbers and Keynote, if you have these popular iWork for iOS apps installed.

You'll learn more about adjusting these app-specific settings later.

USER-INSTALLED APPS

By scrolling toward the bottom of the Settings menu, you'll discover a listing of other individual apps that you have installed on your iPhone or iPad and that have user-adjustable options or settings available. Tap on one app listing at a time to modify these settings. Remember, as you install new apps in the future, additional app listings will be added to this section of the Settings menu and will need to be adjusted accordingly.

KEEP YOUR DEVICE AND DATA PRIVATE: HOW TO ACTIVATE AND USE THE PASSCODE LOCK FEATURE

There are several simple ways to protect the data stored on your iPhone or iPad, and keep it away from unauthorized users. If you want to keep data on your phone or tablet private, the first thing to do is set up and activate the Passcode Lock feature that's built in to iOS 6.

From the Settings app, tap on the General option. Next, tap on the Passcode Lock option to turn on this feature. (By default, the Passcode option is turned off.)

When the Passcode Lock screen appears, tap on the button located at the top of the screen that's labeled Turn Passcode On to activate this security feature.

When the Set Passcode window appears on the phone or tablet's screen (shown in Figure 2.12), use the virtual numeric keypad to create a four-digit security passcode for your device. This code will be requested every time the iPhone or iPad is turned on or woken up from Sleep Mode.

FIGURE 2.12

From the Passcode Lock screen (shown here on the iPad), set and then activate the Passcode Lock feature built into your iOS mobile device. Use it to keep unauthorized people from using your tablet or accessing your sensitive data.

You can enter any four-digit code. Input one digit at a time when the Set Passcode window appears. When prompted, type the same code a second time. When you've done this, the Set Passcode window disappears and the feature becomes active.

Now, from the Passcode Lock screen within Settings, you can further customize this feature. For example, tap on the Require Passcode option to determine when the iPhone or iPad prompts the user to enter the passcode. The default option is Immediately, meaning between when the Lock Screen and Home Screen appears each time the phone or tablet is turned on or woken up.

If you don't believe that a four-digit passcode is secure enough, turn off the Simple Passcode option. When you do this, a Change Passcode window appears, along with the full virtual keyboard. You can now create a more complicated, alphanumeric password to protect your device from unauthorized usage. Anytime you have the option to create a password or passcode on an iOS device, or on your computer or for accessing a website, for example, avoid using something obvious, such as "1234" or your birthday. When possible, mix and match numbers and letters to create your password.

From this screen, if you're using an iPad, you can also determine whether the Picture Frame app option will be displayed on your Lock Screen. This option has a virtual on/off switch associated with it. When it's turned on, the Picture Frame app icon will appear on the Lock Screen. When it's turned off, you cannot turn on the Picture Frame app from the Lock Screen. The app icon to do so will not be displayed.

Also on the Passcode Lock screen is the Erase Data option. If an unauthorized user enters the wrong passcode 10 consecutive times, the iPhone or iPad will automatically erase all data stored on it, if this feature is turned on.

> **❗CAUTION** Activating the Erase Data feature gives you an added layer of security if your tablet falls into the wrong hands. However, to recover the data later, you must have a reliable backup created and stored. Otherwise, that data will be lost forever.

ORGANIZE APPS ON YOUR HOME SCREEN WITH FOLDERS

If you're like most iPhone and iPad users, you'll probably be loading a handful of third-party apps onto your device. After all, there are several hundred thousand third-party apps to choose from. To make finding and organizing your apps easier from the iPhone or iPad's Home Screen, and to reduce onscreen clutter, you can place app icons in folders.

Utilizing the Folders feature is easy. From the Home Screen, press and hold down any app icon until all the app icons begin shaking on the Home Screen. Using your finger, drag one app icon on top of another, to automatically place both of those apps into a new folder.

You can organize your apps in folders based on categories, like Games, Travel, Finance, Productivity, Social Networking, or Bookmarks (shown in Figure 2.13), plus choose your own folder names (or use what's suggested), and then drag and drop the appropriate app icons into the folders you create. After your app icons are organized, simply press the Home button again on the iPhone or iPad to save your folders and display them on your Home Screen.

FIGURE 2.13

On this iPad, a Photography folder has been created. It contains 12 different photography-related apps.

If you later want to remove an app icon from a folder, so that it appears as a stand-alone app icon on your Home Screen, simply press and hold any of the folder icons until all the onscreen icons start to shake. The folder's contents are displayed.

Using your finger, when the app icons are shaking, simply drag the app icons, one at a time, back onto the Home Screen. Each will then be removed from the folder. Press the Home button to finalize this action.

> **TIP**　One feature that's not new to iOS 6, but that's very useful, is the capability to move app icons around on your iPhone or iPad's Home Screen. From the Home Screen, press and hold down any app icon with your finger. When the app icons start to shake, you can use your finger to drag one app icon at a time around on the Home Screen.
>
> Your iPhone or iPad can extend the Home Screen across multiple pages. (Switch pages by swiping your finger from left to right, or right to left when viewing the Home Screen.)
>
> To move an app icon to another Home Screen page, while it's shaking, hold it down with your finger and slowly drag it to the extreme right or left, off of the screen, so that it bounces onto another of the Home Screen's pages.

Although you can customize which app icons will appear on which Home Screen page, the row of up to four app icons displayed at the very bottom of the iPhone's screen (or up to six app icons on the iPad's screen) remains constant. Place your most frequently used apps in these positions so that they're always visible from the Home Screen.

As the app icons are shaking on the Home Screen, you can delete the icons that display a black-and-white "X" in the upper-left corner from your iPhone or iPad by pressing that "X" icon. You'll discover that the preinstalled (core) apps related to iOS 6, like Contacts, Calendar, Reminders, Notes, App Store, and Settings, cannot be deleted. They can only be moved.

ADD FREQUENTLY USED WEB PAGE ICONS TO YOUR HOME SCREEN

Many people constantly return to their favorite websites for updates throughout the day or week. Instead of first accessing the Safari browser on your iPhone or iPad, and then choosing your favorite sites from your Bookmarks list, you can create individual icons for your favorite web pages, and display them on your Home Screen. This allows you to access that web page with a single tap of the finger from the Home Screen.

Depending on the website, when you create a Web Page Icon, it either uses a thumbnail image from the website itself or a pre-designed logo or graphic. In Figure 2.14, the Jason R. Rich icon shows a thumbnail for the JasonRich.com website, while the CNN icon is for CNN.com.

To create a Web Page icon on your Home Screen, access Safari and visit your favorite web page. Next, tap the Share icon that's located next to the Address Bar (shown in Figure 2.15), and tap the Add to Home Screen option that appears.

FIGURE 2.14

A web page icon (such as the one for JasonRich.com or CNN.com) on your Home Screen looks similar to an app icon; however, when you tap it, Safari is launched and the web page that the icon is associated with is loaded automatically.

FIGURE 2.15

To create a web page icon that appears on your Home Screen, use the Add to Home Screen command displayed when you tap the Share icon within Safari (shown here on the iPhone 5).

The menu that appears when you tap on the Share icon contains several features that are new to iOS 6. Learn more about the new features added to Safari in Chapter 13, "Use New Safari Features to Surf More Efficiently."

When you return to your Home Screen, the icon for that web page is now displayed, and looks very much like an app icon. To access that web page in the future, simply tap the appropriate icon on the Home Screen.

ACCESSING THE MULTITASKING BAR

Your iPhone or iPad has the capability to run multiple apps simultaneously. From the multitasking bar, you can quickly switch between apps without first closing one app and launching another.

To access the multitasking bar (shown in Figure 2.16 on the iPad), quickly tap the Home button on your iPhone or iPad twice. At the very bottom of the screen, a horizontal line of app icons that are currently running on your device is displayed. Using your finger, you can scroll left or right to view all the apps. Anytime the multitasking bar is showing, you can also tap on any app to instantly switch to that app.

FIGURE 2.16

The multitasking bar allows you to switch between whichever app you're currently using and any other app that's simultaneously running in the background.

To exit out of the multitasking bar, either tap on an app icon that's displayed on the multitasking bar or press the Home button again once.

> ☑ **TIP**   On the iPad, hold four or five fingers together and drag them from the very bottom of the iPad's screen toward the top to make the Multitasking Bar appear (instead of pressing the Home button twice quickly).

Also, while the Multitasking bar is visible, you can swipe your finger from left to right on the bar and scroll to the Music control panel that is part of iOS 6. This allows you to manage and play music in the background while you're using your iPhone or iPad for other purposes.

Figure 2.17 shows the Music control panel that is accessible from the multitasking bar, without you having to launch the Music app separately. The icon displayed on the extreme left of the Music controls enables you to lock (or unlock) your iOS device's screen rotation.

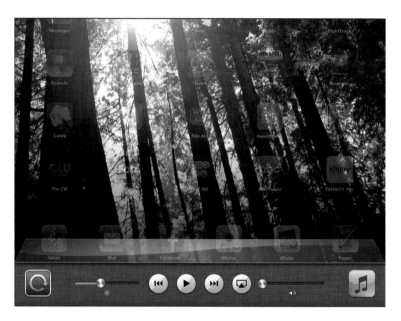

FIGURE 2.17

From the multitasking bar, you can access the Music control panel and play music in the background while you're using your iPhone or iPad for other tasks. This is shown here on the iPad.

> **TIP** The multitasking bar is useful for a variety of things. For example, you can quickly use iOS 6's Select, Select All, Cut, Copy, and Paste commands to move text from one app to another.

> **TIP** If you notice your iPhone or iPad becomes sluggish, it could be a result of too many apps being open at once. In this situation, launch the multitasking bar, press and hold down one app icon until they all start to shake, and then tap on the "X" icon associated with all apps you're not currently using or that do not need to be open. This shuts down those apps, but does not delete them from your iPhone or iPad.

NOTE When viewing the Music controls from the Multitasking Bar, the icon on the left serves as the screen rotation lock. When activated, the screen will not automatically readjust from portrait to landscape mode (or vice versa) when you physically rotate the iPhone, iPad, or iPad mini. On the iPhone, when viewing the Music controls displayed as part of the Multitasking Bar, scroll again from left to right to access the separate, on-screen volume control slider.

3

STRATEGIES FOR FINDING, BUYING, AND USING THIRD-PARTY APPS

In the process of improving its iOS 6 operating system, Apple has once again tinkered with the collection of preinstalled apps that you'll discover on your Home Screen. This collection of apps enables you to begin utilizing your iPhone or iPad for a wide range of popular tasks without first having to find and install additional apps.

However, one of the things that has set the iPhone and iPad apart from its competition, and has made these devices among the most sought after and popular throughout much of the world, is the library of optional apps available for them. Whereas other smartphones or tablets might offer a collection of a few hundred or even a few thousand optional apps, third-party developers have created an ever-growing collection of iPhone and iPad apps that's now in the hundreds of thousands of choices.

All the apps currently available for your iOS device can be found, purchased (if applicable), downloaded, and installed from Apple's online-based App Store.

> **✓ TIP** From the App Store, several Apple-created (or endorsed) iPhone and iPad apps are available. Some of these free apps include iBooks (for download-ing and reading books), Find My Friends (for tracking the whereabouts of your friends and family and allowing them to track your location in real time), Cards (for creating and mailing custom greeting cards from your iOS device), Pod-casts (for downloading or streaming free podcasts), iTunes U (for accessing the incredible collection of personal enrichment and educational content compiled by Apple), the official Twitter app (for managing one or more Twitter accounts from your iPhone or iPad), the official Facebook app (for managing all aspects of your Facebook account), and Find My iPhone. (As an alternative for visiting www.iCloud.com/#Find, this app is used to pinpoint the exact location of a missing iPhone, iPad, and/or Macs.)

APP STORE BASICS

There are two ways to access the App Store: directly from your iPhone or iPad (using the App Store app that comes preinstalled on your device), or using iTunes on your primary computer. The App Store app is used exclusively for finding, pur-chasing (if applicable), downloading, and installing apps directly on your device from the App Store; iTunes on your primary computer is used to access the App Store, but, among many other things, can also be used to access the iTunes Store and Apple's iBookstore to find, purchase (if applicable), download, and install many other types of content.

> **✎ NOTE** In conjunction with the release of iOS 6, Apple has redesigned the layout of the App Store which is accessible from the App Store app.

FREE OR PURCHASED?

As you're about to discover, some apps available from the App Store are free. To download them, you still go through the same process as you do for purchasing an app; however, instead of tapping on the Price icon, followed by the Buy App icon to confirm your purchase, you'll tap on the Free icon associated with the app, followed by an Install App icon. You will not be charged for downloading a free app. You will, however, still need to supply your Apple ID password to confirm the transaction, download, and then automatically install the app.

Before you begin your quest for the perfect collection of apps that will meet your wants and needs, and that will greatly expand what your iPhone and/or iPad is capable of, there are a few things you need to understand about apps in general, which are explained in this chapter.

In addition to apps, you can add a wide range of content to your iPhone or iPad, such as music, movies, TV shows, podcasts, audiobooks, and eBooks. How to acquire and enjoy this content is also mentioned later in this chapter.

HOW NEW APPS INSTALL THEMSELVES

If you're shopping for apps directly from your iPhone or iPad, when you purchase a paid app or download a free app, after you confirm your decision, the app will automatically download and install itself on your device. After it's installed, its app icon appears on your iPhone or iPad's Home Screen and is ready to use.

You can also shop for apps from your primary computer and transfer them to your iPhone or iPad, or sync apps between your various mobile devices using the iTunes Sync process or iCloud.

RESTORING OR REINSTALLING APPS YOU'VE ALREADY DOWNLOADED

To download an app that's already been purchased or downloaded onto another computer or device, in the App Store app on the iPad you're using, tap on the Purchased icon that's displayed at the bottom of the screen. (On the iPhone, tap on the Updates icon, and then tap on the Purchased icon that's displayed at the top of the Updates screen.) All your app purchases to date are displayed.

> **NOTE** At the top of the Purchased screen on the iPhone or iPad, tap on the All tab to view all of the apps you've purchase to date for that device. You also have the option to tap on the Not On This iPhone/Not On This iPad tab to view apps you've acquired in the past, but that are not currently installed on the device you're using.

Instead of a Free or Price icon being associated with each app description, you will see an iCloud icon. Tap on that iCloud icon to download the app (without having to pay for it again) to the iOS device you're currently using. You can only install already purchased apps that are compatible with that iOS device. For example, you can't install an iPad-specific app onto an iPhone or iPod touch.

> ☑ **TIP** From the Settings app, you have the option to have your iOS device automatically download and install any new (and compatible) music, apps, or books purchased using your Apple ID on any other computer or device. To set this up, launch Settings, select the iTunes & App Store option from the main Settings menu, and then adjust the Automatic Downloads options, which include Music, Apps, and Books. You can also decide whether this feature will work with a cellular data Web connection or just when a Wi-Fi Internet connection exists.

WHERE TO FIND APPS, MUSIC, AND MORE

If you're shopping for apps, music, movies, TV shows, podcasts, audiobooks, eBooks, ringtones or other content from your primary computer, with the goal of transferring what you acquire to your iPhone or iPad later via the iTunes sync process or via iCloud, you'll use the latest version of iTunes on your computer.

However, from your iPhone or iPad, acquiring and then enjoying different types of content is done using a handful of different apps. Table 3.1 explains which preinstalled app you should use to acquire and then enjoy various types of content on your iOS device.

Table 3.1   How to Acquire and Enjoy Various Types of Content on Your iPhone or iPad

Content Type	Acquire the Content with This App	Enjoy the Content with with This App
Apps	App Store	The app itself that you download and install
Digital editions of publications (including newspapers and magazines)	Newsstand	The digital publication's proprietary app
Music	iTunes	Music
Movies	iTunes	Videos
TV shows	iTunes	Videos
Podcasts	Podcasts**	Podcasts
Audiobooks	iTunes (or the optional Audible app)	Music (or the optional Audible app)
eBooks*	iBooks (to access iBookstore)	iBooks
PDF files	Mail, iCloud, iTunes Sync	iBooks or another PDF reader app

Content Type	Acquire the Content with This App	Enjoy the Content with with This App
iTunes U Personal Enrichment and Educational Content	iTunes U***	iTunes U
Ringtones (and Alert Tones)	iTunes	Phone, FaceTime, Messages (or other apps that generate audible alarms or ringtones)

* eBooks can also be purchased from Amazon.com and read using the free Kindle app, or purchased from BN.com and read using the free Nook app.

** The Podcasts app is available for free from the App Store. It was developed by Apple and is designed to help you find and experience free podcasts on your iOS mobile device.

*** The iTunes U app serves as a gateway to a vast selection of personal enrichment and educational courses, lectures, workshops and information sessions that have been produced by leading educators, universities and other philanthropic organizations. All iTunes U content is provided for free.

EVERYTHING YOU NEED TO KNOW ABOUT APPS

Apps are individual programs that you install on your iPhone or iPad to give it additional functionality, just as you utilize different programs on your primary computer. For the iPhone or iPad, all apps are available from one central (online-based) location: the App Store.

When you begin exploring the App Store, you'll discover right away that there are literally hundreds of thousands of apps to choose from, which are divided into different categories, including Business, Finance, Lifestyle, News, Games, Education, Entertainment, Photography, Social Networking, Reference, Sports, and Travel.

COMPATIBILITY: DOES THE APP RUN ON MULTIPLE DEVICES?

In terms of compatibility, all iOS apps fall into one of three categories:

1. **iPhone-specific**—These are apps designed exclusively for the various iPhone models that might not function properly on the iPad. Most iPhone-specific apps, however, will run on an iPad, but will not take advantage of the tablet's larger screen.

   Figure 3.1 shows what an iPhone-specific app, in this case Instagram for iPhone, that's running on an iPad looks like. The app functions fine but does not take full advantage of the tablet's larger screen. A useful trick is to tap on the 2x icon in the lower-right corner of the iPad's screen to double the size of what the iPhone app is displaying on the screen (as shown in Figure 3.2). However, in some cases, this causes text and graphics to become slightly distorted.

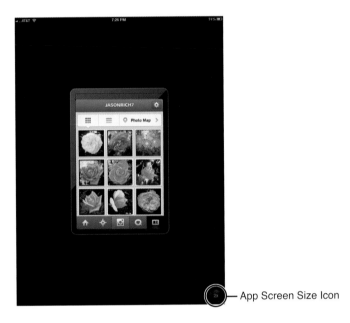

App Screen Size Icon

FIGURE 3.1

Instagram is an iPhone-specific app running on an iPad. It utilizes only a small portion of the tablet's screen that's equivalent to the screen size of an iPhone.

FIGURE 3.2

Tapping the 2x icon doubles the size of the app on the tablet's screen.

2. **iPad-specific**—These are apps designed exclusively for the iPad. They fully utilize the tablet's larger display. They will *not* function on the iPhone or on other iOS devices. iPad apps also function flawlessly on the iPad mini.

3. **Hybrid**—While you may encounter a few exceptions, these are apps designed to work on all iOS devices, including the iPhone and iPad. These apps detect which device they're running on and adapt. When you're reading an app's listing or description, and look at its Price icon, if that icon has a small plus sign in the upper-left corner (as shown in Figure 3.3), this indicates that it is a hybrid app, and will function properly on any model of iPhone or iPad.

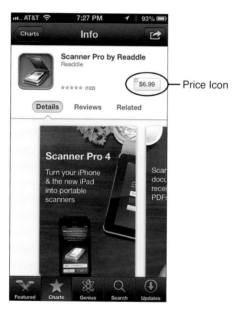

FIGURE 3.3

You can pick out hybrid apps by looking at an app listing or the description's Price icon. If you see a plus sign in the upper-left corner of a Price icon, this indicates it's a hybrid app and will function on any iOS device.

TIP If you own two or more iOS devices, such as an iPhone and an iPad (or an iPod touch), and all of the devices are registered using the same Apple ID account, you can purchase a hybrid (or iPhone-specific) app once but install it on all of your iOS devices. This can be done through iTunes Sync or via iCloud after an app is initially purchased or downloaded.

When you're browsing the App Store from your iPhone, by default it displays all iPhone-specific apps, followed by hybrid apps, but the App Store will not display iPad apps. When you're browsing the App Store from your iPad, iPad-specific, hybrid and iPhone-specific apps are listed. Tap on the Phone or iPad tab that's displayed near the top-center of the screen when viewing many areas of the App Store.

If you're shopping for apps using iTunes on your primary computer, you must click the iPhone or iPad tab that's displayed near the top center of the iTunes screen (shown in Figure 3.4) to select which format apps you're looking for.

iPhone and iPad Tabs

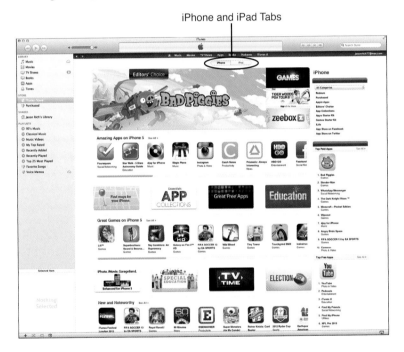

FIGURE 3.4

When shopping for apps using iTunes on your primary computer, click the appropriate tab to indicate which format apps you're looking for, keeping in mind that iPhone-specific apps will run on an iPad (but not take advantage of the tablet's larger screen), but iPad-specific apps will not run on an iPhone.

> **TIP** Because some app developers release the same app in both an iPhone-specific and an iPad-specific format, many iPad-specific apps have "HD" for High-Definition in their title, to help differentiate them from iPhone or Hybrid apps. For example, the popular game Angry Birds is for the iPhone, whereas Angry Birds HD is for the iPad. Most iPhone and all iPad and hybrid apps also function on the iPad mini.

Some iPad-specific apps include the words "for iPad" in their titles, such as GoodReader for iPad, FileMaker Go for iPad, PDF Reader Pro Edition for iPad, or Sid Meier's Pirates! for iPad.

As you look at an app's Description, look at which iOS devices are listed under the Requires heading found within the Information section to determine if a particular app will run on your device. For example, you may discover an iPhone app has been designed specifically for the iPhone 5.

QUICK GUIDE TO APP PRICING

Regardless of whether you use the App Store app from your iPhone or iPad, or visit the App Store through iTunes on your primary computer, you will need to set up an Apple ID account and have a major credit card or debit card linked to the account to make purchases.

TIP If you don't have a major credit card or debit card that you want to link with your Apple ID account so that you can purchase apps from the App Store, you can purchase prepaid iTunes Gift Cards from Apple, or most places that sell prepaid gift cards, such as convenience stores, supermarkets, and pharmacies.

iTunes Gift Cards can be used to make app and other content purchases. iTunes Gift Cards (which are different from Apple Gift Cards, which are redeemable at Apple Stores or Apple.com) are available in a variety of denominations.

The first time you access the App Store and attempt to make a purchase, you are prompted to enter your Apple ID account username and password or set up a new Apple ID account, which requires you to supply your name, address, email, and credit card information. For all subsequent online app purchases, you'll simply need to enter your Apple ID password to confirm the purchase, and your credit card or debit card will automatically be billed. (Or the purchase amount will be deducted from your iTunes Gift Card balance.)

TIP An Apple ID account can also be referred to as an iTunes Store account. To learn more about how an Apple ID account works, or to manage your account, visit www.apple.com/support/appleid. The same Apple ID you use to make purchases though the App Store, iTunes Store, iBookstore or Newsstand can also be used as your username when you're using FaceTime for video conferencing, Messages to access the iMessage service, or to access your iCloud account, for example.

> ☑ **TIP**   Some families opt to share an Apple ID account, so that their iTunes Store, App Store, iBookstore and Newsstand purchases can be shared between their computers and devices. If you share an Apple ID account for content purchases, create a separate Apple ID account for yourself that you can use in conjunction with iMessage, iCloud and FaceTime, for example.

Originally, when the App Store opened, there were two types of apps: free apps and paid apps. The free apps were often demo versions of paid apps (with limited functionality), or fully functional apps that displayed ads in the app. Paid apps were typically priced between $.99 and $9.99.

As the App Store has evolved, additional payment options and fee structures for apps have been introduced, giving app developers new ways to generate revenue, and iPhone and iPad users different methods of paying for apps and content.

The following sections summarize the different types of apps from a pricing standpoint.

FREE APPS

Free apps cost nothing to download and install on your phone or tablet. Some programmers and developers release apps for free out of pure kindness to share their creations with the iPhone- and/or iPad-using public. These are fully functional apps.

There are also free apps that serve as demo versions of paid apps. These are scaled-down versions of apps. In some cases, basic features or functions of the app are locked in the free version, but are later made available if you upgrade to the paid or premium version of the app.

A third category of free apps comprises fully functional apps that display ads as part of their content. In exchange for using the app, you'll need to view ads, which offer the option to click on offers from within the app to learn more about the product or service being advertised.

> ✐ **NOTE**   Many free apps that contain ads will also have a paid app counterpart that's ad-free.

A fourth category of free apps serves as a shell for premium (paid) content that must be loaded into the app to make it fully functional. For example, many newspaper and magazine publishers offer free apps related to their specific publications, but require users to pay for the actual content of the newspaper or magazine, which later gets downloaded into the app.

The final type of free app is fully functional but allows the user to make in-app purchases to add features or functionality to the app, or unlock premium content. The core app, without the extra content, is free, however.

> ✅ **TIP** Some fully functional apps are free because they're designed to promote a specific company or work with a specific service. For example, to use the free HBO Go app, you must be a paid subscriber of the HBO premium cable channel through your cable TV (or satellite) provider. Likewise, to use the free Netflix app, you must be a paid subscriber to this streaming movie service.

When you're looking at an app listing or description in the App Store, is the app is free, it will have a Free icon, instead of a Price icon, associated with it (as shown in Figure 3.5).

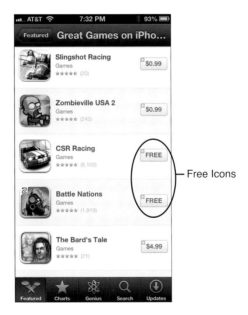

FIGURE 3.5

A free app will have a Free icon displayed in its App Store listing or description (shown here on the iPhone 5).

PAID APPS

After you purchase an app, you own it and can use it as often as you'd like, usually without incurring additional fees (although in-app purchases may be possible). You simply pay a fee for the app upfront, which is typically between $.99 and $9.99. All future upgrades or new versions of the app are free of charge.

In the app listing and description for a paid app, you will see a Price icon displayed for that app, which lists how much the app costs. To purchase the app, tap on this Price icon. It is replaced by a Buy App icon, which needs to be tapped, allowing you to confirm your purchase decision. It is then typically necessary to enter the password associated with your Apple ID account. The cost of the app is charged to the major credit card associated with your Apple ID account or deducted from the balance of your iTunes gift card.

SUBSCRIPTION-BASED APPS

These apps are typically free, and then you pay a recurring subscription fee for content, which automatically gets downloaded into the app. Many digital editions of newspapers, such as the *New York Times* and the *Wall Street Journal*, utilize a subscription app model, as do hundreds of different magazines.

Typically, the main content of the digital and printed version of a publication are identical. However, you can view the digital edition on your iPhone or iPad, and take advantage of added interactive elements built in to the app. If you're already a subscriber to the printed version of a newspaper or magazine, some publishers offer the digital edition free, while others charge an extra fee to subscribe to the digital edition as well. Or you can subscribe to just the digital edition of a publication.

With some magazines, you can download the free app for a specific publication and then, in the app, purchase one issue at a time, such as the current issue or a single past issue. There is no long-term subscription commitment, but individual issues of the publication still need to be purchased and downloaded. Or you can purchase an ongoing (recurring) subscription and new issues of that publication will automatically be downloaded to your iPhone or iPad as they become available.

$\mathcal{P}$ **MORE INFO** Apps that offer subscription-based content always allow you to easily subscribe from within the app, usually with the single touch of an icon. However, if you want to cancel or change your recurring (paid) subscription, you'll need to access the Manage App Subscriptions section of iTunes on your primary computer, or access your Apple ID Account Page from within the App Store app. The link to manage your Apple ID account (and also manage recurring subscriptions) is found near the very bottom of most pages in the App Store app.

Digital editions of magazines and newspapers can be purchased from the Newsstand app. These publications each require their own proprietary app to access and read the publication's content. You will discover digital editions of many popular publications available from the Newsstand app.

TIP You can browse available digital publications and then manage your subscriptions using the Newsstand app that comes preinstalled on your iPhone or iPad.

IN-APP PURCHASES

This type of app might be free, or it might be a paid app. However, as you're actually using the app, you can purchase additional content or add new features and functionality to the app by making in-app purchases. The capability to make in-app purchases has become very popular, and is being used by app developers in a variety of ways.

As you read an app's description in the App Store, if an app requires in-app purchases, it is revealed in the text included in the app description screen. Look for the heading within an apps description that says Top In-App Purchases and tap on it.

CAUTION The price you pay for an app does not translate directly to the quality or usefulness of that app. There are some free or very inexpensive apps that are extremely useful and packed with features, and that can really enhance your experience using your iPhone or iPad. However, there are costly apps (priced at $4.99 or more) that are poorly designed or filled with bugs, or that don't live up to expectations or to the description of the app offered by the app's developer or publisher.

The price of each app is set by the developer or programmer that created or is selling the app. Instead of using the price as the only determining factor if you're evaluating several apps that appear to offer similar functionality, be sure to read the app's customer reviews carefully, and pay attention to the star-based rating the app has received. These user reviews and ratings are a much better indicator of the app's quality and usefulness than the price of the app.

HOW TO SHOP WITH THE APP STORE APP

From your iPhone or iPad's Home Screen, to access the App Store, tap on the blue-and-white App Store app icon. Your device must have access to the Internet via a 3G/4G or Wi-Fi connection.

When you access the App Store via the App Store app (shown in Figure 3.6 on the iPad), you'll discover a handful of command icons at the top and bottom of the screen that are used to navigate your way around the online-based store.

FIGURE 3.6

The main App Store app screen on the iPad. Find, purchase, download, and install apps directly from your tablet.

If you already know the name of the app you want to find, purchase, download, and install, tap on the Search field, which is located in the upper-right corner of the screen in the iPad version. On the iPhone, tap on the Search option displayed at the bottom of the App Store app's screen (as shown in Figure 3.7).

Using the virtual keyboard, enter the name of the app. Tap the Search key on the virtual keyboard to begin the search. You can also perform a search based on a keyword or phrase, such as "word processing," "to-do lists," "time management," or "photo editing."

In a few seconds, matching results are displayed on the App Store screen in the form of app previews. When you access the App Store from your iPhone using the App Store app, iPhone-specific and hybrid apps are displayed.

Search Field

Search Field

FIGURE 3.7

From your iPhone, tap on the Search icon to search for any app in the App Store by name or keyword. Here, the keyword "Sonic" was used to locate the various Sonic The Hedgehog games from Sega that have been adapted for the iPhone and iPad.

Likewise, if you're shopping for apps from your iPad, as you browse the App Store using the App Store app, iPad-specific apps will be displayed if you tap on the iPad tab near the top-center of most areas within the App Store. Hybrid apps will display a plus sign in the upper-left corner their Price icon.

> **TIP** If you use both an iPhone and an iPad, make a point to seek out hybrid apps that will run on both devices. If you only use an iPad, look for iPad-specific apps first, then apps that are designed for both iPad and iPhone. Most apps that are iPhone-specific will run fine on an iPad, but the app's graphics and user interface will be formatted for the iPhone's smaller screen.

> **TIP** At the bottom center of the main App Store screen on the iPad (when using the App Store app) are several command icons, labeled Featured, Charts, Genius, Purchased and Updates. On the iPhone, the icons along the bottom of the screen are labeled Featured, Charts, Genius, Search and Updates. If you don't know the exact name of an app you're looking for, these command icons will help you browse the App Store and discover apps that might be of interest to you.

THE FEATURED COMMAND ICON

Tap on the Featured command icon that is displayed near the bottom of the App Store screen to see a listing of what Apple considers "Featured" apps. These are divided into a handful of categories. For example, Figure 3.8 shows a specialty category, called Amazing Apps on iPhone 5. Either flick your finger from right to left to scroll horizontally through the apps listed, or tap on the See All option that's displayed to the right of the category heading.

Near the top of the screen are large graphic banners that constantly change. In Figure 3.8, the banner simply says "Games," however, it constantly scrolls and often showcases specific apps. These banner graphics promote what Apple considers the "App of the Week," as well as other noteworthy apps the company wants to promote.

On the iPhone or iPad, when looking at any of the app sections after tapping on the Featured option, use your finger to scroll through the displayed app icons, or to view a more comprehensive listing of apps, tap on the See All option that's displayed to the immediate right of each heading.

FIGURE 3.8

View apps that Apple is featuring within specialized categories within the App Store. The category "Amazing Apps for iPhone 5" is shown here.

THE GENIUS APP ICON

The App Store keeps track of all apps you purchase. When you tap on the Genius command icon that's displayed near the bottom center of the App Store screen, the App Store will analyze your past app purchases and offer suggestions for other apps you might be interested in.

> **NOTE** For this feature to work, the Genius feature must first be turned on. You'll be given the option to turn on this feature the first time you tap on the Genius icon within the App Store app.

THE CHARTS ICON

When you tap on the Charts command icon, also located near the bottom center of the App Store app's screen, a listing of Top Paid, Top Free and Top Grossing apps are displayed (shown in Figure 3.9). These charts are based on all app categories. To view charts related to a specific app category, such as Business or Games, first tap on the Charts button, then tap on the Categories button and choose a category.

FIGURE 3.9

From the App Store app on the iPad, tap on the Charts icon at the bottom of the screen to view a list of popular free, paid and top grossing apps.

Three new, category specific charts—Top Free, Top Paid, and Top Grossing—will be displayed. Tap on the See All option to the right of each heading to view up to 300 related apps.

App Store categories include the following:

- Books
- Business
- Catalogs
- Education
- Entertainment
- Finance
- Food & Drink
- Games
- Health & Fitness
- Lifestyle
- Medical
- Music
- Navigation
- News
- Newsstand
- Photo & Video
- Productivity
- Reference
- Social Networking
- Sports
- Travel
- Utilities
- Weather

MANAGE YOUR ACCOUNT AND REDEEM iTUNES GIFT CARDS

When you scroll down to the very bottom of the Featured screen within the App Store, you'll see two command buttons displayed. They're labeled Redeem and Apple ID [Your Apple ID Username].

Tap on the Redeem icon to redeem a prepaid iTunes Gift Card. Tap on the Apple ID [Your Apple ID Username] button to manage your Apple ID account and update your credit card information, for example.

To manage your recurring paid subscriptions, tap on the Apple ID account button that's displayed at the bottom of the Featured page. When the Apple ID window appears (shown in Figure 3.10), tap on the View Apple ID option. When prompted, enter your password. Then, when the Account Settings screen is displayed, scroll down to the Subscriptions heading and tap on the Manage button. You'll then be able to modify or cancel your paid recurring subscriptions to digital newspapers or magazines, for example.

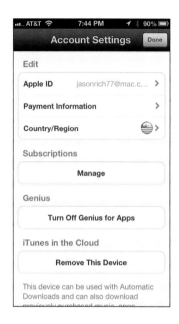

FIGURE 3.10

From the View Account option, you can change or cancel your recurring paid subscriptions for digital editions of newspapers and magazines.

FEATURES OF AN APP LISTING

As you browse the App Store, each screen is composed of many app listings (or more information-packed app previews). Each listing promotes a specific app and displays the app's title, graphic icon or logo, what category the app falls into and its price. Within an app preview (shown in Figure 3.11), the app's title, its logo/ graphic, the app's developer, it's average star-based rating, how many ratings the app has received (the number in parenthesis), the price icon, and a sample screen shot from the app itself is displayed.

> **! CAUTION** Some free apps are, in fact, free. However, they might ulti-mately require you to pay for a content subscription or make in-app purchases to fully utilize the app. App pricing is explained in the section, "Quick Guide to App Pricing."

FIGURE 3.11

A sample app preview contains important, at-a-glace details about that app, including its title and price. Here, a Search was performed on the iPad using the phrase "Microsoft Office," and app preview boxes for several of the 126 search results are displayed.

LEARN BEFORE YOU BUY: ACCESSING THE APP'S DESCRIPTION PAGE

Before committing to a purchase, as you're looking at an app's listing or preview in the App Store, you can tap on its title or graphic icon to view a detailed description. When you do this, the App Store screen is replaced with a detailed description of the app. (On the iPad, a new app description window is displayed.)

An app description screen (like the one shown in Figure 3.12) displays the app's title and logo near the top of the screen, along with its price icon, average start-based rating and the number of ratings it's received.

You'll then see three command tabs, labeled Details, Reviews and Related. Tap on the Details tab to view a detailed description of the app. Tap on the Reviews tab to view a star-based ratings chart for that app, as well as detailed text-based reviews written by your fellow iPhone and iPad users. Tap on the Related tab to view similar apps that are available from the App Store.

Displayed immediately below the Details, Reviews and Related tab are sample screen shots from the app itself. Swipe your finger horizontally to scroll through the sample screen shots, or scroll downwards to view the Details, Reviews or Related information, based on which command tab you've tapped.

FIGURE 3.12
From an app's description screen (shown here for the NFL Pro 2013 app on the iPad), you can learn all about a specific app. This information can help you decide whether it's of interest to you, or relevant to your needs.

What's Offered When You Tap The Details Tab

Displayed immediately below the sample screen shots from the app is a text-based description of the app that has been written and supplied by the app's developer. This description is a sales tool that's designed to sell apps.

Below the Description is information about what new features have been added to the app in the most recent version. Look for the What's New heading. Then, as you scroll downward on this screen, you'll see the Information section. The following headings are displayed, along with related details related to that app:

- **Seller**—Here, the developer or publisher of the app is displayed.

- **Category**—Quickly determine which app category the app falls into, such as Business, Games, Productivity to Finance.

- **Updated**—See when the last update for the app was released.

- **Version**—View the current version number of the app that's available.

- **Size**—This refers to the file size of the app itself. In other words, how much internal storage space it will utilize on your iOS device. Any app-specific data related to this app will require additional storage space.

■ **Rating**—This rating refers to the age-appropriateness of the app. Apps with a 4+ are suitable for all ages. Apps with a 9+ rating are suitable for users over the age of 9, while apps with a 12+ rating are suitable for people over the age of 12. If an app has a 17+ rating, this means it contains material that is most suitable for adults only.

■ **Requires**—Here, the system requirements for the app are listed. This includes which model iPhones and/or iPads the app will function on.

Below the Information section, you'll find the Developer Info link. Tap on this to discover other apps available from the same developer or publisher. Tap on the Version History link to see a description of each version of the app that's been released, as well as what additional features or bug fixes have been incorporated.

If a Top In-App Purchases option is displayed, tap on it to discover what in-app purchases are available related to that app, and determine what they cost.

> ☑ **TIP**   If you're looking at descriptions for game apps, within the Information section, which is displayed when you tap on the Details tab, look for the Game Center logo to determine if that multi-player game is compatible with Apple's Game Center service (and the Game Center app).

What's Offered When You Tap The Reviews Tab

When you tap on the Reviews tab, the App Store Ratings chart will be displayed (shown in Figure 3.13). This graphically shows how many ratings the app has received, as well as its overall average rating and total number of ratings. A top rating is five stars.

Below the App Store Ratings chart, which offers an at-a-glance look at the quality of an app (based on ratings submitted by other iOS mobile device users), you'll see detailed text-based reviews that have been written by other App Store customers.

> ☑ **TIP**   Obviously, an app with a large number of five-star ratings is probably excellent, whereas an app that consistently earns three stars or less is probably not that great or is loaded with bugs.
>
> As you review an app's description, keep scrolling downward, below the star ratings summary chart, and you'll be able to read full reviews that your fellow users have written about that app. These reviews often describe the best features of the app and/or its worst problems.

FIGURE 3.13

Every app description contains an average rating and a rating summary chart. Use it to quickly see what other users think about the app you're currently looking at.

WHAT'S NEW As you're looking at an app's Description screen, when you tap on the Ratings and Reviews tap, above the App Store Ratings chart will be a Facebook "Like" button, which allows you to "Like" the app and share details about it on your Facebook page with your online friends. Simply tap the "Like" button to do this if you have Facebook integration set up on your iOS mobile device. To "unlike" an app you've previously "liked," click the "Like" button again.

What's Offered When You Tap The Related Tab

These are listings for other apps, usually similar in functionality to the app you're looking at.

TIP Additional information about the app can also be obtained from the App Developer Web Site or the App Support website, both of which are operated by the app developer.

On the iPhone, to exit an app's description page and continue browsing the App Store, tap on the left-pointing arrow icon that's displayed near the top-left corner of the screen. On the iPad, tap anywhere outside of the app's description window.

KEEP YOUR APPS CURRENT WITH THE UPDATES COMMAND ICON

One of the command icons that's constantly displayed at the bottom of the App Store app's screen is the Updates icon. This is used to keep your currently installed apps up to date. More information about this feature is included in the section, "Keep Your Apps Up to Date with the Latest Versions."

HOW TO SHOP FROM iTUNES ON YOUR COMPUTER

The second method of finding, purchasing, downloading, installing, and updating apps is to use the latest version of iTunes running on your primary computer. With iTunes running, click the iTunes Store option that is displayed on the left side of the screen, under the Store heading. Your computer must be connected to the Internet to access the iTunes Store.

When the main iTunes Store launches in iTunes, click the App tab that's displayed near the top center of the screen (as shown in Figure 3.14). This will show a similar screen to the Featured page of the App Store when you access it from your iPhone or iPad using the App Store app.

> **⌇ NOTE** Throughout this section, screenshots from iTunes version 10.7 running on a Mac are featured. All the features and functions are the same if you use iTunes on a PC running Windows, but the appearance of the screens might be slightly different. Likewise, if you're using a more recent version of iTunes, the layout of the screens might vary.

FIGURE 3.14

Click the Apps tab that's displayed near the top center of the iTunes screen to access the App Store from within iTunes on your primary computer.

All the functionality of the App Store when accessed through iTunes is the same as when you use the App Store app on your phone or tablet. However, the layout of the screens is slightly different.

For example, near the top center of the App Store when you access it through iTunes, you'll see two command tabs, labeled iPhone and iPad. Click the iPhone icon to view iPhone-specific apps or the iPad option to view iPad-specific apps.

To view apps by category, click and hold down the mouse button on the Apps tab that's displayed near the top center of the App Store screen. A listing of the app categories are displayed in a pull-down menu (as shown in Figure 3.15). Make your selection by clicking it to see a listing of apps by category.

FIGURE 3.15

Choose an app category, such as Business, Finance, Reference, or Travel, to help narrow your search as you begin browsing through the thousands of apps available from the App Store.

As you explore the main App Store screen in iTunes, you'll discover the Top Charts lists displayed along the right margin of the screen. Near the heading at the top of a chart, click the See All option to see a more extensive list of popular apps. You can then sort these by Name, Bestsellers, or Release Date, by choosing a Sort By option from the pull-down menu that appears in the Top Charts screen after you click See All (as shown in Figure 3.16).

FIGURE 3.16

View all the apps from the Top Charts lists to help you quickly determine which apps are the most popular. As you're looking at a Top Charts list, click the View All option. Shown here are the Top Paid Business apps for the iPhone.

To view the Top Charts for a specific app category, first choose the category you want from the App Store pull-down menu near the top center of the screen, and then select your desired category, such as Business, Finance, News, Reference, or Travel.

With a category selected, such as Business, the App Store screen displays New, What's Hot, and All Apps within that category in three separate sections within the main area of the App Store screen. Along the right margin of the screen, the Top Charts listings for Paid Apps, Free Apps and Top Grossing Apps related to your chosen app category are displayed.

The process for viewing an app's description is the same as using the App Store app on your iPhone or iPad. Tap on either the app's title or the graphic icon. This will reveal a full-page description for the app, which includes screenshots, a detailed description, reviews and ratings.

To purchase an app from the App Store when accessed through iTunes on your primary computer, click the Price icon that's displayed in the app's listing or on its description page.

When you purchase an app using your primary computer, it is downloaded and stored on the computer. To transfer it to your iPhone or iPad, you'll need to use the iTunes Sync process, or download it from iCloud (by tapping on the Purchased option in the App Store app on your device).

If you have iTunes Sync configured to automatically transfer your app purchases, during the next sync process, the apps are transferred and automatically installed on your iPhone or iPad.

A backup copy of all apps you purchase (as well as the free apps you download) is retained on your primary computer and stored in your iCloud account. So if you delete an app from your iPhone or iPad, you always have the option of restoring the app from your backup using iTunes or iCloud. You will never be charged again to download an app you've already purchased.

As with the App Store app, when you access the App Store using iTunes on your primary computer, you'll see a Search field in the upper-right corner of the screen. When you perform a search using this search field, however, all relevant iTunes content is displayed, not just iPhone or iPad apps. Each type of content is listed under a separate heading.

QUICK TIPS FOR FINDING APPS RELEVANT TO YOU

As you explore the App Store, it's easy to get overwhelmed by the sheer number of apps that are available for your iOS device. If you're a new iPhone or iPad user, spending time browsing the App Store will introduce you to the many types of apps that are available, and will provide you with ideas about how your phone or tablet can be utilized in your personal or professional life.

However, you can save a lot of time searching for apps if you already know the app's exact title, or if you know what type of app you're looking for. In this case, you can enter either the app's exact title or a keyword description of the app in the App Store's Search field to see a list of relevant matches.

So, if you're looking for a word-processing app, you can either enter the search phrase "Pages" into the App Store's Search field, or enter the search phrase "word processor" to see a selection of word-processing apps.

If you're looking for vertical market apps with specialized functionality that caters to your industry or profession, enter that industry or profession (or keywords associated with it) in the Search field. For example, enter keywords like "medical imaging," "radiology," "plumbing," "telemarketing," or "sales."

As you're evaluating an app before downloading it, use these tips to help you determine whether it's worth installing on your phone or tablet:

- Figure out what type of features or functionality you want to add to your iPhone or iPad.

- Using the Search field, find apps designed to handle the tasks you have in mind. Chances are, you'll easily be able to find a handful of apps created by different developers that are designed to perform the same basic functionality. You can then pick which is the best based on the description, screenshots, and list of features each app offers.

  Compare the various apps by reading their descriptions and viewing the screenshots. Figure out which app will work best for you, based on your unique needs.

- Check the customer reviews and ratings for the app. This useful tool quickly determines whether the app actually works as described in its description. Keep in mind, an app's description in the App Store is written by the app's developer and is designed to sell apps. The customer reviews and star-based ratings are created by fellow iPhone or iPad users who have tried out the app firsthand.

  If an app has only a few ratings or reviews, and they're mixed, you might need to try out the app for yourself to determine whether it will be useful to you. However, if an app has many reviews that are overwhelmingly negative (three stars or less), that's a strong indication that the app does not perform as described, or that it's loaded with bugs, for example.

- If an app offers a free (trial) version, download and test out that version of the app first, before purchasing the premium version. You can always delete any app that you try out but don't wind up liking or needing.

- Ideally, you want to install apps on your iPhone or iPad that were designed specifically for that device, if you have a choice. So if you're using an iPhone 5, choose the iPhone-specific version of an app that's been enhanced for use with the iPhone 5, or if you're using an iPad, download the iPad-specific version of an app.

KEEP YOUR APPS UP TO DATE WITH THE LATEST VERSIONS

Periodically, app developers will release new versions of their apps. To make sure you have the most current version of all apps installed on your iPhone or iPad, while visiting the App Store using the App Store app on your phone or tablet, tap on the Updates command icon that's displayed at the bottom of the screen.

If the updates icon has a red-and-white circle in the upper-right corner of it, this is an indication that one or more of your apps has an update available. The number in the badge (the red circle icon) relates to how many app updates are available, based on the apps currently installed on your device.

Tap on the Updates icon to display a list of apps with updates available, and then tap on the Update All icon or an individual app icon that's displayed on the Updates screen to automatically download the new version of the app and install it. Doing this will replace the older version of the app.

Using the App Store app to check for updates will determine whether there are updated versions for apps currently installed on your device. However, if you check for app updates using iTunes on your primary computer, it will check for updates for all the apps you have ever downloaded using a specific Apple ID account (including backups of apps that are stored on your primary computer or iCloud, but that aren't currently installed on your iPhone or iPad).

To check for app updates from within iTunes on your primary computer, click the Apps option displayed under the Library heading on the left side of the iTunes screen. This will display app listings for every app you've downloaded using that Apple ID account, whether or not it's currently installed on your tablet.

In the lower-right corner of the iTunes screen, when you have the Apps option selected, there is an option that says how many app updates are currently available. Click this option. You can then click individual apps you want to update, or click the Download All Free Updates option that's displayed in the upper-right corner of the My App Updates screen.

After the app updates have been downloaded to your primary computer, perform an iTunes Sync with your iPhone or iPad to transfer the updated versions of the apps currently installed on your device. Or, from your device, access the App Store app, tap on the Purchased icon, and download and install the apps from iCloud.

> **☑ TIP**   To ensure that you have the latest versions of your most commonly used apps installed on your iPhone or iPad, check for app updates once every week or two. Each time Apple releases an update to the iOS operating system, it's common for app developers to also release an updated version of their apps.

4

MAKE THE MOST OF NOTIFICATION CENTER

Many of the apps on your iPhone or iPad are capable of generating messages, alarms, alerts, and/or notifications to inform you that some action needs to be taken.

Mail, for example, alerts you to new incoming emails. Phone (on the iPhone) or FaceTime tells you if and when you've missed a call. Messages gets your attention when someone sends you a text message. Calendar can be set to remind you of your important upcoming appointments, and the Reminders app notifies you whenever an item on one of your to-do lists requires your immediate attention.

If you play games or you're active on Twitter or Facebook, these apps also can notify you when actions need to be taken, or if someone is trying to get in touch with you.

Many apps can also sound off audible alarms, whereas others display alert or banner windows. After you start relying on and using a handful of different apps, it's very easy to become inundated with messages, alerts, alarms, and notifications from them. The solution to managing all of these items as they happen is an app called Notification Center.

NOTE Notification Center is a preinstalled app that's always running. It works with most other apps, serving as a central location to view messages, alert, alarms, and notifications—all of which get displayed in a single window (or in the case of the iPhone, a separate screen). Notification Center is shown in Figure 4.1. You can access this information anytime, when it's convenient for you, regardless of what you're doing on your iPhone or iPad.

FIGURE 4.1

Notification Center is constantly running on your iPhone or iPad. It's shown here on the iPhone 4S. In a single window that appears, it lists all messages, alerts, alarms, and notifications from the various apps that it constantly monitors.

As you're viewing the Notification Center window, tap on an individual item that's listed to instantly launch the relevant app, and have whatever it is that needs your attention quickly displayed on your iPhone or iPad's screen.

So, if you're alerted to an upcoming appointment (as shown in Figure 4.2), simply tap on that alert, the Calendar app will launch, and then your pending appointment is displayed.

FIGURE 4.2

From the Notification Center window, tap on a listing generated by the Calendar app and you'll see details about that particular event. (Shown here on the iPhone 4S.) Keep in mind, you can tap on any listing within the Notification Center window to launch the related app.

> **✓ TIP**   To quickly access the Notification Center window anytime that your iPhone or iPad is turned on, swipe your finger from the very top of the device's screen in a downward direction. This doesn't work, however, from the Lock Screen.

> **✓ TIP**   Thanks to Siri, it's easy to create reminders or alarms, which will ultimately be displayed in Notification Center. To create a reminder (to be stored and accessible from within the Reminders app), activate Siri, say, "Remind me to pick up my dry cleaning tomorrow at 2pm," confirm your request, and the reminder (and a related alarm) will automatically set up (as shown in Figure 4.3). When appropriate, the alarm relating to the Reminder listing will be displayed in the Notification Center window. Refer to Chapter 5, "Using Siri and Dictation to Interact with Your iOS Device," for more information about using your voice to help you control your iPhone or iPad and become more efficient using it.

FIGURE 4.3

Use your voice to quickly create alerts and alarms in the Reminders app, for example, when you take advantage of Siri's capabilities. (Shown here on the iPhone 5.)

NOTIFICATION CENTER'S MAIN WINDOW

Based on how you personalize Notification Center, the app's main window on the iPad or screen on the iPhone will display 1, 5, 10, or 20 messages, alerts, alarms, or notifications from each app that it constantly monitors.

If you have Notification Center set to monitor the FaceTime app and display five alerts from the app at any given time, then when you view the Notification Center window/screen, you will see a summary of the last five incoming FaceTime calls you received. The menu screen within Settings to adjust this is shown in Figure 4.4 on the iPad.

Having Notification Center display only one or five messages from each app will keep the Notification Center window less cluttered, making it easier to quickly determine what needs your attention. However, displaying more messages from each app will inform you about everything that currently requires your attention.

> ✅ TIP You determine which apps Notification Center constantly monitors by making adjustments in Settings. From Settings, tap on the Notifications option.

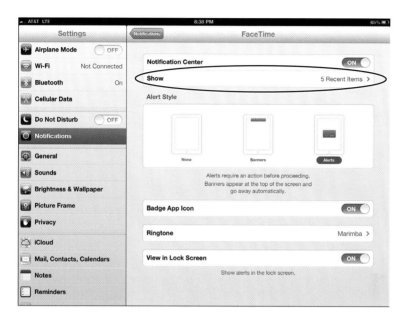

FIGURE 4.4

You decide exactly how many messages, alerts, alarms, or notifications are displayed in the Notification Center window pertaining to each app.

Keep in mind, if 10 apps are being monitored and each app generates 20 new alerts, your Notification Center window displays up to 200 individual listings. It will take you several minutes to review all this information, which isn't necessarily the most productive use of your time. All messages, alerts, alarms, and notifications can be displayed in reverse chronological order by time (based on when each alert is generated), and/or categorized by app for easy reference. When the Notification Center window is displayed, use your finger to scroll downward, as needed, to see the entire list.

> **TIP** To determine how listings are sorted within the Notification Center window, launch Settings, tap on Notifications and then under the Sort Apps heading, tap on Manually or By Time.

When you view the Notification Center window/screen, divider bars with the name of each app that is being monitored are displayed. Below each divider bar are the messages, alerts, alarms, or notifications generated by that particular app. Refer to Figure 4.1 for an example of this for the Reminders and Calendar apps.

> **TIP** To quickly clear the listings in the Notification Center window that relate to a particular app, tap on the circular "X" icon on the extreme right side of a divider bar, and then tap on the Clear icon that appears. Although Notification Center continues monitoring that app, all older listings pertaining to messages, alerts, alarms, or notifications are removed.

At any time, tap on any listing in the Notification Center window to launch the relevant app and deal with what requires your attention, such as a missed call, a new incoming email, or an unread text message.

On the iPad, to make the Notification Center window disappear, tap anywhere on screen that is outside the window. On the iPhone (or iPad) flick your finger in an upward direction, from the bottom of the notification center window toward the top.

> **TIP** Another way to make the Notification Center screen/window disappear is to press the Home button.

The current time is always displayed at the top-center of the Notification Center window, and the time each message, alert, alarm, or notification was generated is displayed on the right side of each listing.

On the left side of each listing, when applicable, a blue dot (shown in Figure 4.5) appears. This dot indicates that it's a new listing, and that you have not yet taken any action relating to it. After you tap on the listing to launch the relevant app, the blue dot automatically disappears.

FIGURE 4.5

A blue dot is displayed on the left side of each listing in the Notification Center window if the listing is new and no action has yet been taken. (Shown here on the iPhone 5.)

WHAT'S NEW Displayed near the top of the Notification screen/ window, can be a Tap To Tweet or Facebook: Tap to Post button. Tapping on the Tap To Tweet buttons allows you to quickly compose and send a tweet message to your Twitter followers from directly within the Notification Center. Tap on the Tap To Post button to compose and publish a Facebook Status Update from within Notification Center. There is no need to first launch the official Twitter or Facebook app.

For these two buttons to function, you first need to turn on Twitter and/or Facebook integration on your iPhone or iPad (which only needs to be done once from within Settings), plus you need to have an active Twitter and/or Facebook account.

It's also necessary to turn on the Share Widget function. To do this, launch Settings, tap on Notifications, and then make sure the Share Widget option is listed under the In Notification Center heading. This happens when you turn on the virtual switch associated with it.

Then, from the Notifications menu screen within Settings, you can move the location of the Share Widget (or the order in which apps are listed) by tapping on the Edit button and then placing your finger on the Move icon (which looks like three horizontal lines) that's associated with each listing. Tap the Done icon when you're finished re-ordering the apps displayed under the In Notification Center heading.

QUICK STRATEGIES FOR PERSONALIZING NOTIFICATION CENTER

By default, Notification Center works with many different apps simultaneously. So, unless you take charge and set preferences for how often these apps should alert you to various things, you could easily discover that Notification Center constantly becomes active and frequently tries to get your attention.

CAUTION If you don't personalize the Notification Center app's settings, by default, any app that is capable of generating a message, an alarm, an alert, or a notification will use Notification Center. Thus, you could easily become distracted and inundated with a vast number of unimportant notifications from apps that you don't consider to be critical.

After all, you might put a very different priority on a missed call from your biggest client than you put on an alert notifying you that your virtual crops are about to wither as you're playing the popular game Farmville, or that construction of a new mushroom house has been completed as part of the game Smurfs' Village.

Notification Center can adapt to your personal needs and priorities, thus keeping you informed only about what you deem to be important.

Customize the settings related to Notification Center through Settings. To do this, launch Settings from the Home Screen. Then, tap on the Notifications option, shown in Figure 4.6 on the iPad.

FIGURE 4.6

After the Settings app is launched, tap on the Notifications option to customize the settings associated with Notification Center, and decide which apps will constantly be monitored.

After you've tapped on the Notifications option in Settings, a listing of apps currently being monitored by the Notification Center app is displayed under the In Notification Center heading. Meanwhile, those apps that are compatible with Notification Center, but that are not currently being monitored, are displayed under the Not in Notification Center heading.

TIP From the Notifications screen of the Settings app, you can determine how you want alerts, alarms and notifications to be displayed in your Notifications Center window. Your options include Manually or By Time. The By Time option lists each item displayed in the Notification Window in chronological order. The Manually option lists items by App (which are displayed alphabetically).

ⓘⓞⓢ⑥ WHAT'S NEW Displayed at the top of the Notifications menu screen within Settings, tap on the Do Not Disturb option to customize this feature.

One at a time, tap on any of the apps listed under the In Notification Center heading to customize the settings associated with how the Notification Center app handles that particular app. The customizable options available to you in the submenu screen that appears varies based on which app you're customizing.

TIP You probably want to customize the settings for each app that Notification Center is monitoring. This is something that needs to be done only once, or whenever you want to change which apps Notification Center constantly monitors.

STEP BY STEP: CUSTOMIZE HOW NOTIFICATION CENTER MONITORS APPS

To customize the Notification Center settings associated with FaceTime, for example, follow these steps:

NOTE Repeat these steps for each app listed under the In Notification Center heading.

1. From the Home Screen, tap on the Settings app icon to launch Settings.
2. Tap on the Notifications option.
3. Choose the FaceTime app from the listing of apps displayed under the In Notification Center heading.
4. The first option at the top of the submenu screen is labeled Notification Center. The option is associated with a virtual on/off switch that is located to the right of the label. When this switch is turned on, Notification Center monitors this app (in this example, FaceTime). If the virtual switch is turned off, Notification Center no longer monitors this app, and messages, alerts, alarms, or notifications generated by this app do not appear in the Notification Center window.

5. If there's an app you don't deem important, turn the virtual switch associated with the Notification Center option to off. For example, if you're using your iPhone or iPad as a business tool, you might want to turn off this setting for Games Center and any games listed (and that are installed on your iPhone or iPad) so that Notification Center does not monitor and display messages, alerts, alarms, or notifications associated with those particular (unimportant) game apps.

> **TIP** You need to turn on or off the Notification Center option for Game Center as well as any individual games installed on your device to eliminate all game-related content from being monitored by Notification Center.

6. Immediately below the Notification Center option that's associated with the virtual on/off switch is another option, labeled Show. Tap on this option to determine how many messages, alerts, alarms, or notifications relating to this particular app display in the Notification Center window at any given time. When you tap on this option, a new submenu screen appears, allowing you to choose between 1 and 20 recent items. Tap on the option of your choice.

7. To exit this submenu screen and return to the main Notifications screen in Settings, tap on the left-pointing arrow icon appearing in the upper-left corner of the submenu screen. In this case, the icon says FaceTime. This will send you back to the previous submenu screen. Again, tap on the left-pointing icon that appears in the upper-left corner of this screen, which in this case is labeled Notifications, to return to the main Notifications screen in Settings.

8. Upon returning to the app listing displayed under the In Notification Center heading, tap on another app label to customize the settings associated with how the Notification Center app handles that app. Repeat the steps outlined here for each app.

> **TIP** If you turn the virtual switch associated with the Notification Center option for a particular app to the off position, this app is no longer displayed within the Notification Center screen (iPhone) or window (iPad). However, you can customize how messages, alerts, alarms, and/or notifications generated by this app are displayed by adjusting the Alert Style, Badge App Icon, and/or View in Lock Screen settings, also displayed in this Settings submenu screen. Again, this is something you need to do with each app.

When you turn off the virtual switch associated with the Notification Center label, that app is removed from the In Notification Center listing, but is now be displayed in the Not in Notification Center list.

WHAT TO DO WHEN ALERTS, NOTIFICATIONS, AND ALARMS GET ANNOYING

If you allow all the compatible apps running on your iPad or iPhone to constantly notify you anytime one of the apps generates a message, an alert, an alarm, or a notification, not only will you discover that the Notification Center window quickly becomes cluttered, but you'll also be distracted by the constant flow of alerts.

To keep your Notification Center window organized, while customizing settings for your apps, follow these basic strategies:

- Turn off the Notification Center option if the app is not important to you.

- Limit the display of recent items that pertain to each app to either one or five.

- For apps like Mail, you can determine how many lines of content are displayed for each new email in the Notification Center window. Choose an option that gives you enough information but doesn't utilize too much onscreen space in the Notification Center window, thus causing clutter. This is a personal preference.

TIP For your most important apps (the ones that keep track of information that's essential to your daily life or work), from the Settings app, tap on the Notifications option, and then for those critical apps, turn on Notification Center. In addition, under the Alert Style option, choose Alerts. Also, turn the virtual switches associated with Badge App Icon, Sounds (if applicable), and View in Lock Screen to the on position.

Doing this allows those essential apps to use audible alerts, if applicable, plus display their own message windows (in addition to or instead of the Notification Center window). Displaying an Alert window requires you to take an action (such as tapping on a specific icon to acknowledge the message), even when the iPhone or iPad is in sleep mode.

STAY INFORMED OF YOUR APPOINTMENTS, DEADLINES, AND RESPONSIBILITIES

For Notification Center to do its job and keep you informed about important appointments, deadlines, and responsibilities, it's important that you fully utilize the Calendar and/or Reminders apps that come preinstalled with iOS 6 on your iPhone or iPad.

> **NOTE** Calendars and Reminders are standalone apps. However, they can easily be integrated with Notification Center so that you are alerted of upcoming appointments, responsibilities, and deadlines.

When you maintain your scheduling and calendar information using the Calendar app (or sync data to this app from your primary computer or a compatible online-based scheduling app), and then set Notification Center to work with Calendar, you will easily be able to stay informed of your upcoming meetings, appointments, deadlines, and responsibilities.

Likewise, if you get into the habit of using the Reminders app to maintain your to-do lists, the alarms and alerts associated with each to-do list item that gets triggered are displayed in the Notification Center window.

HOW TO LIMIT THE CONTENT IN THE NOTIFICATION CENTER WINDOW

Certain apps, like Mail, allow you to choose how much content you get to view for each listing in the Notification Center window. For example, you can opt to view between zero and five lines of an incoming email's content (in addition to the name of the message's sender, its subject, and when it was received).

If specific adjustments relating to how much content for each listing can be viewed in the Notification Center window, this can be customized from within Settings. To choose how much of an incoming email's content you'll see, for example, follow these steps:

1. From the Home Screen, launch Settings.
2. Tap on the Mail, Contacts, Calendars option that's listed under the main Settings menu.

3. In the Mail, Contacts, Calendars submenu, look for the Mail heading, and then tap on the Preview option.

4. From the Preview screen, tap on how many lines of the incoming email you want to preview. This decision impacts what you'll see both in the Mail app itself and in the Notification Center window. Your options include between zero and five lines. Figure 4.7 shows a sample incoming mail listing in which just one line of the message's body is displayed, and Figure 4.8 shows a sample incoming message listing in which five lines of a message's body are displayed.

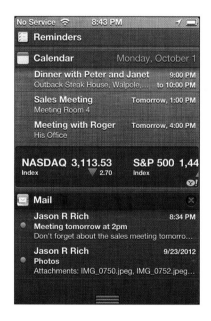

FIGURE 4.7

On this iPhone 4S, the user selected to view one line of each incoming email's body text in the Notification Center window.

FIGURE 4.8

In this example (shown on an iPad), five lines of an incoming email message's body, as well as the sender, the email's subject, and the date it was received, can easily be seen in the Notification Center window.

INFORMATIVE NOTIFICATION CENTER WIDGETS YOU CAN ADD TO YOUR iPHONE

Available on the iPhone, Notification Center widgets are mini apps that appear at the top and/or bottom of the Notification Center window. They display very specific information.

A Weather Widget and Stock Widget come preinstalled in iOS 6 for the iPhone. When turned on and customized, the Weather Widget (which is automatically tied to the Weather app) shows the current weather forecast for your location, but in a concise way.

Meanwhile, the Stock Widget offers a scrolling ticker of the stocks and investments you have stored as part of a personal portfolio using the iPhone's Stocks app (which also comes preinstalled).

When viewing the Weather or Stock widget on the iPhone's Notification Center screen, tap on the widget to launch either the Weather or Stocks app and view related, up-to-date information. In reference to the Weather widget, if you tap on the tiny Y! icon, you can access the relevant Yahoo! Weather webpage.

> **NOTE** From the Weather or Stocks app on your iPhone, customize the settings to determine what data is displayed in the Notification Center window. The Weather Widget or Stocks Widget, which is an optional feature of Notification Center, then pulls data from the respective app and Internet, such as your current city's weather forecast, or details about specific stocks or investments in your portfolio, and display that data in a separate section of the Notification Center window.

> **TIP** To turn off the Weather Widget or Stock Widget so that related data does not appear in your iPhone's Notification Center window, launch Settings, and then tap on the Notifications option. Under the In Notification Center heading, look for the Weather Widget or Stock Widget option and tap on it.
>
> When the Weather Widget (or Stock Widget) submenu screen appears, turn the virtual switch that's associated with Notification Center to the off position. The Weather Widget or Stock Widget is then listed under the Not in Notification Center heading, and when you access the Notification Center window, the widget(s) you turned off no longer appears.

The Weather Widget displays the local weather forecast for wherever you happen to be as long as you have the Location Services feature turned on for the Weather app and the iPhone has access to the Internet.

> **! CAUTION** For the Weather Widget or Stock Widget to work and display current information, your iPhone must have access to the Internet. Otherwise, the most recent data stored on the iPhone (from when the app last had access to the Internet) is displayed. This information can be misleading or outdated.

To customize the Stock Widget, from the iPhone's Home Screen, launch the Stocks app. Next, tap the circular icon containing the letter "i" that appears in the lower-right corner of the screen. To add stocks or investments, tap the plus-sign icon that appears in the upper-left corner of the screen. Or to delete a stock or an investment from the portfolio stored in the app, tap on the red-and-white icon containing the negative sign that's next to the investment you want to remove.

When you've customized your portfolio, tap on the blue-and-white Done icon displayed in the upper-right corner of the screen. This returns you to the main Stocks screen. This is the information that will now appear as part of the Stocks Widget in the Notification Center window.

> **☑ TIP** Instead of relying on the Weather and Stock widget, you can simply use Siri and ask your iPhone or iPad for a weather forecast or an update on your investment portfolio.
>
> To do this, activate Siri, and then when prompted, say something like, "What's today's weather forecast?" or "Do I need an umbrella?" You'll learn more about this feature in Chapter 5.

A third widget you can control is the Share widget. When turned on, it displays a Tap To Tweet and Tap To Post button within the Notification Center screen (iPhone) or window (iPad). These are used to post content to Twitter or Facebook directly from the Notification Center screen or window, without first having to launch the official Twitter or Facebook app.

To turn on the Share widget and choose where it will be displayed within the Notification Center screen or window, launch Settings, tap on Notifications and then select the Share Widget option.

5

USING SIRI AND DICTATION TO INTERACT WITH YOUR iOS DEVICE

Even if you're a jaded iPhone or iPad-user who seldom gets excited by new technological gadgets, it's virtually impossible not to be impressed by the enhancements made to the Siri feature that's incorporated into iOS 6. While Siri was first introduced on the iPhone 4S in conjunction with iOS 5, it's now been enhanced and works with the iPhone 5, 3rd/4th generation iPad, and the iPad mini.

Thanks to Siri, instead of having to utilize the touchscreen to interact with your phone or tablet, and constantly having to use the onscreen virtual keyboard to enter data or information, you can simply use your voice and speak using normal sentences. There are no commands to memorize.

Right from the start, you should understand that Siri doesn't know or understand everything, and it does have limitations in terms of what it can do and which apps it works with. Once

you get accustomed to working with Siri, however, you'll discover this feature can make you much more efficient using your iPhone or iPad.

In addition to using cutting-edge voice recognition, Siri uses advanced artificial intelligence, so it doesn't just understand what you say, it interprets and comprehends what you mean, and then translates your speech to text. And if you don't initially provide the information Siri needs to complete your request or command, you'll be prompted for more information.

(iOS 6) WHAT'S NEW In conjunction with iOS 6, Siri has been given the ability to find and recommend restaurants and then help you quickly make a reservation; plus Siri can now keep you up-to-date on sports scores and related information, while also helping you to find movies and access movie-related information. Using your voice, you can also launch any app, plus interact with a handful of apps, including Facebook and Twitter.

To launch an app, for example, activate Siri and say, "Launch [insert app name]" or "Open [insert app name]." If you want to play a game app that's installed on your iPhone or iPad, say, "Play [insert game name]."

TIP To get the most out of the Siri feature, turn on your iOS device's master Location Services functionality, and then make sure Location Services is set up to work with Siri.

To do this, launch Settings, tap on the Privacy option, and then tap on the Location Services option. Turn On the virtual switch that's associated with Location Services, as well as the virtual switch that's associated with the Siri option.

WHAT YOU SHOULD KNOW BEFORE USING SIRI

For Siri to operate, your phone or tablet must have access to the Internet via a 3G/4G or Wi-Fi connection. Every time you make a request or issue a command to Siri, your iOS mobile device connects to Apple's data center. Thus, if you're using a 3G/4G connection, some of your monthly wireless data allocation is used up (if data allocation is imposed by your wireless service provider).

> **✓ TIP**   Because a Wi-Fi connection is typically significantly faster than a 3G/4G connection, you'll discover that Siri responds faster to your requests and commands when you use a Wi-Fi connection.

You should also understand that heavy use of the Internet, especially when connected via a 3G/4G connection, depletes the battery life of the iPhone or iPad faster. So, if you constantly rely on Siri throughout the day, the battery life of your device will be shorter.

> **! CAUTION**   If your iPhone or iPad is placed in Airplane mode (and Wi-Fi connectivity is turned off), Siri will not function. You'll receive a verbal message stating that Siri is unavailable.

WAYS TO ACTIVATE SIRI

As you go about using your iPhone or iPad, if you want to use the Siri feature, you first must activate it. There are three ways to do this:

- Press and hold the Home button on your iPhone or iPad for two to three seconds.
- Pick up your iPhone and hold it up to your ear. Siri will activate automatically. (However, this iPhone-specific feature first must be turned on from within Settings.)
- Press the Call button on your wireless Bluetooth headset that is paired with your iPhone or iPad. This enables you to use your iOS mobile device from up to 30 feet away.
- If you're using Apple EarPods or an original Apple headset (headphones), tap the middle button on the controls found on the cable.

> **✓ TIP**   If you're using your iOS device in conjunction with a Bluetooth headset, when you activate Siri, to the right of the microphone icon will be a blue speaker icon. Tap on it to choose between using the iPhone's built-in microphone or your headset's microphone when talking to Siri.

When Siri is activated, the message, "What can I help you with?" is displayed near the bottom of the screen, along with a circular microphone icon (shown in Figure 5.1). You'll simultaneously hear Siri's activation tone. Do not start speaking to Siri until this tone is heard. You have about 5 seconds to speak before the microphone deactivates. To reactivate it, simply tap on the microphone icon or repeat one of the previously mentioned steps.

FIGURE 5.1

When Siri is activated, the "What can I help you with?" window appears, and you hear Siri's activation tone. (Shown here on the iPhone 5.)

As soon as you hear Siri's activation tone, speak your question, command, or request. You can either speak into the iPhone or iPad directly, or use a Bluetooth wireless headset that's paired with your phone or tablet.

For the most accurate results when using Siri, speak directly into the iPhone, iPad, or a wireless Bluetooth headset. Try to avoid being in areas with excessive background noise. Speak as clearly as possible so Siri can understand each word in your sentences.

Siri is one of the few features that works from the Lock screen. Thus, even if you have the Passcode Lock feature turned on, someone can potentially pick up your iPhone or iPad and send an email or a text message (using your accounts), or access data from your iPhone or iPad using Siri, without your permission. To keep this from happening, set up the Passcode feature on your device. Then, from within

Settings, turn Off the Siri option that's displayed as part of the Passcode Lock menu screen (shown in Figure 5.2).

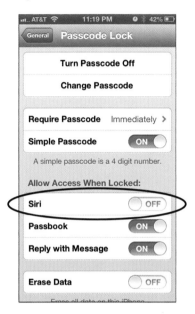

FIGURE 5.2

When you turn off the Siri option displayed on the Passcode Lock menu screen, Siri will not activate from the Lock screen. (Shown here on the iPhone 5.)

SETTING UP SIRI TO WORK ON YOUR iPHONE OR iPAD

Before you start using Siri, you must turn it on from within Settings. Follow these steps to do so:

1. Launch Settings from the Home Screen.
2. From the main Settings menu, tap on the General option.
3. From the General menu screen (shown in Figure 5.3), tap on the Siri option.
4. When the Siri menu screen within Settings is displayed (shown in Figure 5.4), turn on the virtual switch associated with the Siri option by tapping on it. This option is displayed near the top of the screen.
5. Select your language. The default setting is English (United States), however, many other languages are now supported by Siri in conjunction with iOS 6.

FIGURE 5.3

The General menu in Settings displayed the Siri option if it's available on your device.

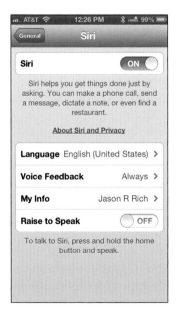

FIGURE 5.4

The Siri menu within Settings.

6. Tap on the Voice Feedback option to determine whether Siri will respond to you verbally for every request you make, or just when using the feature's hands-free mode. If Voice Feedback is turned off, text-based Siri prompts will appear on the iPhone or iPad's screen, but you will not hear Siri's voice.

7. Tap on the My Info icon to link your own Contacts entry with Siri. It's important that you create an entry for yourself in the Contacts app, and fill in all the data fields related to your phone numbers, addresses, email addresses, Twitter username, Facebook account, and so on, and that you properly label each data field. For example, if your Contacts entry has three phone numbers (Home, Work, and iPhone), be sure each has the appropriate label associated with it.

    Likewise, your Home and Work addresses, and the various email addresses you use, should be properly labeled with the Home and Work (or other appropriate) labels. The more information about yourself you include in your Contacts entry, the better Siri will be able to serve you.

> **✅ TIP** Siri also utilizes information stored in the Related People fields available to you from the Add Field option as you create or edit a contact. By tapping on this field, you can add a relationship title, such as *mother*, *father*, *brother*, or *sister* to an entry. Then, when using Siri, if you say, "Call Mom at home," Siri knows exactly to whom you're referring.
>
> However, if you activate Siri and say, "Call my mom at home," the first time you use Siri for this task, you're asked who your mother is. As long as you have a Contact entry for your mother stored in the Contacts app, when you say your mother's real name, Siri links the appropriate contact and remembers this information. This applies to any nickname or title you have for other people, such as "wife," "husband," "son," "daughter, "mother," "father," "dad," or even "Uncle Jack."

8. At the bottom of the Siri menu screen on the iPhone, the Raise To Speak option is listed, and it's associated with a virtual on/off switch. When this switch is turned on, Siri will automatically activate when you pick up the phone and hold it up to your ear.

In addition to customizing the options offered from the Siri menu screen within Settings, it's important that you enable Siri to pinpoint your location. After you complete this procedure, Siri has the basic information needed, as well as access to content stored on your iPhone or iPad, that it needs to function. As you use Siri, it periodically asks you for additional information that you need to supply only once, and it is then saved for future use.

CHECK OUT HOW SIRI CAN HELP YOU!

The great thing about Siri is that you don't have to think too much about how you phrase a command, question, or request. Siri automatically interprets what you say. However, after you activate Siri, you must wait until you hear the activation tone before you begin speaking. Siri is active only when the microphone icon appears purple. If the icon appears stagnant in silver and gray, you must tap on it to reactivate the feature.

When you're finished issuing your command or request or asking a question, simply stop speaking. If additional information is required, Siri will prompt you for it as needed.

To get the most out of using Siri—with the least amount of frustration as a result of Siri not being able to comply with your requests—you must develop a basic understanding of which apps this feature works with, and how Siri can be used in conjunction with those apps.

In general, Siri can be used with most of the apps that come preinstalled with iOS 6, plus Siri can find information on the Internet by performing web searches. You can use Dictation mode, however, in any app where the microphone key appears on the iPhone or iPad's virtual keyboard.

iOS 6 WHAT'S NEW One new feature of Siri that was added to iOS 6 is the ability to launch any app. To do this, activate Siri and say, "Launch [insert app name]." If it's a game you want to play, you can say, "Play [insert game name]." Another option is to say, "Open [insert app name]."

For additional advice about how Siri can be used, activate Siri and say, "Siri, what can you do?" or tap on the information ("i") icon that's displayed next to the "What can I help you with?" message when Siri is activated.

The following sections provide a sampling of what Siri can be used for and tips for how to use Siri effectively. Over time, Apple and third-party app developers will be working to upgrade Siri's capabilities, so you might discover additional functionality as you begin using Siri with various apps.

FIND, DISPLAY, OR USE INFORMATION RELATED TO YOUR CONTACTS

Your Contacts database can store a vast amount of information about people or companies. Every field within a Contact's entry is searchable and can be accessed by Siri. Or you can ask Siri to look up a specific contact for you and display that contact's Info screen on your device's screen.

Again, the more information you include in each entry stored in your Contacts database, the more helpful Siri can be. To have Siri look up and display information stored in Contacts, say something like the following:

- "Look up John Doe in Contacts."
- "What is John Doe's phone number?"
- "What is John Doe's home phone number?" (See Figure 5.5.)
- "What is John Doe's work address?"

> **TIP** When Siri displays the Info screen for a Contact, it is interactive; therefore, you can tap on a displayed phone number to initiate a call, or tap on an email address to launch the Mail app to send email to that address. If you tap on a regular address, the Maps app launches, and if you tap on a website URL, Safari launches and opens that web page.

FIGURE 5.5

When you ask, "What is John Doe's home phone number," the appropriate number from your Contacts database will be displayed.

Siri can also use information stored in your Contacts database to comply with various other requests, such as:

- **"Send John Doe a text message"**—This works if you have an iPhone-labeled phone number or iMessage username or email address saved in John Doe's Contacts entry. On the iPhone, it also works with the phone's SMS text messaging feature if you have a phone number in someone's Contacts entry that's associated with the "mobile" label.

- **"Send John Doe an email"**—This works if you have an email address saved in John Doe's Contacts entry.

- **"Give me directions to John Doe's home"**—This works if you have a home address saved in John Doe's Contacts entry. The newly revamped Maps app launches, and directions from your current location are displayed.

- **"When is John Doe's birthday?"**—This works if you have a date saved in the Birthday field in John Doe's Contacts entry.

- **"What is John Doe's wife's name?"**—This works if you have a spouse's name saved in John Doe's Contacts entry.

INITIATE A CALL

On the iPhone, you can initiate a call by activating Siri and then saying, "Call [name] at home," or "Call [name] at work." This works if that person has a Contacts entry associated with their name, as well as a phone number labeled Home or Work, respectively. You could also say, "Call [name]'s mobile phone," or "Call [name]'s iPhone."

If you request someone's work phone number and Siri finds a contact's name but not a corresponding phone number, Siri responds with, "There is no work number for John Doe in your contacts." This is followed by a listing of whichever phone numbers are available for that contact (shown in Figure 5.6).

> **NOTE** When issuing a command to Siri, you have flexibility in terms of what you say. For example, say, "Call John Doe at work," "Call John Doe work," or "Call the work number for John Doe," and in all these cases, Siri initiates a call to John Doe's work number.

Alternatively, if someone's contact information or phone number is not stored in your iPhone, you can say, "Call" or "Dial" followed by each digit of a phone number. Thus, you'd say, "Call 212 555 1212".

FIGURE 5.6

If you ask for a phone number, for example, that isn't stored in your Contacts database, Siri will respond accordingly with available options.

> **TIP** You can also ask Siri to look up a business phone number or address by saying, "Look up [business name, such as Apple Store] in [city, state]." Or, you could say, "Look up [business type, such as a dry cleaner] in [city, state]."

On the iPhone, when Siri finds the phone number you're looking for, Siri says, "Calling [name] at [location]," and then automatically initiates a call to that number by launching the Phone app. If you're using an iPhone or iPad, Siri has the ability to initiate FaceTime video calls. Use a command, such as, "FaceTime with [insert name]."

FIND YOUR FRIENDS

The optional Find My Friends app is available free from the App Store. If you install it and begin following friends, coworkers, or family members (with their permission), at any time, you can ask Siri, "Where is [name]?" or say, "Find [name]," and Siri finds that person and displays a map showing that person's exact whereabouts. This feature is great for keeping tabs on your kids or teenagers, especially if they miss a curfew or they say they're studying at the library on a Friday evening.

For this feature to work, however, you need to be logged in to your free Find My Friends account via the app.

> ☑ **TIP**   If you're using the Find My Friends app to track your kids' where-abouts, be sure to activate the Restrictions feature on their iOS device so they can not deactivate the Find My Friends app. To do this, launch Settings, tap on the General option and then select the Restrictions option. Adjust the Location Services feature and the Find My Friends feature so your child can't change those settings.

> 🖉 **NOTE**   The optional Apple Store app is also now fully compatible with Siri. Thus, you can use Siri to look up the price for any item sold within the App Store. For example, you can activate Siri and say, "How much is an iPad mini?" Siri will launch the Apple Store app that's installed on your iOS mobile device and display the appropriate product information.

SET UP REMINDERS AND TO-DO ITEMS

If you constantly jot down reminders to yourself on scrap pieces of paper or sticky notes, or frequently manually enter to-do items into the Reminders app, this is one Siri-related feature you'll truly appreciate.

To create a reminder (to be utilized by the Reminders app), complete with an alarm, simply activate Siri and say something like, "Remind me to pick up my dry cleaning tomorrow at 3 PM." As shown in Figure 5.7, Siri creates the to-do item, displays it on the screen for your approval, and then saves it in the Reminders app. On the appropriate time and day, an alarm will sound and the reminder message will be displayed.

> ☑ **TIP**   If you don't want to utilize the Reminders app that comes prein-stalled with iOS 6, you can download a third-party app from the App Store, such as Remember The Milk (www.rememberthemilk.com), that also works with Siri.

FIGURE 5.7
Using your voice, you can create a to-do item in the Reminders app and associate an alarm with it.

> ☑️ **TIP**   When creating a Reminder using Siri, you can provide a specific date and time, such as "tomorrow at 3 pm" or "Friday at 1 pm" or "July 7th at noon."
>
> You can also include a location that Siri knows, such as "Home" or "Work." For example, you could say, "Remind me to feed the dog when I get home," or "Remind me to call Emily when I get to work." Because the Reminders app can handle location-based alerts, you can create them using Siri. You'll learn more about using location-based alerts from Chapter 8, "Organize Your Life with Reminders and Notes."

READ OR SEND TEXT MESSAGES

When you receive a new text message but can't look at the screen, activate Siri and say, "Read new text message." You'll then be given the opportunity to reply to that message and dictate your response.

Using Siri with the Messages app, you can also compose and send a text/instant message to anyone in your Contacts database by saying something like, "Compose a text message to John Doe." You will be asked to select an email address or mobile phone number to use. To bypass this step, say, "Send a text message to John Doe's mobile phone," or "Send a text message to John Doe's iPhone." Then, Siri will say, "What do you want to say to John Doe?" (shown in Figure 5.8). Dictate your text message.

When you're finished speaking, Siri will say, "I updated your message. Ready to send it?" The transcribed message will be displayed on the screen, along with Cancel and Send icons. You can tap an icon or speak your reply.

FIGURE 5.8

Siri asks you to dictate a text message, and then displays the message before it's sent.

CHECK THE WEATHER OR YOUR INVESTMENTS

The Weather app can display a current or extended weather forecast for your immediate area or any city in the world, and the Stocks app (on the iPhone) can be used to track your investments. Both apps work with Siri. However, Siri also has the capability to automatically access the Web and obtain weather information for any city or stock-related information about any stock or mutual fund, for example.

After activating Siri, ask a weather-related questions, such as

■ **"What is today's weather forecast?"**—Siri pinpoints your location and provides a current forecast.

- **"What is the weather forecast for New York City?"**—Of course, you can insert any city and state in your request.
- **"Is it going to rain tomorrow?"**—Siri accesses and interprets the weather forecast, and then vocalizes, as well as displays a response.
- **"Should I bring an umbrella to work?"**—Siri knows the location of your work and can access and then interpret the weather forecast to offer a vocalized and displayed response.

If you have stock-related questions (using the iPhone or iPad), you can ask about specific stocks by saying something like

- "What is [company name]'s stock at?"
- "What is [company]'s stock price?
- "How is [company name]'s stock performing?"
- "Show me [company name] stock."

As you can see in Figure 5.9, when you request stock information, you get a verbal response from Siri along with information about that stock displayed on the iPhone or iPad's screen.

FIGURE 5.9

Just by asking, Siri can tell you how a specific stock is performing.

FIND INFORMATION ON THE WEB OR GET ANSWERS TO QUESTIONS

If you want to perform a web search, you can manually launch the Safari browser, and then use a keyboard to find what you're looking for in the Search field. Or, you can active Siri and ask it to perform the search for you by saying something like

- "Look up the [company] website."
- "Access the website cnn.com."
- "Find [topic] on the web."
- "Search the web for [topic]."
- "Google information about [topic]."
- "Search Wikipedia for [topic]."
- "Bing [topic]." (Bing is a popular search engine operated by Microsoft.)

You also can ask a question and Siri will seek out the appropriate information on the Web.

> **TIP**   Siri is also a mathematical genius. Simply say the mathematical calculation you need solved, and Siri presents the answer in seconds. For example, say, "What is 10 plus 10?", "What's the square root of 24?" or "What is 20 percent of 500?" This feature is particularly useful for helping you calculate the server's tip when you receive the check at a restaurant.

> **NOTE**   When you ask Siri a question that requires your iPhone or iPad to seek out the answer on the Internet, this is done through Apple using Wolfram Alpha. To learn more about the vast topics you can ask Siri about, from unit conversions to historical data, visit www.wolframalpha.com/examples.

SCHEDULE AND MANAGE MEETINGS AND EVENTS

Like many of the apps that come preinstalled with iOS 6, the Calendar app is fully compatible with Siri, which means you can use Siri to create or modify appointments, meetings, or events by using your voice. To do this, some of the things you can say include

- "Set up a meeting at 10:30am."
- "Set up a meeting with Ryan at noon tomorrow."

- "Meet with Emily for lunch at 1pm."
- "Set up a meeting with Rusty about third-quarter sales projections at 4pm on December 12th."

Meetings you create using Siri are added to your iPhone or iPad's Calendar app. Then, if set up correctly, the scheduling data can be synchronized with iCloud (as well as your computers or other iOS devices).

SEND EMAIL AND ACCESS NEW (INCOMING) EMAIL

If you want to compose an email to someone, activate Siri and say, "Send an email to [name]." If that person's email address is listed in your Contacts database, Siri will address a new message to that person. Siri will then say, "What is the subject of your email?" Speak the subject line for your email. When you stop speaking, Siri will say, "Okay, what would you like the email to say?" You can now dictate the body of your email message.

When you're finished speaking, Siri composes the message, displays it on the iPhone or iPad's screen, and then says, "Here is your email to [name]. Ready to send it?" You can now respond "yes" to send the email message, or say "cancel" to abort the message. If the message isn't what you want to say, you can edit it using the virtual keyboard, or ask Siri to "Change the text to…".

SET AN ALARM OR TIMER

Siri can control the Clock app that comes preinstalled on your iOS device so that it serves as an alarm clock or timer. You can say something like, "Set an alarm for 7:30am tomorrow" or "Set a recurring wakeup call for 7:30am" to create a new alarm. Or, to set a 30-minute timer, say, "Set a timer for 30 minutes." A countdown timer will be displayed on the iPhone or iPad's screen, and an alarm sounds when the timer reaches zero.

You can also simply ask Siri, "What's today's date?" or "What time is it?" if you're too busy to look at your watch or the iPhone or iPad's screen, such as when you're driving.

GET DIRECTIONS USING THE MAPS APP

Pretty much any feature you can use the Maps app for—whether it's to find the location or phone number for a business, obtain turn-by-turn directions between two addresses, or map out a specific address location—you can access this functionality using Siri.

To use Maps-related functions, say things like the following:

- "How do I get to [location]?"
- "Show [address]."
- "Directions to [contact name or location]."
- "Find a [business type, such as gas station] near [location]."
- "Find a [business or service name, such as Starbucks Coffee] near where I am."
- "Where is the closest [business type, such as post office]?"
- "Find a [cuisine type, such as Chinese] restaurant near me."

If multiple businesses or locations are found that are directly related to your request, Siri asks you to select one, or all related matches are displayed on a detailed map within in the newly-revamped Maps app using pushpins.

(iOS 6) WHAT'S NEW When asking Siri to look up businesses, landmarks, popular destinations or restaurants, in addition to just displaying a location on a map, Siri now integrates with the Yelp! online service to provide much more detailed information about many destinations and businesses (including restaurants). Plus, in conjunction with the online-based Open Table service, Siri can be used to book a restaurant reservation for you, without you having to call that restaurant.

For example, you can activate Siri and say, "Find Morton's Steak House in Boston." Once found, Siri will display detailed information about that restaurant from Yelp!. As you're looking at this listing on your screen, activate Siri again and say something like, "Book a table for two tonight at 8pm." You will then receive a confirmation for your reservation.

CONTROL THE MUSIC APP

In the mood to hear a specific song that's stored on your iPhone or iPad? Maybe you want to begin playing a specific playlist, you want to hear all the music stored on your iOS device by a particular artist, or you want to play a specific album? Well, just ask Siri. You can control the Music app using your voice by saying things like the following:

- "Play [song title]."
- "Play [album title]."
- "Play [playlist title]."
- "Play [artist's name]."
- "Play [music genre, such as pop, rock, or blues]."

You can also issue specific commands, such as "Shuffle my [title] playlist," or speak commands, such as "Pause" or "Skip" as music is playing. However, Siri is unable to search for and display song or album listings. For example, if you say, "Show music," or "Show song playlists," you will receive a response saying, "Sorry, [your name], I can't search that content." Thus, to use Siri to control your music, you must know what music is stored on your iPhone or iPad.

FORGET STICKY NOTES—DICTATE NOTES TO YOURSELF

The Notes app that comes preinstalled with iOS 6 is used to compose notes using a text editor (as opposed to a full-featured word processor, such as Pages). Siri is compatible with the Notes app and enables you to create and dictate notes.

To create a new note, activate Siri and begin a sentence by saying, "Note that I… " You can also say, "Note: [sentence]." What you dictate will be saved as a new note in the Notes app.

When you use the command "Note," a note is created in the Notes app. It is not accompanied by an alert or alarm. However, if you use the command "Remind me…," Siri creates a reminder listing using the Reminders app, which can be associated with a time/date alarm or a location-based alarm.

> **TIP** Siri's Dictation mode can be used when you are word processing using the Pages app to speed up text entry without having to use the virtual keyboard. For the best results, however, dictate between one and three sentences at a time, have Siri translate your text to speech, and then repeat the process as needed.
>
> Using this feature to translate a significant amount of speech to text uses a lot of your monthly wireless data allocation from your wireless service provider if you're using a 3G/4G connection. At least initially, monitor your data use carefully so you don't go beyond your monthly allocation and receive extra charges on your bill.

SIRI KNOWS ALL ABOUT SPORTS AND MOVIES TOO

If you're looking for the latest scores related to your favorite professional team or sporting event, you can now ask Siri. It's also possible to ask sports-related questions and then have Siri quickly research the answers via the Internet. When it comes to sports, here are some sample questions or requests you can use with Siri:

- "Did the Yankee's win their last game?"
- "What was the score of last night's Patriots game?"
- "What was the score the last time the Yankees and Red Sox played?"

- "Show me the baseball scores from last night."
- "When do the Dallas Cowboys play next?"
- "Who has the most home runs on the New York Mets?"
- "Show me the roster for the Patriots."
- "Are any of the Bruins players currently injured?"

When it comes to movies, Siri can also help you decide what to go see, determine where movies are playing, look up movie times, and provide details about almost any movie ever made. Here are some sample questions or requests you can use with Siri that relate to movies:

- "Where is [insert movie title] playing?"
- "What's playing at [insert movie theater]."
- "Who directed the movie [insert movie title]."
- "Show me the cast from [insert movie title]."
- "What's playing at the movies tonight?"
- "Find the closest movie theater."
- "Show me the reviews for [insert movie title]."
- "What movie won Best Picture in [insert year]."

PRACTICE (WITH SIRI) MAKES PERFECT

Right from the start, Siri will probably understand most of what you say. However, as you begin using this feature often, you will become acquainted with the best and most efficient ways to communicate questions, commands, and requests to generate the desired response.

Keep in mind that Siri translates what you say phonetically, so periodically, you might encounter names or commands that Siri can't understand or match up with correctly spelled information stored on your iPhone or iPad. This occurs most frequently with unusual names that sound vastly different from how they're spelled or used.

! CAUTION   Although Siri might seem human, in reality, it is an iPhone and iPad feature that operates using artificial intelligence and voice recognition software. Before allowing Siri to send any message or text, be sure to proofread it carefully on your device's screen. Keep in mind that some words sound the same when spoken, and Siri might choose the wrong word when translating your speech to text. This could lead to embarrassing situations or dramatically change the meaning of what you intended to say.

As you begin using Siri in your everyday life, you'll quickly discover this feature can streamline how you interact with your iPhone or iPad and make certain tasks much easier to accomplish. Based on the questions you ask, you'll also discover that Siri has a sense of humor. For example, try asking, "Siri, what do you look like?", "Siri, are you attractive?" or "What is the best Smartphone on the market?"

> **! CAUTION**   Theoretically, Siri can be used to control your iPhone or iPad to perform tasks hands-free while you're driving. Although using your iPhone or iPad in hands-free mode while driving might be legal in your state, if this is something you plan to do, proceed with extreme caution and don't allow yourself to be distracted from your primary responsibility, which is driving. Also, seriously consider using a wireless Bluetooth headset.

USE DICTATION MODE INSTEAD OF THE VIRTUAL KEYBOARD

Even if you're using an app that Siri is not yet compatible with, chances are you can still use your iPhone or iPad's Dictation mode. In many situations when the iPhone or iPad's virtual keyboard appears, you'll discover a microphone key located to the left of the spacebar. When you tap on this microphone key, Dictation mode is activated (shown in Figure 5.10).

FIGURE 5.10

Use Dictation mode to enter text using your voice, instead of typing on the virtual keyboard. (Shown here on an iPhone 5 running the Notes app.)

You can now say whatever text you were going to manually type using the virtual keyboard. You can speak for up to 30 seconds at a time. When you're finished speaking, it's necessary to tap the enlarged microphone key on the iPad (shown in Figure 5.11) or the Done key on the iPhone, so that your device can translate your speech into text and insert it into the appropriate onscreen field.

For the fastest and most accurate results, speak one to three sentences at a time, and have your device connected to a Wi-Fi Internet connection.

> **TIP** While using Dictation mode, you can easily add punctuation just by saying it. For example, you can say, "This is a sample dictation period," and Siri will add the period ("."). at the end of the sentence. You can also use words like "open parenthesis" or "close parenthesis," "open quotes" or "close quotes," or "comma," "semicolon," or "colon" as you dictate.

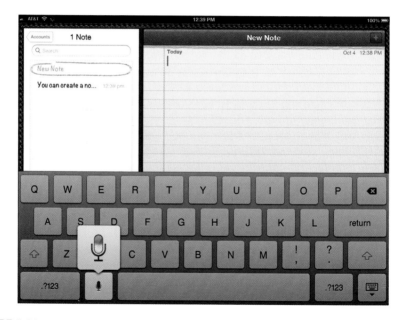

FIGURE 5.11

When you're finished speaking, tap on the enlarged microphone icon so your iPad (shown here) or the Done button on your iPhone to translate your speech into usable text.

6

SYNC AND SHARE FILES USING iCLOUD

iOS 6 includes full integration with Apple's iCloud online-based file-sharing service, which was enhanced with this version of the operating system. Initially, you might think that iCloud is just another cloud-based file-sharing service. However, for iOS 6 users, it does much more than simply allow you to store content on a remote server that's located somewhere in cyberspace. In fact, iCloud introduces a handful of new features and functions to your iPhone or iPad that you'll soon be wondering how you ever lived without. There are several compelling reasons to begin using iCloud with your iOS device (and primary computer).

First, an iCloud account is free. When created, your iCloud account includes 5GB of online storage space for your personal data and files, plus an unlimited amount of additional online storage space for all your iTunes Store, App Store, and iBookstore (and Newsstand) purchases, including apps, music, TV shows, movies, eBooks, audiobooks, ringtones, and so on.

The additional storage space needed to store your Photo Stream and Shared Photo Stream images is also provided, for free, from Apple. Thus, the 5GB of online storage space is used only for your iCloud Backup files or to sync and store app-specific files and data "in the cloud."

An iCloud account also includes a free @icloud.com email address, which you can use to send and receive email from all your devices that are linked to your iCloud account. And iCloud will automatically keep your email account synchronized on all devices.

> **NOTE** If you have an older Apple ID account that has an associated @.mac or @.me email address, it can be used as the email address that's associated with your iCloud account.

If you need to upgrade your iCloud account to utilize additional online storage space, it can be purchased directly from your iOS device for an annual fee (as shown in Figure 6.1).

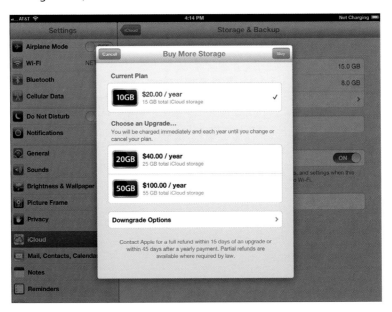

FIGURE 6.1

Launch Settings, select the iCloud option, followed by the Storage & Backup option and then tap on the Change Storage Plan option to acquire additional iCloud online storage space.

> **NOTE** An additional 10GB of online storage is priced at $20 per year (which gives you a total of 15GB, including the 5GB of free online storage). An additional 20GB is priced at $40 per year, and 50GB is priced at $100 per year.

CONTENT SAVED TO iCLOUD IS AVAILABLE ANYWHERE

By default, as soon as you establish a free iCloud account, anytime you acquire and download content from the iTunes Store, a copy of that content automatically gets saved in your iCloud account and immediately becomes available on all of your compatible computers and iOS devices (including Apple TV) that are linked to that iCloud account. This includes all past iTunes purchases and downloads as well.

So, if you hear an awesome new song on the radio while you're out and about, you can immediately purchase and download it from the iTunes Store using your iPhone. As always, that song will become available on your iPhone within a minute.

Then, thanks to iCloud, you'll also be able to access that same newly purchased song from your primary computer, iPad, iPod touch, and/or Apple TV device, without having to repurchase it. This feature also works with TV shows and movies purchased from iTunes, as well as with hybrid apps you want to install on both your iPhone and iPad, for example, without having to purchase that same app twice. The benefit to using iCloud is that syncing can be done from anywhere via the Internet, without using iTunes Sync or requiring a connection between iOS mobile device and primary computer.

If you ever opt to delete any iTunes purchase from your iOS device, for whatever reason, you always have the option of downloading and installing it again, free, from iCloud.

> **TIP** Depending on how you set up the iTunes Store, the App Store, and iBookstore (plus Newsstand) to work with iCloud, you can automatically have all of your computers and iOS devices download all new music, app and eBook content you purchase, or this can be done manually. To adjust these Automatic Downloads settings, launch Settings, select the iTunes & App Stores option, and then turn on or off the virtual switches associated with Music, Apps and Books that are listed under the Automatic Downloads heading.

When turned on for Music on your iPad, for example, if you purchase a new song on your iPhone, it automatically downloads to your tablet as well, assuming the iPad has Internet access via Wi-Fi, unless you've also turned on the Use Cellular Data option that's associated with Automatic Downloads.

Due to their large files sizes, automatic downloads are not possible for TV show episodes, movies or audiobooks acquired from the iTunes Store. However, you can download these purchases manually onto each of your computers and/or iOS mobile devices that are linked to the same iCloud account.

NOTE Although your iTunes music purchases might represent a portion of your overall personal digital music library, chances are, that library also includes CDs (which you have ripped into digital format), as well as online music purchases and downloads from other sources (such as Amazon.com).

For an additional fee of $24.99 per year, you can upgrade your iCloud account by adding the iTunes Match services. This grants you full access to your entire personal digital music library (including non-iTunes purchases) from all of your computers and devices that are linked to your iCloud account. To learn more about iTunes Match, visit www.apple.com/itunes/itunes-match.

ACCESS YOUR PURCHASED iTUNES CONTENT FROM ANY DEVICE

After you have purchased an app, music, a TV show, a movie, an eBook, an audiobook, or another type of content from the iTunes Store, App Store, iBookstore, or Newsstand, that content is automatically available via iCloud to all of your iOS devices, your primary computer, and, depending on the type of content, on your Apple TV. This is automatic, as soon as you set up a free iCloud account.

Because Apple has maintained detailed records of your iTunes, App Store, and iBookstore purchases to date, all content from past purchases also immediately becomes accessible to computers or devices linked to your iCloud account.

Let's look at an example. While using iTunes on your primary computer, suppose you purchase and download the *Never Over* EP released by *American Idol* Season 4 top-4 finalist Anthony Fedorov. The six songs on that EP get immediately downloaded to your computer's hard drive.

Now, thanks to iCloud, those six songs are also instantly made available via your iCloud account to your iPhone, iPad, iPod touch, and/or Apple TV device. So, after purchasing Anthony Fedorov's EP, for example, on your primary computer via iTunes, follow these steps to manually load that same music into your iPad (or another iOS device) via iCloud (assuming you do not have the Automatic Downloads option turned on):

1. Make sure that your iOS device is connected to the Web via a 3G/4G or Wi-Fi connection.

2. Launch the iTunes app on your device. If prompted, when the Apple ID Password window pops up on your screen, use the virtual keyboard to enter your Apple ID password.

3. Tap on the Purchased icon that's displayed near the lower-right corner of the iTunes app's screen. Then, near the top-center of the screen, tap on the Music tab.

> **NOTE** On an iPhone, to access already purchased content, launch the iTunes app, tap on the More icon that's displayed near the bottom-right corner of the screen, tap on the Purchased option, select Music, and then choose the artist or group's name whose music you already own and that you want to download onto the phone.

4. Within a column on the left side of the screen is an alphabetic listing of recording artists and music groups that relate to music you own. For this example, you'd find Anthony Fedorov on this listing. Tap on his name.

5. On the right side of the screen, all songs from Anthony Fedorov that you have purchased and that are stored within your iCloud account are listed. Each listing is accompanied by an iCloud icon (shown in Figure 6.2).

6. Tap on the iCloud icons, one at a time, to select which of Anthony Fedorov's songs you want to download onto your iPad. Or to download all of the songs listed, tap on the iCloud icon associated with the Download All Anthony Fedorov Songs option that's displayed near the top of the screen.

> **TIP** After tapping on the Purchased icon in iTunes on your iPad, tap on the Music, Movies, or TV Shows tab. Each is displayed near the top-center of the screen. If you've acquired audiobooks, an additional tab will be displayed.

Below the Music, Movies, and TV Shows tabs are two additional tabs, labeled All and Not On This iPad (iPhone). Tapping on the All tab lists all content of that type you own, while tapping on the Not On This iPad (iPhone) tab displays only related content you own, but that's not already stored on the device you're using.

FIGURE 6.2

From any device that runs iTunes, you can access and download your previous purchases by tapping on the Purchased icon.

7. Within one to two minutes or so, the new music from Anthony Fedorov's EP, or whatever music you selected to download, will be available to listen to on the iOS 6 device you're currently using.

6. Exit iTunes by pressing the Home button.

7. Launch the Music app on your iOS device.

8. When the Music app launches, Anthony Fedorov's music is now listed when you tap on the Songs, Artists (shown in Figure 6.3) or Albums tabs that are displayed along the bottom of the screen.

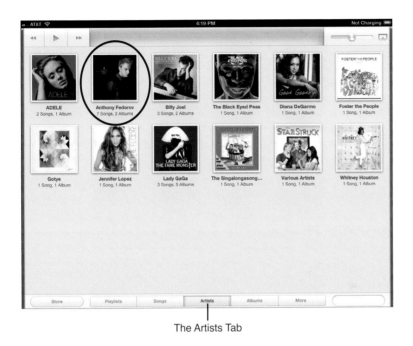

The Artists Tab

FIGURE 6.3

Anthony Fedorov's music was initially purchased from iTunes on a Mac, but was also downloaded (at no additional cost) to an iPad connected to the same iCloud account.

USE iCLOUD TO SYNC YOUR APPS, DATA, DOCUMENTS, AND FILES

Most cloud-based file-sharing services serve mainly as a place in cyberspace to remotely store files. However, you manually have to transfer those files to and from the "cloud." Thanks to iCloud's integration with iOS 6, many of the core apps that come with iOS 6, as well as a growing number of third-party apps, automatically keep data and files created or managed using those apps synchronized with other devices and/or your primary computer that's also linked to the same iCloud account.

From within Settings on your iPhone or iPad, turn on or off iCloud support for all compatible apps on your device. Compatible apps include Contacts, Calendars, Reminders, Safari, Notes, Photos, and Mail (relating only to your free iCloud-related email account).

NOTE Specific information on how to use iCloud with specific prein-stalled apps is covered within later chapters of this book. For example, from Chapter 8, "Organize Your Life with Reminders and Notes," learn how to use the iCloud Sync feature with these two apps, and why using this feature is beneficial.

MORE INFO iCloud is also fully compatible with Apple's optional iWork apps for the iPhone and iPad, which include Pages (word processing), Numbers (spreadsheet management), and Keynote (for digital slide presentations). See the section, "Automatically Transfer Documents Using iCloud" to learn more about this functionality.

When you turn on the iCloud functionality related to the Contacts app, for example, your iOS device will automatically sync your contacts database with iCloud, and all of your computers and/or other iOS devices linked to your iCloud account. Thus, if you add or update a contact entry on your iPhone, that addition or change automatically synchronizes and becomes available within the Contacts app running on your other iOS devices, as well as within the compatible contact management software that's running on your primary computer (such as the Contacts app or Microsoft Outlook on your Mac).

This same functionality also works with the Calendar and Reminders apps, for example. If you add or modify an appointment using the Calendar app on your Mac, or Calendar on your iPad, that new information immediately and automatically synchronizes to all your linked computers and devices.

As you surf the Web using Safari, when you turn on iCloud syncing functionality related to this app, all of your Bookmarks and Bookmark Bar data, along with your Reading List information and open browser window/tabs data are synced via iCloud. Likewise, notes created using the Notes app also sync with the Notes app on your Mac and other iOS mobile devices.

To share your photos between iOS devices, your primary computer, and/or an Apple TV device, you'll need to set up a Photo Stream using iCloud. How to do this is explained later in this chapter.

TIP The Documents & Data setting that's found on the iCloud menu screen within Settings enables you to set up your iOS device to automatically sync (share) documents related to specific apps using iCloud, making them almost instantly and automatically available on your computer(s) and other iOS devices.

This feature works with all iWork for iOS apps (Pages, Numbers, and Keynote), for example.

However, from within Settings, in addition to turning on the Documents & Data feature associated with iCloud from the iCloud menu screen, you also need to turn on the iCloud Sync function for each app from within Settings. How to do this for the iWork apps is described shortly.

CUSTOMIZING iCLOUD TO WORK WITH YOUR APPS

It's important to understand that the app-related synchronization feature offered by iCloud is different from iCloud Backup (which creates a complete backup of your entire iOS device that gets stored online as part of your iCloud account).

When you set up iCloud to work with a specific compatible app, that app automatically accesses the Web, connects to iCloud, and then uploads or downloads app-related files, documents, or data as needed. iCloud then shares (syncs) that app-specific data with your other computers and devices that are linked to the same iCloud account.

To customize which of your compatible iCloud apps utilize iCloud functionality, follow these steps:

1. Launch Settings from your iPhone or iPad's Home Screen.

2. Tap on the iCloud option.

3. When the iCloud menu screen appears (shown in Figure 6.4), at the top of the screen, make sure the Apple ID–linked email address that's associated with your iCloud account is displayed next to the Account option. If it's not, use your existing Apple ID to create or access an iCloud account by tapping on the Account option.

4. Below the Account option is a list of all preinstalled iCloud-compatible apps on your iOS device. To the right of each listing is a virtual on/off switch. To turn on the iCloud functionality associated with a specific app, set its related virtual switch to the on position.

5. When you have turned on the iCloud functionality for all the apps that you want to be able to synchronize via iCloud, exit Settings to save your changes. (Press the Home button to do this.)

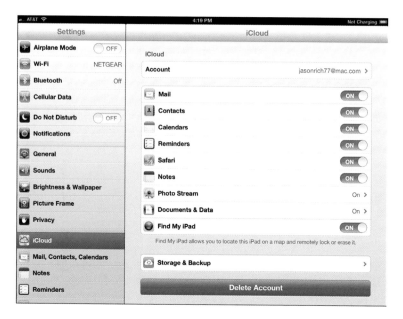

FIGURE 6.4

Turn on or off iCloud functionality for specific apps that come preinstalled with iOS 6 from the iCloud menu within Settings.

6. Repeat this process on each of your iOS devices. So, if you have an iPhone and an iPad, you'll need to turn on the iCloud functionality for Contacts, for example, on both devices to keep Contacts data synchronized via iCloud on both devices.

> **☑ TIP** After you've turned on the iCloud functionality for specific apps, for the various apps on your iOS devices (and your primary computer) to stay synchronized, each computer or device must have access to the Internet. For this use of iCloud on your iPhone or iPad, a 3G/4G or a Wi-Fi Internet connection works fine. For certain other iCloud features, such as Photo Stream and iCloud Backup, your iOS device will require a Wi-Fi Internet connection.

ACCESS YOUR APP-SPECIFIC DATA ONLINE AT iCLOUD.COM

Another benefit of using iCloud to sync your app-specific data is that using any computer or Internet-enabled devices, you can visit www.iCloud.com, log into this website using your iCloud username and password (which is typically your Apple

ID username and password) and then access online-based versions of the Contacts, Calendar, Reminders, and Notes apps. (This is shown on a Mac using the Safari web browser in shown in Figure 6.5). Your most up-to-date data from these apps appears within the online versions of the apps.

FIGURE 6.5

Log into www.iCloud.com to access your app-specific content using online versions of popular iPhone and iPad apps, including Contacts, Calendar, Reminders, and Notes.

So, if you forget your iPhone at home, for example, you can still access your complete Contacts database, your schedule, your to-do lists and your notes from any computer.

Once you log into iCloud.com, click on the on-screen app you want to access. The online apps are almost identical to the iPad versions of the Contacts, Calendar, Reminders, and Notes app.

CREATE A PHOTO STREAM USING iCLOUD

In conjunction with iOS 6, Apple introduced two different types of Photo Streams that work with iCloud. The My Photo Stream option was originally introduced with iOS 5. It allows you to automatically share photos between your own computers and iOS mobile devices that are linked to the same iCloud account. Once set up, this sharing process happens automatically and in the background.

New to iOS 6 is the Shared Photo Streams feature. It works in conjunction with the Photos app (and optional iPhoto app). Shared Photo Streams provide an easy way for you to share an unlimited number of photos that are stored on your iOS mobile device with specific people who you select. This sharing is done using online galleries that are created using iCloud to showcase your selected images.

Using this feature, you can create as many separate Shared Photo Stream galleries as you'd like, add and remove photos from them at anytime, plus choose who is granted access to see and download those photos. From within the Photos app, for example, you could use the Share feature and select Mail, but this option only allows you to share up to five photos at a time with the intended recipients.

The Shared Photo Stream feature allows you to share as many photos as you'd like within each Shared Photo Stream gallery. Each gallery is stored online (via iCloud) and is given a unique URL. When you opt to share a Shared Photo Stream with other people, your iPhone, iPad or computer that you're using to manage the Shared Photo Stream will send your intended audience for those photos an email which provides them with the special webpage address (URL) that's associated with your Shared Photo Stream.

To learn more about the My Photo Stream and Shared Photo Stream features and how they work, be sure to read Chapter 11, "Shoot, Edit, and Share Photos and Videos." However, like all iCloud-related features, on each of your iOS mobile devices and computers, the My Photo Stream and Shared Photo Streams features must be turned on separately. This is done by launching Settings, tapping on the iCloud option, and then turning on the virtual switch that's associated with each Photo Stream option.

> **☑ TIP**   Photo Stream requires that each of your iOS devices has access to a Wi-Fi Internet connection. It does not work with a 3G/4G connection from your iPhone, iPad, or iPod touch. This feature works with both Macs and PCs.

The Photo Stream and Shared Photo Stream feature is compatible with Apple TV, so you can view your favorite digital images on your HDTV at home or at work, as standalone images or as part of an animated slideshow.

> **✐ NOTE**   On your Mac, it is necessary to upgrade to the latest version of the OS X Mountain Lion operating system, as well as the most recent version of iPhoto '11, in order to use the My Photo Stream and the Shared Photo Stream features on your primary computer. You also need to turn on this feature in iPhoto '11.

If you're using a PC, be sure to download the free iCloud Control Panel for Windows v2.0 utility (http://support.apple.com/kb/DL1455), and then turn on the Picture Library feature.

AUTOMATICALLY TRANSFER DOCUMENTS USING iCLOUD

In addition to the iCloud compatibility built in to many of the core (preinstalled) apps that are included with iOS 6, a growing number of other apps also offer iCloud compatibility, and allow you to easily (and automatically) transfer or synchronize app-related documents and files.

This functionality is built in to Apple's iWork apps for the iPhone and iPad, which include Pages (word processing), Numbers (spreadsheet management), and Keynote (for digital slide presentations). Be sure to upgrade your iWork for iOS apps to the latest versions for this functionality to work.

🔍 **MORE INFO** Pages, Keynote, and Numbers are compatible with Microsoft Word, Microsoft PowerPoint, and Microsoft Excel, respectively. For more information on using these apps, see Chapter 19, "Be Productive Using Pages, Numbers, and Keynote."

If you turn on iCloud functionality with Pages, Numbers, Keynote, or other compatible third-party apps, when you create or revise a document, that revision is stored on your iOS device and on iCloud. From iCloud, that same app running on your iOS device (or compatible software running on your primary computer) can access that most recent version of your files or documents within seconds.

So, if you're working with the Pages word processor on your iPhone, your iPad, or the Mac, you always know that when you access a specific Pages document from any compatible device, you're working with the most up-to-date version of that document. The synchronization process happens automatically and behind the scenes, assuming that your iOS devices and primary computer are connected to the Internet.

📝 **NOTE** To use iCloud's "Documents in the Cloud" feature, your iOS device can utilize a 3G/4G or Wi-Fi Internet connection.

The processes for turning on iCloud functionality within compatible apps on your iPhone, iPad, and iPod touch are almost identical. To begin, turn on the Documents & Data option from the iCloud menu within Settings. Then, to turn on the iCloud functionality in Pages on an iPad, for example, follow these steps:

1. From your iOS device, launch Settings from the Home Screen.

2. Scroll down on the main Settings menu until you find the listing of apps stored on your device (shown in Figure 6.6).

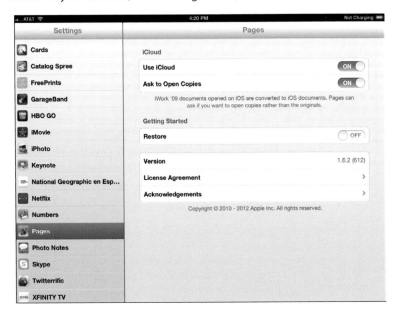

FIGURE 6.6

To control iCloud functionality for apps that don't come preinstalled with iOS 6, scroll down to the specific app listings on the main Settings menu, and tap on the app of your choice, such as Pages (if applicable).

3. Locate the listing for Pages (or the app of your choice) from the Settings menu and tap on it.

4. When the Pages menu screen appears in Settings, tap on the virtual switch that's associated with the Use iCloud option, and switch it to the on position. If you turn this feature to the off position, your documents are stored only on your iPad (in this example), and are not synchronized with other devices via iCloud, because the selected app will not access iCloud via the Internet.

5. Exit Settings. From this point forward, your Pages documents auto-
    matically synchronize with iCloud when your iPad (in this example) has
    Internet access.

6. Repeat this process for each iCloud-compatible app, on each of your
    iOS devices.

USING A UNIQUE APPLE ID FOR iCLOUD

When you first create an iCloud account, you're encouraged to use your pre-
existing Apple ID and username. This is to encourage Apple computer and device
users to use the same Apple ID to make and track all of their iTunes Store, App
Store, iBookstore and Newsstand purchases, plus use that same Apple ID to access
Apple's online-based iMessage instant messaging service, the FaceTime video conferencing service, and utilize all of iCloud's functionality.

If you're the only person who needs access to your iTunes Store, App Store, iBookstore and Newsstand purchases on your own computer(s) and devices, using the
same Apple ID and password for this, as well as to access Apple's other online-
based services is practical and efficient.

However, if you want to share your iTunes Store, App Store, iBookstore and
Newsstand purchases with other family members who have their own iPhone,
iPad, iPod Touch, Mac or PC, but you do not want those other people to be able
to access your iCloud-related files, use your personal iMessage or FaceTime
account, or access your iCloud-related email address, create one shared Apple ID
account for Apple-related online purchases, and then create a second, personal
Apple ID account that you use with some of iCloud's features, as well as iMessage
and FaceTime.

To create and manage your Apple ID account(s), visit https://appleid.apple.
com from any computer or Internet-enabled device. However, when you set up
iCloud, or use iMessage, FaceTime or try to access the iTunes Store, iBookstore or
Newsstand for the first time, you also have the option to create a new Apple ID
account.

> **✓ TIP** From your iPhone or iPad, to view and manage your Apple ID
> account, launch Settings, tap on the iTunes & App Stores option, and then tap on
> the Apple ID option that's displayed near the top of the iTunes & App Store menu
> screen. Tap on the View Apple ID button to access and manage your account, or
> tap on the iForgot button to recover a forgotten Apple ID username or password.

BACKING UP WITH iCLOUD

Until Apple launched iOS 5 and the iCloud service in 2011, creating and maintaining a complete backup of your iOS device on your primary computer required you to use the iTunes Sync process. This option (which is still available) meant that you needed to manually connect your iOS device to your primary computer via the supplied USB cable, and then run iTunes on your computer.

> ☑ **TIP** To use the now antiquated iTunes Sync process requires using the USB cable that came with your iPhone, iPad or iPod touch in order to establish a link between your primary computer and your iOS mobile device. To do this, follow the instructions offered on Apple's website by visiting http://support.apple.com/kb/HT1766.

iOS 6 STILL OFFERS WIRELESS iTUNES SYNC

Today, in addition to using iCloud to wirelessly sync your iOS mobile device and app-specific data, you have two additional options available. You can use the iTunes Sync process or the Wireless iTunes Sync process. If your primary computer and iOS device connect to the same wireless network, you can manually sync your iPhone, iPad, or iPod touch wirelessly. The USB cable connection between your computer and your iOS device is not needed.

> ✎ **NOTE** You can still connect your iPhone (and in some cases your iPad) to a computer via the USB cable to charge your iOS mobile device, without syncing.

Using the Wireless iTunes Sync feature, your wireless iOS device should be plugged in to power and must be linked via Wi-Fi to the same wireless network as your primary computer. After the wireless connection is initiated, you can begin the wireless backup process from within Settings on your iOS device. However, iTunes must be running on your primary computer, and the iTunes Sync over Wi-Fi Connection option that's available when using the iTunes software on your primary computer (a Mac or PC), must be selected.

> ✎ **NOTE** The Wireless iTunes Sync feature enables you to create a full backup of your iOS device and sync app-specific data. The related backup files get stored on your primary computer's hard drive, just as they would if you used the traditional iTunes sync process. This feature does not, however, utilize iCloud.

To create a backup of your iOS device using the Wireless iTunes Sync feature, follow these steps:

1. On your primary computer, launch iTunes.

2. Before you can use the Wireless iTunes Sync process for the first time, connect your iOS device to your primary computer via the supplied USB cable. When the connection between your device and computer is established, on the left side of the iTunes screen, under the Devices heading, click on your iOS device's name.

3. Near the top center of the main iTunes screen, click the Summary tab to see details pertaining to your iOS device.

4. On the Summary screen, use the mouse to add a checkmark to the Sync With This iPhone [iPad] Over Wi-Fi option that's displayed under the Options heading (as shown in Figure 6.7).

FIGURE 6.7

To use the Wireless iTunes Sync feature, it must be turned on from within iTunes on your primary computer and on your iOS device. On your primary computer, click the Sync With This iPhone [iPad] Over Wi-Fi option. iTunes version 10.7 is shown here. The screen looks slightly different if you're running iTunes 11 on your computer.

5. You can now disconnect your iOS device from your primary computer. The USB cable is no longer needed.

6. Make sure that your primary computer and your iOS device are connected to the same wireless network using Wi-Fi on both the computer and iOS mobile device.

7. From your iOS device, launch Settings.

8. Tap on the General option.

9. When the General menu screen appears, scroll down to the iTunes Wi-Fi Sync option, and tap on it.

10. If you haven't already done so, plug in your iOS device to an electrical outlet.

11. On your iOS device, tap the Sync Now button that appears on the iTunes Wi-Fi Sync screen (as shown in Figure 6.8). The Wireless iTunes Sync process will begin. The end result is a backup of your iOS device that's stored on your primary computer's hard drive (just as if you had used the traditional iTunes Sync process by connecting the devices via the supplied USB cable).

FIGURE 6.8

Initiate the Wireless iTunes Sync process from within the Settings app on your iOS device, whether it's an iPhone (shown here), iPad, or iPod touch.

> ✅ **TIP**   After a backup of your iOS device has been created using the iTunes Sync or Wireless iTunes Sync process, you can restore your iOS device (or a new iOS device of the same type) from that backup. For example, you can restore an iPhone from an iPhone backup, or Restore an iPad from an iPad backup. You cannot, however, restore an iPhone from an iPad backup (or vice versa).

When you're reinstalling your iOS device, when prompted, select the Restore From iTunes option, and follow the onscreen prompts.

iCLOUD BACKUP: NO CABLE NEEDED

One additional and useful feature of iOS 6 is the ability to create a complete backup of your iOS device wirelessly, and have the related backup files stored on online ("in the cloud"). Using this feature, your iOS device can be connected to any Wi-Fi Internet connection. Your primary computer is not needed. Thus, the backup can be created from anywhere, and you can later restore your device from anywhere a Wi-Fi Internet connection is present.

TIP When you activate the iCloud Backup feature, if you connect your iOS device to your primary computer, the iTunes Sync process does not work. If you want to create a backup of your device using iTunes Sync and have the backup files stored on your primary computer's hard drive (instead of on iCloud), you need to first turn off the iCloud Backup feature from within the Settings app.

When activated, your iOS device automatically creates a backup to iCloud once per day (when the device is connected to the Internet via a Wi-Fi connection but isn't otherwise in use). For this to happen, your iPhone or iPad also needs to be connected to an external power source. However, at any time, you can manually create a backup of your device to iCloud from within Settings. This can be done when your device is running on battery.

To activate and use the iCloud Backup feature, the process is the same for an iPhone or iPad.

Follow these steps to activate and use the iCloud Backup feature on an iPhone or iPad:

1. Make sure that your iOS device is connected to the Internet via a Wi-Fi connection.

2. From the Home Screen, launch Settings.

3. Tap on the iCloud option.

4. Tap on the Storage & Backup option that's located near the bottom of the iCloud menu screen within Settings.

5. About halfway down on the Storage & Backup screen, tap on the virtual switch that's associated with the iCloud Backup option. Turn the virtual switch to the on position.

6. A new Back Up Now option appears near the bottom of the Storage &
    Backup screen (as shown in Figure 6.9). Tap on it to begin creating a backup
    of your iOS device. The backup file will be stored on iCloud.

FIGURE 6.9

*Manage and launch the iCloud Backup feature from the Storage & Backup screen, accessible
from within the Settings app.*

TIP The first time you use the iCloud Backup feature to create a wireless backup of your iOS device, the process could take up to an hour (or longer),
depending on how much data you have stored on your device.

After the backup process begins, a progress meter is displayed at the bottom of
the Storage & Backup screen within Settings. While the backup is being created
this first time, refrain from using your iOS device. Just kick back and allow the
iPhone or iPad, for example, to connect with iCloud and create the initial backup.

In the future, the iCloud Backup process takes place once per day, automatically,
when your iOS device is not otherwise in use. These backups save all newly created or revised files and data only, so subsequent iCloud Backup procedures are
much quicker.

At the bottom of the Storage & Backup screen within Settings, the time and date
of the last backup is displayed. If, for some reason, the backup process could not

be completed because the device could not connect to the Internet, for example, an error message displays.

At anytime, it's possible to manually create an updated backup via iCloud by tapping on the Back Up Now icon that's displayed on the Storage & Backup screen.

The purpose of creating and maintaining a backup of your device is so that you have a copy of all your apps, data, files, content, and personalized settings stored, if something goes wrong with your device. If and when you need to access the backup to restore your device using iCloud, when prompted, choose the Restore from iCloud option.

iCLOUD: MANY USES, ONE STORAGE SPACE

As you've discovered in this chapter, iCloud is much more than just a typical cloud-based file-sharing service. However, after you set up your free iCloud account, you can choose which of iCloud's features and functions you want to utilize from within Settings on each of your device(s).

You are not required to use all of iCloud's various features. You can turn on only those features you believe are beneficial to you, based on how you typically use your iPhone and/or iPad, and what content, data, and information you want to synchronize or back up to your iCloud account.

> **TIP** If you're like most people and wind up storing a lot of content, data, and files on your iPhone and iPad, for example, and you want to use the iCloud Backup feature with each of your iOS devices, you might need to increase your iCloud online storage space allocation (which means incurring an annual fee).
>
> At the top of the main Storage & Backup screen within Settings, the amount of total online storage space you have available on iCloud is displayed next to the Total Storage heading (refer to Figure 6.8). Below that, the available online storage is listed.
>
> To see how your iCloud online storage is being utilized, tap on the Manage Storage option that's also listed under the Storage heading on the Storage & Backup menu screen. If your online storage allocation is almost filled (or becomes filled), tap on the Buy More Storage option to immediately increase the amount of available online storage space you have available.

7

COMMUNICATE EFFECTIVELY WITH iMESSAGE

Today's tweens and teens have a different way to communicate, and it's quickly spreading to adults as well. Most young people are equipped with a state-of-the-art cellphone or smartphone these days. But, instead of talking with their friends over the phone (and using up minutes of their airtime plan), or even conversing face to face, they often "talk" via text messaging and instant messaging.

Using short, text-based messages, and a special "language" composed of abbreviated terminology, such as "LOL" (meaning "laugh out loud") or "BRB" (meaning "be right back"), people of all ages have begun to rely on text messaging and instant messaging as a convenient way to communicate (as shown in Figure 7.1).

FIGURE 7.1

Text/instant messaging is done using the Messages app. Text-based conversations are formatted to be easy to read and follow.

Every iPhone's service plan has three components: voice, data, and text messaging. Upon subscribing to a plan, iPhone users choose a paid text-messaging plan that allows for the sending or receiving of a predetermined number of text messages per month, or you can pay extra for an unlimited text-messaging plan.

Text messaging using the service offered by your wireless service provider (such as AT&T Wireless, for example) allows iPhone users to send and receive messages and converse with any other cellphone user, regardless of which service provider their phone is registered with. So an iPhone user who uses AT&T Wireless can easily communicate with a cellphone user (even if it's not an iPhone who uses Verizon Wireless or Sprint PCS as a cellular service provider.

On the iPhone, the process of composing, reading, sending, and receiving text messages is done using the Messages app. Because until now text messaging was done through a wireless cellular network (as opposed to via the Internet), this functionality was not available to iPad users.

However, the Messages app can also be used with Apple's own iMessage services. Beyond using the Messages app, there are many optional apps available from the App Store that are compatible with the instant messaging services offered by Yahoo!, Google, Facebook, AIM, and MSN and many other services.

> **NOTE** iMessage is a free text-messaging service operated by Apple that utilizes the Internet (as opposed to a cellular network), and allows iOS mobile device and Mac users to communicate, via unlimited text messages, with other iOS device and Mac users, as long as the devices have access to the Internet.

> **TIP** It's possible to use Siri in order to dictate and send text messages using your voice. To do this, activate Siri and say something like, "Send text message to Jason Rich." When Siri says, "What would you like it to say?," speak your message, and then confirm it (as shown in Figure 7.2). When prompted, tell Siri to send the text message you dictated. This feature works best if details about the person to which you're sending a text message are already stored in your Contacts database.
>
> Siri can also be used to read your newly received text messages, without having to look at or touch the iPhone's screen. You learn more about sending and receiving text messages using Siri in Chapter 5, "Using Siri and Dictation to Interact with Your iOS Device."

FIGURE 7.2

Siri on an iPhone 5 can be used to compose and send text messages using your voice.

BENEFITS OF COMMUNICATING VIA TEXT MESSAGE OR INSTANT MESSAGE

Some of the benefits of using text/instant messaging, as opposed to other forms of communication, such as making a traditional phone call or exchanging emails, include the following:

- You don't have to play phone tag with someone to communicate.
- Text messages can be sent anytime, day or night, and read by the recipient either immediately or whenever convenient.
- Using text messaging does not use up your allocation of airtime minutes, which get depleted when you talk on your cellphone. (However, unless you're using Wi-Fi, instant messaging will use up some of your wireless data allocation.)
- You can conduct multiple text-message–based conversations, with different people, simultaneously, or send the same message to a group.
- Text messaging is often more efficient and saves time versus talking on the phone or composing and sending traditional emails.
- Text messaging enables you to share quick thoughts or tidbits of information, privately, with one person, without engaging in a drawn-out conversation.
- You can attach a photo, a video clip, a location, contact information, or other information within an outgoing text message.
- It's often acceptable to use abbreviations in your text messages to save time while typing, especially if you're communicating casually with friends or family. For example, you could type, "Where R U?" instead of "Where are you?"
- Your iPhone or iPad automatically saves transcripts from all text-based conversations in the Messages app, so you can refer back to them or continue conversations later.

> **!CAUTION** This should be common sense, but if you look around as you're out and about, you'll see it clearly isn't. Under no circumstances should you be attempting to drive and use text messaging on your iPhone or iPad at the same time. Likewise, as you're walking down the street or crossing a busy intersection, don't try multitasking by also sending or reading text messages. Every day, numerous accidents happen (some very serious) as a result of people just like yourself sending or reading text messages when they should be focused on something else.

QUICK START: APPLE'S iMESSAGE SERVICE

Whether your iPhone or iPad is connected to the Internet via a Wi-Fi or 3G/4G connection, using iMessage with the Messages app that comes preinstalled on your device, you now can communicate via text or instant messages with other Macs and iOS mobile device users. Unlike the text-messaging services available through wireless service providers, Apple's iMessage service is free of charge, and it allows for an unlimited number of text messages to be sent and received.

The service also taps into your iPhone or iPad's other functions and allows for the easy sharing of photos, videos, locations, and contacts; plus, it works seamlessly with Notification Center.

> **☑ TIP** When the iMessage service is used with the Messages app, it enables you to send the same text message to multiple recipients. It uses a feature referred to as *group messaging* that enables everyone in that group to participate in the same text-message–based conversation.

The iMessage service is a hybrid between traditional text messaging that people have become accustomed to using on their cellphones, and instant messaging, which is something done on a computer that also involves communicating in real time by exchanging text-based messages (in addition to photos or web links, for example) with the person you're conversing with.

iMessage also enables you to participate in text-based but real-time conversations. You can see when someone is typing a message to you (as they're typing), and then you can view and respond to the message a fraction of a second after it is sent. (When someone is actively typing a message during a conversation on iMessage, a bubble with three periods in it appears.)

> **✎ NOTE** To utilize iMessage with the Messages app, your iPhone or iPad must have access to the Internet. When you're using traditional text messaging (through your wireless service provider), your iPhone must have access to the service's cellular network.

SET UP A FREE iMESSAGE ACCOUNT

Because traditional text messaging is tied to a cellphone, which has a unique phone number, there is no need to have a separate username or account name when using the text-messaging feature through your cellular service provider.

If you know someone's cellphone number, you can send a text message to that person from your cellphone (and vice versa). However, because iMessage is web-based, before using this service, you must set up a free iMessage account, which is tied to either your Apple ID or an existing email address.

The first time you launch the Messages app to use it with the iMessage service, you'll be instructed to set up a free account using your existing Apple ID (as shown in Figure 7.3). Or, instead of using your Apple ID, tap on the Create New Account option to create an account that's linked to another existing email address.

> **NOTE** iPhone users can associate their cellphone number with their iMessage account to send and receive text messages using this service. However, an Apple ID or existing email address can be used as well.

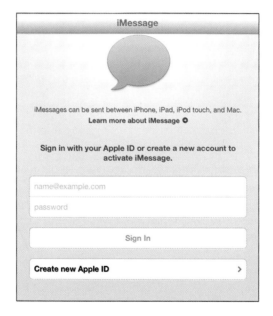

FIGURE 7.3

The first time you use the iMessage service, you'll need to set up a free account that can be linked to your Apple ID or any email address. (The same is true the first time you use FaceTime for videoconferencing.)

> **NOTE** If you already have an Apple ID account, the first time you use iMessage or FaceTime, you should log in using that account information.

> **☑ TIP** If you've upgraded your iPhone to iOS 6, when you first launch Messages, you might discover the app automatically uses your existing Apple ID to establish your free iMessage account. You can modify this within Settings by selecting the Messages option from the main Settings menu, if you want to create a separate Apple ID account for use with these services.
>
> One reason to use multiple Apple ID accounts is to link one with your online purchases and another with iMessage and/or FaceTime. This is useful if your kids or spouse also use an Apple computer or device and you want to share iTunes Store, App Store, iBookstore, or Newsstand purchased content with them, without giving them access to your other data.

To do this, you'll need to complete the information requested from the New Account screen. This includes entering your first and last name and providing an email address. You also need to create and verify a password for the account, plus create a security question and provide an answer to that question. Finally, enter your birth month and day, and choose your country or region.

When the requested New Account information is entered, tap on the blue-and-white Done icon in the upper-right corner of the New Account window. Keep in mind that if you simply enter your existing Apple ID information to set up your iMessage account, and then tap on the Sign In icon, the initial process for establishing an iMessage account is quick.

> **☑ TIP** Just as when you're using FaceTime, the unique Apple ID, email address, or iPhone phone number you use to set up your iMessage account is how people will find you and be able to communicate with you via text/instant messages. So if you want someone to be able to send you text messages via iMessage, that person will need to know the iPhone phone number, Apple ID or email address you used to set up the account. Likewise, to send someone a text message via iMessage, you'll need to know the iPhone phone number, Apple ID or email address the recipient used to set up his or her iMessage account.
>
> If you attempt to send a text message to someone's email address that is not registered with iMessage as an active account, the contents of your intended text message will be sent as a traditional email message and appear in the recipient's email inbox.

PROS AND CONS OF USING iMESSAGE

The biggest benefit to using iMessage over other text-messaging services is that it's free, and you can send/receive an unlimited number of messages. And because iMessage utilizes the Messages app, you'll discover that the app itself nicely integrates with other features, functions, and apps on your iPhone or iPad. Using the Camera app, for example, you can easily snap a photo or shoot a video clip using your iOS mobile device, and then use Messages to send that image or video clip to one or more friends via iMessage (without posting it in a public forum). Or if you're enjoying a cup of coffee at a local cafe, you can quickly share your exact location with a handful of friends and use iMessage to send out an invite for other people to join you.

> **NOTE** Instead of using iMessage, you can also create a text message that contains a photo or webpage link, for example, and send it to any other cell phone using your cellular provider's text messaging service.

If you're away from your iPhone or iPad when an incoming text message arrives, don't worry. The Notification Center app can continuously monitor the Messages app and will inform you of any missed messages in the Notification Center window.

Another convenient feature of iMessage is that you can begin a text-message-based conversation using your iPhone, for example, and then at any time switch to using your iPad or Mac and continue that conversation using the iMessage service. (This feature is not available if you're using the Messages app for text message via your cellular service provider.)

All text messages that are sent and received are saved, in reverse chronological order, and categorized by the person you communicated with. Until you manually delete the conversation, you always have a record of what was said, accompanied by the time and date messages were sent/received.

Currently, one potential drawback to the iMessage service is that to find and communicate with someone, you must know the Apple ID or email address used to set up the person's iMessage account. Thus, you need to know beforehand if they're a Mac, iPhone, or iPad user. However, after you know this, sending and receiving text messages with that person becomes a straightforward process. You can store the person's account information in your Contacts database (which links to the Messages app).

> **TIP** You can also send a message to someone's cell phone number from the Messages app on your iPhone or iPad.

TIPS AND TRICKS FOR USING THE MESSAGES APP

The Messages app, which is used to access the iMessage service on the iPhone or iPad, or for iPhone users to send/receive text messages via their cellular service provider, can be launched from the device's Home Screen.

The Messages app on the iPhone has two main screens: a summary of text-message conversations that's labeled Messages, and an actual conversation screen that's labeled at the top of the screen using the name of the person's you're conversing with (as shown in Figure 7.4). Both of these screens have a handful of icon-based commands available that give you access to the app's features and functions.

FIGURE 7.4

On the iPhone, each text-based conversation you participate in is displayed on a separate screen within the Messages app.

On the iPad, the Messages screen is divided into two main sections. On the left is a listing of previous text-based conversations you've participated in. The heading at the top of this listing (displayed near the upper-left corner of the screen) is Messages, and below it, the names of the people you've previously conversed with using this app.

When Messages is running, the right side of the iPad screen is the active conversation window. From here, you can initiate a new text-message–based conversation or respond to incoming text messages, one at a time.

> **NOTE** When you need to type text messages, the iPhone or iPad's virtual keyboard appears. To give you more onscreen real estate to reread a long conversation, tap on the Hide Keyboard key that always appears near the lower-right corner of the virtual keyboard when it's visible.

CREATE AND SEND A TEXT MESSAGE

The first time you launch Messages on the iPad, the New Message screen will be visible, the cursor will be flashing on the To field, and the virtual keyboard will be displayed. If you have contact information stored in the Contacts app, as soon as you start typing in the To field, Messages attempts to match up existing contacts with the name, cellphone number, or email address you're currently typing. When the intended recipient's name appears (because it's already stored in Contacts), tap on it.

To enter a recipient's name, cellphone number, Apple ID, or email address from scratch, simply type it into the To field using the iPhone or iPad's virtual keyboard.

Using an iPhone, from the Messages screen, tap in the New Message icon that's displayed in the upper-right corner to create a new outgoing text message and establish a new conversation.

> **TIP** After you've sent and received text messages using the Messages app, to initiate a new text-message conversation with someone, tap on the New Message icon that appears in the upper-right corner of the Messages screen on the iPhone, or next to the Messages heading on the upper-left side of the iPad's screen.

To quickly search your Contacts database to find one or more recipients for your text messages, you can also tap on the blue-and-white plus icon in the To field as you're composing a new message. A scrollable list of all contacts stored in Contacts displays, along with a Search field you can use to search your contacts database from within the Messages app.

> ✅ **TIP**   If you're using an iPhone, to use your cellular service provider's text-messaging service to send a message to another cellphone user, enter the recipient's cellphone number in the To field of a new message.
>
> If you're using an iPhone or iPad to send a text message to another iOS mobile device or Mac user via iMessage, in the To field, enter the recipient's Apple ID or the email address the user has linked with his iMessage account. (If the person is using an iPhone, his iMessage account might be associated with his iPhone's phone number, based on how he initially set up the account.)
>
> In your Contacts database, you can create a separate field for someone's iMessage username, or when viewing the person's Contacts listing, simply tap on the appropriate contact information based on how you want to send the text message.

After filling in the To field with one or more recipients, tap on the optional Subject field (on the iPad only) to create a subject for your text message, and then tap on the blank field located to the left of the Send icon to begin typing your text message. On the iPhone, just a blank field for the body of your text message is be available, displayed to the left of the Send icon.

If you're only sending text within your message, enter the text and then tap on the blue-and-white Send icon. Or to attach a photo or video clip to your outgoing text message, tap on the camera icon that's displayed to the left of the field where you're typing the text message.

> ✅ **TIP**   When you tap on the camera icon as you're composing a text message, two command options are displayed (shown in Figure 7.5): Take Photo or Video and Choose Existing. Tap on the Take Photo or Video option to launch the Camera app from within Messages, and quickly snap a photo or shoot a video clip using your iPhone or iPad's built-in camera. How to do this is explained in Chapter 11, "Shoot, Edit, and Share Photos and Videos."
>
> If you already have the photo or video clip stored on your phone or tablet that you want to share, tap on the Choose Existing option to launch the Photos app from within Messages, and then tap on the thumbnail for the photo or video clip you want to attach to the message.
>
> When the photo or video clip has been attached to the outgoing text message, and you've typed any text that you want to accompany it, tap on the Send key to send the message.

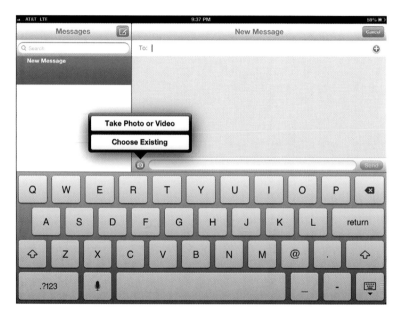

FIGURE 7.5

After tapping on the camera icon, choose to take a photo using your device's built-in camera, or select a photo or video clip that's already stored on your phone or iPad tablet (shown here).

PARTICIPATING IN A TEXT-MESSAGE CONVERSATION

As soon as you tap Send to initiate a new text-message conversation and send an initial message, the New Message window transforms into a conversation window, with the recipient's name displayed at the top center. Displayed on the right side of the conversation window will be the messages you've sent. The responses from the person you're conversing with will be left-justified and displayed in a different color on the screen with text bubbles.

As the text-message–based conversation continues and eventually scrolls off the screen, use your finger to swipe upward or downward to view what's already been said.

> **TIP** Whenever there's a pause between the sending of a message and the receipt of a response, the Messages app automatically inserts the date and time in the center of the screen so that you can later easily track the time period during which each conversation took place. This is particularly helpful if there are long gaps and the conversation did not take place in real time.

On the iPhone, tap on the Edit icon in the upper-right corner of the screen to access command icons for deleting individual text messages, deleting entire text-message conversations, or forwarding a single message (or complete conversation) to someone else. On the iPad, tap on the Share icon to access similar command icons.

> **TIP** From the Messages conversation screen on an iPad, tap on the person-shaped icon that's displayed in the upper-right corner of the conversation window to view the complete Contacts database entry for the person you're conversing with.

To delete entire conversations from within the Messages app, from the Messages screen on the iPhone (or the Messages listing on the right side of the iPad screen), swipe your finger from left to right along the listing for the conversation you want to delete. When the red-and-white Delete icon appears, tap on it to delete that entire conversation (as opposed to individual text messages within a conversation).

> **TIP** To forward a text/instant message you receive, view that message using the Messages app. Tap the Edit button that's displayed in the upper-right corner of the screen, tap on the portions of the message you want to forward, and then tap on the Forward button that's displayed near the bottom-right corner of the screen.

RESPONDING TO AN INCOMING TEXT MESSAGE

Depending on how you set up the Messages app from within Settings, you can be notified of an incoming text message in a number of ways. For example, notification of a new text message can be set to appear in the Notification Center window. Or if the Messages app is already running, a new message alert will be heard and a new message listing will appear on the Messages screen (iPhone) or under the Messages heading on the left side of the iPad screen.

> **TIP** When a new message arrives, a blue dot appears to the left of the new message's listing (under the Messages heading on the iPad or on the Messages screen on the iPhone). The blue dot indicates it's a new, unread text message.

To read the incoming text message and enter into the conversation window and respond, tap on the incoming message listing. If you're looking at the listing in the Notification Center window, for example, and you tap on it, the Messages app launches, and the appropriate conversation window automatically opens.

After reading the incoming text message, use the virtual keyboard to type your response in the blank message field, and then tap the Send icon to send the response message.

RELAUNCH OR REVIEW PAST CONVERSATIONS

From the Messages screen on the iPhone, or from the left side of the screen on the iPad when the Messages app is running, you can view a listing of all saved text-message conversations. The Messages app automatically saves all text messages until you manually delete them.

Under the Messages heading on the iPad (or on the Messages screen on the iPhone), you'll see a listing, displayed in reverse chronological order, of all text-message conversations you've participated in to date. Each listing displays the person's name, the date and time of the last message sent or received, and a summary of the last message sent or received. Tap on any of the listings to relaunch that conversation in the Conversation window. Remember that a blue dot on the left side of the listing indicates an unread message. You can either reread the entire conversation or continue the conversation by responding to the last message that was sent or by sending a new message to that person.

> **TIP** By tapping on one conversation listing at a time, you can quickly switch between conversations and participate in multiple conversations at once.
>
> On the iPhone, to exit the conversation screen you're currently viewing, tap on the left-pointing arrow icon that's displayed in the upper-left corner of the screen. It's labeled Messages.
>
> On the iPad, to exit a conversation, tap on one of the other listings under the Messages heading on the left side of the screen.
>
> To exit the Messages app altogether, press the Home button.

From the Messages screen on the iPhone (or the Messages listing on the iPad that's displayed on the left side of the screen), tap on the Edit icon to quickly delete entire conversations with specific people. To do this, tap on the red-and-white icon that's displayed next to the listing under the Messages heading once you tap the Edit icon.

> **☑ TIP** You can set up Notification Center to alert you of new incoming text messages in the Notification Center window. This setup is done once from within the Settings app. You can also set it up so that your iPhone or iPad displays a banner or an alert on the screen, shows a Badge App Icon, and/or displays a message on the Lock Screen when a new incoming text message arrives.
>
> To adjust these settings, launch the Settings app from the Home Screen, tap on the Notification option, and then adjust the Notification Center, Show, Alert Style, Badge App Icon, Show Preview, Repeat Alert, and View in Lock Screen options that are displayed under the Messages heading.

> **☑ TIP** When you're using Messages on the iPhone, near the top of each conversation screen will be three command buttons, labeled Call or Email, Face-Time, and Contact. Tap the Call button to initiate a phone call with that person (from an iPhone). Tap on Email to compose and send an email message to the person you're currently conversing with using the Messages app. The Mail app will automatically load, and the To field of the message will be filled in with the recipient's email address.
>
> Tap on the FaceTime icon to initiate a FaceTime videoconference if both you and the person you're conversing with using Messages and an active FaceTime account.
>
> Tap on the Contact icon to view the person's entry within your device's Contacts database, if the entry exists, or to create an entry for the person you're currently conversing with using Messages. While viewing a Contacts entry, you can tap on any phone number (when using an iPhone) to dial that number and initiate a call.

CUSTOMIZE THE MESSAGES APP

In Settings, you can customize several settings related to the Messages app. To do this, launch Settings from the Home Screen, and then tap on the Messages option that's displayed in the main Settings menu.

In the Messages setup window, you can turn on or off the iMessage service altogether, plus make adjustments that are relevant to sending and receiving text messages from your iOS 6 device. For example, by adjusting the virtual switch associated with the Send Read Receipts option to the on position, you will be notified when someone readers your text messages. Thus, if you send someone important or timely information via text message, you will be notified when it's received, and don't have to worry about whether the intended recipient received your message.

On the iPhone (as shown in Figure 7.6), you can also set preferences for using text messages (SMS and MMS messages) versus iMessage. On the iPad, the customizations available from within Settings pertain exclusively to the iMessage service.

FIGURE 7.6

In Settings, you can customize the Messages app to work with your cellular service provider's text-message service and/or Apple's iMessage service, plus you can personalize a handful of related options.

LEARN TO UNDERSTAND TEXT-MESSAGING ABBREVIATIONS

The key to becoming a highly skilled communicator when using text/instant messaging is to understand the lingo and abbreviations associated with this form of communication.

> **MORE INFO** In addition to using abbreviations, a "fluent" text-message communicator will use emoticons to convey emotions. A smiley or frown face are examples of emoticons created using the punctuation keys on the virtual keyboard. To see additional emoticons and discover how they're used, visit http://messenger.msn.com/Resource/Emoticons.aspx.

! CAUTION Beware of the iPhone or iPad's auto-correction feature when texting. When turned on, your iOS device will automatically "fix" misspelled or incorrectly typed words. However, this auto-correction feature is not always accurate, especially if you're using abbreviations in your text messages, and could result in an embarrassing situation.

To turn on or off the Auto-Correction feature, launch the Settings app and select the General option from the main Settings menu. Scroll down to the Keyboard option, and tap on it. Tap on the virtual on/off switch associated with the Auto-Correction feature to turn it on or off.

As a general rule, whether you're composing text messages, email, or documents or using an instant messaging app on your iOS device, proofread everything carefully before tapping the Send icon.

TIP When using the Messages app, you can take advantage of keyboard shortcuts and or special keyboard layouts to increase your text entry speed and accuracy, plus give you a greater selection of special characters, symbols and emoticons, for example. To create keyboard shortcuts, launch Settings, tap on the General option, and then tap on the Keyboard option. To create a new Keyboard Shortcut that can be used from any app, including Messages, tap on the Add New Shortcut… button.

To activate and be able to use a special keyboard layout, such as the Emoji keyboard (which offers hundreds of symbols and emoticons), launch Settings, tap on the General option, and then tap on the Keyboard option. From the Keyboard menu (within Settings), tap on the Keyboards option. Then, from the Keyboards menu, tap on the Add New Keyboard… option, and select the Emoji option by tapping on it. Now, when you're using the iPhone, iPad or iPad mini, for example, and the virtual keyboard is displayed, between the "123" key and the Dictation key (the microphone) will be a globe-shaped icon. Tap on this new keyboard key to reveal the alternate keyboard layout (shown in Figure 7.7 on the iPad mini).

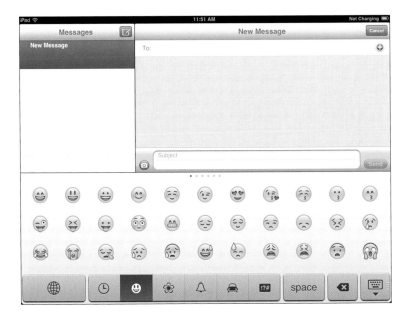

FIGURE 7.7

You can use alternative keyboard layouts, such as Emoji, to gain access to special letters, symbols, and emoticons.

IN THIS CHAPTER

- Discover new ways to manage information on your iOS device
- Create and manage to-do lists using the Reminders app
- Use the Notes app to create, manage, share and sync notes between your iPhone, iPad and Mac(s)

8

ORGANIZE YOUR LIFE WITH REMINDERS AND NOTES

If you have a busy life, and most of us do, your iPhone or iPad can be used to help you manage your schedule and day-to-day appointments, plus allow you to stay in contact with the people you know (and manage those contacts using the Contacts app), while also helping you maintain one or more detailed to-do lists. Plus, instead of using traditional sticky notes or cocktail napkins to jot notes to yourself, the Notes app is ideal for note taking, keeping track of ideas and managing text-based information that does not require the full functionality of a word processor, such as Pages.

Using the Reminders app, you can easily manage multiple to-do lists simultaneously, and add alarms and deadlines to individual to-do items, plus you can be reminded of responsibilities, tasks, or objectives exactly when you need this information, based on your geographic location or a

predetermined time and date. The Reminders app works nicely with Siri, Notification Center and iCloud, which makes synchronizing your app-related data a straightforward process.

> **NOTE** The Notes app works nicely with the iPhone or iPad's Dictation feature (so you don't have to manually type notes into the app), plus you can now sync your notes with iCloud (and your other iOS mobile devices and/or computers).

> **NOTE** The features and functions offered by the Reminders and Notes apps are virtually identical on the iPhone, iPad, and iPod Touch. However, due to varying screen sizes, the location of specific command icons, options, and menus sometimes varies. However, after you get to know how the app functions in general, you'll easily be able to switch between using it on your iPhone or iPad, for example, without confusion.

On the iPad, all information relevant to a specific app or function is typically displayed on a single screen. On the iPhone, however, that same information is often split up and displayed on several separate screens.

If you're an iPad mini user, you'll discover that the version of the Reminders app available to you is identical to the iPad version. It does not allow you to create location-based alerts and associate them with list items. However, you can create a date/time-based alert/alarm, plus add a Priority and Notes to each item added to a list. How to do this will be explained shortly.

USE REMINDERS TO MANAGE YOUR TO-DO LISTS

If you've just acquired a new iPhone or iPad, you'll discover an app that's preinstalled on your device, called Reminders. On the surface, this is a straightforward to-do list manager, however, it offers a plethora of interesting and useful features.

> **NOTE** Reminders is just one option for managing to-do lists on your iPhone or iPad. If you use the Search feature in the App Store (with the keyword "to-do list"), you'll find many more apps created by third parties that can be used for this purpose but that offer different features.

For starters, you can create as many separate to-do lists as you need to properly manage your personal and professional life, or various projects you're responsible for.

> **TIP** To make juggling a wide range of tasks, and keeping track of deadlines and your ongoing responsibilities an easier process, every item on your to-do list can be given unique alarms, which can be associated with specific times and/or dates. On the iPhone, each alert can also be location-based or be given a separate Priority (choose between None, Low, Medium, or High).

Because your iPhone has GPS capabilities, it always knows exactly where it is. Thus, you can create items within your to-do lists and associate one or more of them with an alarm that alerts you when you arrive at or depart from a particular geographic location, such as your home, your office, or a particular store.

For example, you can have your morning to-do list or call list automatically display on your iPhone's screen when you arrive at work, if you associate just one item on that list with a location-based alarm. Or if you're maintaining a list of office supplies you need to purchase at Staples, you can have your shopping list that was created using Reminders, pop up on the screen when you arrive at your local Staples office supply superstore. Again, only one item on the list needs to have a location-based alarm associated with it.

In addition, you can have a reminder alarm set to warn you of an upcoming deadline, and then have a second alarm alert you when that deadline has actually arrived. This can be displayed on your iPhone or iPad's screen within the Notification Center screen/window, or as separate Alerts or Banners, depending on how you have the Reminders app set up to work with your device.

> **TIP** To set up Reminders to work with Notification Center and/or display on-screen Alerts or Banners, launch Settings, tap on the Notifications option, and then tap on the listing for the Reminders app. You can then customize the settings on the Reminders menu screen within Settings (shown in Figure 8.1). Refer to Chapter 4, "Make the Most of Notification Center," to learn more about using any app with the Notification Center functionality of your iPhone or iPad.

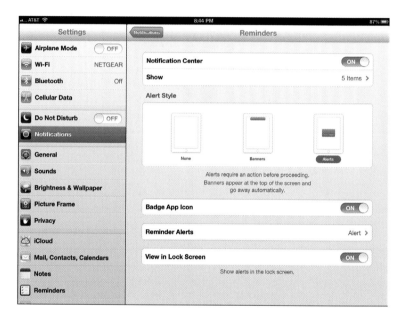

FIGURE 8.1

Customize how you want Reminders to get your attention through Notification Center and/or using Alerts or Banners from this Settings menu screen (shown here on the iPad).

KEEP UP TO DATE WITH REMINDERS

When you launch Reminders for the first time, on the iPhone, a blank to-do notepad will be displayed. On the iPad, on the left side of the screen, you will see the control center for this app. On the right side of the screen will be a simulated sheet of lined paper, with the heading Reminders at the top. This serves as your blank to-do notepad (as shown in Figure 8.2).

To begin creating a single to-do list under the default Reminders heading, tap on the top empty line of the simulated sheet of paper, or tap on the plus sign icon that's displayed near the upper-right corner of the screen. The virtual keyboard appears. Enter the first item to be added to your to-do list, and then tap on the Return key on the keyboard.

When you tap on the Return key, an empty check box will appear in the margin, to the left of the to-do list item you just entered. You can mark the completion of this task later by tapping on this check box in order to add a checkmark to it. The item is then automatically moved to the master Completed list. However, as soon as you're done entering the to-do list item, you can tap on it to make the Details window appear. From this window, you can set a Remind Me alarm by tapping on the Remind Me On A Day option. Or you can tap on the Show More option to set a Priority for the to-do item or add text-based Notes to the item.

> **✓ TIP** If you're managing multiple to-do lists, you can also assign the to-do item to a specific list.

FIGURE 8.2

Using Reminders, you can create and manage one or more to-do lists. (Shown here on the iPad.) Each list can have as many separate items as you wish.

When you scroll down to the bottom of the Details window, you'll see a Delete option. Tap on it to delete the item from your list. As soon as make any changes to a to-do list item, if you have iCloud functionality turned on for the Reminders app, your additions, edits or deletions will almost immediately sync with iCloud, assuming your iOS mobile device has access to the Internet. See the section, "Reminders Also Works With iCloud," to learn more about how the Reminders app integrates with iCloud to sync app-specific data.

On the iPhone only, if you tap on the Remind Me option in the Details box, you can choose between two options, which include Remind Me On a Day or Remind Me At A Location. To set a date-specific alarm, turn the virtual switch associated with Remind Me On a Day to the on position, and then tap on the date and time line that appears below it to set the date and time for the alert.

☑ TIP Prior to using a location-based alarm on your iPhone, if you'll be using this feature when running errands, one at a time, use the Maps app to find the locations of the businesses or stores you'll be visiting, and then save them as contacts in your Contacts database.

For example, if you'll be creating a grocery list using the Reminders app, from the Maps app, find the address of your supermarket using the Search feature of the Maps app. Enter "Shaw's Supermarket, Sharon, MA," for example. Include the business name, city and state in the Maps search.

When the location of the supermarket is displayed on a map, tap the blue-and-white > icon to reveal details about the supermarket's address and phone number.

Scroll down on the screen to the Add To Contacts icon, and tap on it. An entry for the supermarket (complete with its address) will be stored in your Contacts database, and will now be accessible from the Reminders app, so you can use it with the location-based reminders feature.

To set an alarm based on a location, turn on the virtual switch associated with the Remind Me At A Location option, choose the desired location you want the alert to be associated with, and then decide whether you want to be alerted when you arrive or when you leave that destination. On the iPad, you can only set an alarm based on a date and time.

☑ TIP If you get into the habit of using the Mac version of Reminders (which comes bundled with OS X Mountain Lion), you can create location-based alerts on your Mac and they'll sync with your iPhone via iCloud. Location-based alerts do not, however, currently work on Reminders running on the iPad.

☑ TIP When you opt to associate an alert with a location, you have the option to choose your current location, select your Home or Work address, or choose an address from your Contacts database. You also have the option to set a priority with each to-do list item. Your Priority options include None, Low, Medium, and High.

While setting a Priority for a list item displays that item with one, two or three exclamations points to signify its importance, adjusting an item's Priority does not automatically change its location within the list. Rearranging the order of items on a list needs to be done manually.

To do this, while looking at a list, tap on the Edit button. Then place your finger on the Move icon that's associated with the list item you want to move and drag it upwards or downwards to the desired location within the list. Tap the Done button to save your changes.

Again, these alarms can be associated with each item in each of your to-do lists. You also have the option to create a to-do list item but not associate any type of alert or alarm with it.

When any alarm is generated for a to-do list item, a notification automatically appears within your iOS device's Notification Center screen/window, assuming that you have this feature turned on.

When it comes to managing your to-do list and accomplishing tasks listed in it, as you complete each listing, tap on the check box associated with that item. This causes a check mark to appear in the check box, and causes the to-do list item to be moved to the Completed section.

On the iPhone, to view the Completed listing, tap on the icon in the upper-left corner of the main Reminders screen (it looks like three horizontal lines), and then tap on the Completed option.

On the iPad, the Completed section is displayed on the left side of the screen. At any time, you can view your list of completed items by tapping on the Completed heading.

TIP One additional feature of the Reminders app is that you can create a separate to-do list associated with each day on the calendar. To do this on the iPhone, access the Lists screen (shown in Figure 8.3), and then tap on the Today option, or at the bottom of the Lists screen, scroll to the day you want to create, edit or view a separate list for.

On the iPad, tap on the Today option on the left side of the screen, or tap on any date within the monthly calendar that's displayed in the lower-left corner of the screen.

NOTE When you associate any list item with a date, that item will also appear on a list created for that date. By looking at a particular day's list, you can see everything you need to do that day, even if items are actually saved within different lists.

FIGURE 8.3

The list management screen of the Reminders app shown on the iPhone 5.

MANAGE MULTIPLE TO-DO LISTS SIMULTANEOUSLY WITH REMINDERS

To create multiple to-do lists using Reminders on the iPhone, follow these steps:

1. From the main Reminders screen, tap on the List Management icon displayed in the upper-left corner of the screen (it looks like three horizontal lines).

2. From the Lists screen that appears, tap on the Create New List option.

3. Using the virtual keyboard, type a name or title for the new to-do list.

4. Tap on the Done icon.

5. Begin adding individual to-do items to the list (as shown in Figure 8.4).

To create multiple to-do lists using Reminders on the iPad, follow these steps:

1. From the main Reminders screen, tap on the Create New List option.

2. Using the virtual keyboard, type a name or title for the new to-do list.

3. Tap on the Done icon.

4. Begin adding individual to-do items to the list.

FIGURE 8.4

Whenever you create a new to-do list, you can give it a unique title or name. Then, begin adding to-do items to that list, one at a time. Each individual to-do item can have a deadline and/or alarm associated with it.

HOW TO DELETE AN ENTIRE TO-DO LIST

When viewing the List screen on the iPhone or the List column on the iPad, find the listing for the to-do list you want to delete and swipe your finger from left to right across it. When the Delete button appears, tap on it.

Or, while looking at the List screen, tap on the Edit button, and that tap on the negative sign icon that's associated with the list you want to erase. When in Edit mode, to change the order of your lists, place your finger on the icon that looks like three horizontal lines that's associated with a list, and drag it upward or downward.

To exit Edit mode, tap on the Done icon.

HOW TO VIEW YOUR INDIVIDUAL LISTS

On the iPhone, from the main Reminders screen, tap on the List Management icon that's displayed in the upper-left corner of the screen (with the three horizontal lines) to view the Lists screen. It displays all of the separate to-do lists currently stored on your device, along with the Completed listing. Tap on any list from the Lists screen to view that list.

To view to-do items associated with a specific date, scroll through the date options displayed near the bottom of the screen and tap on a day.

On the iPad, a listing of all the separate to-do lists currently stored on your device can be found on the left side of the screen. Tap on the list's name that you want to view. The selected list is displayed on the right side of the screen.

On the calendar that's displayed in the lower-left corner of the screen, you can tap on a specific date to view upcoming deadlines or due dates associated with specific to-do list items, and/or view lists associated with a specific day.

> **TIP** To quickly find items in any of your to-do lists, tap on the Search field. On the iPhone, it's displayed at the top of the Lists screen. On the iPad, the Search field is displayed in the upper-left portion of the main Reminders screen. Use the virtual keyboard to enter any text that is associated with what you're looking for, and then tap the Search key on the keyboard.

After you get into the habit of entering all of your to-do list items, upcoming deadlines, or various other tidbits of information into the Reminders app, you'll quickly discover that it can be used to manage many types of information in your personal and professional life.

Chances are, you'll quickly find that Reminders, when used with Notification Center, iCloud, and Calendar, for example, is a wonderfully powerful to-do list management tool that's extremely versatile and customizable to meet your unique needs.

> **TIP** To save time and make the most use of the Reminders app, get into the habit of using it with Siri. To create a new to-do list item, activate Siri and begin your command with the words, "Remind me to…" You can also say, "Add [insert item] to my [insert list title] list."
>
> As you speak your to-do list items, you can associate date or location alerts to them. For example, if you say, "Remind me to pick up my dry cleaning tomorrow at 2pm." Siri adds a to-do list item to your default to-do list and associate an alarm with it.
>
> On the iPhone, activate Siri and say, "Remind me to feed the dog when I get home," and Siri displays a reminder (and play an audible alert) when you get home.

REMINDERS ALSO WORKS WITH iCLOUD

In conjunction with iOS 6, the Reminders app is now fully supported by iCloud. You can set up each of your iOS mobile devices and your Mac(s) to sync this Reminders data with iCloud, and then all of your to-do lists and items will remain synced across all of your computers and devices in almost real-time. This happens continuously, automatically and in the background (as along as each device or computer has access to the Internet).

To set this up, first create an iCloud account and configure your iPhone or iPad to work with this feature. Then, launch Settings and tap on the iCloud option. Turn on the virtual switch associated with the Reminders option (shown in Figure 8.5). The device you just did this on will now sync Reminders-specific data with iCloud automatically.

Repeat this process on your other iOS mobile devices that are linked to the same iCloud account, as well as on your Mac (select iCloud from within System Preferences).

FIGURE 8.5
Turn on iCloud sync functionality on your iPhone and/or iPad.

Once Reminders begins syncing your app-specific data with iCloud, using any computer or Internet-enabled mobile device, you always have the option to visit www.iCloud.com, sign in using your Apple ID and Password (or iCloud username and password), and then access the online-based Reminders app which will be populated with all of your to-do list data from your iPhone, iPad and/or Mac(s).

> **NOTE** If you also use a Mac that's running OS X Mountain Lion, this latest version of the Mac operating system now comes with preinstalled Reminders and Notes apps that are fully compatible with and work just like the iPhone editions of these apps.

PERFORM BASIC TEXT EDITING AND NOTE TAKING WITH THE NOTES APP

While the Reminders app allows you to create, edit, view and maintain detailed to-do lists that can be synced between your iOS mobile devices and Mac(s), the Notes app serves as a basic text editor that allows you to create, edit, view and manage notes.

> **NOTE** While the Notes app offers very basic formatting functionality, if you need the features and functions of a full-featured word processor, you'll definitely want to use the Pages app or another word processing app on your iPhone or iPad. Notes is designed more for basic note taking, not word processing.

Just like Reminders, the Notes app comes preinstalled with iOS 6 on the iPhone, iPad and iPod touch. In addition, a similar Notes app comes preinstalled on Macs running OS X Mountain Lion, so if you set up this app to work with iCloud, all of your notes remain synced on all of your computers and/or iOS mobile devices that are linked to the same iCloud account.

On the iPhone, the Notes app has two main screens—one that lists each of your note titles and serves as a menu for accessing them (shown in Figure 8.6), and a second for actually creating and viewing each note on a virtual yellow lined notepad (shown in Figure 8.7).

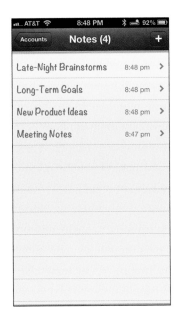

FIGURE 8.6
This Notes list screen displays the heading of each individual note stored on your iPhone. Tap on the listing to view a note.

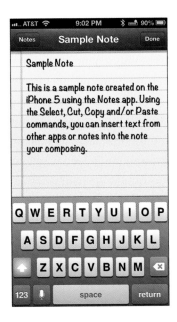

FIGURE 8.7
From the note editing screen on the iPhone, you can create, edit or view individual notes.

On the iPad, the listing of notes is displayed on the left side of the screen, while the right side of the screen displays the individual notes (shown in Figure 8.8).

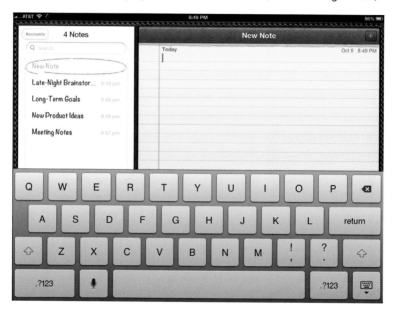

FIGURE 8.8

The iPad displays all aspects of the Notes app on a single screen.

To create a new note, tap on the plus-sign icon that's displayed near the top-right corner of the iPhone or iPad's screen. On the virtual yellow-lined page, begin typing your note using the virtual keyboard, or activate the Dictation function.

> **NOTE** By default, the first line of text you enter into a new note will become that note's title, and is what will be displayed on the Notes listing screen/column.

> **TIP** When using the Dictation function with the Notes app, you can speak for up to 30 seconds at a time, allow the iPhone or iPad to translate what you've said into text and insert that text into your note, and then you can repeat the process as needed. Edit your text using the virtual keyboard.

When you're done typing, dictating or editing a note, exit out of the app altogether and your note will be saved. Or, hide the virtual keyboard by tapping on the Hide

Keyboard key (displayed in the lower-right corner of the keyboard on the iPad) and then use one of the four command icons that are displayed along the bottom of the screen. On the iPhone, when you're done typing or viewing a note, tap on the Done key. The four command icons for that page will be displayed (shown in Figure 8.9).

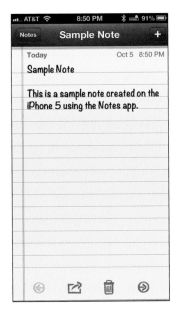

FIGURE 8.9
The Notes app offers four command icons along the bottom of the screen.

The left pointing arrow allows you to flip one page back in your virtual notebook and view a previous note page. The right pointing arrow icon allows you to flip one page forward within your virtual notebook.

Tap on the trash can icon to delete the note you're currently viewing. From the Notes listing screen (on the iPhone) or column (on the iPad), swipe your finger from left to right across an note's title to delete it. Tap on the Delete button to confirm your deletion decision.

! CAUTION If you have Notes set up to sync with iCloud and your other iOS mobile devices and/or Mac(s), as soon as you delete or change a note, those changes will be reflected almost immediately on iCloud and on your other computers and/or iOS mobile devices that are linked to the same account.

Tap on the Share button to send the note to one or more recipients via email, print the note using an AirPrint-compatible printer, or copy the note to your iPhone or iPad's virtual clipboard (so you can then paste the contents of the note into another app).

> **TIP** The Notes app works with the Select, Select All, Copy, Cut and Paste features of iOS 6. Thus, you can select and copy text from one note and then paste it into another note or into another app altogether.

As you're creating or viewing a note, press and hold your finger on any word to make the Select All, Copy, Cut and/or Paste menu options appear. You'll also see a Define option displayed (shown in Figure 8.10).

Tap on Define to look up the definition of the selected work. A pop-up window displaying the definition will be displayed. When you use this feature for the first time, you're promoted to download the Dictionary that can accompany the Notes app. This process takes just 5 to 10 seconds and only needs to be done once.

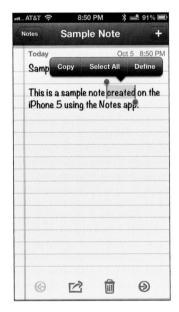

FIGURE 8.10

As you're typing text into the Notes app, hold your finger on a word and tap on the Define option to view a definition (and the correct spelling) of that word.

To customize the appearance of your text within your notes, launch Settings, scroll down to the Notes option, and then select which font you want to use. Your options include Noteworthy, Helvetica or Marker Felt.

> **TIP** Syncing notes with iCloud works exactly the same as syncing Contacts, Calendars or Reminders app-specific data, however, once iCloud is set up on your iOS device, you need to turn on the iCloud syncing function that's specific to the Notes app from the iCloud menu screen within Settings. (Refer back to the "Reminders Also Works With iCloud" section earlier in this chapter.)

Once you set up the Notes app to sync app-specific data with iCloud, access the iCloud.com website (www.icloud.com) at anytime using any computer or Internet enabled device, log into your account using your Apple ID and password (or iCloud username and password), and then tap on the Notes icon to use the online-based Notes app, which will be populated with all of your Notes data from your iPhone, iPad and/or Mac(s).

The Notes app's functionality is relatively basic and straightforward. However, this app comes is particularly handy to jot down ideas or memos, without having to worry about formatting text (as you would when using a word processing app). To help keep you organized, the time and date you create each note is automatically saved in conjunction with the note itself.

IN THIS CHAPTER

- Learn to use new features of the Maps app
- Use the Maps app to obtain turn-by-turn directions between two locations.
- Find and display any address, land-mark, point-of-interest or business on a map

NAVIGATING WITH THE NEWLY REVAMPED MAPS APP

In conjunction with iOS 6, Apple has redesigned the Maps app from scratch. This app no longer relies of Google Maps. Instead, Apple has created and implemented a proprietary vector-based mapping system that displays highly detailed maps on the iPhone or iPad's screen.

> **TIP** As you're viewing a map, it's almost always possible to zoom in or out using either a reverse-pinch or pinch figure gesture, or a double-tap on the area of the map you want to zoom in or out of.

If you're a veteran iPhone or iPad user, you'll discover that the Maps app offers some really exciting and visually inter-esting new features, and is much better integrated with Siri, for example, than the older versions of the app.

Keep in mind, the Maps app requires Internet access to function. Although the app works with a Wi-Fi connection, if you plan to use the app's turn-by-turn directions feature, you'll need to use a 3G/4G connection (which will use up some of your monthly wireless data allocation with each use), since you'll be in motion and will quickly leave the wireless signal radius of any Wi-Fi hotspot. Using the Maps feature with Siri (via a 3G/4G connection) requires even more wireless data usage.

NOTE When the new Maps app was first released in conjunction with iOS 6, many users experienced glitches with the app, which Apple quickly acknowledged. By the time you read this, a revised version of the new Maps app will most likely be released that addresses and fixes at least some of these problems.

However, instead of using the Maps app for navigation, you'll find a handful of similar apps available from the App Store (listed in the Navigation category). You can also use Safari on your iPhone or iPad to visit a navigation website, such as Mapquest.com or Google Maps (https://maps.google.com).

TIP To get the most use out of the Maps app, the main Location Services feature within your iPhone or iPad (as well as Location Services for the Maps app) must be turned on. To do this, launch Settings, tap on the Privacy option, and then tap on Location Services. From the Location Services menu screen, turn on the virtual switch that's displayed near the top of the screen (associated with Locations Services), and then scroll down and make sure the virtual switch that's associated with the Maps app is also turned on.

GET THE MOST FROM USING NEW MAPS APP FEATURES

Compared to previously-related versions of the Maps app, the iOS 6 edition offers a handful of new features, like detailed turn-by-turn spoken and displayed directions, interactive 3D map views, and a visually stunning Flyover map view (for many cities and metropolitan areas). If you're familiar with the older versions of the Maps app, what you'll discover missing is the popular Google Street View.

CAUTION Just as when using any GPS device for turn-by-turn directions, do not rely 100 percent on the directions you're given. Pay attention as you're driving and use common sense. If the Maps app tell you to drive down a one-way street or drive along a closed road, for example, ignore those directions and seek out an alternate route. Don't become one of those people who literally drive into a lake or over a cliff because their GPS told them to. (Yes, this does happen.)

In addition, real-time traffic conditions can be graphically overlaid onto maps (which show traffic jams and construction, for example), and when you look up a business, restaurant, point-of-interest or landmark, the Maps app now seamlessly integrates with Yelp! in order to display detailed information about specific locations. The Yelp! information screens for each location are interactive, so if you're using an iPhone and tap on a phone number, you can initiate a call to that business or restaurant, for example.

TIP To enhance the capabilities of the Yelp! integration, download and install the optional (and free) Yelp! app from the App Store. Without the Yelp! app, when appropriate, the Maps app will transfer you to the Yelp! website.

NOTE Yelp! is a vast online database that contains more than 30 million reviews related to local businesses, stores, restaurants, hotels, tourist attractions and points-of-interest. Reviews are created by everyday people, who share their experiences, thoughts and photos. However, beyond user-provided reviews, Yelp! also offers details about many businesses and restaurants.

While Maps offers a lot of functionality packed into a stand-alone app, it's also designed to work in conjunction with many other apps, such as Contacts, as well as your iOS device's Siri feature. For example, as you're viewing any entry within your Contacts database, when you tap on an address, the Maps app launches and displays that address on a map. You can then quickly obtain detailed directions to that location.

Plus, as you learned from Chapter 5, "Using Siri and Dictation to Interact with Your iOS Device," you can utilize many features built into the Maps app using voice commands and requests. For example, regardless of what you're doing on the iPhone or iPad, it's possible to activate Siri and say, "How do I get home from here?" or "Where is the closest gas station?" and then have the Maps app provide you with the directions and map you need.

> **☑ TIP**   Anytime you're viewing a map within the Maps app, tap on the My Location icon (which looks like a northeast-pointing arrow) that's displayed near the bottom-left corner of the screen to pinpoint and display your exact location on the map. Your location is displayed using a pulsating blue dot (shown in Figure 9.1). If for some reason the Maps app loses its Internet signal temporarily, tap on this My Location icon again to reestablish your location.

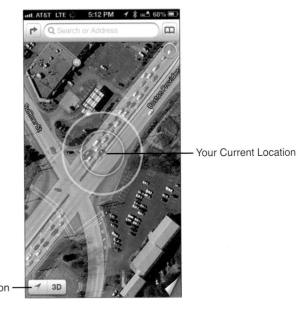

Your Current Location

Current Location Icon

FIGURE 9.1
Tap on the My Location icon (near the lower-left corner of the screen) to pinpoint and display your exact location on a map using a pulsating blue dot.

OVERVIEW OF THE MAPS APP'S SCREEN

The main screen of the Maps app offers a streamlined interface (compared to older versions of the app). Displayed near the top-left corner of the screen is the Directions icon. Tap on it to enter a Start and End location, and then obtain detailed driving, walking or public transportation directions between those two points.

> **NOTE** Depending on the two points you enter, walking directions may not be applicable or viable. Currently, if you seek out public transportation directions, you'll be redirected to the App Store to seek out an alternate app. Thus, if you're relying on public transportation to get around a popular city, such as Manhattan, Washington, DC, Boston, London or Paris, download an app specifically designed for that public transportation system. Use the Search option within the App Store to find one of these apps. For example, enter the search phrase "London Tube Map" to find a variety of interactive apps that will help you navigate your way around London's subway/train system.

Displayed near the top-center of the Maps app screen is the Search field. Use it to find and map out any address. Here, you can enter a complete address (house/building number, street, city, state), or provide less specific information, such as just a city, state or country.

For example, within the Search field, enter United States to see a map of the entire country. Or, enter California to view a map of the state. You also have the option to enter Los Angeles, California to view a more detailed map of the city, or you can enter a specific street address located within Los Angeles to view it on a detailed map that shows specific streets (and street names).

This Search field is also used to find businesses, restaurants, points-of-interest, landmarks and/or tourist destinations. How to use this feature will be explained shortly. Keep in mind, once the Maps app finds the location you're looking for, you can zoom in or zoom out manually on that map to see more or less detail. Plus, you can change the Map view and switch between the Standard, Hybrid, Satellite, 3D and/or Flyover view (each of which will be explained shortly).

> **TIP** Within the Search field, enter the name of any contact within your Contacts database to find and display an address for that contact. As you perform a search, the contents of your iOS device (including the Contacts app) is searched, followed by a web-based search, if applicable.

Anytime a specific location is specified on the map, such as results of a Search, those results will be displayed using a virtual red push-pins. Tap on a push-pin to view more details about that location and to access a separate Location screen (iPhone) or window (iPad).

As you're looking at the main Maps screen, however, look to the upper-right corner to find the Bookmarks icon. Just like Safari, the Maps app allows you to store bookmarks for specific locations. When you tap on the Bookmarks icon, three command tabs are displayed at the bottom of the screen/window. They're labeled Bookmarks, Recents and Contacts.

Tapping on the Bookmarks tab will reveal a list of previously saved bookmarked locations. Tap on the Edit button to edit, delete or reorder this list, or swipe your finger from left to right across a Bookmark listing to delete it.

Tap on the Recents tab to view a list of recently searched or viewed locations. To clear this list, tap on the Clear button that's displayed near the top-left corner of the screen.

When you tap on the Contacts tab, the All Contacts listing will be displayed. This shows a comprehensive list of all entries stored within your Contacts database. Whether you're looking at the Bookmarks, Recents or All Contacts list, tap on one of the listings to view that location on a map.

Again, as you're looking at the main Maps screen, the center area of the display is used to showcase maps. Remember, in most cases, you can zoom in or zoom out on the map you're looking at. You can also use your finger to move around within that map and see other areas of it.

Displayed near the bottom-left corner of the screen is the My Location icon (it looks like a northeast-pointing arrow). At anytime a map is displayed, tap on this icon to locate and display (or update) your current location on the map. This feature is useful if you look up another destination and then want to quickly see where you're located in comparison to that other location. However, when you're using the Maps app for turn-by-turn directions, your iPhone/iPad will keep track of your location in real-time and display this on the map as you're in motion.

As you're viewing a Standard, Hybrid or Satellite map, tap on the 3D button that's displayed near the bottom-left corner of the screen to switch to a 3D view. Many people find the 3D view more visually interesting, although it doesn't reveal any new on-screen information that could not be seen using the Maps app's Standard, Hybrid or Satellite views.

> **TIP** When you're viewing a map of a popular city or metropolitan area, the 3D button is automatically replaced by the Flyover icon. The Flyover feature offers a true, three-dimensional looking map of a city from the perspective of an airplane cockpit. From this view, use your finger to move around on the screen and see a bird's eye view of a city, which is visually impressive and highly-detailed.

When you look at the lower-right corner of the main Maps app's screen, you'll notice a virtual flap. Tap on this flap to reveal the app's menu screen.

THE MAPS APP'S MENU SCREEN

The Maps app's menu screen (shown in Figure 9.2) displays four command buttons and three command tabs. The four command buttons are labeled Drop Pin, Print, Show (or Hide) Traffic and List Results.

FIGURE 9.2

The Maps app menu screen offers several command icons and map view command tabs.

THE DROP PIN COMMAND

When you tap on the Drop Pin option, the full Maps screen returns. Now, tap anywhere on that map to place a virtual push-pin. The new push-pin is displayed in purple, instead of red. You can view detailed information about that particular location, including its exact address. You can then tap on that push-pin to view an information window (iPhone) or screen (iPad) that offers a handful of menu options, such as Directions To Here, Directions From Here, Add To Contacts, Share Location, Add To Bookmarks and Report A Problem.

THE PRINT COMMAND

If you have a wireless printer linked to your iPhone or iPad via AirPrint, tap on the Print button to create a print out of whatever is displayed on the screen, whether it's a detailed map, a text-based list of turn-by-turn directions to a destination, or a listing of search results (such as restaurants or gas stations in a particular area).

When you tap on the Print button, the Print options screen/window will be displayed. Select an AirPrint-compatible printer and the number of copies you want printed, then tap on the Print button. If you have a color printer linked to your iPhone or iPad, you can print maps (or color-coded directions) in full-color.

THE SHOW TRAFFIC OPTION

Regardless of which map view you're looking at, you can have real-time traffic information superimposed on the map. This feature can help you avoid traffic jams and construction, and allows you to seek an alternate route before you get stuck in the traffic.

NOTE Mild traffic is showcased on a map using yellow, while heavy traffic is depicted in red. When construction is being done on a roadway, separate construction icons (displayed in yellow or red) are displayed on the map.

TIP The Show Traffic feature works much better when you're viewing a zoomed-in version of a map that shows a lot of street-level detail. Figure 9.3 shows heavy traffic conditions (a dashed red line) along Hollywood Blvd. in Hollywood, California (in front of the famous Mann's Chinese Theater).

THE LIST RESULTS OPTION

When you perform a search using the Search field that's displayed near the top-center of the screen, you'll often discover multiple search results showcased on the map using red virtual push-pins. Tap on the List Results button to view an interactive, text-based listing of these search results (shown in Figure 9.4). When you tap on a single result from the List Results screen/window, you can view much more detailed information about that result.

So, if you enter "Apple Store, Los Angeles, CA" into the Search field, locations of all of the nearby Apple Stores are displayed. Tap on the List Results button to view a listing of each result, which includes its street address and Yelp! star-based rating. You can then tap on the right-pointing arrow icon that's displayed to the right of the listing to display a more detailed Location Screen, or tap on the listing itself to view it on the map.

FIGURE 9.3

A dashed red line along a roadway indicates heavy traffic when you have the Show Traffic feature turned on within the Maps app.

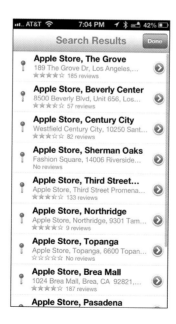

FIGURE 9.4

The List results screen shows a text-based and interactive summary of search results.

> **TIP** When viewing a List Results screen (iPhone)/window (iPad), tap on the Done button or any specific listing to return to the main map view. When you tap on a listing, the location of that listing is highlighted on the map. To view the Location screen for that listing, tap on the right-pointing arrow icon (>) that's displayed to the right of a listing on the List Results screen.

THE STANDARD, HYBRID AND SATELLITE TABS

Displayed along the bottom of the Maps menu screen are the three map view command tabs—Standard, Hybrid and Satellite. The Standard map view (shown in Figure 9.5) displays a traditional-looking, multi-colored map on the screen. Street names and other important information is labeled and displayed on the map.

FIGURE 9.5
The Standard map view shows a traditional, multi-colored map with street names and other points-of-interest listed on it.

The Satellite view uses high-resolution and extremely detailed satellite imagery to show maps from an overhead view, while the Hybrid map view (refer back to Figure 9.1) showcases the same satellite imagery, but overlays and displays street names and other important information, similar to the information you'd see using the Standard view.

> ☑ **TIP**   Anytime you're viewing a map, you can switch between Map views. Then from the main Maps screen, tap on the My Location icon to display your exact location on the map, and/or tap on the 3D icon to add a three-dimensional element to the map. (If a Flyover view is available, the Flyover icon will be displayed instead of the 3D icon.)

OBTAIN TURN-BY-TURN DIRECTIONS BETWEEN TWO LOCATIONS

The turn-by-turn directions feature introduced in the iOS 6 edition of the Maps app is not only easy-to-use, it's also extremely useful. Begin using this feature from the main Maps app screen. Tap on the Directions icon that's displayed near the top-left corner of the screen.

The Start and End field, as well as the reverse directions, driving, walking and public transportation icons are displayed (shown in Figure 9.6). Within the Start field, the default option is your current location. However, to change this, tap on the field and enter any starting address. Then tap on the End field and enter any ending address:

FIGURE 9.6

Fill in the Start and End fields to obtain detailed, turn-by-turn directions between any two locations that you choose.

TIP Within the Start and End field, you can enter a Contact entry's name, a full address, a city and state, just a state, or just a country. You can use two letter state abbreviations and you don't have to worry about using upper and lower-case letters. The app will understand what you're typing either way. For example, you can type "New York, NY," "new york, ny" or "New York, New York" and get the same result. This goes for contacts or business names as well.

When the Start and End fields have been filled in, tap on the car-shaped icon near the top-center of the screen to access detailed driving directions. Or, tap on the person-shaped icon to obtain walking directions between those two locations. If public transportation is available, tap on the bus-shaped icon. When you seek public transportation guidance, the Maps app will refer to you to the App Store and display several different Routing Map options compatible with public transportation systems in that region.

Next, tap in the Route button that's displayed near the upper-right corner of the screen. An route overview map (shown in Figure 9.7) is displayed. The green push-pin represents your starting location, and the red-push pin represents your ending location. If you selected Driving directions, the Maps app will display between one and three possible routes between the Start and End locations.

FIGURE 9.7

A sample route overview map shows your Start and End location on one map, plus up to three possible driving routes to get there.

The primary route (Route 1) will be outlined on the route overview map with a dark blue line, and have a corresponding Route 1 flag. If available, one or two alternate routes will be outlined with light blue lines, and be labeled Route 2 and Route 3.

> **TIP** Turn on the Show Traffic option to display current traffic conditions along the three routes, and then choose the one with the least congestion or construction. Tap on the Route 1, Route 2 or Route 3 flag to select your route. (Route 1 is the default selection.)

Tap on the Start button that's displayed near the upper-right corner of the screen to begin the real-time, turn-by-turn directions. Just like when using a stand-alone GPS device, a voice guides you through each turn, while also displaying related information on the main map screen (shown in Figure 9.8).

FIGURE 9.8

The Maps app shows detailed, turn-by-turn directions on the map screen, plus speaks to you as you're driving.

While the turn-by-turn directions are being displayed, the Standard map view will be used. Tap on the screen to display your ETA, as well as how much time is left in your trip and the distance from your destination. This is displayed along the top of the screen. Tap the Overview button to return to the route overview map, or tap the End icon to exit out of the turn-by-turn directions feature and return to the main Maps screen.

Follow the voice and on-screen prompts until you reach your destination. If you press the Home button, you can return to the Home Screen and launch another app (while the Maps feature is still running), and then return to the turn-by-turn directions by tapping on the green bar that says Touch To Return To Navigation. It's displayed near the top of the screen. (This also works when you launch another app via the multitasking bar.)

TIP Displayed to the immediate left of the Start and End field when you tap on the Directions button is a Swap button. Tap it to switch the addresses you have in the Start and End fields in order to obtain "reverse" directions.

NOTE Tap on the Directions Overview icon that's displayed near the lower-left corner of the screen to switch from the map view to a text-based turn-by-turn directions listing. Tap the Done button to exit out of this view.

TIP When using your iPhone or iPad and the Maps app for real-time, turn-by-turn directions, the iOS device will be in use and accessing the Internet extensively. This will drain the device's battery faster. If you use this feature from your car often, consider investing in a car charger that plugs into your car's 9-volt plug. This way, your iPhone/iPad's battery will remain charged (and can actually recharge) while it's being used.

CAUTION Using the Maps app for turn-by-turn directions via a 3G/4G Internet connection requires a significant amount of wireless data usage. Using this feature will quickly deplete your 3G/4G monthly wireless data allocation (unless you've subscribed to an unlimited wireless service plan).

LOOK UP CONTACT ENTRIES, BUSINESSES, RESTAURANTS, LANDMARKS, AND POINTS-OF-INTEREST

One of the other primary uses of the Maps app is to find and display addresses, contacts, businesses, points-of-interest or landmarks on a map screen. To do this, from the main Maps screen, type what you're looking for into the Search field. In Figure 9.9, Gillette Stadium, Foxboro, MA, was entered into the search field.

FIGURE 9.9

Gillette Stadium (home of the New England Patriots) in Foxboro, MA, is shown here using the hybrid and 3D map view on an iPhone 5.

Here are some examples of what you can enter into the Search field:

- A full address for almost any location in the world. This will display a map of that specific location.
- An intersection (such as 42nd street and Broadway or Hollywood and Highland).
- A city and state. This will display a map of that area.
- A state. This will display a state map.
- A country. This will display a country-wide map.

- A person or business name from your Contacts database. This will display the corresponding address on a map.

- The name of a business, restaurant, or point-of-interest followed by the city and state.

- Just the name of a business, restaurant, or point-of-interest. The Maps app will look in the most recent search area for what you're looking for, or if it's a known landmark (such as The White House or the Empire State Building), for example, the app will find and display it.

- The type of business or service you're looking for. For example, type gas station, hospital, seafood restaurants, or post office.

> **TIP** If you're looking for businesses or services in your immediate area, tap on the My Location icon first, so the iPhone or iPad pinpoints your location, and then enter what you're searching for. No city or state needs to be entered. If you don't tap on the My Location icon first, you need to enter what you're looking for, followed by the city, a comma, and the state, in order to find local search results. Otherwise, the Maps app defaults to the last search location.

USE THE INTERACTIVE LOCATION SCREENS TO FIND MORE INFORMATION

Once search results are displayed on the map, in the form of virtual push-pins, tap on any push-pin to view an information banner for a location on a map. In Figure 9.10, a search for Apple Store locations in Los Angeles was performed and displayed on the map.

Tap on one push-pin, and then on tap on the left side of the information banner to obtain "quick" turn-by-turn directions from your current location. Or, tap on the right-pointing arrow icon (>) on the right side of the listing to view an interactive Location screen (iPhone)/window (iPad).

A separate Location screen/window (shown in Figure 9.11) displays details about that search result using details from the Maps app, the Internet and from Yelp!. Tap on the Info tab on the Location screen/window to view the phone number, address, website URL, and/or other information for that search result. What information is displayed will depend on whether it's a business, restaurant, point-of-interest or tourist attraction, for example.

FIGURE 9.10

A search for Apple Stores in the Los Angeles area was performed. The results are shown as red virtual push-pins on this hybrid view map.

FIGURE 9.11

A detailed Location screen/window combines location information with details about that location obtained from Yelp!. In this example, a Location window for Morton's Steak House in New York City is shown on the iPad.

> 📝 **TIP**   When looking at multiple search results on a map (refer to Figure 9.10), access the Maps menu screen and tap on List Results to view a text-based, interactive listing of the search results (refer to Figure 9.4).

As you scroll down on the Location screen/window, you'll see a Directions To Here and Directions From Here option. Tap on either of these to obtain directions to or from your current location to the address listed on the screen.

Tap on the More Info On Yelp! button to launch the Yelp! app or visit the Yelp! website to view more detailed information about that location.

You'll also discover an Add To Contacts button (used to create a new Contacts entry using information from the Location screen), Add to Bookmarks button (used to create and store a bookmark for the location within the Maps app's Bookmarks menu), Share Location button (which allows you to email or text/instant message details about the location to someone else), and a Report A Problem button (used to report errors in the location data to Apple).

Tap on the Reviews tab to view Yelp!-related star-based ratings and text-based reviews from other Yelp! users, or tap on the Photos tab to view photos of that location, including photos uploaded by other Yelp! users. You can also contribute your own star-based rating, review or photos for a location.

> 📝 **TIP**   If you look up information about a restaurant, for example, the Location screen will include Yelp!-related information, including the type of food served, the menu price range (using dollar sign symbols), the hours of operation, and potentially a website link that will allow you to view the restaurant's menu. You can also determine if the restaurant delivers, or accepts reservations.
>
> If reservations are accepted, use the optional Open Table app to make reservations online, activate Siri and say, "Make a reservation for [insert number of people] for [insert day and time]," or initiate a call from an iPhone to the restaurant by tapping on the phone number field.

If you perform a search for a particular type of business or restaurant and multiple search results are displayed on the map, access the Maps app's menu and tap on List Results to view a text-based listing of the search results. You can then tap on any listing to view its Location screen/window.

> **TIP** When viewing a map, a compass often appears near the upper-right corner of the screen. When you tap on the My Location icon, the Map will be displayed using a north-facing orientation. If you double-tap on the My Location icon, the map will orientate itself in the direction you're traveling.

THE MAPS APP'S FLYOVER VIEW

While the 3D feature makes looking at Standard, Hybrid and Satellite maps more interesting, the Flyover map view that's available for many major cities is just plain cool, although it doesn't really serve a navigation purpose. This feature, however, can be used to help you get acquainted with the layout of a city and allow you to take a virtual tour of its skyline from your iPhone or iPad.

When it's available, the 3D icon that's normally displayed near the lower-left corner of the Maps screen will be replaced with the Flyover icon (which looks like a building). Tap on it to switch to a stunning Flyover map view (shown in Figure 9.12).

FIGURE 9.12

The Flyover view of New York City shown on the iPad.

> ☑️ **TIP** When using the 3D or Flyover view, you can zoom in or out on the map, plus change the perspective by placing two fingers on the screen and moving them up or down together. You can also use just one finger to move up, down, left or right to view a different area of the map and scroll around.

CUSTOMIZE MAP-RELATED SETTINGS

To customize a handful of settings related to the Maps app, launch Settings and tap on the Maps option. From the Maps menu screen, it's possible to adjust the Navigation Voice Volume, show distances in Miles or Kilometers, automatically have the iPhone/iPad translate Map Labels into English, and/or adjust the size of on-screen labels.

10

MAKE THE MOST OF SOCIAL NETWORKING APPS

There are more than one billion active users worldwide on Facebook, 500 million Twitter users, and a fast-growing following for the Google+ and Instagram online social networking services. In recent years, these services have redefined how people communicate, and the evolution is rapidly continuing. New features for sharing news, photos, information, gossip, ideas, videos, web URLs, and other content are continuously being introduced and incorporated into these services.

One reason services like Twitter and Facebook have become so popular is that people are able to manage their accounts and become active within these massive online communities from virtually anywhere—and at any time (24/7)—using their computer, Smartphone (iPhone), or tablet (iPad).

For iPhone, iPod touch, or iPad users, staying active on Facebook, Twitter, Instagram, Google+, LinkedIn, and other online social networking services is easy, thanks to a collection of apps currently available from the App Store.

Plus, you can update your Facebook Status or compose and send a tweet to your Twitter followers from directly within a handful of apps that come preinstalled on your iPhone or iPad (including Photos and Safari), as well as directly from the Notification Center screen (iPhone) or window (iPad), thank to iOS 6's integration with these two services.

If you're already active on Twitter, Facebook, Google+, Instagram, LinkedIn, or another popular online social networking site, start by downloading the free "official" apps for any or all of these services:

- Both the official Facebook and official Twitter apps are available from the App Store, however, you can also download and install them from within Settings. To do this, launch Settings, tap on the Facebook or Twitter option, and then tap on the Install button that's displayed near the top of the screen.

- The official Google+, Instagram and LinkedIn apps are free iPhone apps that work flawlessly on the iPad, but they don't take advantage of the iPad's larger screen beyond allowing you to tap on the 2x icon to double the size of the iPhone-formatted screens.

> **☑ TIP** Before you can compose and send Facebook Status Updates or tweets to your Twitter followers directly from almost any app that has a Share button or menu, it is necessary to turn on Facebook and/or Twitter integration with your iPhone or iPad. To do this, launch Settings, tap on Facebook or Twitter, and then on the Facebook or Twitter menu screen, enter your username and password where prompted. If you have multiple Twitter accounts, add them (one at a time) to the Twitter menu screen within settings. Then, once you install the official Facebook and/or Twitter apps onto your iOS device, it'll be necessary to log into each service again using the app, by entering your service-specific username and password.

As you'll discover later in this chapter, beyond the "official" apps for the popular online social networking services, there is a vast selection of third-party (free and paid) apps that also allow you to manage your Twitter, Facebook, Google+, LinkedIn, Instagram, or other online social networking accounts. These apps all offer slightly different features and functions. Some are iPhone-specific, whereas others are iPad-specific or hybrid apps that work on all iOS devices.

NOTE As long as your iOS device is connected to the Internet, you can use a specialized app to manage any of your online social networking accounts from virtually anywhere. For example, if you're out and about with your iPhone, you can snap and edit a photo, and then immediately tweet that photo to your followers, or upload it to Facebook, for example, all in a matter of seconds, while also updating your status.

TIPS FOR USING THE OFFICIAL TWITTER APP

If you have an active Twitter account, you'll need to install the official Twitter app on your device, plus add your existing Twitter account information to your iOS mobile device from within Settings, so that you can begin sending tweets from within other iOS 6 apps, such as Photos and Safari. If you don't yet have a free Twitter account, you can set one up in just minutes from within the official Twitter app or from within Settings (by selecting the Twitter option from the main Settings menu).

MORE INFO Want to learn more about what Twitter is and how it works? Using any web-enabled computer or device, visit http:// support.twitter.com/groups/31-twitter-basics.

TIP To create a free Twitter account, launch Settings and select the Twitter option. From the Twitter screen, tap on Add Account, then tap on the Create New Account icon. When prompted fill in the fields displayed in the New Account window that appears (shown in Figure 10.1).

When all the fields in the Sign Up screen have been filled in, tap on the Create My Account option. When the welcome screen appears, you're ready to begin tweeting and following other Twitter users. This can be done using the official Twitter app or another third-party app designed for use with Twitter on your iPhone, iPod touch, or iPad.

FIGURE 10.1

You can create a new Twitter account in seconds from within Settings on your iPhone or iPad. Access Twitter's New Account screen and fill in the blank fields.

CUSTOMIZING THE OFFICIAL TWITTER APP

In addition to adding your existing Twitter account information within Settings, to take advantage of Twitter's integration within iOS 6, if you plan to use the official Twitter app to send and receive tweets and manage your account(s), you'll need to configure the app as well.

After downloading and installing the official Twitter app on your iOS device, launch the app from the Home Screen. Decide whether or not you want Twitter to be able to use your Current Location when the pop-up window asking this appears. Either tap OK to allow Location Services to work with the Twitter app, or tap the Don't Allow button to turn off this feature.

If you have not yet entered your Twitter account details into Settings on your iPhone or iPad, displayed on the Hello screen for the app, you'll discover two command buttons. They're labeled Sign In and Sign Up. If you already have one or more active Twitter accounts, tap the Sign In button. When the Add Account screen appears, enter your Twitter username and password using the device's virtual keyword. When you're done, tap on the Save button. After your account is authorized, the main Twitter screen will appear.

On the iPad, running down the center of the screen is your main Twitter feed (also referred to as your Timeline). Along the left margin of the screen (shown in Figure 10.2) are four command icons, with the following command options listed below it: Home, Connect, Discover, and Me.

FIGURE 10.2

The official Twitter app on the iPad. You can view your Timeline, plus access most of the app's main commands and features from this screen.

In the upper-right corner of the main Twitter screen (on the iPhone or iPad) is the Compose Tweet icon. Tap on this to compose a new tweet using the tablet's virtual keyboard (as shown in Figure 10.3). After the tweet (which can be up to 140 characters in length) is created, tap on the Send icon to publish it.

> **NOTE** The official Twitter app for the iPhone offers the same functionality as the iPad version; however, the screen layout and the position of various command icons will be slightly different.

FIGURE 10.3

In this New Tweet window you can compose and send a tweet from within the official Twitter app.

TIP To customize the Twitter tap, tap on the Me icon that's displayed near the lower-right corner of the iPhone app's screen, and on the left side of the iPad app's screen, and then tap on the gear-shaped icon displayed under your account heading on the Me screen. From here, you can either edit your profile or adjust app-specific settings, including the Notification options associated with the app.

From this Settings screen (shown in Figure 10.4), you can also control specific features in the app, such as the Image and Video Service you'll use when attaching photos or video clips to your outgoing tweets, the image quality of the photos you'll send, and whether you want to turn on or off the sound effects associated with this app.

FIGURE 10.4

The Settings screen within the Twitter app allows you to customize app-specific settings.

USING THE OFFICIAL TWITTER APP

After it's configured to work with your Twitter account, you can manage one or more Twitter accounts using the official Twitter app. On the iPad (refer to Figure 10.2), the commands for doing this are displayed on the left side of the screen and include Home, Connect, Discover, and Me.

On the iPhone, the main commands for using Twitter are displayed as icons at the bottom of the official Twitter app screen (as shown in Figure 10.5). At the upper-right corner of the screen is the Compose Tweet button used for composing new outgoing tweets (messages).

The main screen area is where your Twitter feed (or Timeline) is displayed. Use the Home, Connect, Discover and Me command icons to access sub-menus and features associated with the Twitter app, as well as to manage your account(s). On the main screen, the Search and Compose Tweet command icons are also displayed.

> **NOTE**   On the iPhone, the Search option is available at the top of the screen when you first tap on the Discover command icon. It's not displayed on the main screen.

FIGURE 10.5
The main screen of the official Twitter app on an iPhone 5.

Here's a quick summary of how these features are used:

- **Home**—Return to the main timeline screen of the Twitter app.
- **Connect**—View recent Interactions or Mentions related to your username (@username). Tap on either the Interactions tab to see tweet-based conversations you've participated in, or tap on the Mentions tab to see tweets that contain a reference to your Twitter username.
- **Discover**—See major news stories unfolding on Twitter, recent activity of people you're following, and what the current Trends are. You can also obtain recommendations about who to follow, browse categories to find new people or organizations to follow, or find your real-life friends who are also active on Twitter using options available from the Discover screen.
- **Me**—Access details about your Twitter account(s). You can see how many tweets you've sent, the number of people following you, and how many people you're following. Tap on any of these listings to view a detailed list. Tap on the gear-shaped icon to adjust app-specific settings or modify your profile. Tap the Account icon (which looks like two heads) to switch between your Twitter accounts, or tap on the Mail icon to read direct messages you have waiting or send new Direct Messages via Twitter. You can also view your own Twitter timeline and view the recent tweets you've composed and sent.

- **Search**—Tap the Search icon on the main page (iPad) or use the Search field displayed at the top of the Discover screen (iPhone) to look up a Twitter user or any keyword to find people or tweets that are of interest, based on topics.
- **Compose Tweet**—Compose an outgoing tweet to your followers. A tweet can be up to 140-characters long, and contain a photo, website link (URL) and/or your current location.

COMPOSE AN OUTGOING TWEET

Using the official Twitter app, to compose an outgoing tweet, tap on the Compose Tweet icon. When the New Tweet screen with the virtual keyboard appears, begin composing your tweet. Remember, you have up to 140 characters per tweet.

TIP At the top center of the New Tweet window, under the New Tweet heading is the Twitter account from which you'll be sending the outgoing tweet. If you are managing multiple Twitter accounts using the app, tap on this heading to select which account the tweet should be sent from. An Accounts window listing each account username is displayed.

TIP You can use Siri or the Dictation feature to compose a tweet using your voice. To use Siri, begin your command by saying the word "Tweet." For example, activate Siri and say, "Tweet: I just got to Starbucks." This can be done anytime, regardless of what app you're running.

However, when you're looking at the Compose Tweet screen/window, either from the official Twitter app or when you select Tweet from the Share menu of any compatible app, instead of typing your message, tap on the microphone button to activate the iPhone or iPad's Dictation feature, and then dictate your message.

Keep in mind, when composing a tweet, the @ symbol is used to address your tweet to a specific person or to mention specific Twitter users in a tweet. The hash symbol (#) is used to identify a topic or subject within a tweet, known as a hashtag.

Tap on the camera-shaped icon to either take a photo using your iOS device's built-in camera or attach a photo to your tweet that's already store on your device. Tap on the Location icon (displayed to the immediate right of the camera icon) to manually attach your exact location to the tweet using your device's Location Services (GPS) capabilities.

> ☑ **TIP** In the lower-right corner of the New Tweet window (displayed as you're composing an outgoing tweet) is a counter that shows the number of characters remaining. The counter starts at 140 and counts downward with each new character you type as part of your tweet. If you add a photo or website address (URL) to your tweet, this will take up some characters.

To keep your tweets short, it's acceptable to use abbreviations. To send your tweet after it's composed, tap on the Send icon that's displayed in the upper-right corner of the New Tweet window. Or, to abort the process, tap on the Cancel button that is displayed in the upper-left corner of the New Tweet window.

> ☑ **TIP** If there are phrases or long words you use often, instead of having to constantly type them using the virtual keyboard built in to your iOS device, you can use the iOS 6's keyboard shortcuts feature. To set up this feature, launch Settings. Tap on the General option, and then from the General screen, scroll down to the Keyboard option.
>
> Under the Shortcuts heading you can add your own shortcuts. For example, you can create an RL shortcut for the phrase, "I am running late." After you create the shortcut, you simply need to type RL, and your iOS device will expand this to "I am running late" in compatible apps, including Twitter.
>
> Using keyboard shortcuts enables you to save time when entering commonly used words, phrases, or sentences. It can also help reduce typos and errors while composing messages.
>
> The keyboard shortcuts feature can be used with most other apps as well that require data entry using the virtual keyboard.

SENDING TWEETS FROM OTHER APPS

Thanks to iOS 6's Twitter integration, you can compose and send tweets (with app-specific attachments) from the Photos and Safari app, as well as other apps that have a Share menu. To do this, simply tap on the Share button or access the Share menu within the app you're using (shown in Figure 10.6). If Twitter integration is offered, a Twitter button will be displayed as part of the Share menu.

Tap the Twitter button, and a New Tweet screen (iPhone) or window (iPad) will be displayed. You can then compose and send your tweet from whatever app you're using. If you're using the Photos app, for example, you can select a photo to be included as an attachment. From Safari, you can tweet the webpage's URL that you're currently viewing.

FIGURE 10.6

Tap on the Twitter button found within the Share menu of many apps.

From the Notification Screen (iPhone) or window (iPad), tap on the Tap To Tweet button to compose and send a tweet anytime your device has access to the Internet, regardless of what app you're currently using.

REPLYING TO TWEETS AND OTHER TWITTER FEATURES

As you're viewing your Timeline, if there's a tweet you want to reply to, tap on that tweet listing. On the iPhone, a separate screen showcasing just that tweet will be displayed. On the iPad, the tweet is displayed in an enlarged on-screen window. Displayed below the selected message are four command icons (shown in Figure 10.7). Here's a summary of how these command are used:

■ **Reply**—The command icons associated with the Reply option looks like a left-pointing arrow. Tap on it to compose a public reply to the selected tweet you're viewing. This causes a Reply To window to appear. At the start of your message, the @Username will already be filled in with the username of the person you're replying to and anyone else mentioned within that tweet.

■ **Re-Tweet**—Tap on the square-shaped icon composed of two arrows to re-tweet the selected message to your followers. It appears on your own time-line, but credit is automatically given to the tweet's original author. You can also use the Quote Tweet option that allows you to attach another tweet to your own before sending it.

- **Favorite**—The star-shaped icon is used to tag a tweet as a Favorite and include it in your Favorites list.
- **More**—This icon looks like three dots. Tap on this icon to reveal a menu of additional options, such as Copy Link or Mail Link. Additional options will also be offered (see Figure 10.7). The Copy Link feature will only appear if the tweet you're looking at has a website URL listed within it.

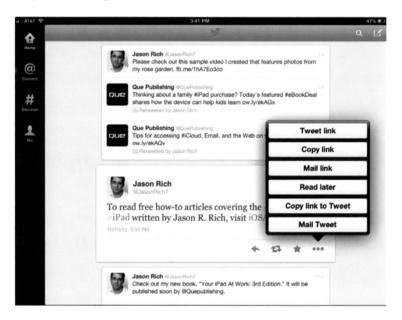

FIGURE 10.7

Tap on the More icon to reveal a menu of additional features you can use to manage tweets.

> **TIP**   If you're viewing a tweet in a foreign language, you can instantly translate it to the native language of your iOS device by tapping on the Translate option. A window with the translation of the selected message will be displayed.

Tap on the Mail Tweet option to email the contents of the selected message to someone from within the Twitter app without first having to launch the Mail app. When you use this command, the selected tweet will automatically be embedded in the body of the outgoing email message. You just need to fill in the To field and tap Send.

The Copy Link to Tweet option allows you to save the URL for that particular tweet in your iOS device's virtual clipboard. You can then use the Paste command to insert that information into another app.

HOW TO RE-TWEET MESSAGES

As you're reviewing your Timeline, which includes tweets composed by the various people you're following, if you stumble upon a particular tweet that you'd like to share with your own Twitter followers, instead of retyping the message from scratch, select it and then tap on the Retweet option to copy that tweet and send it to your followers from your Twitter account.

> **☑ TIP** In addition to communicating with your followers and the people you're following on Twitter, you can join in on virtual conversations happening between strangers. There are several ways to join in on a conversation about a specific topic.
>
> First, use the Search option to find a specific topic based on a keyword or phrase. When using Twitter, topics or subjects are highlighted by a hash symbol (#) in front of the topic. This is referred to as a hashtag. For example, if you want to find a Twitter conversation relating to the iPad, you'd do a search for the hashtag #iPad. (Some people refer to the hash symbol as the number sign symbol or as a pound sign.)
>
> Another way to find Twitter-based conversations to join in on is to view the ever-changing list of Trending Topics, tap on a topic that's of interest, and then respond to particular tweets from strangers that are displayed.
>
> To view a list of trending (currently popular) topics, tap on the Discover command icon, and scroll down to the Trends heading.
>
> The Trends list updates constantly, as the most current topics people are discussing and tweeting about on Twitter change. Often, trending topics relate to late-breaking news stories or celebrity gossip, but they're always based on the most-tweeted-about subjects or topics.

> **🔍 MORE INFO** With 30.2 million followers (as of October 2012), recording artist Lady Gaga (@LadyGaga) is one of the most-followed celebrities on Twitter. With just more than 28.8 million followers, recording artist Justin Bieber (@JustinBieber) is also extremely popular.
>
> Actor Wil Wheaton (@wilw), best known from the movie *Stand By Me* and the TV series *Star Trek: The Next Generation,* is one of many celebrities who is extremely active on Twitter and who interacts with his fans/Twitter followers. He has more than 2.1 million followers.
>
> To view a listing of the Top 1000 most popular people, businesses, and organizations on Twitter, visit http://twitaholic.com.

! CAUTION Although virtually every celebrity, politician, professional athlete, author, or public figure has a presence on Twitter, there are also many impersonators and impostors out there.

To make sure you're following the actual celebrity or public figure that you intend, look for a blue-and-white check mark icon next to that person's username. This indicates that their identity has been verified by Twitter.

IF YOU'RE CONCERNED ABOUT PRIVACY, DON'T SHARE YOUR LOCATION

One of the features built into the Twitter and Facebook apps (and iOS 6 integration) is that when composing and sending a tweet to your followers or composing and publishing content on Facebook (which can potentially be seen by the general public), your exact location can automatically be attached to the outgoing message.

So, if you're concerned about privacy, turn off the Location Services feature of within your iOS device entirely, or just turn off Location Services related to Twitter and/or Facebook. To do this, launch Settings, tap on the Privacy option, and then tap on the Location Services option.

Next, you can turn off the master Location Services virtual switch that's displayed near the top of the screen to prevent all apps from pinpointing and using your location information, or you can leave it on, but scroll down on the Location Services menu screen and turn off the Location Services feature associated with just Twitter or Facebook.

If you're sharing digital photos or video clips shot using your iPhone or iPad on an online social networking service, such as Twitter or Facebook, by default, those images or videos have geo-tagging information (the exact location where the photo or video was shot) saved in conjunction with the digital file. To avoid sharing this location information, from the Location Services menu within Settings, also turn off the Location Services option that's associated with the Camera and Photos apps, as well as any other photography-related apps used to capture, edit or share your digital pictures or videos.

MANAGE YOUR FACEBOOK ACCOUNT WITH THE OFFICIAL FACEBOOK APP

When it comes to online social networking, Facebook is by far the most popular service of its type in cyberspace. Its functionality goes well beyond what Twitter (which is basically a micro blogging service) offers.

> **NOTE** Creating and managing a Facebook account is free, and it can be done from virtually any device that connects to the Internet, including an iPhone or iPad. To create a new Facebook account, using Safari, visit www.Facebook.com and complete the Sign Up form. You can also create an account from within the official Facebook app. After your account is set up, complete your online profile, and then invite people you already know to become your friends on Facebook.

In addition to posting updates for your Facebook friends, which can include short tidbits about what you're up to or what's on your mind, Facebook enables you to share photos (or video clips) and multi-image photo albums, send/receive private email, participate in real-time chats with your friends, participate in online special-interest groups, play multiplayer games (like Words with Friends), and interact with people in a wide range of other ways.

Much of Facebook's functionality is offered to iPhone and iPad users via the official Facebook apps, which are also among the all-time-most-popular apps offered from the App Store, according to Apple.

The official Facebook apps for iPhone and iPad are available, for free, from the App Store. The appropriate version of the app can also be installed from within Settings on your device. Although there are also many third-party apps designed to be used with Facebook (some of which cost money), the official Facebook apps are the only ones designed and endorsed by Facebook.

> **TIP** You can download and install the official Facebook app, and then customize its app-specific settings from within Settings on your iPhone/iPad. Launch Settings and tap on the Facebook option to access the Facebook menu screen. From this screen, you also need to set up Facebook integration with iOS 6, so that it works with Notifications Center and other compatible apps, like Photos and Safari.

When using the official Facebook app on your iPad (held in landscape mode), the screen is divided into two columns. The column displayed on the right side of the screen enables you to see which of your Facebook friends are currently online. By tapping on any friend listing, you can initiate a real-time text-based chat. On the iPhone, access the Chat feature from the main menu. It then opens a separate Chat screen.

To access the Facebook app's main menu, which enables you to access your profile and News Feed, plus access Facebook features such as Messages, Nearby, Events, Friends, Photos, and Chat, tap on the Menu icon that's displayed in the upper-left corner of the screen. It looks like three horizontal lines.

Located next to the Menu icon are icons that enable you to manage your friend requests, messages, and notifications.

Everything you're able to do using the Facebook app is done by accessing the main menu or through command icons that are displayed along the top of the screen.

Also on the iPad, when either the Menu column (on the left side of the screen) or Chat column (on the right side of the screen) are visible, you can make one of them disappear by swiping your finger sideways in the direction that will close the menu or online friends list.

> **TIP** As you're looking at someone's contact information on their Profile page (or any other screens within the Facebook app), if you tap on an email address, the Mail app launches and you'll be able to send an email to that person. The To field is filled in automatically with the recipient's email address. Likewise, if you tap a website URL, Safari launches and automatically loads that website. Or, if you're using an iPhone and you tap on a phone number, your iPhone initiates a call to that number.

Here's a summary of what functionality is offered when you tap on any of the Facebook app's main menu (shown in Figure 10.8):

- **Search**—Find people or other content-related information on Facebook using the Search field that's displayed at the top-left corner of the app's main menu screen.

- **Your Profile**—The profile you create on Facebook can be as brief or as detailed as you'd like. This is one way people can find you and get to know you using this service. As you create your Facebook profile, keep in mind that just about everything you enter is keyword searchable, from your age and sexual orientation to your political affiliation and favorite movies or TV shows.

From the Profile section of the app, you can view your Wall or Info screen, share photos, create posts to be displayed on your public Wall, update and display information about yourself (within the Info section), manage your photo albums, and see a list of your Facebook friends.

FIGURE 10.8
The main menu of the official Facebook app shown here on the iPad mini.

- **News Feed**—This feature is somewhat similar to Twitter. You can read short messages that your Facebook friends have posted. These short messages can include text and be accompanied by a photo, video clip, or website URL. Using News Feed is a quick and easy way to keep track of what all of your Facebook friends are up to. From the News Feed screen, you can also share photos, post your own status, or check in and share your current location.

- **Messages**—Manage your Facebook messages from the Messages screen. This includes private messages sent between you and other Facebook members, as well as missed instant messages you received.

- **Nearby**—Based on your current location, this feature on the iPad enables you to view a detailed map that showcases where your other Facebook friends (who are currently online) are located, based on when they last used the Check-In feature. On the iPad, recent check-ins from friends are displayed as a listing.

- **Events**—Facebook automatically keeps track of everyone's birthday and notifies you when any of your Facebook friends are having a birthday. To see a listing of upcoming birthdays, tap on the Birthdays icon after tapping on the Events icon. Facebook users also can send and respond to electronic invitations for parties, gatherings, or events. Tap on the Events icon to read invites sent by others or to send out your own digital invite for a party or gathering that you're planning.

- **Friends**—Tap on this option to view and manage your list of Facebook friends and to visit their respective Facebook pages.

- **Chat**—At any given time, this option allows you to see which of your Facebook friends are currently online, and then you can initiate a real-time, text-based chat with any of those people. In addition to text-based chats, you can participate in real-time videoconferences with your Facebook friends, for free. On the iPad, the Chat feature is displayed on the right side of the screen whenever the main menu is not displayed and the tablet is being held in landscape mode. On the iPhone, Chat is a separate menu option that leads to the Chat screen.

- **App Center**—Utilize any of the iOS-compatible Facebook apps that you have activated with your account, including a growing selection of multiplayer games. Some optional apps, such as Yelp!, can also be launched from within the Facebook app.

- **Photos**—This option enables you to manage the individual photos or photo albums that you have uploaded to Facebook and that you're sharing with others.

> **! CAUTION** Although you can upload and share an unlimited number of photos on Facebook, when you upload your images, their resolution and file size are automatically diminished. Thus, this is a great way to share your images but not a good method for maintaining an online backup or archive of your digital photo library.

- **Account Settings**—Manage the Account Settings, Privacy Settings, and Help Center that's associated with your account.

- **Log Out**—This command is used to sign off from Facebook. If you don't sign out, even if you exit the Facebook app, you will remain logged into your account and the app will continue running in the background.

- **Privacy & Terms**—To maintain your privacy and ensure you're not disclosing or sharing too much information about yourself on Facebook, periodically review the ever-changing privacy settings associated with this app.

> **TIP** From this main menu screen, you also have the option of adding more Facebook pages to the menu by tapping on the Like icon associated with many Facebook pages and apps. You can also join groups and have them displayed on the menu.

> **MORE INFO** Want to learn more about Facebook and how it works? Visit www.facebook.com/help/ from any Internet-enabled computer or device.

UPDATE YOUR STATUS, CHECK-IN, OR UPLOAD PHOTOS

When viewing your News Feed (a menu option), displayed near the top of the official Facebook app's screen are three command tabs, labeled Status, Photo and Check-In. Tap on the Status tab to update your Facebook Status. This is information that will be published on your wall and that can be viewable by the general public (if you have your privacy settings adjusted to allow this).

> **NOTE** To adjust your Facebook privacy settings, access the app's Menu and tap on the Account Settings options. From the Settings menu, tap on Privacy.

Tap on the Photo tab to upload one or more photos from the Photos app to Facebook. You can then add tags and captions to your photos. Use the Check In feature to share your exact location with others and add a comment about where you are, who you're with and what you're doing.

UPDATE YOUR FACEBOOK STATUS FROM OTHER APPS

Thanks to iOS 6's new Facebook integration, you can update your Facebook Status from directly within the Notification Center screen (iPhone) or window (iPad) by opening Notification Center (swipe your finger downwards from the top of the screen, regardless of which app is running), and then tap on the Tap To Post button.

You can also update your Facebook Status, and include app-specific content within your status update from within Photos, Safari or almost any other app that has a Share button. Tap on the app's Share button to access the Share menu, and then tap on the Facebook option. A Facebook Status Update screen (iPhone) or window (iPad) is displayed (shown in Figure 10.9).

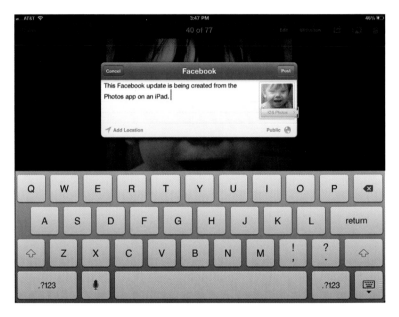

FIGURE 10.9
Compose and send a Facebook Status Update from any compatible app that has a Share button or Share feature, such as Photos or Safari.

When the Facebook window appears, type your message using the virtual keyboard. You can also dictate your message using the Dictation feature. If you want to add your current location to the outgoing message, tap on the Add Location option that's displayed in the lower-left corner of the window/screen. To decide who will be able to access your update, tap on the lower-right corner of the screen/window where it says Public, Friends, Friends Except Acquaintances, Only Me, or Close Friends, and choose your selection.

Tap on the Post button to publish your Facebook update, as long as your iPhone/iPad has access to the Internet. Just like with Twitter, Facebook integration must first be activated from within Settings.

> **TIP** If you access the Facebook option using the Share menu within Photos (or another photography app), you'll be able to embed a photo into your Facebook Status Updates. Likewise, if you use the Share option from within Safari, you can share a webpage URL within your updates. If you use the Tap To Post button within Notification Center, for example, you can only include text within your update.

OTHER SPECIALIZED APPS FOR ONLINE SOCIAL NETWORKING

Although you could opt to use their respective "official" apps to connect to Twitter, Facebook, Google+, Tumblr, Instagram, or other popular online services, in the App Store you'll find many third-party apps (not all of which are free) that allow you to interact with these popular online social networking services and utilize features often not offered by the official apps.

TIP To find third-party apps designed to work with your favorite online social networking services that might offer enhanced functionality—such as the capability to more easily upload photos, create albums, tag photos, and/or share digital images online—visit the App Store. In the App Store's Search field, enter the name of the online social networking service you're interested in, and then take a look at the various apps that are listed. Although you can always use the "official" app for that service, which is free, you might decide that one of the third-party paid apps will be more useful to you.

When you visit the App Store, tap on the Categories option, and then select Social Networking to see a complete list of available apps that can somehow be used to interact with services like Twitter, Facebook, Google+, Instagram, LinkedIn, etc. You'll find literally thousands of iPhone-specific, iPad-specific, and hybrid apps to choose from.

MORE INFO LinkedIn is a popular online social networking site that caters specifically to business professionals, entrepreneurs, consultants, free-lancers, and small-business operators. The primary focus of this service is on professional networking.

Setting up a LinkedIn account is free, as is downloading and using the official LinkedIn app (which is available from the App Store). However, from the App Store, you'll also find third-party apps like the iPad-specific LinkPad ($1.99), which also allows you to manage your LinkedIn account.

NOTE To learn more about LinkedIn and how you can fully utilize it, visit http://learn.linkedin.com/new-users.

SEESMIC PING

If you're active on multiple online social networking sites, this iPhone/iPad app (free) allows you to compose and send a single post but have it simultaneously get published to all of your accounts. It supports Facebook, Twitter, MySpace, Flickr, WordPress, Blogger, LinkedIn, and dozens of others.

When composing a message, you can easily attach a photo or web URL, and the app will shrink the size of the related URL(s) automatically as needed. The app also integrates with the Photos and Maps app, so you can share photos taken or stored on your iOS device and/or share your exact location with others. Pingle also maintains an archive of all messages you've sent out from the app.

The easy-to-use Seesmic Ping app is a real timesaver if you want to keep all your online social networking accounts up to date without having to constantly post separate messages or updates to each account. After you set up Seesmic Ping to work with all of your accounts, you can also send messages from the www.Seesmic.com website.

TWITTERIFIC FOR TWITTER

Twitterific is also a hybrid iPhone/iPad-specific app that automatically adjusts its displays based on the device you're using. It is a powerful app used for managing one or more Twitter accounts.

The basic Twitterific app is free; however, you can upgrade to a premium (ad-free) version for $4.99. One nice feature of this app is that your Twitter feed will be color-coded, so you can easily differentiate between tweets you've sent, tweets you've responded to, other people's tweets, tweets that have been re-tweeted, and responses to your tweets.

The app also enables you to find, follow, unfollow, or block users easily; create and save searches; track trending topics; and attach a photo, your location, or website URLs to your tweets as you compose them.

INSTAGRAM

Now owned by Facebook, Instagram is an online social networking site that works something like Twitter, except instead of composing and sharing text-based messages, you can post one photo at a time, include a caption, as well as tags for that photo. Your followers (and potentially the general public) can then post comments about your photos.

When using in conjunction with the cameras built into your iPhone or iPad, the official Instagram app (and the Instagram service) offer a fun way to share your life with others through photos that you can take and upload instantly from anywhere.

One of the great features of the Instagram app is that you can edit a photo using pre-created filters (shown in Figure 10.10), and make them look amazing (or add special effects to them) with a single tap on the screen. You can also add frames or borders around your images before posting them.

FIGURE 10.10

Easy add special effects, filters, borders or frames to your images before publishing them on Instagram.

Instagram is easy to use, plus it now integrates with Facebook, Twitter, Foursquare, Tumblr, and Flickr, so you can post your Instagram photos within your other online social networking accounts simultaneously. The app and the service are free.

> **TIP** Using an optional app, such as InstaCollage, you can quickly create multi-image collages using your Instagram photos, and then publish those collages on Instagram with a tap on the screen. Or, if you visit www.StickyGram.com, you can link to your Instagram account and have custom, 2" x 2" refrigerator magnets created from your Instagram photos ($14.99 per sheet of nine magnets).

YOUTUBE

Over the years, YouTube has evolved from being just a way to watch free videos into becoming an online-based community that allows people to watch, comment on and share videos. Since the launch of the iPhone and iPad, the official YouTube app came bundled with the iOS operating system. This is no longer the case with iOS 6. However, you can download the newly-redesigned, official YouTube app from the App Store for free. It allows you to manage your YouTube account and watch streaming videos, as long as your iPhone/iPad has an Internet connection.

> **❗CAUTION** Streaming video content to your iPhone or iPad requires a tremendous about of wireless data usage. If you're using a Wi-Fi connection, this isn't an issue. However, if you're using a 3G/4G Internet connection with a monthly data allocation, watching YouTube videos will quickly use up that data allocation.

IN THIS CHAPTER

- How to use new features iOS 6 brings to the Camera and Photos apps
- How to use tips and tricks for shooting, editing, and sharing photos and videos
- Take panoramic photos using the iPhone's Camera app

11

SHOOT, EDIT, AND SHARE PHOTOS AND VIDEOS

People love taking photos, and thanks to the two digital cameras built in to the latest iPhones and iPads, plus the improvements made to the Camera and Photos apps with iOS 6, it's never been easier or more fun to shoot, edit, view, print, and share your digital images or video clips.

The iPhone 5, for example, offers an improved 8MP rear-facing camera, along with the enhanced Camera and Photos apps that come preinstalled with iOS 6. Thus, it's possible to take crystal-clear photos and create large and vibrant, full-color prints from the digital files. The trick to taking crystal clear images, however, is to hold the iPhone or iPad as steady as possible when shooting an image.

☑ **TIP** The iOS 6 version of Photos app that comes preinstalled on your iPhone or iPad now enables you to edit and/or digitally enhance your photos after they're shot, as opposed to just viewing, printing, and sharing them. Now, if a photo you shoot appears slightly too light (overexposed) or too dark (underexposed), you can often fix it with a tap of the finger. You can also correct red-eye or crop and rotate images stored on the phone or tablet.

By tapping on the Share icon (a square icon with an arrow coming out of it) within the Photo app, you can easily share your images in several ways. You can attach up to five photos to an outgoing email message from within Photos, attach a photo to a text/instant message, tweet a photo to your Twitter followers, or upload a photo directly to your Facebook page. You can also sync your images with your primary computer or share your digital images with all your computers and iOS devices by setting up a Photo Stream via iCloud.

Using your digital images with other apps is also easier than ever, thanks to iOS 6. You can assign a photo to a contact in the Contacts app, use a photo as your Lock Screen or Home Screen wallpaper, or easily copy a photo into another app, such as Pages or Keynote.

(iOS 6) **WHAT'S NEW** Two of the most useful features added to the Camera and Photos apps in conjunction with iOS 6 are the ability to shoot panoramic shots from your iPhone's camera (using the Camera app), and then edit those images and upload them to Facebook from within the Photos app on either an iPhone or iPad.

Although the Share button within Photos allows you to select and share up to five photos at a time via email, using the iCloud's new Shared Photo Stream feature, you can create an online-based photo album that contains as many images as you'd like, and then share those photos with specific people you select. This provides an easy way to share many photos and also decide exactly who gets to see them.

The Camera and Photos apps also work in conjunction with many third-party apps, so you can use specialized editing tools or share your photos online in a variety of different ways. For example, there's the optional Instagram app for uploading photos and adding special effects to them via your Instagram account. Or, if you want to order prints of photos directly from your iPhone or iPad, and have them shipped to your door within a few days, you can use one of several apps (such as FreePrints) that are available from the App Store.

METHODS FOR LOADING DIGITAL IMAGES INTO YOUR iPHONE OR iPAD

Before you can view, edit, print, and share your favorite digital images, you first need to shoot them using the Camera or Photo Booth app, or transfer images into your iOS device.

> **NOTE** Some third-party apps, including Instagram, also allow you to access and use your iPhone or iPad's built-in cameras, without using the Camera app.

Aside from shooting images using one of your iOS device's built-in cameras, there are several ways to import photos into your iOS device, and then store them in the Photos app:

- Use the iTunes sync process to transfer photos to your device. Set up iTunes to sync the image folders or albums you want, and then initiate an iTunes sync or wireless iTunes sync from your primary computer.

- Load photos from a Photo Stream (via iCloud). Later in this chapter, how to work with Photo Stream is explained.

- Receive and save photos sent via email. When a photo is embedded in an email, hold your finger on it for a second or two until a menu appears, giving you the option to save the image (within the Camera Roll folder of the Photos app), or copy the image to your device's virtual clipboard (after which you can paste it into another app). This feature, along with other Share options, is shown using the Mail app on a iPad in Figure 11.1.

- Receive and save photos sent via text message or Twitter. Tap on the image you receive using the Messages app, and then tap on the Copy command. When viewing the image in full-screen mode, tap on the Share button, and then select the Save To Camera Roll option or Open in iPhoto option, for example.

- Save images directly from a website as you're surfing the Web. Hold your finger on the image you're viewing within a website. If it's not copy-protected, after a second or two a menu appears, enabling you to save the image or copy it to your device's virtual clipboard (after which you can paste it into another app).

- Use the optional Camera Connection Kit ($29, available from Apple Stores or Apple.com) to load images from your digital camera or its memory card directly into your iPhone or iPad.

FIGURE 11.1

If you receive a digital photo attached to an incoming email, you can save the image in the Camera Roll by holding your finger on the image thumbnail (within the email), and then tapping on the Save Image option when it appears.

> **NOTE** When you use the Save Image command, the image will be stored within the Camera Roll album of Photos. You can then view, edit, enhance, print, or share it.

THE NEW AND IMPROVED CAMERA APP

The Camera app that comes preinstalled with iOS 6 has been given some enhancements, yet it still remains very easy to use if you want to snap a photo or shoot a video clip. To begin using the Camera app, launch it from your device's Home Screen.

The main camera viewfinder screen (shown in Figure 11.2) appears as soon as you launch the Camera app on an iPhone, iPod touch, or iPad. The main area of the screen serves as your camera's viewfinder. In other words, what you see on the screen is what you'll photograph or capture on video.

FIGURE 11.2

From the Camera app's main screen (shown here on the iPhone 5), you can snap digital photos or shoot video. The app looks similar on the iPhone and iPad and works pretty much the same way.

Along the bottom of the screen are several command buttons and icons. In the lower-left corner, you'll see a thumbnail image of the last photo or video clip you shot. Tap on it to view that image or video clip by automatically launching the Photos app.

At the bottom center of the screen on the iPhone, or on middle-right side of the screen on the iPad, is the camera's shutter button. Tap on this to snap a photo or to start and stop the video camera. In Camera mode, tap on this camera-shaped shutter button to snap a photo. You'll hear a sound effect, and a single photo will be saved. In Video mode, the camera-shaped icon transforms into an oval with a dim red dot inside it. The dot gets brighter when you tap on it to begin shooting a video clip.

In the lower-right corner of the Camera screen is the Camera/Video virtual switch. Tap on it to move the switch to the left and place the Camera app into Camera mode for shooting digital photos. Or move the virtual switch to the right to shoot video.

As you know, the latest iPhone and iPad models each have two built-in cameras—one in the front, and one on the back of the device. The front-facing camera makes it easier to snap photos of yourself or participate in videoconferences, for example.

The rear-facing camera (which allows you to take higher-resolution photos or video) allows you to photograph whatever you're looking at that's facing forward. Tap on the icon located in the upper-right corner of the screen on the iPhone (or the lower-right corner of the screen on the iPad) to switch between cameras.

On the iPad, displayed near the bottom-left of the main Camera screen is the Options icon. Tap on it to reveal the Grid option. When it's turned on, a "Rule of Thirds" grid gets displayed on the main screen (your viewfinder when in Camera mode). How to use the Rule of Thirds while shooting to better compose and frame your shots is explained later in this chapter.

On the iPhone, the Options button that's displayed near the top-center of the screen enables you to turn on/off the Rule of Thirds grid, as well as the HDR mode that's built in to the Camera app. You'll also discover the Panorama button here that allows you to shoot gorgeous panoramic images with ease. (This is a feature that's currently exclusive to the iPhone.)

Also on the iPhone, in the upper-left corner of the main Camera screen, you'll see an icon labeled Auto. You can turn this feature on or off. It controls whether the iPhone will automatically use the built-in flash when needed as you're shooting photos or video with the rear-facing camera.

> ## 🔍 MORE INFO   The HDR mode in the Camera app stands for High Dynamic Range. It can be used with the rear-facing camera only. When turned on, this feature captures the available light differently and can help you compensate for a photo that would otherwise be over- or underexposed.
>
> When HDR mode is turned on, your iPhone saves two images each time you tap the shutter button to snap a photo. One utilizes HDR mode and the other does not. You can later view the images, choose which you like best, and discard the other one. The drawback to using HDR mode is that it takes several extra seconds to store both images each time you snap a photo, and this slows down the Camera app.

HOW TO SNAP A PHOTO

Snapping a single digital photo using the Camera app is simple. Follow these steps:

1.   Launch the Camera app from the Home Screen.

2.   Make sure the virtual switch is set to Camera mode and the shutter button icon looks like a camera.

3.   Tap on Options to turn on or off the Grid feature as you see fit, as well as the HDR feature on the iPhone.

4. Choose which of your device's two built-in cameras you want to use by tapping on the camera selection icon.

5. Compose or frame your image by holding up your iPhone or iPad and pointing it at your subject.

6. Select what the main subject of your photo will be, such as a person or an object. Tap your finger on the screen where your subject appears in the viewfinder. An autofocus sensor box appears on the screen at the location you tap. Where this box is positioned is what the camera focuses on (as opposed to something in the foreground, in the background, or next to your intended subject).

> ☑ **TIP**   As you're holding your iPhone or iPad to snap a photo or shoot video, be sure your fingers don't accidentally block the camera lens that's being utilized. On the more recent iPhone models, next to the rear-facing camera lens is a tiny flash. Keep your fingers clear of this as well.

> ✐ **NOTE**   If you're taking a group photo (up to 10 people), the camera app detects this and multiple auto focus sensors will appear on all of your subject's faces.

7. If you want to use the Camera app's zoom feature, use a pinch motion on the screen. A zoom slider (shown in Figure 11.3) appears near the bottom of the screen. Use your finger to move the dot within the slider to the right to zoom in, or to the left to zoom out on your subject.

8. On the iPhone, tap on the Flash icon that's displayed neat the top-left corner of the screen. You have three flash-related options. When turned on, the flash will activate for every picture you take. When turned off, the flash will not activate at all, regardless of the lighting conditions. When you select Auto, the Camera app will activate the flash when it deems additional light is needed. If you have HDR mode turned on (iPhone only), the flash will not work.

9. When you have your image framed within the viewfinder, tap on the shutter button to snap the photo. Or tap the Volume Up (+) button on the side of your iPhone. You'll see an animation of a virtual shutter closing and then reopening on the screen, indicating that the photo is being taken. At the same time, you'll hear an audio effect.

FIGURE 11.3

As you're framing an image, you can zoom in (or out) on your subject using the onscreen zoom slider. Use a pinch finger gesture on the screen to make this slider appear, and then move the slider to the right or left to increase or decrease the zoom level.

10. Within 1 and 5 seconds the photo will be saved on your device in the Camera Roll album of Photos. You can now shoot another photo or view the photo using the Photos app.

HOW TO SHOOT A PANORAMIC PHOTO

On the iPhone, to take advantage of the new panoramic shooting mode to snap a photo of a landscape, city skyline or a large group of people, for example, follow these steps:

1. Launch the Camera app.

2. Make sure the Camera app is in Camera mode (as opposed to video mode).

3. Tap on the Options button that's displayed near the top-center of the screen.

4. Tap on the Panorama button.

5. Position your iPhone's viewfinder to the extreme left of your wide angle shot.

> ✅ **TIP** If you tap on the large arrow icon within the viewfinder, you can switch the panning direction from right to left, instead of left to right as you're capturing a panoramic shot.

6. Tap the shutter button icon and then slowly and steadily move your iPhone from left to right. If you go too fast, a message appears on the screen telling you to slow down (shown in Figure 11.4).

FIGURE 11.4

The new Panorama shooting mode is ideal for capturing vast landscapes, city skylines or large group photos.

7. The panorama slider will move from left to right as you capture your image. You can tap the shutter button again when you're done, or continue moving the iPhone to the right until the entire length of the image has been captured.

8. The panoramic photo will be saved within the Camera Roll folder of the Photos app. You can then view, edit and/or share it on the iPhone's screen from within Photos.

> ✅ **TIP** When viewing a panoramic photo, hold your iPhone in landscape mode. However, when shooting a panoramic shot, you should hold the iPhone in portrait mode.

HOW TO SHOOT VIDEO

From the Camera app, you can easily shoot video. Follow these basic steps for shooting video on your iPhone or iPad:

1. Launch the Camera app from the Home Screen.

2. Set the Camera app to Video mode with the Camera/Video virtual switch, and make sure the shutter button icon shows a dim red dot.

3. Choose which camera you want to use. You can switch between the front- and the rear-facing camera at any time.

4. On the iPhone, tap on the Flash icon that's displayed neat the top-left cor-ner of the screen. You have three flash-related options. When turned on, the flash will activate as you're shooting video. When turned off, the flash will not activate at all, regardless of the lighting conditions. When you select Auto, the Camera app will activate the flash and keep it on as a constant light source when it deems additional light is needed.

5. Hold your iPhone or iPad up to the subject you want to capture on video. Set up your shot by looking at what's displayed on the screen.

6. When you're ready to start shooting video, tap on the shutter button. The red dot will get brighter and blink. This indicates you're now filming. Your iPhone or iPad captures whatever images you see on the screen, as well as any sound in the area.

7. As you're filming video, notice a timer displayed in the upper-right corner of the screen. Your only limit to how much video you can shoot is based on the amount of available memory in your iOS device and how long the bat-tery lasts. However, this app is designed more for shooting short video clips, not full-length home movies.

8. Also as you're filming, tap anywhere on the screen to focus in on your sub-ject using the app's built-in autofocus sensor.

9. To stop filming, tap again on the red dot shutter button. Your video footage will be saved. You can now view, edit, and share it from within the Photos app or the optional iMovie app, for example.

> **TIP**   Although the Photos app enables you to trim your video clips as well as view and share the videos, if you want to edit your videos, plus add titles and special effects, you'll definitely want to purchase and use Apple's feature-packed iMovie app, which is available from the App Store ($4.99). For more information about iMovie, visit www.apple.com/apps/imovie.

USE PHOTO BOOTH TO SNAP WHIMSICAL PHOTOS

In addition to the Camera app, the Photo Booth app that comes preinstalled with iOS 6 on the iPad enables you to shoot photos and immediately incorporate one of eight special effects, which are displayed on the main viewfinder screen as you're shooting. When an image is shot using Photo Booth, it's saved in the Camera Roll folder of Photos and can easily be viewed, edited, enhanced, printed, or shared. Photo Booth offers a more whimsical option for snapping photos using the front- or rear-facing camera of your iPad.

TIPS FOR SHOOTING EYE-CATCHING PHOTOS

Even though you're using a smartphone or tablet to shoot photos, as opposed to a full-featured, digital SLR or point-and-shoot digital camera, you can still use basic photo composition and framing techniques to snap professional-quality images.

> **TIP** On the iPhone 5, 3rd/4th generation iPad or the iPad mini, for example, the rear-facing camera offers superior resolution and takes better photos, so use this camera (as opposed to the front-facing camera) as often as possible to get the highest-quality results.

To generate the best possible in-focus, well-lit, and nicely framed images when shooting with your iPhone, iPod touch, or iPad, follow these basic shooting strategies (many of which also apply when shooting video):

- Pay attention to your light source. As a general rule, the light source (such as the sun) should be behind you (the photographer) and shining onto your subject. When light from your primary light source shines directly into your camera's lens (in this case your iPhone or iPad), you'll wind up with unwanted glares or an overexposed image.

- As you look at the viewfinder screen, pay attention to shadows. Unwanted shadows can be caused by the sun or by an artificial light source. When shadows show up in your images, they can be distracting. Make sure shadows aren't covering your subject(s).

> **TIP** If your human subject is wearing a hat, for example, this can place an annoying shadow across the subject's face. Or if your subject is standing under a tree in daylight, shadows from the tree's branches and leaves will often cover your subject.

When you're shooting indoors using the iPhone's flash, this too will generate shadows. Try to keep your subject at least two or three feet away from a wall or backdrop to reduce shadows, and don't get too close to your subject.

- When you're using the flash, red-eye often becomes a problem. To avoid this, try to shine more light on your subject and not rely on the flash. Or step farther away from your subject physically but use the zoom to move in closer.

TIP Like any camera, the flash built in to your iPhone has an optimal range that generates the best lighting results. If you're too close to your subject when using the flash, the photo will come out overexposed. If you're too far away, the photo might turn out underexposed. You can compensate by moving closer or farther away from your subject but then use the zoom feature when necessary.

NOTE When you use the digital zoom built into the Camera app, a photo's image quality will be reduced the further you zoom in. It also becomes even more essential to hold the iPhone steady as you're taking pictures when you use the zoom feature.

- Candid photos of people are great for showing emotion, spontaneity, or true life. The key to taking great candid photos is to have your camera ready to shoot and to be unobtrusive so that your subjects don't become self-conscious when they have a camera aimed at them. Try to anticipate when something interesting, surprising, or funny, or that will generate a strong emotion, will happen, and be ready to snap a photo. Also, don't get too close to your subject. You're better off being several feet away and using the zoom so that you, as the photographer, don't become a distraction.

- As you get ready to tap the shutter icon and snap a photo, hold your iOS device perfectly still. Even the slightest movement could result in a blurry image, especially in low-light situations.

TIP As you're looking at your primary subject through the "viewfinder" (the iPhone or iPad's screen when using the Camera app), tap on the intended subject on the screen once to set the Autofocus and Auto Exposure Lock. A blue square will appear on the screen over your subject. This informs the iPhone or iPad about what you want your primary subject to be, and ensures the best possible focus and available lighting utilization.

The automatic face detection feature, used for taking photos of people, can auto focus on up to 10 faces simultaneously, ensuring each appears crystal clear in a group photo.

■ If you're shooting in poor light, take advantage of the iPhone's HDR feature by turning it on.

TIP On the iPhone, it's possible to launch the Camera app directly from the Lock Screen in order to save time when you want to shoot a photo. Place you finger on the camera icon that's displayed on the Lock Screen and flick upwards to quickly launch the Camera app, and then use the Volume Up button on your device as your shutter button to snap a photo.

■ When shooting portraits of people or specific objects, make sure you use the Camera app's autofocus sensor box to focus in on your subject. As you look through the viewfinder, tap on the main subject's face, for example. This will ensure that the Camera app focuses in on the person, and not something in the foreground, in the background, or to the side of your subject.

■ As you're framing your subject(s) in the viewfinder, pay attention to what's in the foreground, in the background, and to the sides of the subject. These objects can often be used to frame your subject and add a sense of multi-dimensionality to a photo. Just make sure that the autofocus sensor of the Camera app focuses in on your intended subject, and not something else in the photo, to ensure clarity.

■ The best way to improve the overall quality of your photos when shooting with your iPhone, iPad, or iPod touch (or any digital camera) is to incorporate the Rule of Thirds when you're framing or composing each shot.

HOW TO USE THE RULE OF THIRDS WHEN SHOOTING

It's a common mistake for amateur photographers to hold their camera directly up to their subject, point it at the subject head-on, center the subject in the frame, and snap a photo. The result is always a generic-looking image, even if it's well-lit and in perfect focus.

Instead, as you look at the viewfinder screen to compose or frame your image, utilize the Rule of Thirds. This is a shooting strategy used by professional photographers, but it's very easy to take advantage of, and the results will be impressive.

Image a tic-tac-toe grid being superimposed on your camera's viewfinder. Or tap on the Options icon when shooting with the Camera app and turn on the Grid feature (shown in Figure 11.5). The center box in the tic-tac-toe grid corresponds to the center of the image you're about to shoot as you look at the viewfinder screen.

Instead of framing your subject in this center box, reframe the image so your subject is positioned along one of the horizontal or vertical lines of the grid, or so that the main focal point of the image is positioned at one of the grid's intersection points.

FIGURE 11.5

It's easier to utilize the Rule of Thirds for composing an image when the Grid feature of the Camera app is turned on. This grid appears on the viewfinder screen, but not in the images you shoot.

🔍 **MORE INFO** In some cases, you might find it easier to use a stand or even a tripod for your iPhone or iPad to help hold it steady as you're snapping a photo. Joby (http://joby.com/gorillamobile), for example, offers several different mini-tripod and stand products for use with your iOS device.

✅ **TIP** As you're shooting, instead of holding the camera head-on, directly facing your subject, try shooting from a different perspective, such as from slightly above, below, or to the side of your subject. This will allow you to create more visually interesting images.

Using the Rule of Thirds when framing your images will take a bit of practice, but if you use this shooting technique consistently and correctly, you'll discover that the quality of your images will vastly improve. Of course, you also want to take into account lighting, as well as what's in the foreground, in the background, and to the sides of your main subject. And be sure to tap your creativity when choosing your shooting angle or perspective for each shot.

> **TIP** When you're shooting a subject in motion, capture the subject moving into the frame, as opposed to moving out of it, while also taking into account the Rule of Thirds.

USING THE PHOTOS APP TO VIEW, EDIT, ENHANCE, PRINT, AND SHARE PHOTOS AND VIDEOS

You can launch the Photos app from your iOS device's Home Screen or from within the Camera app by tapping on the image thumbnail icon displayed in the lower-left corner of the main Camera app screen.

First and foremost, you'll want to use the Photos app to view images stored on your iOS device. On the iPhone, the functionality of the Photos app is almost identical to the iPad version; however, the appearance of some of the screens and the position of certain command icons and menus will be different (due to the smaller size of the iPhone's screen). On the iPhone, for example, instead of a single Video Images screen, you'll see a separate Albums screen, followed by a Photos screen.

VIEWING PHOTOS AND VIDEOS (iPAD)

The View Images screen on the iPad (shown in Figure 11.6) has multiple viewing tabs displayed at the top center of the screen labeled Photos, Photo Stream (if applicable), Albums, and Places.

> **TIP** The Places tab appears only when photos are stored that include geo-tagging information. The Photo Stream only appears when you have this feature turned on.

On the iPad, tap on the Photos tab to see thumbnails of all images stored on your tablet (refer to Figure 11.6), regardless of which album they're stored in. Use your finger to move upward or downward and scroll through your images. When the Photos tab is active, the Slideshow and Edit buttons will be displayed in the upper-right corner of the screen. Tap Slideshow to create a slideshow of your images and adjust specific settings, such as transition effects and what music will be played.

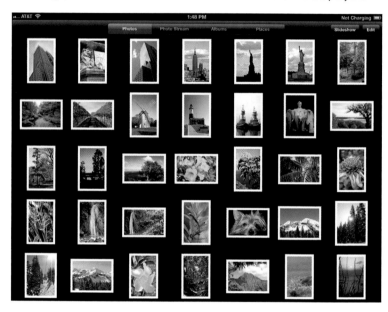

FIGURE 11.6

From the View Images screen, tap on the Photos tab to view thumbnails of all images stored on your tablet in the Photos app.

On the iPad, when viewing your image thumbnails by tapping on the Photos tab, tap on Edit button, select one or more images, and then tap on the Share button (displayed in the upper-left corner of the screen) to share the selected images. Tap on the button associated with how you want to share the selected images (Mail, Photo Stream, Facebook, etc.).

From the Share menu, tap on the Copy icon to move the selected image(s) to your iPad's virtual clipboard, and then be able to paste them into another app.

Instead of tapping on the Share button, tap on the Delete button to erase the selected images from your iOS device altogether. In the upper-right corner of the screen, an Add To and Cancel button will also be seen.

> **TIP** When you transfer images to your iPhone or iPad via iTunes Sync from your primary computer, you will be able to view and edit these images, but you will not be able to delete them from the Album on your iOS mobile device they were imported into. To delete those images from your iPhone or iPad, you'll need to edit the Album on your primary computer and then re-sync the Album.

Tap on the Add To button to copy the selected images into another existing Album or a New Album that you can create when prompted. Tapping on the Cancel button will exit this screen.

From the main View Images screen, tap on the Albums tab (displayed at the top center of the screen) to view thumbnails representing the individual albums that contain your photos. By default, all photos and videos shot using the Camera app will be saved in the Camera Roll album. From this screen, tap on any Album thumbnail to reveal thumbnails of the images stored within it.

From the main View Images screen, tap on the Places icon to see a map showcasing where images were shot. This geo-tagging feature works with all photos shot using your iPhone or iPad, or with images shot with a digital camera that has a geo-tagging feature. If none of the images stored on your iOS device have geo-tagging associated with them, this Places feature will not be displayed.

In the Photos app, the thumbnails for video clips shot using the Camera app will also be displayed. However, in the lower-left corner of a video clip's thumbnail will be a movie-camera icon, and in the lower-right corner the length of the video will be displayed (as shown in Figure 11.7).

FIGURE 11.7

The thumbnails for video clips stored in the Photos app look a bit different than those for photos. Video clips have a video-camera icon in the lower-left corner and the length of the video displayed in the lower-right corner of its thumbnail.

VIEWING PHOTOS AND VIDEOS (iPHONE)

The iPhone version of Photos offers the same core functionality of the iPad, but the user interface is a bit different. Along the bottom of the iPhoto screen are the three command icons, labeled Albums, Photo Stream, and Places.

When you tap on the Albums button, you'll see listings for each Album, including Camera Roll, in the main area of the screen. Tap on Photo Stream to view your main Photo Stream, as well as the Shared Photo Streams you create. Tap on Places to view a map that depicts where images were taken (assuming geo-tagging information is attached to the photos.)

From the Albums screen, tap on any listing to open an Album and view thumbnails that depict each photo within that Album. You can then tap on the Edit button to select one or more images and then Share them, use the Add To button to move them into another Album, or tap on the Delete button to delete them from your iPhone altogether.

VIEW AN IMAGE IN FULL-SCREEN MODE

When viewing thumbnails of your images, tap on any single image thumbnail to view a full-screen version of it. As you're then viewing an image, tap on it to make the various command icons for editing and sharing the image appear on the screen (as shown in Figure 11.8). Tap on the Edit button to reveal the image editing options offered within the Photos app.

To exit the single-image view and return to the multi-image thumbnail view of an Album, tap anywhere on the screen to make the command icons appear, and then tap on the left-pointing arrow-shaped icon that's displayed in the upper-left corner of the screen. The word displayed in this icon will be the Album name the photo is stored in, such as Camera Roll.

As you're viewing a single image in full-screen mode, on the iPad along the bottom of the screen will be a filmstrip depiction of all images stored in the current album, or all images stored on your iOS device if you were previously in Photos viewing mode.

Also on the iPad, in the upper-right corner are at least three command icons used for editing, viewing slideshows, and sharing images. If you have AirPlay functionality available, an AirPlay icon will also be displayed.

On the iPhone, the Edit command is displayed in the upper-right corner of the screen, and the Share command icon is displayed in the lower-left corner of the screen (as shown in Figure 11.9).

FIGURE 11.8

When viewing an image in full-screen mode, tap anywhere on that image to reveal the command icons you'll use to ultimately edit, enhance, and share that image.

FIGURE 11.9

On the iPhone, the positions of the Edit and Share commands are different than on the iPad, but the functionality is the same.

EDITING PHOTOS AND VIDEOS

After selecting a single image to view in full-screen mode, tap on the Edit button to access the Edit commands for photos.

> **TIP** When you tap on the thumbnail for a video clip, you'll have the option to play that clip in the Photos app. Or you can tap anywhere on the screen (except for the Play icon in the center of the screen) to access the video trimming (editing) feature, as well as the Share icon and the trash can icon (used to delete the video clip from your iOS device).
>
> To trim a video clip, look at the filmstrip display of the clip located at the top of the screen, and move the left or right editing tabs accordingly to define the portion of the clip you want to edit. The box around the filmstrip display turns yellow, and the Trim command icon appears on the right side of the screen. Before tapping on Trim, tap on the Play icon to preview your newly edited video clip. If it's okay, tap on the Trim icon to save your changes. Two additional command icons will appear, labeled Trim Original and Save As New Clip. Trim Original alters the original video clip and replaces the file, whereas the Save As New Clip option creates a separate file and keeps a copy of the original clip.

COMMANDS FOR EDITING PHOTOS

When you tap on the Edit command icon while viewing a single image in full-screen mode, the following command icons are displayed on the screen. These icons provide the tools for quickly editing and enhancing your image. On the iPhone, these command options are displayed as graphic icons, whereas on the iPad, their purpose is spelled out. The commands available include the following:

- **Rotate**—Tap on this icon once to rotate the image counterclockwise by 90 degrees. You can tap the Rotate icon up to three times before the image returns to its original orientation.

- **Enhance**—Tap on the Auto-Enhance feature to instantly sharpen the photo and make the colors in it more vibrant. You should notice a dramatic improvement in the visual quality, lighting, detail, and sharpness of your image. Once you tap the Auto-Enhance feature, it works automatically.

- **Red-Eye**—If any human subject in your photo is exhibiting signs of red-eye as a result of your using a flash, tap on the Red-Eye icon to digitally remove this unwanted discoloration in your subject's pupils.

- **Crop**—Tap on this icon to crop the image and reposition your subject in the frame. If you forgot to incorporate the Rule of Thirds while shooting a photo, you can sometimes compensate by cropping a photo. You also can cut away unwanted background or zoom in on your subject, based on how you crop it. When the crop grid appears, position your finger in any corner or side of the grid to determine how you'll crop the image. When you're done, tap on the Crop icon to confirm your changes.

> **☑ TIP** If you're cropping an image by moving around the cropping grid using your finger, if you first tap on the Constrain icon, this forces the basic dimensions of your image to stay intact. This allows you to make perfectly sized prints later, without throwing off the image dimensions.

- **Revert to Original**—On this iPad, tapping on this icon instantly removes all your edits and returns the photo to its original appearance.
- **Undo**—On the iPad, if you tap Undo, the last edit you made to the image is undone but any other edits remain intact. On the iPhone, tap the Cancel button.
- **Save**—After you've used the various editing commands to edit or enhance your image, tap on the Save command to save your changes.
- **Cancel**—Tap on this icon to exit the photo-editing mode of the Photos app without making any changes to the photo you're viewing.

PRINTING PHOTOS

iOS 6 is fully compatible with Apple's AirPrint feature, so if you have a photo printer set up to work wirelessly with your iOS device, you can create photo prints from your digital images using the Print command in the Photos app. Follow these steps to print an image:

1. Launch the Photos app from the Home Screen or by tapping on the photo thumbnail in the Camera app.
2. From the main View Images screen, tap on any thumbnail to view an image in full-screen mode. (You might need to open an album first by tapping on the Album's thumbnail, if you have the Albums viewing option selected.)
3. Tap on the full-screen version of the image to make the various command icons appear.
4. Tap on the Share icon.
5. From the Share menu, select the Print option.
6. When the Printer Options submenu appears, select your printer, determine how many copies of the print you'd like to create, and then tap on the Print icon.

MORE INFO   To print wirelessly from your iOS device using the Air-Print feature, you must have a compatible printer. To learn more about AirPrint, and to configure your printer for wireless printing from your iPhone or iPad, visit http://support.apple.com/kb/HT4356.

TIP   Many one-hour photo processing labs (within pharmacies, as well as stores like Wal-Mart or Target), allow you to email photos directly from your iPhone or iPad to their lab, and then be able to pick up prints that same day (often within an hour). There are also photo lab services that have special apps which allow you to select photos stored on your iOS mobile device, upload them to a lab, and then have prints mailed to you within a few days.

Walgreens for iPad, RitzPix, FreePrints, SnapFish, and Kodak Kiosk Connection are among the apps that allow you to order prints directly from your iPhone or iPad.

TIP   When emailing a photo to a lab (or someone who will be print-ing them on their home photo printer), to achieve the best possible prints, send the images in Full Size mode from your iOS device. To do this, after filling in the Email fields and tapping Send, tap on the Actual Size button on the iPhone when the image quality menu appears. On the iPad, tap on the Images option that's displayed to the right of the Front field, and then when the Image Size options appear, tap on the Actual Size tab.

SHARING PHOTOS AND VIDEOS

The Photos app offers several new ways to show off and share your favorite digi-tal images. As you're looking at a photo in full-screen mode on the iPad, tap on the Slideshow icon to create a slideshow of your images and view it on your iPad screen. (You can also connect your tablet to an HD television or monitor to display your slideshow, or connect it to your home theater system via Apple TV.)

On the iPhone, iPod touch, or iPad, to access some of the other ways you can showcase and share your favorite images using the Photos app, tap on the Share icon, and then tap on one of the menu options.

HOW TO EMAIL A PHOTO

From either the iPhone or iPad, when looking at thumbnails for images within an Album, tap on the Edit button to select between one and five images and then tap on the Share icon. Select the Mail option and fill in the To field when prompted. If you want, edit the Subject field and/or add text to the body of the email, and then tap the Send button.

When viewing a single image, tap on the Share button, select Mail, fill in the To field, edit the Subject and, if you want, add text to the body of the message (shown in Figure 11.10), and then tap the Send button.

FIGURE 11.10

You can send an email with one to five photos attached to it from within the Photos app.

ASSIGN A PHOTO TO A CONTACT

To link an image stored in the Photos app to a specific contact in the Contacts app, follow these steps:

1. From within the Photos app, select a single photo and view it in full-screen mode.

2. Tap on the image while in full-screen mode to make the various command icons appear.

3. Tap on the Share icon.

4. Tap on the Assign to Contact option.

5. An All Contacts window, displaying the names associated with all your contacts, will be displayed. Scroll through the listing, or use the Search field to find the specific entry with which you want to associate the photo.

6. Tap on that person's or company's name from the All Contacts listing.

7. When the Choose Photo window opens, use your finger to move or scale the image. What you see in the box is what will be saved.

8. Tap on the Use icon to save the photo and link it to the selected contact.

9. When you launch Contacts and access that person's entry, you will now see the photo you selected appear in that entry.

USE A PHOTO AS A HOME SCREEN OR LOCK SCREEN WALLPAPER IMAGE

See Chapter 2, "Tips and Tricks for Customizing Settings," for information about how to customize your Home Screen and Lock Screen using digital images stored on your iOS device.

TWEET A PHOTO OR PUBLISH A PHOTO ON FACEBOOK

Twitter and Facebook functionality has been integrated into several iOS 6 apps, allowing you to compose and send tweets or Facebook Status Updates from within those apps. Photos is one of the apps that integrates with Twitter and Facebook, allowing you to select a photo and share it with your followers, along with an accompanying text-based message.

To tweet a photo, after tapping the Share icon while viewing a single photo in fullscreen mode, select the Tweet option. Compose your tweet message (which will already have the selected image attached), and then tap the Send icon.

To post a photo to Facebook with an optional text-based message, tap the Facebook button within the Share menu. From the Facebook window (shown in Figure 11.11), tap on Add Location to include where you're sending the posting from, or tap in the lower-right corner of the window to decide which of your Facebook friends will be able to view the photo once it's published.

FIGURE 11.11

From the Photos app on your iPhone or iPad, you can send an image directly to your Facebook page as part of a Status Update.

COPYING A PHOTO

From within the Photos app, you can store a photo in your iOS device's virtual clipboard, and then paste that photo into another compatible app. To copy a photo into your device's virtual clipboard, follow these steps:

1. From within the Photos app, select a single photo and view it in full-screen mode.

2. Tap on the image while in full-screen mode to make the various command icons appear.

3. Tap on the Share icon.

4. Tap on the Copy Photo option. The photo will now be stored in the virtual clipboard.

5. Launch a compatible app and hold your finger down on the screen to use the Paste option and paste your photo from the clipboard into the active app.

DELETING PHOTOS STORED ON YOUR IOS DEVICE

To delete photos stored in the Photos app on the iPad, access the main View Images screen and tap on the Photos tab. Next, tap on the Edit button, select the images to be deleted and tap on the Delete button.

On the iPhone, from the Albums screen, tap on any of the album listings. When the album opens and reveals the thumbnails for the images stored in that album, tap on the Edit button. Select the images to be deleted and then tap on the Delete button.

EDIT YOUR PHOTOS WITH THIRD-PARTY PHOTOGRAPHY APPS

The latest version of the Photos app, introduced with iOS 6, enables you to do some basic edits and enhancements to any photo you snap using your iPhone, iPod touch, or iPad, or that you somehow transfer into your device. If you want vastly more powerful editing tools available to you from your device, be sure to purchase and download the optional iPhoto app ($4.99) from the App Store.

As you explore the Photography section of the App Store, however, you'll find literally hundreds of other apps that can be used to shoot, edit, view, achieve, print and share your digital photos. Some of these apps offer functionality that's not otherwise offered using the Camera, Photos or iPhoto apps.

CREATE AND MANAGE A PHOTO STREAM VIA iCLOUD

You already know that you can easily transfer images into your iOS device and export them from your device using various methods. One feature of iOS 6 is the capability to create and manage a Photo Stream via iCloud.

A Photo Stream enables you to store a collection of up to 1,000 of your digital images on iCloud, and automatically sync those images with your computer(s) and all of your iOS devices, including Apple TV. Thus, your most recent images are always readily available to you, and you never have to worry about backing them up or manually transferring them to a specific computer or device.

To create and use the Photo Stream feature of iCloud, you need to set up a free iCloud account. Then, from within Settings on your iOS device, tap on the iCloud option. Then, turn on the Photo Stream option. To utilize this feature and be able to upload and download photos to and from your iOS device, a Wi-Fi Internet connection is required.

> ☑ **TIP** You can store any image from your Photo Stream on your iOS device indefinitely. As you're viewing an image from your Photo Stream, tap on the Share icon and select the Save To Camera Roll option.

Your Photo Stream will be connected to the Apple ID or email address you linked with your iCloud account.

CREATE AND MANAGE A SHARED PHOTO STREAM VIA iCLOUD

The Photo Stream feature is a tool designed to make it easy for you to sync your latest digital photos between your own computer(s), Apple TV device and iOS mobile devices that are linked to the same Apple ID/iCloud account.

Shared Photo Stream, however, is a tool that allows you to share groups of photos with other people via the Internet (and iCloud). Once you have the Photo Stream feature turned on, as well as an active iCloud account, from the Photos app, tap on Albums and open an Album that contains the images you want to share (or tap on Photos on the iPad to view all photos stored within the Photos app).

Tap the on the Edit button, and then select one or more images. Next, tap on the Share button and select the Photo Stream option. From the Add To A Photo Stream screen, either select an already existing Shared Photo Stream to add the selected photos to, or tap on the New Photo Stream option.

If you create a New Photo Stream, the Photo Stream screen will be displayed. In the To field, enter one or more email addresses for people with whom you want to share the Shared Photo Stream (shown in Figure 11.12). Within the Name field, enter a title for your Shared Photo Stream, and then turn on or off the Public Website option. (If the Public Website option is turned On, anyone who visits www. iCloud.com will potentially be able to view your images.)

Tap on the Next button to continue. You can then add an optional text-based comment to your photo stream. Tap the Post button to publish the Shared Photo Stream online. Within a few minutes, your photos will be uploaded to iCloud and a special website URL will be assigned to them. At the same time, your iOS device will send an email to the recipients you selected and provide them with this unique URL so that they can view your shared images (shown in Figure 11.13).

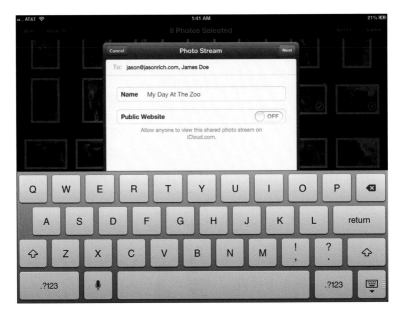

FIGURE 11.12

As you're creating a Shared Photo Stream, you can decide who will be able to see it and send an email to those people that contains a special URL to access those photos.

FIGURE 11.13

The people who you invite to view your images published as part of a Shared Photo Stream will receive an email.

If the recipients are iPhoto '11 (Mac) users or iOS device users, they'll be able to view your images or download them into their iPhoto '11 software or Photos app. Otherwise, they'll just be able to view the photos online by visiting the unique URL assigned to your Shared Photo Stream.

You can create and edit as many Shared Photo Streams as you desire, and make each available to different people, if you choose to. You can also delete a Shared Photo Stream at anytime by tapping on the Photo Stream button within the Photos app, opening a Shared Photo Stream, tapping the Edit button, and then selecting which photos you want to delete. Tap the Delete button to continue. From the Select Photos screen, however, you can also add photos to an existing Shared Photo Stream.

12

MAKE AND RECEIVE CALLS WITH AN iPHONE

Although your iPhone is capable of handling a wide range of tasks, one of its core, fundamental purposes is to serve as a feature-packed cellphone. Your iPhone is capable of making and receiving voice calls using a wireless service provider that you selected when the phone was acquired. The Phone app that comes preinstalled on your iPhone offers a vast selection of calling features that make it easy to stay in touch with people.

> **TIP** If you're an iPad user, you can make and receive Voice over IP (Internet-based) phone calls using the Skype app. These calls can be made to (or received from) any landline or cell phone. You also can participate in Skype-to-Skype calls for free. Skype can also be used for free videoconferencing with Mac, PC, iOS mobile device or

Android mobile device users. (Using FaceTime for video conferencing only works with other Mac or iOS mobile device users.)

The iPhone or iPad version of Skype is also ideal for saving money when you're making international calls from the U.S., or to avoid hefty international roaming charges when you're calling home to the U.S. when traveling overseas.

After you set up and activate your new iPhone with a wireless service provider and choose a calling plan, it's capable of receiving incoming calls and enables you to make outgoing calls using the Phone app.

In the United States, several wireless service providers now offer the iPhone. When you purchase an iPhone, you must decide, in advance, which wireless service provider you'll sign up with (a two-year service agreement with a hefty early termination fee is typically involved).

NOTE It is possible to pay full price for an iPhone to get an unlocked version that works with any compatible wireless service provider, without signing up for a two-year contract, but the purchase price for the phone will be hefty.

Choose a wireless service provider that offers the best coverage area where you'll be using it, the most competitively priced calling plan based on your needs, and the extra features you want or need.

TIP From Apple's website, you can compare iPhone rate plans for wireless service providers that support the iPhone. In the U.S., visit https://static.ips.apple.com.edgekey.net/ipa_preauth/content/catalog/en_US/index.html.

Not all wireless service providers enable iPhone users to talk and surf the Web at the same time. Likewise, some offer better international roaming coverage than others, while some are more generous when it comes to monthly wireless data allocation. When it comes to the iPhone 3GS, iPhone 4, iPhone 4S, or iPhone 5, the iPhone hardware is slightly different based on which wireless service provider you choose, so you can't switch after you've acquired the iPhone.

TIP For your iPhone to make or receive calls, it must be turned on and *not* in Airplane mode. A decent cellular service signal, which is displayed in the upper-left corner of the screen in the form of bars, is also a necessity. The more bars you see (up to five), the stronger the cellular signal (which is based on your proximity to the closest cell towers). For more on Airplane mode, see Chapter 2, "Tips and Tricks for Customizing Settings."

ANSWERING AN INCOMING CALL

Regardless of what you're doing on your iPhone, when an incoming call is received, everything else is put on hold and the Phone app launches, unless the iPhone is turned off or in Airplane mode, in which case calls automatically go to voicemail.

To control the volume of the ringer, press the Volume Up or Volume Down buttons on the side of your iPhone; or to turn off the ringer (which causes the phone to vibrate when an incoming call is received), turn on the Mute button on the side of the iPhone.

> **TIP** While your iPhone is still ringing, to silence the ringer immediately and after five to 10 seconds, send an incoming call to voicemail (without answering it), press the Power button or Volume Up or Volume Down button once. To send the incoming call immediately to voicemail, double tap on the Power button, or tap the Decline icon displayed on the screen.
>
> You can also silence the iPhone's ringer while you're in a meeting or at the theater, for example, by switching on the Mute button (located on the side of the iPhone, above the Volume Up button). Your phone will then vibrate instead of ring when an incoming call is received. To control the Vibrate feature, launch Settings and tap on the Sounds option.

There are several ways to answer an incoming call. If you're doing something else on your iPhone and it starts to ring, the caller ID for the incoming caller appears, along with a green-and-white Answer icon and a red-and-white Decline icon (as shown in Figure 12.1). Tap the Answer icon to answer the call. If you tap Decline or wait too long to answer the call, it will automatically go to voicemail.

If you're using the iPhone 5 with the EarPods that came with it (or you've purchased Apples EarPods separately for your older iPhone model), or you're using Apple's original earbuds or a wireless Bluetooth headset with any iPhone model, you can answer an incoming call by pressing the Answer button on the headset.

Phone Handset Icon

FIGURE 12.1

Your iPhone will notify you when an incoming call is received. You can then answer or decline that call.

iOS 6 **WHAT'S NEW**   There are two new features offered by the Phone app in conjunction with iOS 6 that can be used to manage incoming calls. When you receive an incoming call, displayed to the right of the Decline and Accept buttons (or the Slide To Answer slider on the Lock Screen), you'll see a phone handset icon (refer to Figure 12.1). Place your finger on this icon and flick upwards to reveal two additional command buttons, labeled Reply with Message and Remind Me Later (shown in Figure 12.2).

When you tap on Reply with Message, a menu containing three pre-written text messages, along with a Custom… button will be displayed. Tap on one of the three message buttons to send that message to the caller via text/instant message. Or tap on the Custom… button to type a custom message that will be sent to that caller. (The incoming call will also be transferred to voicemail.)

To customize the three pre-written messages available from the Reply With Message option, launch Settings, tap on the Phone option, and then tap on the Reply With Message option. Displayed on the Reply With Message menu screen (shown in Figure 12.3) are three fields with the default messages, "I'll call you later,"

"I'm on my way," and "What's up?" Tap on one of these fields to replace the default message with your own. The new, pre-created messages display when you access the Reply With Message option anytime an incoming call is received.

The other new option for managing incoming calls is the Remind Me Later option. When you tap on this button, the incoming call is sent to voicemail, but you can quickly set a reminder (and alarm) for yourself to call that person back in one hour, when you leave your current location or when you get home. (For these last two options to function, Locations Services related to the Phone app must be turned on from within Settings.)

FIGURE 12.2

Reply With Message and Remind Me Later are two new ways to manage incoming calls without actually answering them.

If the iPhone is in Sleep mode when an incoming call is received, unlock the phone by swiping your finger from left to right on the Slide to Answer slider, which automatically takes the phone out of Sleep mode, unlocks it, and answers the incoming call (as shown in Figure 12.4). Again, if you ignore the incoming call, it gets sent to voicemail after several rings.

FIGURE 12.3

From within Settings, create your own pre-written messages that can be sent to incoming callers when using the Reply With Message option.

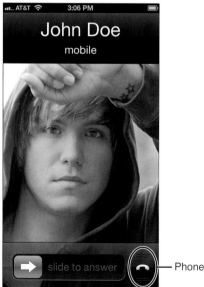

Phone Handset Icon

FIGURE 12.4

If your iPhone is in Sleep mode when a call is received, slide your finger along the Slide to Answer slider to unlock the phone and answer the call.

✓ TIP If you're too busy to answer an incoming call on your iPhone, you can let the call go to voicemail (so that the caller can leave you a message), or you can set up call forwarding so that the incoming call automatically gets rerouted to another phone number, such as your home or office number. To set up call forwarding, and turn this function on or off as needed, launch Settings, and then tap on the Phone option.

From the Phone menu in Settings, you can view your iPhone's phone number, set up and turn on call forwarding, turn on or off call waiting, and decide whether you want your iPhone's number to be displayed on someone's caller ID when you initiate a call.

Also from Settings, you have the option to turn on or off the International Assist feature, which makes initiating international calls much less confusing.

After you answer an incoming call, again you have a few options. You can hold the iPhone up to your ear and start talking, or you can tap the Speaker icon and use your iPhone as a speakerphone (assuming you're not in a public area where doing this will annoy the people around you). You also can use the phone with a wired or wireless headset, which offers hands-free operation. The headset option is ideal when you're driving, plus it offers privacy (versus using the iPhone's speaker phone option). If you're using Apple EarPods or Apple's original earbuds as a phone headset, especially when driving, only insert one ear bud and use them with one ear, not two.

! CAUTION If you're driving, choose a headset that covers only one ear, or use the Speaker option for hands-free operation. Refrain from holding the phone up to your ear or covering both ears with a headset. (See the section, "A Few Thoughts About Wireless Headsets," for headset considerations.) Make sure you're familiar with state and local laws in your area related to the use of cellphones while driving. Some jurisdictions limit or prohibit using a cellphone while driving, even if the phone is a hands-free model, and many other areas across the country are considering similar legislation. If you're on the road a lot and need to use your iPhone to make calls while driving, check with AAA (www.aaa.com) or the Insurance Institute for Highway Safety (www.iihs.org/laws/cellphonelaws.aspx) for information about the laws in other localities where you might be driving.

Many people find it convenient to use a wireless Bluetooth headset with their iPhone. You'll learn more about headsets later in this chapter. When using a Bluetooth headset, you don't need to hold the phone up to your ear to carry on a conversation. If you're using a headset, tap on the headset's answer button when you receive an incoming call to answer it. There's no need to do anything on your iPhone.

As soon as you answer an incoming call, the Phone apps screen will change, giving you access to the Call In Progress screen (shown in Figure 12.5). This screen contains several command icons: Mute, Keypad, Speaker, Add Call, FaceTime, Contacts, and End. At the top of the screen, the caller's information and a call timer are displayed.

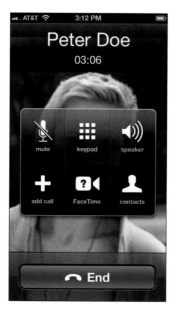

FIGURE 12.5

The main Call In Progress screen on the iPhone appears when you're participating in an incoming or outgoing call.

NOTE When you receive an incoming call, if the caller ID for that caller matches up with a contact stored in your Contacts database (in the Contacts app), that person's name, which number the call is from (Home, Work, Mobile, etc.), and the caller's photo (if you have a photo of that person linked to the contact) are displayed (refer to Figure 12.1).

If there's no match in your Contacts database, the regular caller ID data will be displayed, which might include the person's name, phone number, and the city and state the call is originating from. However, not all incoming calls display all this information.

You could receive calls labeled Private or Unknown; or just the phone number, along with the city and state from which the call is originating, might be listed.

Here's a summary of the command icons available to you from the Call In Progress screen during a phone conversation (after you answer a call or after your outgoing call connects):

▪ **Mute**—Tap on this icon to turn off your iPhone's microphone. You can still hear what's being said to you, but the person you're speaking with cannot hear you. (When you're ready to be heard again, make sure you turn off the Mute feature by tapping on this icon again.)

▪ **Keypad**—Replace the current menu screen with the numeric telephone keypad. This is necessary for navigating your way through voicemail trees (for example, when you're told to press 1 for English, press 2 to speak with an operator, press 3 to connect to a call center, and so on).

▪ **Speaker (or Audio Source)**—Tap the Speaker icon to switch from Handset mode (in which you hold the iPhone up to your ear to have a phone conversation) to Speaker mode, which turns your iPhone into a speakerphone. If you're using your iPhone with a headset, a third Headset option will be listed, and this menu feature will be labeled Audio Source as opposed to Speaker.

▪ **Add Call (+)**—During a conversation with someone, you can initiate a conference call and bring a third party into the conversation by tapping on Add Call. How to do this is described later in this chapter.

▪ **FaceTime**—If the person you're talking to on your iPhone is also calling from an iPhone, and both devices have access to an Internet connection, tap on the FaceTime icon to switch from a traditional phone call to a real-time videoconference using the FaceTime app. You also can initiate a FaceTime call and launch the FaceTime app by tapping on this icon.

NOTE You can participate in FaceTime video conference calls, for free, with iPhone, Mac, iPad, or iPod touch users. For this feature to work, in most cases, your iPhone requires a Wi-Fi Internet connection (although some wireless service providers now allow FaceTime to be used with a 3G/4G connection.) Both parties need to have active FaceTime accounts, and be able to access the FaceTime service using their computer or iOS mobile device when a FaceTime call connection is initiated.

▪ **Contacts**—While you're conversing on the phone, you can access your Contacts database and look up someone's information by tapping on this option.

■ **End**—At any time during a phone conversation, tap on the large red-and-white End button to terminate the call. Or tap the end call button on your headset, if applicable. Unlike when you use a landline phone, you need to tap the End button to end a call after you say goodbye (as opposed to hanging up the receiver on a traditional phone), unless the person you're speaking with disconnects first.

> **TIP** Depending on your wireless service provider, you might be able to participate in a phone conversation and surf the Web at the same time by taking advantage of iOS 6's multitasking capabilities. To launch another app, press the Home button and tap on its app icon from the Home Screen. Or to access the multitasking bar, double-tap on the Home button, and then tap on any app icon that appears in the multitasking bar.
>
> When you view the Home Screen while still on the phone, near the top of the Home Screen will be a green-and-white banner that shows, "Touch to return to call," along with a call timer. Tap on this green bar to return to the Phone app.
>
> Keep in mind that your phone conversation can continue while you're using other apps. While some wireless service providers enable you to talk and web surf at the same time, others don't. Even if this is the case, you can still access and use other iPhone apps during a phone conversation. (In some cases, you can talk and surf the web at the same time using only a Wi-Fi connection, not a 3G/4G connection.)

RESPOND TO A CALL WAITING SIGNAL WHILE ON THE PHONE

As you're chatting it up with the person you're speaking with on the phone, if you have the Call Waiting feature turned on (it's controllable from the Settings app), and if someone else tries to call you, you hear a call waiting tone, and a related message appears on your iPhone's screen.

> **TIP** When you accept a second incoming call via Call Waiting, the command icons on your iPhone change. You can merge the two calls by tapping on the Merge Calls icon (creating a three-way conference call) or using the Swap icon to switch between calls (always keeping one party on hold). This is much easier to do when you're using a corded headset (EarPods), wireless Bluetooth headset, or a hands-free car kit, so you can talk while looking at the iPhone's screen.

The second caller's caller ID information will be displayed on the screen, along with several command icons and buttons. Here's what each of these commands is used for:

- **Ignore**—Disregard the incoming call (send it to voicemail) and continue speaking with the person you're already on the phone with.
- **Hold Call + Answer**—Place the person you're speaking with on hold and answer the new, incoming call. You can then switch back to the original conversation, or merge the two calls and create a conference call.
- **End Call + Answer**—Disconnect from the person you're speaking with and answer the new, incoming call.
- **Reply with Message**—Send the caller a pre-written text message, and send the call to voicemail.
- **Remind Me Later**—Set a reminder for yourself to call the person back, and send the call to voicemail.

> **TIP** When the call waiting signal goes off on your iPhone, typically only you will hear it. Thus, the person you're speaking with on the other end of the line will not know you've received another call. So before tapping Hold Call + Answer or End Call + Answer, be sure to tell the person you were originally speaking with what's going on.

If you select the Hold Call + Answer option, the original person you were speaking with is placed on hold, and you'll be connected to the call waiting caller. The Call In Progress screen will show a Merge Calls and a Swap Calls button (shown in Figure 12.6). Tap on Merge Calls to bring both parties together and speak with everyone at the same time, or tap on Swap in order to switch back and forth between calls (always leaving one party on hold).

While engaged in a conference call on your iPhone, the names of the parties you're speaking with (or their caller ID phone numbers) are displayed near the top of the screen (shown in Figure 12.7). Tap on the > icon to the right of the names to reveal a new screen that enables you to place either party in the conference call on hold. To reestablish the conference call, tap on the Merge Calls icon again.

While you're engaged in a three-way call (with two other parties), you can tap on the Add Call option again to add more parties to the conference call.

FIGURE 12.6

If you accept a call waiting call, you can merge the two calls together or switch between them.

Use the > icon to manage calls during a conference call

FIGURE 12.7

When you're engaged in a conference call, you can place one party on hold and continue speaking with the other parties by tapping on the > icon displayed near the top-right corner of the screen.

MAKING CALLS FROM YOUR iPHONE

There are several ways to initiate a phone call from your iPhone; however, you typically must first launch the Phone app. Then, you can do the following:

- Dial a number manually using the keypad.
- Access a listing from your Contacts database (from within the Phone app), choose a number, and dial it.
- Use Siri (which is explained in Chapter 5, "Using Siri and Dictation to Interact with Your iOS Device"). This can be done anytime, regardless of what app is running on your iPhone (or if you're looking at the Home Screen, for example).
- Redial a number from your Recents call log.
- Select and dial a phone number from the Phone app's Favorites list.
- Redial a number used by someone who left you a voicemail message
- Dial a number displayed in another compatible app, such as Maps, Mail, Safari, or Contacts. When you tap on the phone number, it dials that number and initiates a call using the Phone app.

MANUAL DIALING

To initiate a call by manually dialing a phone number, follow these steps:

1. Launch the Phone app from the Home Screen.
2. Tap on the Keypad icon displayed at the bottom of the screen (as shown in Figure 12.8).
3. Using the numeric phone keypad, dial the number you want to reach, including the area code. (If you're making an international call, include the country code as well.)
4. If you make a mistake when entering a digit, tap the Backspace key displayed to the right of the Call button.
5. When the 10-digit phone number is entered and displayed at the top of the screen, tap the green-and-white Call button to initiate the call. If you're making an international call, entering additional digits will be required.
6. The display on the iPhone will change. A "Calling" message is displayed until the call connects, at which time the Call Menu screen is displayed.

FIGURE 12.8

A telephone numeric keypad appears when you tap on the Keypad option (displayed at the bottom of the screen) within the Phone app.

✓ **TIP** You can use Siri to dial a phone number. To do this, activate Siri and say, "Dial 2 1 2 5 5 5 1 2 1 2," speaking each digit.

📝 **NOTE** As you enter a phone number using the keypad, if that number is already stored in your Contacts database (within the Contacts app), the person's name automatically displays at the top of the screen, just below the phone number you entered.

You can also use the Cut, Copy, and Paste features of iOS 6 to copy a phone number displayed in another app, and then paste it into the phone number field on the Keypad screen. Or, if you tap on a phone number that's displayed within the Contacts app or while surfing the web using Safari, for example, the Phone app will automatically launch and a call to that number will be initiated. (In Safari, you'll need to confirm your request.)

DIALING FROM A CONTACTS ENTRY IN THE PHONE APP

From within the Phone app, you can look up any phone number stored in your personal Contacts database that's associated with the Contacts app. The Phone and Contacts apps work nicely together on your iPhone. To use this feature, follow these steps:

1. Launch the Phone app from the Home Screen.

2. Tap on the Contacts icon displayed at the bottom of the screen.

3. An alphabetized listing of the contacts stored in the Contacts app will be displayed. At the top of the screen is a blank Search field. Using your finger, either scroll through the alphabetized list of contacts or use the iPhone's virtual keyboard to find a stored listing.

4. Tap on any listing to view its complete Contacts entry. This might include multiple phone numbers, such as Home, Work, and Mobile. From a contact's entry screen, tap on the phone number you want to dial.

5. The display on the iPhone will change. A "Calling" message is displayed until the call connects, at which time the Call Menu screen is displayed.

USE SIRI TO INITIATE CALLS

After you have added entries into your Contacts database using the Contacts app, you can use Siri feature to dial someone's phone number by speaking into the iPhone.

To use Siri to initiate a call, activate the Siri feature, and when you hear the audio prompt, say, "Call [insert name] at [insert location, such as home or work]," or "Call mom on her cell."

The first time you refer to your mom, dad, or grandma, for example, Siri will ask you who that person is, so that person can be matched up with their Contacts entry. Siri then remembers this information, so when you say, "Call dad at work," Siri knows exactly who you're talking about. This information can also be entered manually within the Contacts app by filling in the Related People field.

Using Siri, you can also say, "Dial," and then speak the digits of a phone number to initiate a call.

INITIATING A CONFERENCE CALL

During a typical phone conversation with one other person, you can initiate a conference call and bring a third party into the call. To do this, from the Call In Progress screen, tap on the Add Call (+) icon. The Call In Progress screen will be replaced by the All Contacts screen (which includes a listing of all contacts stored in your Contacts database), as well as a blank Search field.

You can either look up the phone number you want to add to your conference call or tap on the Keypad icon (displayed at the bottom of the screen) to manually enter the phone number. When you do this, the Call In Progress screen changes slightly. The Add Call and FaceTime command icons are replaced by Merge Calls and Swap icons. During this process, the person you were speaking with will be placed on hold. Tap Merge Calls to make both calls active and initiate the conference call. Or tap Swap to switch between calls, one at a time.

MANAGING YOUR VOICEMAIL

Your unique iPhone phone number, provided by your wireless service provider, comes with voicemail, which allows people to leave you messages if you're not able to speak with them when they call.

Just as with any voicemail service, you can record your outgoing message, play back missed messages from your iPhone, or call your iPhone's voicemail service and listen to your calls from another phone.

RECORD YOUR OUTGOING MESSAGE

To record your outgoing voicemail message, which is what people will hear when they call your iPhone and you don't answer, follow these steps. Or you can have a computer-generated voice instruct callers to leave a message.

1. Launch the Phone app from the Home Screen.

2. Tap on the Voicemail icon, displayed in the lower-right corner of the screen.

3. In the upper-left corner of the Voicemail screen (shown in Figure 12.9), tap on the Greeting icon.

4. From the Greeting screen, tap on the Default option to skip recording a message and have a computer voice use a generic message. Or tap on the Custom option to record your own outgoing voicemail message.

5. After you tap the Custom option, it will be highlighted in blue. Tap on the Record icon that's displayed in the lower-right corner of the Greeting screen. Hold the phone up to your mouth and begin recording your message.

6. A sample message might say, "Hello, you've reached [insert your name]. I am not available right now, but please leave your name and phone number, and I will return your call as soon as possible. Thank you for calling."

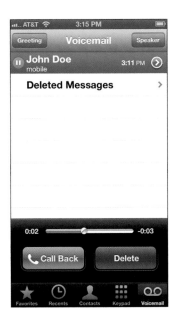

FIGURE 12.9

The Voicemail screen on the iPhone. From here, you can listen to your messages or choose to record an outgoing greeting.

7. When you're done recording, tap on the Record button again. You can now play back your message by tapping on the Play icon, or tap on the Save icon (displayed in the upper-right corner of the screen) to save your message and activate it.

HOW TO PLAY AND DELETE VOICEMAIL MESSAGES

If you receive an incoming call that you either missed or opted to avoid answering (such as that dreaded call from your mother-in-law or a bill collector), you can listen to the voicemail message the caller left, either from your iPhone or by calling your iPhone's voicemail from another phone.

LISTEN TO VOICEMAIL FROM YOUR iPHONE

From your iPhone, to listen to and then save or delete an incoming voicemail message, follow these steps:

1. Launch the Phone app from the Home Screen.
2. Tap on the Voicemail icon that's displayed in the bottom-right corner of the screen.

3. Under the Voicemail heading seen at the top of the screen will be a listing of missed voicemail messages (refer to Figure 12.9). Tap on any of the messages to highlight it.

> **NOTE** When you see a blue dot to the left of a voicemail message listing, this indicates it's a new, unheard message. After you listen to the message, the blue dot disappears. When you tap on the message to listen to it, the blue dot will transform into a Pause/Play icon.

4. Near the bottom of the screen, you will see a slider that depicts the length of the message, along with Call Back and Delete icons.

5. After a message is highlighted, tap on the small play/pause icon that appears to the left of the message listing. The message will begin playing. It might, however, take a few seconds for the message to load. A brief pause should be expected.

6. As your message plays, the dot on the timer slider near the bottom of the screen moves to the right. You can listen to parts of the message again by moving this slider around with your finger.

7. When you're done listening to the message, you can leave the listing alone (which keeps the message saved on your phone), or you can tap the Delete icon to erase it. You also have the option to call back the person who left the message by tapping on the Call Back icon.

8. To exit the voicemail options, tap on any of the other command icons displayed at the bottom of the Phone app's screen, or press the Home button on your iPhone.

> **TIP** You might find it easier to listen to your voicemail messages via speaker phone, by first tapping on the Speaker icon in the upper-right corner of the voicemail screen.

> **TIP** If you accidentally delete an important voicemail, don't panic. From the voicemail screen, scroll to the very bottom of your voicemail message list and tap on the Deleted Messages icon. Tap on the message you want to undelete to highlight it, and then tap on the Undelete icon.

LISTEN TO YOUR iPHONE'S VOICEMAIL FROM ANOTHER PHONE

You also have the option to use another phone to call your iPhone's voicemail service and listen to the messages that were left. Follow these steps:

1. From any other phone besides your iPhone (including a landline or another cellphone), dial your iPhone's phone number.

2. When your iPhone's voicemail picks up, press the * key on the phone you're calling from.

3. When prompted by the computer voice, enter the numeric password that's associated with your voicemail.

> ☑ **TIP** To set or change your voicemail password, launch the Settings app and tap on the Phone option. From the Phone menu in Settings, scroll down to the Change Voicemail Password option and tap on it. When the Password screen appears, use the keypad to create and enter a password. To change a password, first enter your current password, tap Done, and then enter a new voicemail password.

4. Follow the voice prompts to listen to or delete your messages.

5. As you're listening to your messages:
   - Press 1 to play back your messages.
   - Press 5 to hear details about a message, including the incoming phone number and the time/date it was recorded, as well as the message length.
   - Press 7 to delete the current message.
   - Press 9 to save the message.
   - Press # to skip the current message.
   - Press 0 for more options.

6. Hang up when you're finished listening to your voicemail messages.

CREATE AND USE A FAVORITES LIST

From within the Phone app, you can create a Favorites list, which is a customized list of your most frequently dialed contacts. To access this list, launch the Phone app, and then tap on the Favorites icon that's displayed near the bottom-left corner of the screen.

To add a contact to the Favorites list, tap on the plus-sign (+) icon that you see in the upper-right corner of the screen. Select any listing from your Contacts database and tap on it. When the complete listing for that entry appears, tap on the specific phone number you want listed in your Favorites list. The newly created Favorites listing appears at the end of your Favorites list.

> **TIP** Each favorites entry can have one name and one phone number associated with it. So, if a Contact entry has multiple phone numbers listed, choose one. Or, if you want quick access to someone's home, work, and mobile number from your Favorites list, create three separate entries for that person. When you create the entry in Favorites, the type of phone number it is (Home, Work, Mobile, iPhone, and so on) is displayed to the right of the person's name. A Favorites listing can also relate to someone's FaceTime identifier (their iPhone number, Apple ID, or the email address they used to set up their FaceTime account.)

To edit the contacts already listed in your Favorites list, tap on the Edit icon in the upper-left corner of the screen. After tapping Edit, you can change the order of your Favorites list by holding your finger on the rightmost icon next to a listing, and then dragging it upward or downward to the desired location. Or you can delete a listing by tapping on the red-and-white negative-sign icon displayed to the left of a listing. When you're finished making changes, tap on the Done icon that's displayed in the upper-left corner of the screen.

> **TIP** As you're viewing your Favorites list, tap on the blue-and-white right-pointing arrow icon. You'll see it to the right of each listing. This enables you to view that person's entire entry from within your Contacts database.

To dial a phone number listed in your Favorites list, simply tap on its listing. The Phone app automatically dials the number and initiates a call.

ACCESSING YOUR RECENTS CALL LOG

The Phone app on your iPhone automatically keeps track of all incoming and outgoing calls. To access this detailed call log, launch the Phone app from the Home Screen, and then tap on the Recents command icon displayed at the bottom of the screen.

At the top of the Recents screen are two command tabs, labeled All and Missed, along with an Edit command icon. Tap on the All tab to view a detailed listing of all incoming and outgoing calls, displayed in reverse-chronological order. Missed incoming calls are displayed in red. Tap on the Missed tab to see a listing of calls you didn't answer. Tap on the Edit icon to delete specific calls from this listing.

> **TIP** Missed calls will also be displayed in the Notification Center window on your iPhone or as an icon badge or alert on your Home Screen, depending on how you set up Notifications for the Phone app within the Settings app. To customize the Notifications options for the Phone app, launch Settings from the Home Screen and tap on the Notifications option. From the Notifications screen in Settings, tap on the Phone option. You can adjust how your iPhone alerts you to missed calls by personalizing the options on this Phone screen.

Each listing in the Recents call log displays the name of the person you spoke with (based on data from your Contacts database or the Caller ID feature) or their phone number. If it's someone from your Contacts database, information about which phone number (home, work, mobile, or such) the caller used appears below the name.

If the same person called you, or you called that person, multiple times in a row, a number in parentheses indicates how many calls were made to or from that person. This is displayed to the right of the name or phone number.

On the right side of the screen, with each Recents listing, is the time the call was made or received. To view the Contacts entry related to that person, tap on the right-pointing blue-and-white arrow icon that's associated with the listing. At the top of a contact's entry screen are details about the call itself, including its time and date, whether it was an incoming or outgoing call, and its duration.

To call someone back who is listed in the Recents list, tap anywhere on that listing, except for on the blue-and-white arrow icon.

DO YOU TALK TOO MUCH? KEEPING TRACK OF USAGE

Every iPhone voice plan comes with a predetermined number of talk minutes per month. Some plans offer unlimited night and weekend calling, but calls made or received during the day count against your monthly minute allocation.

> **CAUTION** Contact your wireless service provider (or read your service agreement carefully) to determine the time period that's considered prime daytime, versus night or weekend, as it varies greatly. Unlimited night and weekend calling does not start until 9:00 p.m. with some wireless service providers. If you have a truly unlimited calling plan, however, this is not a concern.

To keep track of your monthly usage, launch the Settings app and tap on the General option. From the General screen within Settings, scroll down to the Usage option and tap on it. Scroll to the bottom of the Usage screen, and tap on the Cellular Usage option.

Or for the exact number of minutes used thus far during the current billing period, contact your wireless service provider by phone or via the company's website. If you go over your monthly minute allocation, you will be charged a hefty surcharge for each additional minute used.

> **TIP** Each of the wireless service providers that support the iPhone offer a free app for managing your wireless service account. It's available from the App Store. Use it to manage all aspects of your account, pay your monthly bill, and view your voice, data, and text-messaging use at any time. You can also set the alert option in the app to remind you each month when the bill is due for payment.

CUSTOMIZING RINGTONES

Thanks to the iTunes Store, you can purchase and download custom ringtones for your iPhone. You can use one ringtone as your generic ringtone for all incoming calls, or you can assign specific ringtones to individual people.

> **TIP** To shop for ringtones, launch Settings, select Sounds, and from the Sounds menu screen, tap on the Ringtone option. Tap on the Store button that's displayed near the top-right corner of the Ringtone menu screen (within Settings).
>
> When you purchase and download a new ringtone, it becomes available on your iPhone's internal ringtones list. Most ringtones from the iTunes Store cost $1.29 each.

To choose a default ringtone that you'll hear for all your incoming calls, launch Settings and select the Sounds option. From the Sounds menu screen, scroll down to the Ringtone option and tap on it. A complete listing of ringtones stored on your iPhone is displayed (as shown in Figure 12.10).

iOS 6 comes with more than two dozen ringtones preinstalled that you can choose from. From the Ringtones screen in Settings, tap on a ringtone to listen to it and select it as your new default. Or, at the top of this screen, tap on the Store button to shop for more via the iTunes Store (an Internet connection is required).

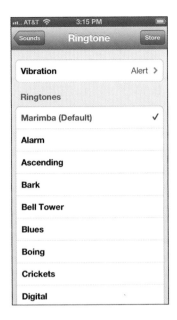

FIGURE 12.10

The Ringtones listing on your iPhone displays more than two dozen preinstalled ringtones, plus any ringtones you purchase and download from the iTunes Store.

CUSTOM RINGTONES FOR SPECIFIC CONTACTS

To assign a custom ringtone to a specific person so that you hear it when that person calls your iPhone, follow these steps:

1. Launch the Contacts app from the iPhone's Home Screen.

2. From the All Contacts screen, find the specific contact with whom you want to link a custom ringtone. You can scroll through the listing or use the Search field to find a contact.

3. When the contact is selected and you're looking at that Contacts entry, tap the Edit icon that's displayed in the upper-right corner of the screen.

4. From the Info screen that displays that contact entry's data, scroll down to the Ringtone field and tap on it.

5. When the Ringtone screen appears, select a specific ringtone from the list that you want to assign to the contact and tap on it. You can choose a specific song (purchased from iTunes) or ringer sound that reminds you of that person.

6. Tap on the Save icon to save your selection and return to the contact's Info screen. Tap on the Done icon to save your changes.

7. When that contact calls you, the ringtone you hear will be the one you just linked to that contact (as opposed to the default ringtone).

A FEW THOUGHTS ABOUT WIRELESS HEADSETS

Many states have outlawed using a cellphone while driving unless you have a wireless headset or hands-free feature on your phone. Although the speakerphone feature of your iPhone counts as a hands-free feature, to ensure the best possible call quality while you're driving, invest in a wireless Bluetooth headset.

Not only can you use a wireless Bluetooth headset while driving, but you can keep it on your person throughout the day and use it whenever you make or receive calls using your iPhone. This allows you to keep your hands free while you're talking, or to easily access other apps or iPhone features during a phone conversation. If you invest in only one accessory for your iPhone, and you plan to use the iPhone to make and receive phone calls, a wireless Bluetooth headset is a worthwhile investment (although a good-quality iPhone case is also highly recommended).

Bluetooth wireless headsets are priced as low as $20 but can cost as much as $200. If you want to ensure the highest-quality phone conversations possible, so that people can hear you and you can hear them, even if there's background noise present, invest in a good-quality Bluetooth wireless headset that includes a noise-canceling microphone and a good-quality speaker. Plus, choose a headset that's comfortable to wear and that has a long battery life.

Although you have literally hundreds of wireless Bluetooth headsets to choose from, some of the best ones on the market, that work perfectly with an iPhone, are available from a company called Jawbone (www.Jawbone.com). Jawbone has several wireless Bluetooth headset models available, including the Jawbone Era ($129.99) and Jawbone Icon ($99.99). Both models are available online, at stores like Best Buy, or wherever cellphone accessories are sold.

TIP The first time you use a wireless Bluetooth headset (or any Bluetooth device) with your iPhone, you must turn on the Bluetooth feature on your phone and then "pair" the device with your iPhone. To prepare your iPhone for this, launch the Settings app, tap on the General menu option, and from the General menu screen, tap on the Bluetooth option.

Turn on the virtual switch associated with the Bluetooth option, and then follow the "pairing" directions that came with your headset to finish the process. Your headset then appears under the Devices heading on the Bluetooth screen within Settings, and the Bluetooth icon is displayed in the upper-right corner of the screen, next to the battery life indicator.

13

USE NEW SAFARI FEATURES TO SURF MORE EFFICIENTLY

Chances are, if you know how to use a Mac or PC, you already know how to surf the Web using a browser such as Safari, Microsoft Internet Explorer, Firefox, or Google Chrome, for example, on your computer.

The Safari web browser on your iPhone (shown in Figure 13.1) or iPad (shown in Figure 13.2) offers the same basic functionality as the web browser for your desktop or laptop computer, but it's designed to maximize the iPhone or iPad's touchscreen and screen size.

FIGURE 13.1

The main screen of the Safari web browser on the iPhone 5.

FIGURE 13.2

The main screen of the Safari web browser on the iPad.

With the release of iOS 6, Apple enhanced the Safari app, giving it a handful of new features that make web surfing a more enjoyable, secure, and efficient experience.

WHAT'S NEW Three of the many new or enhanced features added to the iOS 6 version of Safari are iCloud tabs (for syncing open web browsers); the capability to create, manage, and access a Reading List (even when offline); and the capability to send tweets or Facebook updates directly from within Safari. Plus, the iOS 6 version of Safari continues to fully integrate with iCloud, so all of your saved bookmarks can automatically be synced with the web browser on your primary computer, as well as with your other iOS devices.

As you'd expect from your iPhone or iPad, surfing the Web using the Safari app is a highly customizable experience. For example, you can hold your device in Portrait or Landscape mode while surfing.

On most websites, you can also zoom in on or zoom out of specific areas or elements, such as a paragraph of text or a photo, using the reverse-pinch finger gesture (to zoom in) or the pinch gesture (to zoom out), or by double-tapping on a specific area of the screen to zoom in or out.

Although many improvements have been made to the web-surfing capabilities of Safari on the iPhone and iPad, what's still missing is Adobe Flash compatibility. Adobe Flash is a website programming language used to generate many of the slick animations you see on websites. Unfortunately, these animations won't be visible when you access a Flash-based website using the iOS version of Safari.

If you want limited Flash compatibility on your iPhone or iPad, try using a third-party web browser app, such as Photon Flash Web Browser for iPhone ($3.99) or Photon Flash Web Browser for iPad ($4.99). Both versions are available from the App Store and offer compatibility with some (but not all) Flash-based content you'll encounter on the Web.

TIP Using your voice, you can instruct Siri to find information for you on the Web. For example, after activating Siri, = say, "Find me information about [insert topic]." Siri will respond, "If you'd like, I can search the web for [insert topic]." Respond "yes" to initiate an online search.

Or you can instruct Siri to "Find [insert topic] on the web," and Siri automatically launches Safari and initiate a search. The relevant search engine listings are displayed on your iPhone's screen. When speaking with Siri, you're also able to mention a website by name. For example, you can say, "Find www dot Jason Rich dot com" to find search engine listings for my website.

✅ TIP If you see a photo or graphic that you like when surfing the web, to save it within the Camera Roll folder of the Photos app, place and hold your finger on it for a second or two. When the Save Image button appears, tap on it. You also have the option to Copy the image to the virtual clipboard built into iOS 6. Once the content is copied into the clipboard, you can paste it into another app.

CUSTOMIZE YOUR WEB SURFING EXPERIENCE

If you have iOS 6 running on your iPhone or iPad, the latest version of Safari is already available to you from the Home Screen. However, you can customize your web surfing experience at any time from within Settings.

To do this, launch Settings from the Home Screen, and then tap on the Safari option. When the Safari menu screen appears (as shown in Figure 13.3), you'll see a handful of customizable menu options. Here's a summary of what each is used for:

■ **Search Engine**—As you use Safari, in the upper-right corner of the screen is a blank Search field, which is used to find what you're looking for on the Web via a search engine, such as Google, Yahoo!, or Bing. This option enables you to select your default (favorite) Internet search engine. So if you select Google as your default, whenever you perform a search using Safari's Search field, the browser automatically accesses Google to obtain your search results.

FIGURE 13.3

Customize your web surfing experience when using Safari from within Settings on your iOS device.

> **☑ TIP** Regardless of which Internet search engine (Google, Yahoo!, or Bing) you select to be your default from within the Settings app, you can always add the other two (or any other search engine) to your Bookmarks or Bookmarks Bar, so that you can access the other search engines directly, by pointing Safari to www.Google.com, www.Yahoo.com, www.Bing.com, and so on.

▪ **AutoFill**—One of the more tedious aspects of surfing the Web is constantly having to fill in certain types of data fields, such as your name, address, phone number, and email address.

This feature, when turned on, remembers your responses, and automatically inserts the data into the appropriate fields. It also pulls information from your own contacts entry in the Contacts app. To customize this option and link your personal contact entry to Safari, tap on the AutoFill option, turn on the Use Contact Info option (as shown in Figure 13.4), and then tap on My Info to select your contact entry in Contacts. You can also set whether Safari remembers usernames and passwords for specific websites you visit.

FIGURE 13.4

To avoid constantly having to enter your personal info when you visit various websites, link your own contact entry in Contacts to Safari from within the Settings app.

- **Open Links (iPhone only)**—Instead of using onscreen tabs, Safari on the iPhone creates separate windows for each web page that's open. You can quickly switch between viewing open web pages by tapping on the Pages icon that's displayed in the lower-right corner of the Safari screen.

- **Open New Tabs in Background (iPad only)**—When turned on, this feature enables you to open up new web pages in separate tabs while remaining on the web page you're currently viewing. Then, when you're ready, you can tap on the other tab(s) to view the additional websites.

- **Always Show Bookmarks Bar (iPad only)**—This feature enables you to constantly display your Bookmarks Bar as you use Safari so that your favorite websites are literally only one tap away. Although this feature adds convenience and speed to your web browsing experience, it also takes up one line of valuable onscreen real estate. When it's turned off, the Bookmarks Bar is displayed automatically anytime you manually enter a website URL into the Address field, or when you use the Search field. It then disappears from the screen.

- **Private Browsing**—By default, Safari automatically keeps track of every website you visit in the History folder (which is accessible from the Bookmarks icon). It also remembers data you type into certain data fields on websites when you use AutoFill. If you turn on Private Browsing, however, none of this information gets saved on your iPhone or iPad. Thus, it becomes much more difficult (although not impossible) for someone to track what you've been doing on the Web. So if you're concerned about privacy, consider turning on this feature.

- **Accept Cookies**—Many websites use cookies to remember who you are and your personalized preferences when you're visiting that site. This is actually data that gets saved on your iPhone or iPad but that's accessible by the websites you revisit. When this option is turned on, Safari accepts cookies from websites you visit, or whenever a cookie is supplied (based on the option you select). When it's turned off, this information will not be saved. Thus, you will need to reenter specific information, such as your username and password or particular preferences, each time you visit that site.

- **Clear History**—Using this feature, you can delete the contents of Safari's History folder that stores details about all the websites you have visited.

- **Clear Cookies and Data**—Use this command to delete all cookies related to websites you've visited that Safari has stored on your iOS device.

- **Use Cellular Data**—This option allows your iPhone or iPad to use the cellular data service (as opposed to a Wi-Fi Internet connection) to download Reading List information to your device so that it can be read offline. While this feature is convenient, it also utilizes some of your monthly wireless data allocation, which is why there's an on/off option associated with it.

- **Fraud Warning**—This feature helps prevent you from visiting impostor websites designed to look like real ones, which have been created for the purpose of committing fraud or identity theft. It's not foolproof, but keeping this feature turned on gives you an added level of protection, especially if you use your iOS device for online banking and other financial transactions.

- **JavaScript**—Some website designers use a programming language called JavaScript to control the functionality of a website. You can turn off this feature, which in turn will limit what some websites you visit will do. However, for the ordinary person, leaving the JavaScript feature turned on is fine. You might want to turn off this feature to reduce the amount of wireless data you use when connected to the Internet with a 3G/4G connection, if you have a monthly allocation.

- **Block Pop-ups**—When turned on, this feature prevents a website you're visiting from creating and displaying extra windows or opening a bunch of unwanted browser pages. The default for this option is turned on. You will probably enjoy your web surfing experience more if you leave it that way.

- **Advanced**—In addition to the History folder and cookies, Safari maintains information about sites you've visited in a Website Data folder, which you can delete manually by tapping on the Advanced option, followed by the Website Data option. At the bottom of the Website Data screen, tap on the red-and-white Remove All Website Data icon to delete this content. (Or access this file to determine which websites someone else has visited while using your device.)

> **TIP** As you make changes within Settings relating to Safari, they are automatically saved, and those changes take effect the next time you launch the Safari app. When you're finished customizing the Safari app in Settings, press the Home button to exit Settings and return to the Home Screen.

HOW TO USE TABBED BROWSING WITH SAFARI

Safari's Title bar contains the various command icons used to navigate the Web. On the iPhone, it's divided into two sections that are constantly displayed along the top and bottom of the Safari screen. At the top of the Safari screen on the iPhone, you'll see the Address bar and the Search field. Along the bottom of the screen, the Left and Right navigation icons, along with the Share, Bookmarks, and Open Links icons, are displayed.

If you're using Safari on an iPad, the Title bar also displays all of Safari's command icons along the top of the screen. Immediately below the Title bar, if you have the option turned on, your personalized Bookmarks Bar will be displayed. Below the Bookmarks Bar, the Tabs bar becomes visible if you have more than one web page loaded in Safari at any given time.

SWITCHING BETWEEN WEB PAGES ON AN iPHONE

The iPhone version of "tabbed browsing" involves Safari opening separate browser windows for each active web page. By tapping on the Pages icon that's constantly displayed near the bottom-right corner of the Safari screen, you can quickly switch between browser windows (shown in Figure 13.5) by flicking your finger on the screen from right to left or left to right.

FIGURE 13.5

On the iPhone, after tapping the Pages icon, swipe your finger left to right or right to left to switch between multiple web browser windows that can simultaneously be loaded in Safari.

When you're viewing the Pages screen, tap on the New Page icon (displayed in the lower-left corner of the screen) to create a new (empty) browser window and then manually surf to a new website (by typing a URL into the Address bar, using the Search field, or selecting a saved bookmark).

> **TIP** On an iPhone, up to eight browser windows can be open simultane-
> ously. On an iPad, you can create up to nine browser window tabs.

Tap the Done button (displayed in the lower-right corner of the screen) to exit the
Open Links screen and return to the main Safari web browser screen. Or tap on one
of the web page thumbnails as you scroll through them on the Pages screen.

TABBED BROWSING ON THE iPAD

When you tap on a link in a web page that causes a new web page to automatically open, a new tab in Safari is created and displayed (shown in Figure 13.6).

Open Safari Browser Tabs

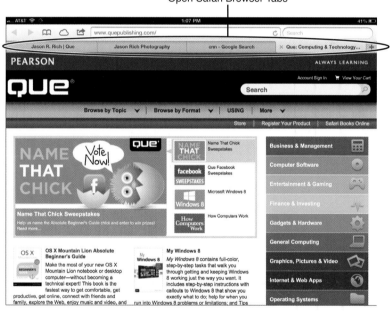

FIGURE 13.6
*Instead of separate windows, Safari on the iPad uses onscreen tabs that enable you to instantly
switch between web pages that are simultaneously open.*

As you're viewing a web page, you can simultaneously open another web page
by tapping on the plus icon that is displayed to the extreme right of the Tab bar.
When you do this, a new tab is created, and you can visit a new web page without
closing the previous page.

Along the Tab bar on the iPad, you can have multiple web pages accessible at once. Simply by tapping on a tab, you can instantly switch between web pages. To close a tab, tap on the small x that appears on the left side of that tab.

DISCOVER THE NEW iCLOUD TABS FEATURE OF SAFARI

You already know that iCloud can be set up to sync app-specific data between your iPhone, iPad, Mac(s) and PC(s) that are linked to the same iCloud (Apple ID) account. In addition to syncing your Safari Bookmarks, Bookmark Bar and Reading List information, the iOS 6 version of Safari also syncs, in real-time, your open browser windows.

Thus, if you're surfing the web on your Mac and have one or more browser windows open, you can pick up your iPhone or iPad, tap on the iCloud Tabs option, and then open that same browser window(s) on your mobile device (or vice versa), without having to re-enter the webpage's URL.

On the iPhone, to access the iCloud Tabs feature and view the browser windows open on your computer(s) and/or other mobile devices that are linked to the same iCloud account, tap on the Bookmarks icon and then select the iCloud Tabs option.

On the iPad, the iCloud icon is displayed along the Title Bar, in between the Bookmarks and Share icons. When you tap on the iCloud Tabs option, a separate screen (iPhone) or window (iPad) appears that lists open browser window on each computer or device. Tap on a listing to open that browser window on the device you're using.

> **! CAUTION**   With this feature turned on, as you're surfing the web on your iPhone or iPad, someone can literally follow along and see what web pages you're visiting in real-time online by tapping on the iCloud Tabs option while using Safari on your computer.

REMOVE SCREEN CLUTTER WITH SAFARI READER

Safari Reader works on the iPhone and iPad and enables you to select a compatible website page; strip out graphic icons, ads, and other unwanted elements that cause onscreen clutter; and then read just the text (and view related photos) from that web page on your iOS device's screen.

The Safari Reader works only with compatible websites, including those published by major daily newspapers and other news organizations. If the feature is available while you're viewing a web page, a Reader button (as shown in Figure 13.7) is displayed next to that web page's URL in the Address field of Safari.

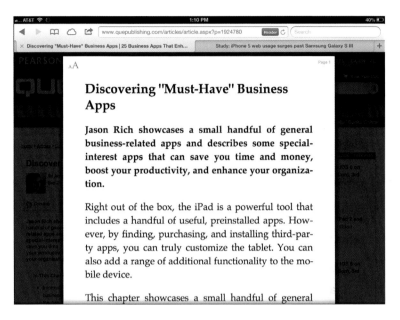

FIGURE 13.7
When you see a Reader button appear in the Address bar of Safari, you can open that content in the Reader window and view it clutter free.

When you see the Reader button displayed, tap on it. An uncluttered screen (iPhone) or window (iPad) that contains just the article or text from that web page, along with related photos, is displayed. Use your finger to scroll up or down.

In the upper-left corner of the Reader window, tap on the aA icon to increase or decrease the size of the onscreen text. To exit the Reader window and return to the main web page, tap anywhere in the margins of the screen, outside the Reader window.

> **TIP** Tap on the Share icon in the Reader window (or Safari's Title bar) to add the article to your Reading List, or share it using one of the other methods offered from the Share menu.

CREATE AND MANAGE READING LISTS

As you're surfing the Web, you'll often come across specific web pages, articles, or other information that you know you'll want to refer to later. From within Safari, you can always create a bookmark for that website URL and have it displayed in your Bookmarks list or on your Bookmarks Bar, or you can add it to your Reading List, which is another way to store web page links and content that's of interest to you.

iOS 6 WHAT'S NEW The iOS 6 version of Safari allows the Reading List feature to download entire webpages for offline viewing, as opposed to simply storing website addresses that you are able to refer back to later. While this feature will download text and photos associated with a webpage, it will not download animated graphics, video or audio content associated with that page.

As you're reading a website or web-based article, for example, to add it to your personalized Reading List for later review, tap on the Share icon and select the Add to Reading List option. Figure 13.8 shows an example of a Reading List.

FIGURE 13.8

Creating a Reading List is another way to store links related to specific content on the Web that you want to easily be able to find again and access later.

When you want to refer to items stored in your Reading List, from Safari, tap on the Bookmarks icon, and then tap on the Reading List option. A listing of your saved web pages or articles previously saved to your Reading List is displayed.

> **TIP** Like your Bookmarks list and Bookmarks Bar, the items stored in your Reading List can automatically be saved to iCloud, and almost instantly made available on any other computer or iOS device that's linked to your iCloud account. See the section, "Create, Manage, and Sync Safari Bookmarks," for details on setting up these features for backup to iCloud.

NEW OPTIONS FOR SHARING WEB CONTENT IN SAFARI

There will probably be times when you're surfing the Web and come across something funny, informative, educational, or just plain bizarre that you want to share with other people, add to your Bookmarks list, or print, for example. The iOS 6 version of Safari makes sharing web links extremely easy, plus it now gives you a handful of new options.

Anytime you're visiting a web page that you want to share with others, tap on the Share icon to reveal a menu that's chock-full of new features (as shown in Figure 13.9).

FIGURE 13.9

The Share icon in Safari offers a handful of new options, like the capability to send a tweet (via Twitter) from within the web browser.

On the iPhone, the Share icon is displayed near the bottom center of the Safari screen. On the iPad, the Share icon can be found to the immediate left of the Address bar.

The following options are available from the Share icon:

■ **Mail**—To share a website URL with someone else via email, as you're looking at the web page or website you want to share, tap on the Share icon and select the Mail option. In Safari, an outgoing email window will appear.

Simply fill in the To field with the recipient's email address, and tap the Send icon (as shown in Figure 13.10). The website URL automatically is embedded within the body of the email, with the website's heading used as the email's subject. Before sending the email, you can add text to the body of the email message or change the Subject.

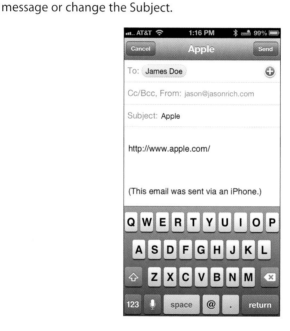

FIGURE 13.10

In Safari, you can email information about a website to one or more recipients without exiting Safari and opening the Mail app.

■ **Message**—Tap on this option to send a link to the webpage you're viewing to one or more other people via text or instant message using the Messages app. Just fill in the To field and tap the Send button. You can also add a text-based message along with the link.

■ **Tweet**—If you have an active Twitter account that's set up for use with iOS 6, tap on the Tweet option from the Share menu to create an outgoing tweet that automatically has the website URL attached.

When the Tweet window appears (shown in Figure 13.11), enter your tweet message (up to 140 characters, minus the length of the website URL). Tap the Send icon when the tweet message is composed and ready to share with your Twitter followers.

FIGURE 13.11

Send out a tweet to your Twitter followers from within Safari, and automatically include a link to the web page you're viewing.

TIP If you're managing multiple Twitter accounts from your iOS device, within the outgoing tweet window, tap on the From field, and then select from which of your Twitter accounts you want to send the tweet you're composing.

- **Facebook**—Thanks to Facebook integration within iOS 6, when you tap on the Facebook option, you can update your Facebook Status and include details about the webpage you're viewing in Safari.

- **Add to Home Screen**—In addition to saving a website URL in the form of a bookmark or within your Reading List, another option is to save it as a Home Screen icon. This feature is explained later, in the "Launch Your Favorite Websites Fast with Home Screen Icons" section.

- **Print**—In Safari, you can wirelessly print a website to any AirPrint-compatible printer that's set up to work with your iOS device. To print a web page, tap on the Print command. From the Printer Options screen, select the printer you want to use, and then choose the number of copies you want printed. Tap the Print icon at the bottom of the Print Options window to send the web page document to your printer.

- **Copy**—Use this command to copy the webpage URL you're looking at to the virtual clipboard that's built into iOS 6. You can then paste that information into another app.

- **Bookmark**—Tap on this option to add a bookmark to your personal Bookmarks list or Bookmarks Bar that's stored in Safari. You can later access your bookmarks by tapping on the Bookmark icon.

  When you opt to save a bookmark, an Add Bookmark window appears (as shown in Figure 13.12). Here, you can enter a title for the bookmark and decide whether you want to save it as part of your Bookmarks list or in your Bookmarks Bar.

FIGURE 13.12

You can save a website URL as a bookmark in your Bookmarks list or to be displayed as part of Safari's Bookmarks Bar.

> ☑ **TIP** To access your Bookmarks list, tap on the Bookmarks icon that's displayed next to the Share icon in Safari, and tap on the Bookmarks icon to view your personalized list of saved website bookmarks.

■ **Add to Reading List**—Instead of adding a web page URL to your Bookmarks list or Bookmarks Bar, you can save it in your Reading List for later reference. To access your Reading List, tap on the Bookmarks icon, and then tap on the Reading List option.

> ✐ **NOTE** When using Safari on the iPhone, you can maintain a Bookmarks Bar (if you sync this data from a computer or other iOS device); however, to conserve onscreen space, the Bookmarks Bar is not displayed across the top of the Safari screen like it is on an iPad. Instead, on an iPhone, the Bookmarks Bar is displayed as an additional Bookmark folder when you tap on the Bookmarks icon.

CREATE, MANAGE, AND SYNC SAFARI BOOKMARKS

Thanks to the fact that Safari is fully integrated with iCloud, if you have an active iCloud account, your iOS device automatically syncs your Bookmarks and related Safari data with your other iOS devices, as well as the compatible web browsers on your primary computer(s).

To activate this iCloud sync feature, launch Settings from the Home Screen, and then tap on the iCloud option. When the iCloud menu screen appears, make sure your iCloud account is listed at the top of the screen, and then make sure the virtual on/off switch associated with the Safari option is turned on.

Your Bookmarks list, Bookmarks Bar, open browser windows (tabs) and Safari Reading List will now automatically be continuously synced with your iCloud account. Thus, when you add a new bookmark while surfing the Web on your iPad, within seconds that same bookmark will appear in your Bookmarks list on your iPhone and on Safari that's running on your Mac, for example.

LAUNCH YOUR FAVORITE WEBSITES FAST WITH HOME SCREEN ICONS

If you regularly visit certain websites, you can create individual bookmarks for them. However, to access those sites, you'll still need to launch Safari from your iPhone or iPad's Home Screen, tap on the Bookmarks icon, and then tap on a specific bookmark listing to access the related site.

An alternative that will save you time is to create a Home Screen icon for each of your favorite websites (as shown in Figure 13.13). To create a Home Screen icon, surf to one of your favorite websites. After it loads, tap on the Share icon, and choose the Add to Home Screen option.

FIGURE 13.13

Create Home Screen icons for your favorite websites so that you can launch them directly from your iOS device's Home Screen with a single tap. All four icons displayed near the top of this iPhone 5 Home Screen represent webpages.

A new Add to Home window appears. It displays a thumbnail image of the website you're visiting and enables you to enter the title for the website (which will be displayed below the icon on your device's Home Screen). Keep the title you choose short. When you've created the title (or if you decide to keep the default title that Safari creates), tap on the Add icon that's displayed in the upper-right corner of the window.

> **NOTE** When you use the Add to Home feature in Safari, if you're creating a shortcut for a website designed to be compatible with an iPhone or iPad, a special website-related icon (as opposed to a thumbnail) is displayed. The CNN logo icon displayed within Figure 13.13 is an example of this.

Safari closes, and you are returned to your device's Home Screen. Displayed on the Home Screen will be what looks like a new app icon; however, it's really a link to your favorite website. Tap on this icon to automatically launch Safari from the Home Screen and load your web page.

After a Home Screen icon is created for a web page, it can be treated like any other app icon. You can move it around on the Home Screen, add the icon to a folder, or delete the icon from the Home Screen.

> **iOS 6 WHAT'S NEW** Another new feature built into the iOS 6 edition of Safari for the iPhone is the web browser's full-screen mode (shown in Figure 13.14). It works great on the iPhone 5. To access full-screen mode, rotate the iPhone to landscape mode (sideways), and tap on the Full Screen icon that's displayed near the lower-right corner of the screen. The Title Bar and command icons normally displayed at the top and bottom of the app's screen disappear. To exit out of full screen mode, tap on the Full Screen icon (which continues to appear in the lower-right corner of the screen).

Full Screen Mode Icon

FIGURE 13.14

On the iPhone, the iOS 6 version of Safari offers a new full screen mode.

14

MANAGE YOUR EMAIL EFFICIENTLY

If you're someone who's constantly on the go, being able to send and receive emails from virtually anywhere there's a 3G/4G or Wi-Fi Internet connection enables you to stay in touch, stay informed, and be productive from wherever you happen to be. Managing one or more email accounts from an iPhone or iPad has just gotten a bit easier, thanks to the improvements made to the Mail app that comes preinstalled with iOS 6.

WHAT'S NEW This latest edition of the Mail app offers the new VIP List feature. It allows you to assign certain important people in your life, who regularly send you emails, a "VIP" designation. Those incoming emails from your boss, important clients, close friends or family members, for example, are then marked with a special star-shaped icon in your regular Inbox, but they're also gathered into their own VIP mailbox for easy reference.

As you use the iOS 6 edition of the Mail app, you also notice a slightly more streamlined user interface. For example, to refresh your Inbox, you simply need to swipe your finger downwards on the inbox screen (iPhone) or within the inbox column on the left side of the Mail app's screen (iPad).

In addition, as you're composing an email, it's now possible to insert a photo or video clip that's stored on your iPhone or iPad into the body of an email from directly within the Mail app. (In the past, this needed to be done from the Photos app, which continues to be possible.)

Another new Mail app feature is the ability to create separate Signatures for each email account you're managing from your iPhone or iPad. In the past, the Signature you created was used for all email accounts.

The Mail app offers a comprehensive set of tools, features, and functions to help you compose, send, and receive emails from one or more existing accounts. So from your iPhone or iPad, you can simultaneously manage your personal and work-related email accounts, as well as the free email account that's provided to you when you set up an iCloud account.

Before you can begin using the Mail app, it's necessary to set up your existing email accounts from within Settings. This process takes just a few minutes.

If you don't yet have an email account, there are several ways to get one. You can sign up for a free Apple iCloud account, which includes an email account. In addition, Google offers free Gmail email accounts (http://mail.google.com), and Yahoo! offers free Yahoo! Mail accounts (http://features.mail.yahoo.com), both of which are fully compatible with your iOS device's Mail app.

HOW TO ADD EMAIL ACCOUNTS TO THE MAIL APP

To initially set up your iOS device to work with your existing email account(s), launch Settings from the Home Screen. This process works with virtually all email accounts, including Yahoo! Mail, Google Gmail, AOL Mail, iCloud Mail, Microsoft Exchange, and other email accounts established using industry-standard POP3 and IMAP email services.

If you have an email account through your employer that doesn't initially work using the setup procedure outlined in this chapter, contact your company's IT department or Apple's technical support for assistance.

NOTE The process for setting up an existing email account to use with your iPhone or iPad and the Mail app needs to be done only once per account.

Follow these steps to set up your iOS device to work with each of your existing email accounts:

1. From the Home Screen, launch Settings.

2. Tap on the Mail, Contacts, Calendars option.

3. When the Mail, Contacts, Calendars menu screen appears, tap on the Add Account option that's displayed near the top of the screen, below the Accounts heading.

4. From the Add Account screen, select the type of email account you have. Your options include iCloud, Microsoft Exchange, Google Gmail, Yahoo! Mail, AOL Mail, Microsoft Hotmail, and Other (shown in Figure 14.1). Tap on the appropriate option. If you have a POP3 or IMAP-compatible email account that doesn't otherwise fall into one of the provided email types, tap on the Other option, and follow the onscreen prompts.

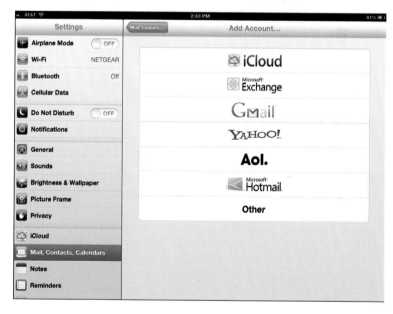

FIGURE 14.1

Choose the type of email account you'd like to add by tapping on the appropriate menu option.

If you have an existing Yahoo Email account, for example, tap on the Yahoo icon. When the Yahoo! screen appears (shown in Figure 14.2), use the iPhone or iPad's virtual keyboard to enter your account name, email address, password, and a description for the account.

FIGURE 14.2
If you're setting up a Yahoo! Mail account, tap on the Yahoo! option, and then fill in the email account–related fields that appear on the screen using your existing email account details, such as your email address and password.

> ☑ **TIP**   As you're adding an email account from within Settings, the account name should be your full name or whatever you want to appear within the From field of emails (alongside your email address) that you compose and send from your iPhone or iPad using that email account. You can opt to use just your first name, a family name (such as "The Anderson Family"), or a nickname, based on what you want to share with the recipients of your emails. The Description can be anything that helps you personally differentiate that account from your other accounts, such as Home Email, Work Email, or Yahoo! Email. The email account Description is something that only you see on your device.

5. Tap on the Next button that's located in the upper-right corner of the window.

6. Your iOS device connects to the email account's server and confirms the account details you've entered. The word Verifying appears on the screen.

7. After the account has been verified, a new window with options is displayed. They're probably labeled Mail, Contacts, Calendars, Reminders and Notes, although depending on the type of email account you're setting

up, not all of these options may be available. Each option has a virtual on/ off switch associated with it. The default for many of these options is On. They're used to determine what additional app-specific data can be linked with the Mail account, such as your Contacts database, the schedule from your Calendar app, your to-do list from the Reminders app, or your notes from the Notes app.

> **!CAUTION** If you're already syncing app-specific data for Contacts, Calendar, Reminders and/or Notes with iCloud, do not also sync them with Yahoo!, Google or a Microsoft Exchange-compatible account, or you could wind up with duplicate records or entries in each app. In other words, if you're already syncing your app-specific data, such as your calendar or contacts with Google, don't also sync this information using iCloud.

8. Tap on the Save button that's located in the upper-right corner of this window. An "Adding Account" message will briefly be displayed.

9. Details about the email account you just set up are added to your iOS device and become immediately accessible via the Mail app.

10. If you have another existing email account to set up, from the Mail, Contacts, Calendars screen in the Settings app, tap on the Add Account option again, and repeat the preceding procedure. Otherwise, exit the Settings app and launch the Mail app from the Home Screen.

Depending on the type of email account you're setting up for use with your iPhone or iPad, the information you're prompted for varies slightly. For example, to set up an existing Microsoft Exchange email account, the prompts you need to fill in during the email setup procedure include Email Address, Domain, Username, Password, and a Description for the account.

To set up an existing iCloud email account, enter your existing Apple ID and password. To set up a Gmail or AOL Mail account, enter your name, email address, and password, as well as an account description.

After the account is set up, it is listed within Settings, under the Accounts heading, when you tap on the Mail, Contacts, Calendars option.

> **✓ TIP** When you purchase a new iOS device, it comes with free technical support from AppleCare for 90 days. If you purchased AppleCare+ with your iOS device, you have access to free technical support from Apple for two years. This includes the ability to make an in-person appointment with an Apple Genius at

any Apple Store, and have someone set up your email accounts on your iPhone or iPad for you.

To schedule a free appointment, visit www.apple.com/retail/geniusbar. Or call Apple's toll-free technical support phone number and have someone talk you through the email setup process. Call 800-APL-CARE (275-2273).

HOW TO CUSTOMIZE MAIL OPTIONS FROM SETTINGS

To customize options available within the Mail app, launch Settings, and select the Mail, Contacts, Calendars option. Then, on the Mail, Contacts, Calendars screen (shown in Figure 14.3), you will see a handful of customizable features pertaining to how your iOS device will handle your email accounts.

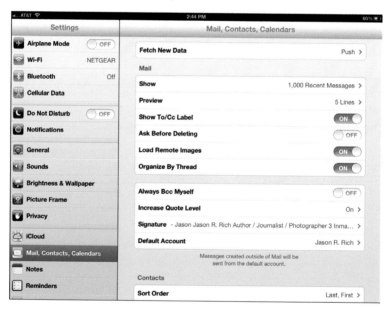

FIGURE 14.3

From Settings, you can customize a handful of settings relating to the Mail app.

At the top of the Mail, Contacts, Calendars screen is a listing of the individual email accounts you have already linked with the Mail app using the directions found earlier in this chapter, in the section "How to Add Email Accounts to the Mail App."

Below the Accounts heading on the Mail, Contacts, Calendars screen in Settings is the Fetch New Data option. Use this to determine how often your iOS device will automatically access the Internet to check for and download new incoming email messages from each email account's server.

> ☑ **TIP**   From the Fetch New Data screen, you can turn on or off the Push feature. When turned on, your iPhone or iPad automatically accesses and displays new incoming emails as they arrive on your email account's server. When the Push feature is turned off, you can select how often you want your iOS mobile device to check for new emails. Your options include: Every 15 minutes, Every 30 Minutes, Hourly or Manually.
>
> The benefit to using the Fetch feature set to Manually is that you can greatly reduce the amount of wireless data usage you utilize. This is important if you have a monthly 3G/4G wireless data allocation through your wireless service provider. If you have an account that offers unlimited wireless data, or you utilize a Wi-Fi connection, this is not a concern.
>
> In iOS 6, when you tap on the Advanced option that's displayed near the bottom of the Fetch New Data screen, you can set up separate Push or Fetch guidelines for each email account you're managing from your iPhone or iPad.

Getting back to the user-adjustable options available to you from the Mail, Contacts, Calendars menu screen within Settings, by scrolling down on this screen, you'll see the Mail heading. Below this heading are a handful of customizable options relating to how the Mail app manages your email accounts and email messages:

- **Show**—This feature determines how many messages within a particular email account the Mail app downloads from the server and displays at any given time. Your options include 50, 100, 200, 500 and 1,000 Recent Messages. (This impacts how much of your device's internal storage is utilized by the Mail app to store email messages and related data.)

- **Preview**—As you look at your Inbox (or any mailbox) using the Mail app, you can determine how much of each email message's body text will be visible from the mailbox summary screen, in addition to the From, Date/Time, and Subject. You can choose None, or between one and five lines of the email message.

> ☑ **TIP**   The Preview option also impacts the email-related notifications that appear within the Notification Center screen (iPhone) or window (iPad), if you assign Notification Center to continuously monitor the Mail app. You can adjust this in Settings by tapping on the Notifications option under the main Settings menu.

■ **Show To/Cc Label**—Decide whether or not to view the To and Cc fields when viewing the preview screen for emails.

■ **Ask Before Deleting**—This option serves as a safety net to ensure that you don't accidentally delete an important email message from your iOS device. When this feature is turned on, you're asked to confirm your message deletion request before an email message is actually deleted. At least until you become comfortable using the Mail app, it's a good idea to leave this feature turned on. Keep in mind that, by default, you cannot delete email messages stored on your email account's server. When you delete a message from the Mail app, it is deleted from only your iPhone or iPad but is still accessible from other devices. On your iOS device, it might also appear in the Trash folder that's related to that email account, depending on how it is set up.

■ **Load Remote Images**—When an email message has a photo or graphic embedded in it, this option determines whether that photo or graphic is automatically downloaded and displayed with the email message. You can opt to have your iOS device refrain from automatically loading graphics with email messages. This reduces the amount of data transferred to your iPhone or iPad (which is a consideration if you're connected to the Internet via 3G/4G). You always have the option to tap on the placeholder icon in the email message to manually download the graphic content in a specific message, including photos.

■ **Organize by Thread**—This feature enables you to review messages in reverse chronological order if a single message turns into a back-and-forth email conversation, in which multiple parties keep hitting Reply to respond to messages with the same Subject. When turned on, this makes keeping track of email conversations much easier, especially if you're managing several email accounts on your iPhone or iPad. If it's turned off, messages in your Inbox are displayed in reverse chronological order, as they're received, and are not also grouped together by subject.

■ **Always Bcc Myself**—To ensure that you keep a copy of every outgoing email you send, turn on this feature. A copy of every outgoing email will also be sent to your Inbox if this feature is turned on. Typically, all outgoing messages automatically get saved in a Sent folder that's related to that account. If your email account type does not allow you to access sent emails from another computer or device, using the Bcc Myself option compensates for this.

■ **Increase Quote Level**—When turned on, anytime you Reply to a message or Forward a message, the contents of that original email appear indented, which makes it easier for the reader to differentiate between the message you add and the original message being replied to or forwarded. This option impacts message formatting, not actual content.

- **Signature**—For every outgoing email that you compose, you can automatically add an email signature. The default signature is "Sent from my iPhone" or "Sent from my iPad." However, by tapping on this option within Settings, you can use the virtual keyboard to create customized signatures for each email account. A signature might include your name, mailing address, email address, phone number(s), and so forth.

- **Default Account**—If you're using the Mail app to manage multiple email accounts, when you Reply to a message or Forward a message, it is always sent from the email account the message was originally sent to. However, if you tap on the Compose New Email icon to create a new email from scratch, the email account that message is sent from is whichever you have set up as the Mail app's Default account. If you wish to change this account for a specific email, simply tap on the From field as you're composing a new email and select one of your other accounts.

After you make whatever adjustments you want to the Mail app-related options from within Settings, exit Settings by pressing the Home button in order to return to the Home Screen. You're now ready to begin using the Mail app to access and manage your email account(s).

TIPS FOR VIEWING YOUR INCOMING EMAIL

The Mail app has three main purposes. It allows you to do the following:

- Compose and send new email messages, or respond to emails.
- Read incoming email messages.
- Manage one or more of your email accounts simultaneously, and keep your incoming and outgoing emails well organized.

When you launch the Mail app on your iPhone or iPad, the Inbox for your various email accounts is displayed. You can opt to display incoming messages for a single email account, or display the incoming messages (in reverse chronological order, based on when each was received) from all of your email accounts by selecting the All Inboxes option.

Even though Mail enables you to simultaneously view incoming emails from multiple accounts within a single listing, behind the scenes, the app automatically keeps your incoming and outgoing emails, and your various email accounts, separate. So if you opt to read and respond to an email from your work-related Inbox, for example, that response is automatically sent out from your work-related email account and saved in the Sent Folder for that account.

> ☑ **TIP**   The Mail app is fully compatible with Siri. If you want to read your new (incoming) email messages, for example, activate Safari and say, "Read my new email." Siri displays a list of new email messages on the iPhone or iPad's screen.
>
> Or if you want to compose an email, activate Siri, and say, "Send an email to [insert name]." If multiple email addresses are stored in your Contacts database for that person, Siri asks you which email address to use, based on the Home, Work or Other label associated with each. You can, however, tell Siri to "Send an email to [insert name] at [insert location, such as Home or Work]," to inform Siri which email account to utilize. This saves you a step when communicating with Siri.
>
> Siri then prompts you to dictate the subject of the email. Once you speak what the subject line of the email should say, Siri asks, "What would you like the email to say?"
>
> When you hear the prompt tone, start dictating the body of your email message. You can speak for up to 30 seconds at a time. For the best results, however, keep your dictation short and simple. After you stop speaking, Siri displays the message on the iPhone or iPad's screen, and asks whether you're ready to send it.
>
> More information about using Siri can be found in Chapter 5, "Using Siri and Dictation to Interact with Your iOS Device."

Viewing all the Inboxes for all of your accounts simultaneously makes it faster to review your incoming emails, without having to manually switch between email accounts.

If you have multiple email accounts being managed from your iOS device, to view all of your Inboxes simultaneously, or to switch between Inboxes, follow these steps:

1. Launch the Mail app.
2. The Inbox you last looked at will be displayed.
3. Tap on the left-pointing, arrow-shaped Mailboxes icon that's displayed in the upper-left corner of the screen to select which Inbox you want to view. They're all listed under the Inboxes heading.
4. From the menu that appears, the first option displayed under the Inboxes heading is All Inboxes. Tap on this to view a single listing of all incoming emails. Or tap on any single email account that's listed under the Inboxes heading.

> ☑ **TIP**   Displayed under the Inboxes heading is the new VIP mailbox listing. Tap on this to view only emails from your various inboxes that have been received by people you've added to your VIP List. When you tap on the VIP option, these

emails are displayed in a single mailbox, although the list is comprised of VIP messages from all of the accounts you're managing on your iPhone or iPad. You'll learn more about using the VIP List feature of the Mail app shortly.

Below the VIP listing under the Inboxes heading is a Flagged listing. This allows you to view separate mailbox comprised of only emails you've previously flagged as being important. Again, this is a comprehensive listing of flagged incoming emails from all of the accounts you're managing on your iPhone or iPad. (In reality, however, the Mail app keeps the messages sorted behind the scenes, based on which email account each is associated with.)

5. When you tap on your option, the Inbox screen returns, and the incoming emails (from the account or accounts you selected) are displayed. You can modify this option at any time.

FETCH NEW DATA

You can set up your iOS device to automatically access the Internet and retrieve new email messages by tapping on the Fetch New Data option within Settings, and then adjusting its settings. Or simply make sure that the Push option either for the entire Mail app, or for specific email accounts, is turned on.

NOTE The Push allows your iPhone or iPad to continuously monitor your email service and download new messages as they arrive. The Fetch feature allows you to determine how often your iOS mobile device connects to the mail service (as opposed to continuous monitoring). Using the Fetch feature, you can also set it up so your iPhone or iPad only check for new emails when you manually Refresh the mailbox.

To adjust these settings, launch Settings and select the Mail, Contacts, Calendars option. Then, scroll down to the Fetch New Data option and tap on it.

From the Fetch New Data screen, you can turn on the Push option, which means the iPhone or iPad accesses new emails automatically. Or you can turn off the Push option but set the Fetch option to check for new emails every 15 minutes, every 30 minutes, hourly, or manually.

TIP As you're looking at any of your inboxes within the Mail app, to manually check for new emails and refresh the inbox, swipe your finger in a downwards direction on the inbox screen (iPhone) or along the inbox column on the left side of the screen (iPad).

COMPOSING AN EMAIL MESSAGE

In the Mail app, you can easily compose an email from scratch and send it to one or more recipients. To compose a new email, tap on the Compose icon. On an iPhone, the Compose icon can always be found in the lower-right corner of the screen within the Mail app. On an iPad, the Compose icon is displayed in the upper-right corner of the screen within the Mail app.

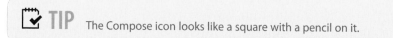 **TIP** The Compose icon looks like a square with a pencil on it.

When you tap on the Compose icon, a blank New Message email message template appears on the iPhone or iPad's screen. On the iPhone, you will see a New Message screen displayed. On the iPad, a New Message pop-up window appears. Using the virtual keyboard, fill in the To, Cc, Bcc, and/or Subject fields (as shown in Figure 14.4). At the very least, you must fill in the To field with a valid email address for at least one recipient. The other fields are optional.

FIGURE 14.4

Tap on the Compose icon to create an email from scratch and send it from your iOS device.

You can send the same email to multiple recipients by either adding multiple email addresses to the To field or by adding additional email addresses to the Cc and/or Bcc fields.

If you're managing one email account from your iOS device, the From field is auto-matically be filled in with your email address. However, if you're managing multiple email addresses from the iPhone or iPad, tap on the From field to select which email address you want to send the message from. The default account is other-wise used.

> **TIP** As you fill in the To field when composing an email, the Mail app automatically accesses your Contacts database and matches up entries based on what you type in the To field. This can save you time because you don't have to manually enter email addresses. If you know that the person you're sending an email to already has an entry within your Contacts database, you can type that person's name, as opposed to their email address, in the To field.

Next, tap on the Subject field and use the virtual keyboard to enter the subject for your message. As you do this, the subject appears at the very top center of the Compose window (replacing the New Message heading).

> **TIP** When using almost any app with a Share icon or menu, to compose and send an email that contains app-specific content, without first launching the Mail app, tap on the Share icon or menu option and select Mail.
>
> A New Message screen appears with the related app-specific content already attached to that outgoing email message. Use the virtual keyboard to compose your email, and then tap on the Send icon. The email message is sent and you are returned to the app you were using.
>
> Meanwhile, as you're viewing a Contact's entry within the Contacts app, if you tap on an email address within that entry, a New Message screen (iPhone) or window (iPad) appears, and you can compose and send an email message to that person from within the Contacts app.
>
> On an iPhone, you can also tap on any phone number listed to initiate a phone call with that contact, without first launching the Phone app. To send a text/instant message to that person (via the Messages app) from within the Contacts app, scroll down to the bottom of their Contacts entry and tap the Send Message button.

To begin creating the main body of the outgoing email message, tap in the main body area of the message template on the screen, and begin using the virtual keyboard (or the external keyboard you're using with your iPhone or iPad) to compose your message. You also have the option to tap on the Dictation key and then dictate your message using iOS 6's Dictation feature. To learn more about Dictation, refer to Chapter 5.

> **! CAUTION** If you have the Auto-Capitalization, Auto-Correction and/or Check Spelling feature(s) turned on, which are adjustable from within Settings, as you type, the iPhone or iPad will automatically correct anything that it perceives as a typo or misspelled word.
>
> Be very careful when using these features because they are notorious for plugging the wrong word into a sentence. Especially if you're creating important business documents and emails, make sure you proofread whatever you type on your iPhone or iPad carefully before sending it. Typically, these features are helpful, but they do have quirks that can lead to embarrassing and unprofessional mistakes.
>
> To turn on or off the Auto-Capitalization, Auto-Correction and/or Check Spelling features, launch Settings, tap on the General option, select the Keyboard option, and then turn on or off the virtual switch that's associated for each option that's displayed within the Keyboard menu screen.

The Signature you set up from within Settings for the selected From account is automatically displayed at the bottom of the newly composed message. You can return to Settings to turn off the Signature feature, or change the signature that appears. (To do this, launch Settings, tap on the Mail, Contacts, Calendars option, and then tap on the Signature option that's displayed below the Mail heading.)

When your email is fully written and ready to be sent, tap on the blue-and-white Send button that's displayed in the upper-right corner of the Compose window. In a few seconds, the message is sent from your iOS device, assuming that it is connected to the Internet. A copy of the message appears in your Sent or Outbox folder.

As a message is being sent, a "Sending" notification appears near the bottom of the Mail app's screen.

> **TIP** The Mail app enables you to format your outgoing email messages and include **bold**, *italic*, and/or underlined text (as well as combinations, like ***bold-italic text***).

To format text in an email message you're composing, type the text as you normally would using the virtual keyboard. After the text appears in your email, hold your finger on a word to make the Select, Select All, Paste, Insert Photo or Video and Quote Level command tabs appear above that word.

Tap on Select, and then use your finger to move around the blue dots that appear to highlight the text you want to modify. Select the word, phrase, or sentence, for example, that you want to highlight using bold, italic, and/or underlined text.

When the appropriate text is highlighted in blue, (if necessary) tap the right-pointing arrow that appears above the text (next to the Cut, Copy, and Paste commands), and then tap on the **B**/U option. A new menu appears above the highlighted text with three options, labeled Bold, Italics, and Underline. Tap on one or more of these tabs to alter the highlighted text (as shown in Figure 14.5).

FIGURE 14.5
The Mail enables you to use bold, italic, and/or underlined text in the body of your outgoing email messages.

INSERT A PHOTO OR VIDEO INTO YOUR OUTGOING EMAIL

As you're composing an outgoing email, if you want to insert a photo or video clip that's stored on your iPhone or iPad into that email, place and hold your finger anywhere in the body of the email where you want to embed that photo or video.

> **NOTE** On the iPhone, tap on the right-pointing arrow that's displayed to the right of the Select, Select All and Paste commands to access the Insert Photo or Video option.

Within a second, the Insert Photo or Video tab is displayed. Tap on it. The Photos screen (iPhone) or window (iPad) appears. Select the photo you want to insert into the email from the appropriate Album by selecting an Album and then tapping on an image or video thumbnail. The photo/video you selected is previewed within the Choose Photo window. Tap on the Use button to insert the photo (or video clip) into your email.

You can repeat this process to include multiple images within an email (up to five), keeping in mind that the overall file size associated with the outgoing email can not exceed 5MB.

> **TIP** Once you insert a photo into an outgoing email on the iPad, to the right of the Cc/Bcc, From: field a new option that says Images: [insert file size] is displayed. To alter the image file size (and by default, the resolution) of the attached photo(s), tap on the Images option. Under the From field, an Image Size option appears. To the right of this option are four command tabs, labeled Small, Medium, Large, and Actual Size. Each is accompanied by the file size of the image(s) you're sending. Tap on one of these options.
>
> On the iPhone, once you tap the Send button, you may be asked to select an image resolution for the Photo(s) you've attached to the outgoing email.
>
> If you know the photo(s) will be made into prints later, send the images using the Actual Size option. This will, however, have a greater impact on your wireless data usage if you're using a 3G/4G connection and have a monthly usage allocation.

USING SELECT, SELECT ALL, CUT, COPY, AND PASTE

The iOS operating system offers Select, Select All, Cut, Copy, and Paste commands, which are accessible from many iPhone or iPad apps, including Mail. Using these commands, you can quickly copy and paste content from one portion of an app to another, or from one app into another app, whether it's a paragraph of text, a phone number, or a photo.

To use these commands, use your finger to hold down on any word or graphic element on the screen for one or two seconds, until the Select and Select All tabs appear above that content. To select a single word or select what content you want to copy or cut, tap on the Select tab. Or to select all the content on the screen, tap the Select All tab.

After text (or a graphic element, such as a photo) is selected, tap on the Cut tab to delete that selected content from the screen (if this option is available in the app you're using), or tap the Copy tab to save the highlighted content in your iPhone or iPad's virtual clipboard.

Now, move to where you want to paste that saved content. This can be in the same email or document, for example, or in another app altogether. Choose the location on the screen where you want to paste the content, and hold your finger on that location for two or three seconds. When the Paste tab appears, tap on it. The content you just copied is pasted into that location.

> **TIP** In the Mail app, as you use the Select, Select All, Cut, Copy, and Paste commands, notice a Quote Level option that appears on the menu above the highlighted text or content that you select. Tap on this to increase or decrease the indent of that content, which impacts how it's formatted on the screen.

HOW TO SAVE AN UNSENT DRAFT OF AN EMAIL MESSAGE

If you want to save a draft of an email (in your Draft folder, for example), without sending it, as you're composing the email message, tap on the Cancel button that appears in the upper-left corner of the Compose message window. Two command buttons appear, labeled Delete Draft and Save Draft. To save the unsent draft, tap on Save Draft.

If you have a saved but unsent draft of an email, you can return to it later to modify and/or send it. To do this, from the main Inbox screen within Mail, tap on the left-pointing Mailboxes icon that looks like an arrow (displayed near the upper-left corner of the screen). From the Mailboxes screen, scroll down to the Accounts heading, and tap on the listing for the email account from which the email draft was composed. When you see a list of folders related to that email account, tap on the Drafts folder (a number in a gray oval appears to the right of the Drafts folder name, indicating there are draft email messages stored in it). When you see the listings for the saved draft emails, tap on the appropriate listing to open that email message. You can now edit the message or send it.

> ☑ **TIP** Aside from including photos or videos within an email, to send an email message that contains another type of content or file attachment, such as a Pages document, those attachments must be sent from within a specific app, not from the Mail app.
>
> A Pages, Word, or PDF document can be sent from within Pages, a Numbers or Excel (spreadsheet) file can be sent from within Numbers, and up to five photos per email can be sent from within the Photos app, for example. In a compatible app, tap on the Share icon, and then select the Mail option.

TIPS FOR READING EMAIL

If you're managing multiple email accounts with your iPhone or iPad, it's important to understand that while the Mail app enables you to view email messages in all your accounts simultaneously (when you're looking at the All Inboxes view), the app actually keeps messages from your different accounts separate.

Also, as you view your incoming email messages, by default, the app groups emails together by message thread, allowing you to follow an email-based conversation that extends through multiple messages and replies. When turned on, this feature displays emails in the same thread in reverse chronological order, with the newest message first, and then displays all previous emails and your replies in sequence.

> ☑ **TIP** To send and receive emails from your iPhone or iPad using the Mail app, your iOS device must be connected to the Internet via a Wi-Fi or 3G/4G connection. Keep in mind that emails with large attachments, such as photos, Microsoft Office documents, or PDF files (sent from within specific apps) deplete your monthly wireless data allocation from your wireless service provider much faster, as does having your iOS device automatically check for new incoming emails often.

After you launch the Mail app, you can access the Inbox for one or more of your existing email accounts, compose new emails, or manage your email accounts. Just like the Inbox on your main computer's email software, the Inbox of the Mail app (shown in Figure 14.6 on an iPhone, and Figure 14.7 on an iPad) displays your incoming emails.

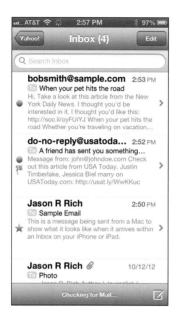

FIGURE 14.6

The Inbox screen of the Mail app displays a listing of your incoming emails on the iPhone 5.

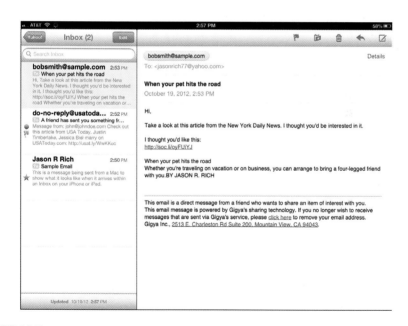

FIGURE 14.7

On the iPad, the Inbox, displayed on the left side of the Mail app's screen, provides a listing of your incoming emails.

TIP As you're looking at the inbox for any of your email accounts (or the All Inboxes mailbox), to the left of each email message preview you may see a tiny graphic icon (refer to Figure 14.6 and Figure 14.7). A blue dot represents a new and unread email (or an email that's been marked as unread). A solid blue star represents a new and unread email from someone on your VIP list, while a star-outline icon represents a read email from someone on your VIP list.

An orange flag icon displayed to the left of an email preview means that you have manually flagged that message (or message thread) as urgent. A curved, left-pointing arrow icons means that you have read and replied to that message, while a right-pointing arrow icon means you've read and have forwarded that message to one or more people.

If no tiny icon appears to the left of a email preview listing, this means the message has been read and is simply stored in that inbox (or mailbox). You have not done anything special in regard to that message, such as replied to it or flagged it as urgent.

THE MAIL APP'S INBOX

When you're viewing your Inbox(es), a list of the individual emails is displayed. Based on the customizations you make from the Settings app that pertain to the Mail app, the Sender, Subject, Date/Time, and up to five lines of the message's body text can be displayed for each incoming message listing.

On the iPhone, when viewing your Inbox and the listing of incoming (new) email messages, tap on any message listing to read that message in its entirety. When you do this, a new message screen appears. At the bottom of this screen is a series of command icons for managing that email.

On the iPad, the email message that's highlighted in blue on the left side of the screen is the one that's currently being displayed, in its entirety, on the right side of the screen. Tap on any email listing on the left side of the screen to view the entire message on the right side of the screen. Icons at the top of the screen are used for managing that email.

At the top of the Inbox message listing are two command icons, labeled Mailboxes (or the name of the mailbox you're viewing) and Edit. In between these two icons is its heading, along with a number that's displayed in parentheses. This number indicates how many new, unread messages are currently stored in your Inbox.

Just below this Inbox's heading is a Search field. Tap on this Search field to make the iPhone or iPad's virtual keyboard appear, allowing you to enter a search phrase and quickly find a particular email message. You can search the content of the Mail app using any keyword, a sender's name, or an email subject, for example.

THE EDIT BUTTON

Located on top of a mailbox's message listing (to the right of its heading) is a command button that's labeled Edit. When you tap on this button, you can quickly select multiple messages from a mailbox, such as your inbox, to delete or move to another mailbox (or folder) (as shown in Figure 14.8).

> **TIP** If you tap on the Mark button that's displayed to the right of the Delete and Move buttons, you can flag or mark one or more emails as Read at the same time.

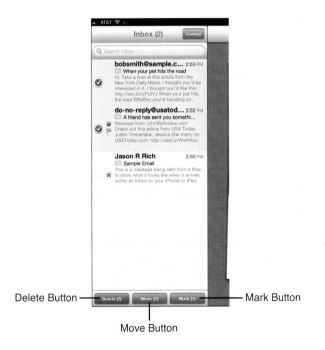

Delete Button — Move Button — Mark Button

FIGURE 14.8

Tap the Edit button to manage your incoming messages, delete them in quantity, or move them to another mailbox or folder to keep them organized.

After you tap the Edit button, an empty circle icon appears to the left of each email message preview listing. To move or delete one or more messages from the current mailbox's listing (which could be your Inbox, VIP, Flagged, Junk/Spam or Read mailbox, tap on the empty circle icon for that message. A red-and-white check mark fills the empty circle icon when you do this, and the Delete and Move command icons displayed at the bottom of the screen become active. (For some types of email accounts, a Delete All button is also displayed, allowing you to select and delete all messages within that mailbox at the same time.)

After you've selected one or more messages, tap the Delete icon to quickly delete one or more messages simultaneously from the mailbox (which sends them to the Trash folder), or tap the blue-and-white Move icon, and then select which folder you want to move those email messages to.

> **TIP** In Edit mode while reviewing a mailbox, you can select one or more messages and move them from one mailbox into another by selecting the Move command.
>
> On the iPhone, from a mailbox screen, tap on the Edit icon (that's displayed in the upper-right corner of the screen). Tap on one or more messages you want to select and then move. When the messages are selected and have a checkmark next to them, tap on the Move icon displayed at the bottom of the screen. A list of available mailboxes relating to that email account is displayed. Tap on the mailbox in which you want to store that email. It will then be removed from your the original mailbox (such as the inbox), but appear within the newly selected mailbox.
>
> Or as you're reading a single email on the iPhone, tap on the Move icon that's displayed at the bottom of the screen, and then choose a mailbox that's associated with that email account to store the message in.
>
> On the iPad, to use the Move command, as you're viewing a mailbox on the left side of the screen, tap the Edit button that's displayed in the upper-right corner of the mailbox's column. Tap on the email messages you want to select and then move. A checkmark appears next to each selected message.
>
> Tap on the Move icon after you've selected one or more messages. A list of available mailboxes is displayed on the left side of the iPad's screen. Tap on the mailbox to which you want to move the messages.
>
> Or as you're reading an email message, tap on the Move icon that's displayed near the upper-right corner of the screen, and then choose a mailbox that's associated with that email account to store the message in. The mailbox options are displayed on the left side of the screen.

To exit this option without doing anything, tap on the blue-and-white Cancel icon that's displayed at the top of the Inbox listing, to the right of the Inbox heading.

HOW TO DELETE INDIVIDUAL INCOMING MESSAGES

On your iPhone or iPad, as you're looking at the listing of messages in your Inbox (or any mailbox), you can also delete individual messages, one at a time. Swipe your finger from left to right over a message listing. A red-and-white Delete icon will appear on the right side of that email message listing (shown in Figure 14.9). Tap on this Delete icon to delete the message.

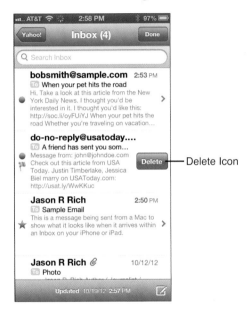

FIGURE 14.9

Swipe your finger from left to right over a single email message listing to make the Delete icon appear, allowing you to delete the message from your Inbox and send it to the Trash folder.

TIP Another way to delete a message from your Inbox, or any mailbox, is to tap on a message listing to view that message. To then delete the message, tap on the Trash Can icon. On the iPhone, the Trash Can is displayed at the bottom center of the screen. On the iPad, it's displayed in the upper-right corner of the screen. Doing this immediately sends the message to the Trash folder and removes it from its current folder, such as your Inbox.

HOW TO VIEW YOUR EMAILS

When a single email message is selected from the Inbox listing, that message is displayed in its entirety. At the top of the message, you'll see the From, To, Cc (if applicable), Bcc (if applicable), Subject, and the Date/Time it was sent.

In the upper-right corner of the email message is a blue Hide command. If you tap on this, some of the message header information will no longer be displayed. To make this information reappear, tap on the Details command that appears in the upper-right corner of the message.

As you're reading an email, tap on the flag icon to "flag" that message and mark it as urgent, or mark the email as unread. These options appear within a pop-up menu. When you flag a message, an orange flag becomes associated with that message, which is displayed in the message itself (to the right of the date and time), and within the inbox (mailbox) the message is stored in. Plus, from your Inboxes menu, if you tap on the Flagged option, you can view a separate mailbox that contains only flagged (urgent) messages.

> **☑ TIP** As you're reading email on the small screen of your iPhone (or even on the iPad screen), if the text is difficult to see, you can automatically increase the size of all text displayed in the Mail, Contacts, Calendar, Messages, and Notes apps by adjusting the Accessibility option within Settings.
>
> To make this font size adjustment, launch Settings. Select the General option and then tap on the Accessibility option. From the Accessibility menu screen, tap on the Large Text option. You can now select the font size you'd like your iOS device to use when displaying your emails and other content from the Contacts, Calendar, Messages, and Notes app.

You might want to mark a message as Unread, so when you refer to your emails later, you'll know you still need to respond to or reread that message.

TAKE ADVANTAGE OF THE MAIL APP'S NEW VIP LIST FEATURE

In addition to flagging individual messages as important, you can have the Mail app automatically highlight all emails sent from particular senders who you deem as important, such as your boss, important clients, close friends or family members. Once you add a sender to your VIP List, all of their incoming emails are marked with a star-shaped icon, instead of a blue dot icon that represents a regular, new incoming email.

To add someone to your VIP List, as you're reading any email from that person, tap on the From field (their name/email address). A Sender screen (iPhone) or window (iPad) appears. At the bottom of this window, tap on the Add To VIP button. This adds and keeps that sender on your custom VIP list until you manually remove them.

To later remove someone from your VIP list, read any of their email messages and again tap on the From field. When the Sender window appears, tap on the Remove From VIP button (which has replaced the Add To VIP button).

Now, as you're reviewing your inbox for a specific email account, the All Inboxes mailbox, or any other mailbox for that matter, any messages from people on your VIP list have a star displayed to the left of their email listings.

> **☑ TIP**   From the Mailboxes menu within Mail, you can also tap on the VIP listing to view a special mailbox that displays only incoming emails from people on your VIP list. Using the VIP List feature helps you quickly differentiate important emails from spam messages and less important incoming emails that don't necessarily require your immediate attention.

HOW TO DEAL WITH INCOMING EMAIL MESSAGE ATTACHMENTS

The Mail app enables you to access certain types of attachment files that accompany an incoming email message. Photos (in the .JPEG, .GIF, and .TIFF format), audio files (in the .MP3, .AAC, .WAV, and .AIFF format), video clips, and PDF files, as well as Pages, Keynote, Numbers, Microsoft Word, Microsoft Excel, and Microsoft PowerPoint files, can all be viewed or accessed from the iPhone or iPad using the Mail app.

If an incoming email message contains an attachment that is not compatible or accessible from your iOS device, you will see that an attachment is present but you won't be able to open or access it. In this case, you need to access this content from your primary computer.

To open an attached file using another app, in the incoming email message, tap and hold down the attachment icon for one to three seconds. If the attachment is compatible with an app that's installed on your iPhone or iPad, you're given the option to transfer the file to that app or directly open or access the file using that app.

ORGANIZE EMAIL MESSAGES IN FOLDERS

Email messages appearing in your Inbox, for example, can easily be moved into another folder, allowing you to better organize your emails. Here's how to do this:

> **✐ NOTE** Not all email account types allow for folders to be created. In some cases, you're limited to the default folders that are already related to that account, such as Inbox, Sent, Read, Trash and Spam. (The default folders vary by account type.)

1. From the Inbox listing, tap the Edit button that's located above the Inbox listing. Or, if you're viewing an email message, tap on the Move icon (it's shaped like file folder.) On the iPhone, the Move icon can be found at the bottom of the screen. On the iPad, it's located in the upper-right corner of the screen.

2. When you tap the Move icon (as shown in Figure 14.10), the various folders available for that email account are displayed. Tap on the mailbox to which you want to move the message. The mailboxes available vary for different types of email accounts, and might vary depending on whether you have created your own mailboxes using the Mail app.

3. The email message will be moved to the folder you select.

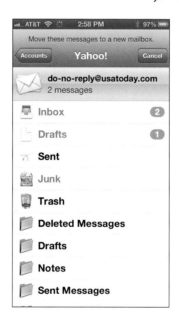

FIGURE 14.10

To move a file, tap on the Move icon, and then tap on the name of the mailbox to which you want to move the message. The message will be transferred from your Inbox to that other mailbox.

> **✓ TIP** As you're managing incoming and outgoing emails, the Mail app uses the default mailboxes that are already associated with that email account, such as Inbox, Drafts, Sent, Trash, and Junk. However, for many types of email accounts (but not all), you can create your own mailboxes as well, and then move individual messages into those mailboxes, to customize the way you organize them.
>
> To create a custom mailbox for use with an email account (assuming that your existing email account allows for this feature), from the Inbox, tap on the Mailboxes icon. When the Mailboxes screen appears, under the Accounts heading, choose one of your accounts for which you want to create a mailbox, and tap on its listing. A listing of the existing mailboxes for that account will be displayed.
>
> Tap on the Edit button that appears near the top of the screen. Then, tap on the New Mailbox icon that appears near the bottom of the screen. Enter the name of the mailbox you want to create, and then tap on the Save button. Your new mailbox is now displayed with that email account. The process works the same on the iPhone and iPad, but the position of the various icons varies slightly.

FORWARDING, PRINTING, AND REPLYING TO MESSAGES

From the Mail app, you can forward any incoming message to someone else, reply to the message, or print the email by tapping on the left-pointing, curved-arrow icon that's displayed when you're viewing an email. On an iPhone, the curved-arrow icon is displayed at the bottom of the screen. On an iPad, it can be found in the upper-right corner of the main Inbox screen (next to the Trash Can icon).

When you tap on this icon, as you're reading any email message, a menu will be displayed with the following three options: Reply, Forward, and Print.

To reply to the message you're reading (and respond to the sender), tap on the Reply icon. A blank email message template appears on the screen. Refer to the "Composing an Email Message" section for details on how to write and send an email message from the Mail app.

To forward the email you're reading to another recipient, tap on the Forward icon. If there's an attachment associated with this email, you're be asked, "Include attachments from original email?" and you'll see two options displayed on the screen, labeled "Include" and "Don't Include." Tap on the appropriate response.

When you opt to forward an email, a new message template appears on the screen. However, the contents of the message you're forwarding appears in the body of the email message. Start the message-forwarding process by filling in the To field. You can also modify the Subject field (or leave the message's original Subject), and then add to the body of the email message with your own text. This text appears above the forwarded message's content.

> **TIP** To forward an email to multiple recipients, enter each person's email address in the To field of the outgoing message, separating each address with a comma (,). Thus, you'd type **Jason@JasonRich.com, JasonRich77@yahoo.com** in the To field to forward or send the message to these two recipients simultaneously. Or tap on the plus icon (+) that appears to the right of the To field to add more recipients.

When you're ready to forward the message to one or more recipients, tap on the blue-and-white Send button that appears. Or tap the Cancel button to abort the message-forwarding process.

If you have a wireless printer set up to work with your iOS device (using the AirPrint feature built in to the iOS 6 operating system and some printers), you can tap the Print icon that appears when you tap the left-pointing curved-arrow icon as you're reading an email.

> **TIP** As you're reading emails, you'll discover that all the touchscreen finger motions you've learned work on the section of the iOS device's screen that's displaying the actual email messages. You can scroll up or down and/or zoom in or out. Plus, you can use the Select, Cut, Copy, and Paste features built in to the iOS operating system to manipulate the contents of an email message and utilize that content in other apps, for example. Or you can select, cut, and paste a portion of one email and insert it into another email message you're composing.

IN THIS CHAPTER

- How to use new features added to the Calendar and Contacts apps
- Implement strategies for staying organized, on time, and productive with your iOS device
- Keep your calendar and contact-related data synced between your iOS mobile devices, computer(s), and online apps

15

CALENDAR AND CONTACT MANAGEMENT STRATEGIES

Veteran iPhone or iPad users will immediately discover some nice improvements to the iOS 6 editions of the Contacts and Calendar apps. The majority of the Contact app's improvements related to iOS 6 come in the form of integration with other apps, which can now more readily access your calendar information and personal contacts database. This enables you to utilize contact data from the Contacts app without actually launching Contacts, for example. Yet the information you need will be placed exactly where you need it, such as in the To field of an email, a tweet, or a text message you're composing.

In keeping with iOS 6's theme of inter-app integration, the Calendar and Contacts apps are fully compatible with iCloud, which makes synchronizing your app-related data a straightforward process. You can also more easily synchronize data

with online-based calendars or contact management apps related to Microsoft Exchange, as well as Google, Yahoo! or Facebook.

Plus, Calendar can easily be set up to work with Notification Center, so all of your alerts, alarms, reminders, and notifications are consistently displayed in one place—the Notification Center screen (iPhone) or window (iPad)—that's constantly available to you. See Chapter 4, "Make the Most of Notification Center," for information on how to set up and use Notification Center with these and other apps.

Best of all, Calendar and Contacts are among the apps that come preinstalled with iOS 6, so they're immediately available to you, without your having to first visit the App Store.

> **NOTE** The features and functions offered by the Calendar and Contacts apps are virtually identical on the iPhone, iPad, and iPod Touch. However, due to varying screen sizes, the location of specific command icons, options, and menus sometimes varies. However, after you get to know how each app functions in general, you'll easily be able to switch between using them on your iPhone, iPad, or Mac (running OS X Mountain Lion), for example, without confusion.

On the iPad, all information relevant to a specific app or function is typically displayed on a single screen. On the iPhone, however, that same information is often split up and displayed on several separate screens.

GET ACQUAINTED WITH THE CALENDAR APP

With its multiple viewing options for keeping track of the scheduling information stored in it, the iOS 6 version of the Calendar app for the iPhone or iPad is a highly customizable scheduling tool that enables you to easily sync your scheduling data with your primary computer's scheduling software (such as Microsoft Outlook on a PC or Calendar/iCal on a Mac) or an online-based scheduling application (from Google, Yahoo!, Facebook or that's Microsoft Exchange-compatible).

SYNC APP-SPECIFIC DATA WITH ONLINE-BASED APPS

To sync your calendar or contacts data with Yahoo!, Google or Microsoft Exchange-compatible software, instead of using iCloud, launch Settings and tap on the Mail, Contacts, Calendars option. Under the Accounts heading, tap on Add Account… Then, choose which type of account you want to sync data with, such as Microsoft Exchange, Gmail (Google) or Yahoo!. Tap on your option.

When prompted, enter your Name, Email address, Password and an Account Description (as well as any other information related to your account that's requested). After your account is verified, a menu screen within Settings related to that account lists app-specific options, such as Mail, Contacts, Calendars, Reminders and/or Notes. Turn on the virtual switch associated with any or all of these options. Your iPhone or iPad automatically and continuously syncs your app-specific data on your iOS device with your online-based account. So, if you turn on the virtual switch associated with Calendars, your event data is continuously synchronized.

To sync scheduling and/or contact-related data with Facebook, launch Settings and tap on the Facebook option. When prompted, enter your Facebook user-name and password. Then, near the bottom of the Facebook menu screen within Settings, turn on the virtual switch that's associated with Calendar and/or Contacts. Periodically tap on the Update All Contacts option as you add new online Facebook friends. Calendar and/or contacts data is imported from Facebook and incorporated into your Calendar and/or Contacts apps.

Both the Calendar and Contacts app also work seamlessly for syncing data between your iOS mobile devices, Mac(s) and PC(s) that are linked to the same iCloud account. To set up this feature, launch Settings, tap on the iCloud option, and then turn on the virtual switch associates with Calendar and/or Contacts. This only needs to be done once on each device or computer that's linked to the same iCloud account. Your app-specific data automatically remains synced.

> **TIP** Once you turn on iCloud functionality in conjunction with Calendar or Contacts, at anytime and from any computer or Internet-enabled device, you can access online-based versions of the Contacts and Calendar apps that are popu-lated with your own data. To do this, visit www.iCloud.com and log in using your Apple ID and password (or iCloud username and password), and then tap on the Calendar or Contacts app icon that's displayed on the screen.

From within Calendar, you can also share some or all of your schedule information with colleagues and maintain several separate, color-coded calendars to keep per-sonal and work-related responsibilities, as well as individual projects, listed sepa-rately, while still being able to view them on the same screen.

> **MORE INFO** For details about syncing Calendar data with a Yahoo! account, visit http://mobile.yahoo.com/iphone. For directions on how to sync the Calendar app with a Google account, visit http://support.google.com/a/users/bin/answer.py?hl=en&answer=138740.

CONTROLLING THE VIEW

Launch Calendar from your iOS device's Home Screen, and then choose in which viewing perspective you'd like to view your schedule data. Your options include these:

- **Day**—This view displays your appointments and scheduled events individually, based on the time each item is scheduled for (as shown in Figure 15.1).

FIGURE 15.1

The Day view of the Calendar app lets you see your schedule broken down one day at a time, in one-hour increments. (Shown here on the iPad.)

On the iPhone, the Day view displays the date at the top of the screen, and then an item-by-item listing of your scheduled appointments and obligations, displayed in chronological order, based on the time each is scheduled for on that day.

On the iPad, the Day display is split into two sections. You'll see the date, along with a small calendar for the month, and a summary listing of appointments and/or events displayed on the left side of the screen. On the right side of the screen is an item-by-item listing of your scheduled appointments and obligations, displayed in chronological order, based on the time each is scheduled for on that day.

> **TIP** Use the Day view of the Calendar app to see a detailed outline of scheduled appointments and events for a single day. Swipe your finger to scroll up or down to see an hour-by-hour summary of that day's schedule.

On the iPhone, tap on the left or right arrows displayed at the top of the screen, to the right and left of the date, to view another day's schedule.

On the iPad, tap the left or right arrows displayed at the bottom of the screen, or tap a particular month and day icon, also displayed at the bottom of the screen, to view another day's schedule.

■ **Week**—This view uses a grid format to display the days of the week along the top of the screen and time intervals along the left side (shown in Figure 15.2). With it, you have an overview of all appointments and events scheduled during a particular week (Sunday through Saturday).

Use the small icons at the bottom of the screen to change the date range you want to view in the main portion of the screen.

FIGURE 15.2

The Calendar app's Week view shown here on the iPad. To view it on the iPhone, rotate the device to landscape mode.

> **TIP** On the iPhone, to see the Week view, first tap the List, Day or Month view tab at the bottom of the screen, and then rotate your iPhone from portrait mode to landscape mode to automatically switch to the Week view. You can then swipe your finger from left to right, right to left, and/or up and down on the screen to scroll through your appointments in the Week view of the Calendar app.

■ **Month**—This month-at-a-time view enables you to see a month's worth of appointments and events at a time. Tap any single day to immediately switch to the Day view to review a detailed summary of appointments or events slated for that day. On an iPad, this requires a double-tap on a specific day.

> **TIP** On the iPhone, use the left and right arrows, displayed to the right and left of the Month and Year, to quickly jump between months as you view the calendar in Month view.
>
> On the iPad, tap on the small year and month icons, displayed at the bottom of the screen, to quickly jump between months as you view the calendar in Month view. You can also use the arrow icons displayed to the right and left of the month display at the bottom of the screen to change the month you're viewing.

■ **Year** (iPad Only)—This Year view in Calendar enables you to look at 12 mini-calendars and see a color-coded preview of your schedule (with minimal detail displayed). For example, use this view to block out vacation days, travel days, and so on, and get a comprehensive view of your overall annual schedule.

■ **List**—See a complete summary listing of all appointments and events stored in the Calendar app. You can tap on an individual listing to see its complete details. This is a fast and convenient way to see your upcoming appointments in chronological order. Using this view, you can scroll through upcoming events and appointments without knowing their exact date. It also enables you to more easily use the Calendar app as a to-do list manager (instead of the Reminders app).

> **TIP** Regardless of which view you select, at any time, you can view the current day's schedule by tapping the Today button that's located in the lower-left corner of the screen. On the calendar itself, the current date is always highlighted in blue.

HOW TO ENTER A NEW APPOINTMENT

Regardless of which calendar view you're using, follow these steps to enter a new appointment:

1. Tap the plus icon that's displayed in the upper-right corner of the screen on the iPhone or the lower-right corner of the screen on the iPad. This causes an Add Event window to be displayed (shown in Figure 15.3).

FIGURE 15.3
The Add Event window on the iPad looks identical to the Add Event screen on the iPhone.

> **NOTE** When you're using the Calendar app, all appointments, meetings, and other items you enter are referred to as "events."

2. The first field in the Add Event window is labeled Title. Using the virtual keyboard, enter a heading for the appointment or event, such as "Lunch with Rusty," "Ryan's Soccer Practice," "Call Email," or "Mandatory Sales Meeting at Work."

3. If there's a location associated with the event, tap the Location field that's located below the Title field, and then use the virtual keyboard to enter an address or a location. Entering information into the Location field is optional. You can be as detailed as you want when entering information into this field.

4. To set the time and date for the new appointment to begin and end, tap the Starts and Ends field. A new Start & End window is displayed, temporarily replacing the Add Event window.

5. When viewing the Start & End window, tap the Starts option so that it becomes highlighted in blue, and then use the scrolling Date, Hour, Minute, and AM/PM dials to select the start time for your appointment.

6. After entering the start time, tap on the Ends option, and again use the scrolling Date, Hour, Minute, and AM/PM dials to select the end time for your appointment. Or if the appointment lasts the entire day, tap the All-Day virtual switch, moving it from the off to the on position.

7. After you enter the start time and end time for the appointment, you must tap the blue-and-white Done button to save this information and return to the Add Event window.

    If the appointment you're entering repeats every day, every week, every two weeks, every month, or every year, tap the Repeat option, and choose the appropriate time interval. The default for this option is Never, meaning that it is a nonrepeating, one-time-only appointment.

8. To set an audible alarm for the event, tap the Alert option displayed below the Repeat option in the Add Event window. The Event Alert window temporarily replaces the Add Event window.

9. In the Event Alert window, tap to specify when you want the audible alarm to sound to remind you of the appointment. Your options are None (which is the default), At Time of Event, 5 minutes before, 15 minutes before, 30 minutes before, one hour before, two hours before, one day before, or two days before. When you tap your selection, a check mark that corresponds to that selection displays on the left side of the window.

10. Tap the blue-and-white Done button that's displayed in the upper-right corner of the Event Alert window to save the information and return to the Add Event screen.

> **☑ TIP** After you've added an alert, a Second Alert option displays in the Add Event window. If you want to add a secondary alarm to this appointment, tap the Second Alert option, and when the Event Alert window reappears, tap on the time when you want the second alarm to sound. Again, don't forget to tap on the Done button.
>
> This is useful if you want to be reminded of an appointment or deadline several hours (or days) before it's scheduled to occur, and then again several minutes before, for example. You can pick the time periods between the two alarms.

11. When you return to the Add Event window, if you're maintaining several separate calendars in the Calendar app, you can choose in which calendar you want to list the appointment or event by tapping on the Calendar option and then selecting the appropriate calendar.

> **TIP** Tap on the Invitees option within the Add Event window to invite others to the event via email. You can manually type names or tap the plus-sign icon to add contacts from your Contacts database. The person you add as an invitee is sent an email automatically, allowing them to respond to the invite. The Calendar app keeps track of RSVPs for event attendees.

It is essential that you tap the blue-and-white Done button to save the new appointment information and have it displayed in your calendar. Tap the Cancel icon (displayed in the upper-left corner of the Add Event, Start & End, Repeat, or Event Alert window), to exit that window without saving any new information.

> **TIP** As you scroll down in the Add Event window, you will see an optional URL and Notes field. Using the virtual keyboard, enter a website URL that somehow corresponds to the event. Or tap on the Notes field and type notes pertaining to the appointment (or paste data from other apps in this field).

USE SIRI TO ENTER NEW EVENTS INTO THE CALENDAR APP

Instead of manually entering appointment or event information into your iPhone or iPad using the virtual keyboard, or importing/syncing scheduling data from another computer or device, you always have the option to use Siri. To create a new Event within the Calendar app using your voice, activate Siri and say something like:

- "Set up a meeting at 11am with John Doe at his office."
- "Meet with Rusty today at 2:30pm."
- "New appointment with Dr. Doe on Wednesday, July 11th at 4:00pm."
- "Schedule a dinner with Rusty at Morton's Steak House in Boston on Saturday, July 7th at 6:00pm."

VIEWING INDIVIDUAL APPOINTMENT DETAILS

From any calendar view in the Calendar app, tap an individual event (appointment, meeting, and so on) to view all the details related to that item.

When you tap on a single event listing, a new window opens. In the upper-right corner of the window/screen is an Edit icon. Tap it to modify any aspect of the event listing, such as the title, location, start time, end time, alert, or notes.

To delete an event entry entirely, tap the red-and-white Delete Event icon that's displayed at the bottom of the Edit window. Or when you're done making changes to an Event entry, tap on the blue-and-white Done button that's displayed in the upper-right corner of the window.

> **TIP**   The Calendar app works with several other apps, including Contacts and Notification Center. For example, in Contacts, you can enter someone's birthday in a record, and that information can automatically be displayed within the Calendar app.
>
> To display birthday listings, for example, from within Calendar, tap the Calendars button, which is displayed in the upper-left corner of the screen, and then tap on the Birthdays option to add a check mark to that selection. All recurring birthdays stored in your Contacts app will now appear in Calendar.

QUICKLY FIND APPOINTMENT OR EVENT DETAILS

In addition to viewing the various calendar views offered within the Calendar app, to find individual appointments, use the Search field. On the iPhone, the in-app Search field can be found at the top of the screen when you tap on the List option (displayed at the bottom of the screen for viewing events). On the iPad, the Search field can always be found in the upper-right corner of the Calendar app.

Tap the Search field, and then use the virtual keyboard to enter any keyword or phrase associated with the appointment you're looking for.

Or from the iPhone or iPad's Home Screen, swipe your finger from left to right to access the Spotlight Search screen. In the Search field that appears, enter a keyword, search phrase, or date associated with an appointment. When a list of relevant items is displayed, tap the appointment you want to view. This launches the Calendar app and displays that specific appointment.

> ☑ **TIP**　Using Siri, say something like, "When is my next appointment with [insert name]?" You can also say, "Show me my schedule for Wednesday," or ask, "What's on my calendar for July 7?" in order to quickly find an event stored within the Calendar app. If you enter information into the Location field as you're creating events within the app, you can later ask Siri, "Where is my next meeting?"

VIEWING ONE OR MORE COLOR-CODED CALENDARS

One of the handy features of the Calendar app is that you can view and manage multiple color-coded calendars at once on the same screen, or you can easily switch between calendars.

To decide which calendar information you want to view, tap the Calendars icon that is displayed in the upper-left corner of the screen. When the Show Calendars window appears, select which calendar or calendars you want to view on your device's screen by tapping on their listings.

You can view one or more calendars at a time, or you can select to view data from all your calendars on one screen simultaneously. Each calendar is color-coded, so you can tell entries apart when looking at multiple calendars on the screen at once. If you're using color-coding on your Mac with the Calendar app, for example, this coding transfers to your iOS device when you sync Calendar data. Otherwise, each time a new Calendar is created within the Calendar app, a color will be assigned to it by the app.

CUSTOMIZING THE CALENDAR APP

There are many ways to customize the Calendar app beyond choosing between the various calendar views. For example, you can set audible alerts, and/or use on-screen Alerts and Banners to remind you of appointments, meetings, and events. You can also display Calendar related information within the Notification Center screen (iPhone) or window (iPad).

> ☑ **TIP**　To customize the audio alert generated by the Calendar app, launch the Settings app, and then select the Sounds option.
>
> Make sure the Calendar Alerts option, displayed in the Sounds screen of Settings, is turned on. If this option is turned off, a text-based message displays on the iPhone or iPad's screen as an event reminder instead of an audible alarm sounding.

If you are able to receive meeting or event invites from others, from the Settings app, tap on the Mail, Contacts and Calendars option. Then scroll down to the Calendars heading and make sure the New Invitations Alerts option is turned on. This enables you to hear an audible alarm when you receive a new invitation.

Also from this screen, under the Calendars heading, determine how far back in your schedule you want to sync appointment data between your primary computer and your iOS device. Your options include Events 2 Weeks Back, Events 1 Month Back, Events 3 Months Back, Events 6 Months Back, and All Events.

ADJUSTING TIME ZONE SUPPORT

When the Time Zone Support option is turned on and you've selected the major city that you're in or near, all alarms are activated based on that city's time zone. However, when you travel, turn off this option. With Time Zone Support turned off, the iPhone or iPad determines the current date and time based on the location and time zone you're in (when it's connected to cell network or Internet), and adjusts all your alarms to go off at the appropriate time for that time zone.

To access the Time Zone Support feature, follow these steps:

1. Launch the Settings app.

2. Select the Mail, Contacts, Calendars option.

3. Scroll down to the options listed under Calendars, and then tap on Time Zone Support.

4. When the Time Zone Support screen appears, you will see a virtual switch for turning this feature on or off. When it's turned on, below the switch is a Time Zone option. Tap it, and then choose your home city (or a city in the time zone you're in).

When turned off, Time Zone Support displays event times in your Calendar and activates alarms based on the time zone selected. So if New York City (Eastern Time Zone) is selected, and you have an appointment set for 2:00 p.m. with an accompanying alarm, you see that appointment listed at 2:00 p.m. and hear the alarm at 2:00 p.m. Eastern Time, regardless of where, or in what time zone, you're actually physically located.

> **TIP** Just as with Contacts, Reminders, and Notes, you can sync your app-specific Calendar data with iCloud so that your schedule becomes accessible on all of your iOS mobile devices, as well as your Mac(s) or PC(s) that are linked to the same account. When you do this, you can also visit www.iCloud.com, log in using

your Apple ID and password (or iCloud username and password) and then use the online-based version of the Calendar will to view your scheduling data from any computer or Internet-enabled device.

USE CONTACTS TO KEEP IN TOUCH WITH PEOPLE YOU KNOW

The art of networking is all about meeting new people, staying in contact with them, making referrals and connections for others, and tapping the knowledge, experience, or expertise of the people you know to help you achieve your personal or career-related goals.

In addition to the contacts you establish and maintain within your network, your personal contacts database might include people you work with, customers, clients, family members, people from your community whom you interact with (doctors, hair stylist, barber, dry cleaners, and so on), your real-world friends, and your online friends from Facebook, for example.

NOTE Contacts is a powerful and customizable contact management database program that works with several other apps that also came preinstalled on your iPhone or iPad, including Mail, Calendar, Safari, FaceTime, and Maps, as well as optional apps, like the official Facebook and Twitter apps.

THE CONTACTS APP IS HIGHLY CUSTOMIZABLE

Chances are, the same contacts database that you rely on at your office or on your personal computer at home can be synced with your iPhone or iPad and made available to you using the Contacts app.

Of course, Contacts can also be used as a standalone app, enabling you to enter new contact entries as you meet new people and need to keep track of details about them on your iOS device.

The information you maintain in your Contacts database is highly customizable, which means you can keep track of only the information you want or need. For example, within each contact entry, you can store a vast amount of information about a person, including the following:

- First and last name
- Name prefix (Mr., Mrs., Dr., and so on)

- Name suffix (Jr., Sr., Ph.D., Esq., and so on)
- Job title
- Company
- Multiple phone numbers (work, home, cell, and so on)
- Multiple email addresses
- Multiple mailing addresses (work, home, and so on)
- Multiple web page addresses
- Facebook, Twitter, Skype, Instant Messenger, or other online social networking site usernames

You can also customize your contacts database to include additional information, such as each contact's photo, nickname, spouse's and/or assistant's names, birthday, and Instant Messenger usernames, as well as detailed notes about the contact.

When you're using the Contacts app, your entire contacts database is instantly searchable using data from any field within the database, so even if you have a database containing thousands of entries, you can find the person or company you're looking for in a matter of seconds. And with the iOS 6 version of Contacts, you can now link contact entries together.

THE CONTACTS APP WORKS SEAMLESSLY WITH OTHER APPS

After your contacts database has been populated with entries, you'll discover that the Contacts app works with other apps on your iPhone and/or iPad. Here are just some of the ways your device's other apps can work with the Contacts app:

- When you compose a new email message from within Mail, in the To field you can begin typing someone's full name or email address. If that person's contact information is already stored within Contacts, the relevant email address automatically displays in the email's To field.
- If you're planning a trip to visit a contact, from the Maps app, you can pull up someone's address from your Contacts database and obtain driving directions to the person's home or work location.
- If you include each person's birthday in your Contacts database, that information can automatically be displayed in the Calendar app to remind you in advance to send a card.
- As you're creating each Contacts entry, you can include a photo of that person—by either activating the Camera app from the Contacts app to snap a photo or using a photo that's stored in the Photos app—and link it with the

contact. You can also insert photos of Facebook friends into the app auto-matically. See the section called, "How to Add a Photo to a Contacts Entry," later in this chapter.

- From within FaceTime, you can create a Favorites list of people you video-conference with often. You will compile this list from entries in your Contacts database, but you can access it from FaceTime. On the iPhone, the Favorites list for the Phone app and FaceTime are the same. On the iPad, launch the FaceTime app, tap on the Favorites command icon, and then tap the plus-sign icon to add each new contact to the Favorites list.

- From the Messages app, you can access your Contacts database when fill-ing out the To field as you compose new text messages to be sent via iMes-sage, text message or instant message. As soon as you tap on the To field, an All Contacts window appears, allowing you to select contacts from your Contacts database (or you can manually enter the recipients' info).

- If you're active on Facebook or Twitter, you have the option to add each con-tact's Facebook username or Twitter username within their Contacts entry. When you do this, the app automatically downloads each entry's Facebook profile picture and inserts it into your Contacts database.

When you first launch the Contacts app, its related database will be empty. However, you can create and build your database in two ways:

- You can sync the Contacts app with your primary contact management appli-cation on your computer, on your network, or on an online (cloud)-based service, such as iCloud.

- You can manually enter contact information directly into the app.

Ultimately, as you begin using this app and come to rely on it, you can enter new contact information or edit entries either on your iOS device or in your primary contact management application, and keep all the information synchronized, regardless of where the entry was created or modified.

WHO DO YOU KNOW? HOW TO VIEW YOUR CONTACTS

From the iPhone or iPad's Home Screen, tap the Contacts app to launch it.

On the iPhone, what you'll see when the Contacts app launches is the All Contacts screen, which displays an alphabetical listing of your contacts. Along the right side of the screen are alphabetic tabs, and a Search field is located near the top of the screen.

On the iPad, on the extreme left side of the screen are alphabetic tabs. Near the upper left of the screen, you'll see the All Contacts heading. Below it is a Search field. After you have added entries in your contacts database, they are listed alphabetically on the left side of the screen, below the Search field (as shown in Figure 15.4).

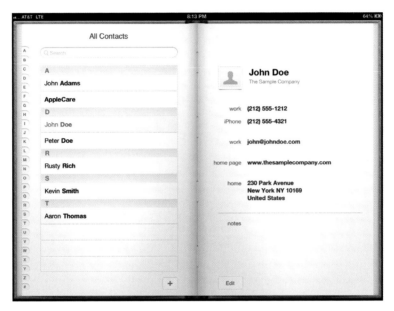

FIGURE 15.4

On the iPad, the All Contacts listing and individual listings are shown on the left and right side of the screen, respectively. On the iPhone, this information is divided into two separate screens.

> **TIP** If you tap the Search field, you can quickly find a particular entry by entering any keyword associated with an entry, such as a first or last name, city, state, job title, or company name. Any content in your Contacts database is searchable from this Search field.
>
> You can also tap a letter tab on the screen to see all entries "filed" under that letter by a contact's last name, first name, or company name, depending on how you set up the Contacts app from within the Settings app's Mail, Contacts, Calendars option.

On the iPhone, to see the complete listing for a particular entry, tap on its listing from the All Contacts screen. A new screen shows the specific contact's information (shown in Figure 15.5).

FIGURE 15.5

A sample contact entry from the Contacts app displayed on the iPhone 5.

On the iPad, to see the complete listing for a particular entry, tap on its listing from the All Contacts display on the left side of the screen. That entry's complete contents will then be displayed on the right side of the screen.

> ☑ **TIP** In addition to using the search field in the Contacts app, you can quickly find information from within this app by accessing the Spotlight Search screen from your iPhone or iPad's Home Screen.
>
> To use the Spotlight Search screen, start on the first Home Screen page, and swipe your finger from left to right across the display. The Spotlight Search screen enables you to search for content within your entire iOS device (including the Contacts app).

If you're using Siri, you can quickly find and display any contact within your Contacts database by activating Siri and saying, "Find [insert name] within Contacts." The appropriate info screen for that contact will be displayed.

MEET SOMEONE NEW? CREATE A NEW CONTACTS ENTRY

To create a new Contacts entry, tap the plus icon. On the iPhone, it's displayed in the upper-right corner of the All Contacts screen. On the iPad, the plus icon can be found near the bottom center of the Contacts screen. When you do this, the main Contacts screen is replaced by an Info screen, and the virtual keyboard appears.

> **NOTE** As you're creating each Contacts entry, you can fill in whichever fields you want. You can always go back and edit a contact entry to include additional information later.

Within the Info window are a handful of empty fields related to a single Contacts entry, starting with the First Name field (shown in Figure 15.6). By default, the fields available in this app include First Name, Last Name, Company, Photo, [Mobile] Phone Number, Email Address, Ringtone, Text Tone, Home Page (Website) URL, Address, and Notes.

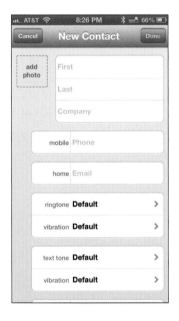

FIGURE 15.6

From this Info screen, you can create a new contact and include as much information pertaining to that person or company as you want. (Shown here on the iPhone 5.)

> **TIP** When creating or editing contacts, it's extremely important to associate the correct labels with phone numbers, email address, and address data.
>
> For each phone number you add to a contact's entry, for example, it can include a Home, Work, Mobile, iPhone or Other label (among others). For many of the features of iOS 6 that utilize data from your Contacts database to work correctly, it's important that you properly label content you add to each Contacts entry. This is particularly important if you'll be using Siri.

Some of these fields, including Phone, Email, and Mailing Address, allow you to input multiple listings, one at a time. So you can include someone's home phone, work phone, and mobile phone numbers within the entry. Likewise, you can include multiple email addresses, and/or a home address and work address for an individual.

Begin by filling in one field at a time. To jump to the next field, tap it. So, after using the virtual keyboard to fill in the First Name field, tap on the Last Name field to fill it in, and then move on to the Company field, if applicable, by tapping it.

> **TIP** For each type of field, the virtual keyboard modifies itself accordingly, giving you access to specialized keys. You can change the label associated with certain fields (which are displayed in blue) by tapping the field label itself. This reveals a Label menu, offering selectable options for that field.
>
> For example, the Label options for the Phone Number field include Mobile, iPhone, Home, Work, Main, Home Fax, Work Fax, Pager, and Other. At the bottom of this Label window, you can tap the Add Custom Label option to create your own label if none of the listed options applies.
>
> Tap the label title of your choice. A check mark appears next to it, and you are returned to the Info window.

As you scroll down in the Info window and fill in each field, at the bottom of the window you'll discover an Add Field option. Tap this to reveal a menu containing at least 14 additional fields you can add to Contacts entries, such as a Middle name, Job Title, Nickname, Instant Message username, Twitter username, (Facebook) Profile, and Birthday (as shown in Figure 15.7 on the iPad). There's also a field to add Related People, such as the names of your contact's mother, father, parent, brother, sister, child, friend, spouse, partner, assistant, manager, or other. You can also add your own titles for the Related People field.

A green-and-white plus icon that is displayed next to a field (on the left) means that you can have multiple entries for that field, such as several phone numbers, email addresses, or mailing addresses.

If there's a field displayed that you don't want to utilize or display, you can tap the red-and-white minus sign icon to delete the field from the Info window.

FIGURE 15.7

From the Add Field option, choose what additional information you want to include in a particular contact's entry, such as the person's birthday, spouse's name, Twitter username (@Username), or Instant Message username. This information can automatically be used by other apps.

Each time you add a new mailing address to a contact's entry from within the Info screen, the Address field expands to include a Street, City, State, ZIP, and Country field.

> **TIP** In the Notes field, you can enter as much information pertaining to that contact as you want. Or you can paste content from another app into this field using the iOS's Select, Copy, and Paste commands, and using the multitasking capabilities of your iPhone or iPad to quickly switch between apps.

After you have filled in all the fields for a particular entry, tap the Done button, which is displayed in the upper-right corner of the Info window. Your new entry gets added to your contacts database.

HOW TO ADD A PHOTO TO A CONTACTS ENTRY

To the immediate left of the First Name field is a square box that says Add Photo. When you tap this field, a submenu with two options—Take Photo and Choose Photo—is displayed.

Tap Take Photo to launch the Camera app from within the Contacts app and snap a photo to be linked to the Contacts entry you're creating. Or tap on the Choose Photo option. In this case, the Photos app launches so that you can choose any digital image that's currently stored on your iOS device. When you tap the photo of your choice, a Choose a Photo window displays on the Contacts screen, enabling you to move and scale the image with your finger.

After cropping or adjusting the photo selected, tap the Use icon that's displayed in the upper-right corner of the Choose Photo window to link the photo with that contact's entry (as shown in Figure 15.8).

FIGURE 15.8

Linking a photo with someone's Contacts entry enables you to visually identify the person as you're reviewing your contacts.

> **TIP** If you use an iPhone, or FaceTime on your iPad, from the Ringtone option in the Info window, you can select the specific ringtone you hear each time that particular contact calls you. Your iPhone or iPad has 25 preinstalled ringtones (with Marimba being the default). From iTunes, you can download thousands of additional ringtones, many of which are clips from popular songs.

EDITING OR DELETING AN ENTRY

As you're looking at the main Contacts screen, you can edit an entry by tapping on its listing from the All Contacts screen. This results in the complete entry being displayed for that contact. To edit the contact, tap on the Edit icon. The Edit icon is displayed in the upper-right corner of the screen on the iPhone, but near the bottom of the screen on the iPad.

When the Info window appears, tap any field to modify it using the virtual keyboard. Delete any field(s) altogether by tapping on the red-and-white minus sign icon associated with it.

You can also add new fields within an entry by tapping any of the green-and-white plus sign icons and then choosing the type of field you want to add.

When you're done editing a Contacts entry, again tap the Done button.

> **TIP** To delete an entire entry from your Contacts database, as you're editing a contact entry and looking at the Info window for that entry, scroll down to the bottom of it and tap the Delete Contact option.

INTERACTIVE CONTACTS ENTRIES

Whenever you're viewing a Contacts entry, tapping a listed email address causes the Mail app to launch, which enables you to compose an email message to that person. The To field of the outgoing email is automatically filled in with the email address you tapped on from within Contacts.

> **TIP** On the iPhone, tap any phone number listed in a Contacts entry to dial that phone number and initiate a call. Or at the bottom of the contact entry's Info screen, tap on the Send Message or FaceTime icon to either send a text message to that person or initiate a FaceTime videoconference.

Likewise, from within an entry, tap any website URL that's listed, and the Safari web browser launches and automatically displays the appropriate web page.

This also works with the Twitter field (if you have the Twitter app installed). Tap on someone's Twitter username to send a tweet. The appropriate @Username appears at the beginning of the tweet automatically.

> **TIP** If you tap on a street address, this automatically launches the Maps app, which displays that address. (At this point, you can tap on the Directions icon to obtain directions to that contact's location.)

HOW TO LINK CONTACT ENTRIES TOGETHER

Depending on how you use the Contacts app, you might find it useful to group contacts based on relationships. For example, you might have duplicate listings that contain different information for the same person. By linking these contacts, it makes it easier for you to organize people who have separate entries, such as for the Home and Work information. When you do this, all entries for that person appear as one single entry within the Contacts app, and their combined information can be viewed on a single screen.

When you're in edit mode, modifying content in a contact's entry, scroll down to the bottom of the window or screen to link contact entries together.

On the iPhone, tap on the Link Contact icon that's displayed under the Linked Contacts heading, and then choose one or more contact entries to link to the one you're editing.

On the iPad, you link contacts by scrolling down below the red-and-white Delete contact icon when editing an entry. Tap on the small icon with a silhouette of a head with a plus sign next to it to link this contact with one or more other contacts already in your database.

SHARING CONTACT ENTRIES

From the main Contacts screen, tap a contact that you want to share details about. When the contact's entry is displayed, scroll down to the bottom of the entry until you see the Share Contact button displayed. Tap it. You can then choose to share the contact's details with someone else via email or text/instant message.

If you choose email, an outgoing email message form displays on your iPhone or iPad's screen. Fill in the To field with the person or people you want to share the contact info with. The default subject of the email is Contact. However, you can tap this field and modify it using the virtual keyboard.

If you choose Message, an instant/text message screen (iPhone) or window (iPad) is displayed, allowing you to fill in the To field with the names or text/instant message usernames or mobile phone numbers for the people you want to share the information with.

The Contacts entry you selected (stored in .vcf format) is already embedded in the outgoing email or text/instant message. When you've filled in all the necessary fields, tap the blue-and-white Send icon. Upon doing this, you are returned to the Contacts app.

The recipient(s) will quickly receive your email or message. When he/she clicks on the email's attachment (the contact entry you sent), it can automatically be imported into their contact management application as a new entry, such as in the Contacts app on their Mac, iPhone or iPad. If the recipient doesn't have a compatible app, they can simply view the contact information using compatible software.

> **☑ TIP** If someone shares a Contacts entry with you via email, when you're viewing the incoming email on your iPhone or iPad, tap the email's attachment. The Contacts entry that was emailed is displayed in a window. At the bottom of this window, as the recipient of the contact's information, tap the Create New Contact or Add to Existing Contact option to incorporate this information into your Contacts database.

ADDITIONAL WAYS TO MAKE CONTACT FROM WITHIN CONTACTS

When you're viewing any single contact, in addition to the Share Contact button you see displayed, you'll notice three other command buttons, including Send Message, FaceTime, and Add to Favorites. Tap on the Send Message icon to send that person a text/instant message via the Messages app. Or tap on the FaceTime app to initiate a FaceTime videoconference with that person.

If you tap on the Add to Favorites button, that contact will appear in your Favorites list that's displayed in the Phone and FaceTime apps.

16

iOS 6 GAMING

The latest iPhone and iPad models are chock-full of ways to entertain yourself. Thanks to their crisp touchscreens and superior sound systems, not to mention the built-in three-axis gyro and accelerometer, your iOS device is able to offer truly immersive interactive gaming experiences.

> **TIP** To hear the sound effects and music that accompany most games, plug in the Apple EarPods that came with your iPhone 5, or consider buying a pair of EarPods separately ($29). EarPods represent Apple's re-design of typical headphones. They work great with all iOS mobile devices for experiencing stereo music and audio—when playing games or using the Music or Videos app, for example.

Because your iPhone or iPad also connects directly to the wireless Web, you can easily engage in multiplayer games in various ways, so you can challenge others in high-action or

turn-based games whether your opponents are sitting next to you on a couch, are located across town, or they're on the opposite side of the country (or planet).

Simply by visiting the App Store or becoming active on Apple's Games Center, you'll find literally thousands of fun, challenging, cutting-edge, and often addictive games, developed by some of the most talented and imaginative video and computer game developers in the world.

So, whether you have five minutes in between meetings and want to experience some type of puzzle game, or you want to immerse yourself for hours at a time in an intricate computer-generated world, you'll find plenty of gaming experiences that cater to your wants, needs, time constraints, and skill level.

Some games are iPhone/iPod touch–specific or iPad-specific, meaning they're designed to work only on that device. However, others are hybrid apps that work on all iOS devices and can easily be shared between your devices via iCloud. For hybrid apps, you need to purchase each game only once to experience it on your iPhone, iPad, and iPod touch.

> **TIP** As you browse the App Store, look for games that are enhanced for the iPad. The games that are enhanced for the iPad will often have "HD" or "for iPad" as part of their title. These are often iPad-specific games that must be purchased separate from the iPhone version.

> **WHAT'S NEW** If you're an iPhone 5 user, look for a growing number of game titles, like Lili, Superbrothers: Sword & Sworcery EP, Sly Gamblers: Air Supremacy, Pocket Planes, Super Hexagon, Galaxy on Fire 2 HD, Wild Blood, Tiny Tower, Order & Chaos, and Jetpack Joyride, that are being promoted as "Enhanced For iPhone 5." These games take advantage of the phone's larger Retina display and faster processor.

MANY DIFFERENT GAMING EXPERIENCES ARE AT YOUR FINGERTIPS

The games available from the App Store are divided into different categories or genres. Some of the types of gaming experiences you can experience on your iPhone, iPad, or iPod touch include:

- **Action/Adventure**—From character-based games to high-action shoot'em-ups, iOS games feature highly detailed graphics, realistic sound effects, and plenty of fast-paced challenges.

■ **Action/Puzzle Challenges**—Games like Tetris, the massively popular Angry Birds series (shown in Figure 16.1), and Bejeweled Blitz (shown in Figure 16.2) are among the many types of action-based puzzle games that make you think and test your reflexes. The best puzzle games are easy to learn, difficult to master, and extremely addicting.

FIGURE 16.1

Angry Birds and its sequels are among the most popular games of all time for the iPhone and iPad. They offer countless hours of whimsical challenges.

FIGURE 16.2

Bejeweled Blitz is a colorful, fast-paced puzzle game that's been enhanced for play on the iPhone 5, but that also looks fantastic on older iPhone models and on the iPad.

- **Casino and Card Games**—Some of these games faithfully re-create the casino experience (slot machines, roulette, craps, and so on), whereas others allow you to compete against real players or computer-controlled opponents as you play popular card games, like blackjack, many variations of poker, or solitaire. The Solitaire app from Mobility Ware is one of many solitaire games offered from the App Store. It's shown on the iPhone 5 in Figure 16.3.

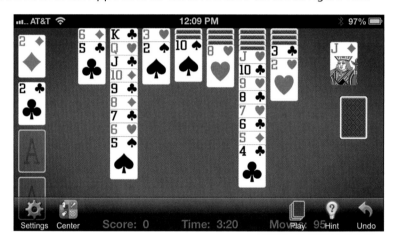

FIGURE 16.3

Card games and casino simulations of all kinds are available for the iPhone or iPad. Shown here is just one popular version of Solitaire from MobilityWare.

- **Classic Arcade and Video Games**—Pac-Man, Sonic the Hedgehog 2, Space Invaders, Asteroids, Centipede, and many others have been faithfully re-created for play on the iPhone and/or iPad, complete with their original graphics and sound effects.

> ☑ **TIP** To make classic arcade games, as well as action/adventure games, more realistic, a company called ThinkGeek (www.thinkgeek.com) offers a removable joystick attachment that sticks onto your iPad's screen, called the Joystick-It Arcade Stick that gives you more arcade-like control over the onscreen action. It's priced at $8.99.
>
> The Fling for iPad, from Ten One Design ($19.95, http://tenonedesign.com/fling.php), offers similar game-controller functionality but utilizes a totally different design. This is more of a removable thumb pad that attaches to the iPad's screen.
>
> The iCade accessory for iPad from Ion Audio ($99.99, www.ionaudio.com) is actually a wooden housing that your iPad gets inserted into. iCade transforms the

tablet into what looks like a tabletop coin-op arcade machine, complete with a full-size joystick controller and eight arcade-style buttons. It can be used to play more than 100 classic arcade games from Atari (like Asteroids, Centipede, and Battlezone), which are sold separately from the App Store.

- **Classic Board Games**—Faithful adaptations of classic board games, such as Monopoly, chess, checkers, backgammon, Life, Dominoes, Clue, Trivial Pursuit, Boggle, Scrabble, Uno, Risk, and Yahtzee, are all available for the iPhone and iPad as single or multiplayer games.

- **Crossword Puzzles**—If you're looking for crossword puzzle challenges, the options are extensive. There's the subscription-based NYTimes Crosswords app (shown in Figure 16.4) that re-creates each day's puzzle that's published in the *New York Times* newspaper. This app also includes a massive archive of 4,000-plus past puzzles. You'll also find dozens of other crossword puzzle apps available from the App Store.

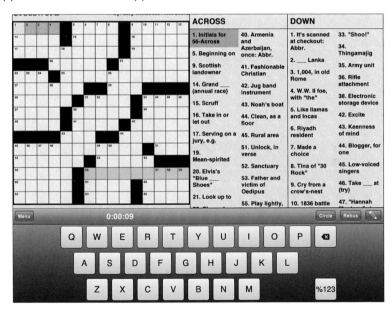

FIGURE 16.4

If you're a fan of crossword puzzles, be sure to check out the NYTimes Crosswords app. Try your hand at solving the actual puzzles that appear in the popular daily newspaper, plus access a massive archive of past crossword puzzles.

- **Simulations**—These games allow you to immerse yourself in a computer-generated, virtual world that can re-create a real-life environment or enable you to experience the most imaginative of scenarios. You can build and manage the city of your dreams by playing SimCity Deluxe for iPad, wield a mighty sword in a game like Infinity Blade II, become a sniper in Arcade Super Sniper: War on Terror, or help Papa Smurf build and manage a colorful Smurf village in Smurfs' Village (shown in Figure 16.5). There are also flight simulators, in which you can pilot all sorts of aircraft, or you can become the lead zookeeper of your own virtual zoo when you play Tap Zoo.

FIGURE 16.5

Smurfs' Village is an extremely popular game that's suitable for all ages. It's also an example of a free game that offers in-app purchases. As a result, it has become one of the highest-grossing iPhone and iPad apps ever. It's shown here being played on an iPad.

- **Sports Simulations**—These are games based on real-life sports, such as golf, baseball, basketball, football, and NASCAR. In many cases, the games re-create real-life professional athletes and/or teams using actual stats, and faithfully re-create the arenas, stadiums, courses, or tracks where the real-life sports take place. In fact, the more you know about the real-life sport when playing some of these simulations, the better you'll be at playing them. There are also less realistic sports games, like NBA Jam by EA Sports for iPad, that focus more on arcade-style action as opposed to realism.

> **TIP** If you're an avid golfer but can't make it out to the links in person, try playing the very realistic game Tiger Woods PGA Tour 12 (shown in Figure 16.6).

FIGURE 16.6
Tiger Woods PGA Tour 12 for iPad is one of many very realistic sports simulation games you can play on your tablet.

- **Sudoku Puzzles**—Challenge your mind with the many versions of Sudoku that are available from the App Store. Also available are other types of word- and number-based puzzle challenges, like many different Word Search games. Social Sudoku is one of more than 100 Sudoku apps available for the iPhone and iPad. It's shown in Figure 16.7 being played on an iPad.

In each of these game categories, you'll find many different game-play experiences. Although some of the games are adaptations of popular video games originally designed for Nintendo, Sony, Microsoft, Sega, or Atari gaming systems, for example, the iOS editions of these games often take full advantage of the features and functionality that are unique to the iPhone and/or iPad.

FIGURE 16.7

The Social Sudoku game is one of many Sudoku puzzle challenges available from the App Store for the iPhone and iPad.

> 📝 **TIP**   One of the most popular online-based multi-player games is called Words With Friends. It's is a turn-based, Scrabble-like, word building game that allows you to participate in up to 20 separate games with different people at the same time.
>
> A free, advertiser supported and a separate paid (ad-free) version for Words With Friends (shown in Figure 16.8) are available, but both offer identical game play and offer optional in-app purchases. While you're playing against other people via the Internet, you can chat with them (or taunt them) in real-time using text messages.
>
> One great feature of Words with Friends is that it's just as easy to find a total stranger to compete against safely as it is to invite a friend or loved one to play against you.

FIGURE 16.8
More than 20 million people from around the world have begun playing Words With Friends. It's a fun and challenging multi-player game for people over the age of eight.

Because your iOS device can connect to the Web, you're able to experience real-time multiplayer games and compete against friends, co-workers, your kids, or total strangers. In fact, Apple's own online-based Game Center (accessible through Game Center–compatible games, or the Game Center app that comes preinstalled on your iOS device) offers a free online forum in which you can meet and compete against others as you experience a growing number of popular multiplayer games.

Thousands of games are available from the App Store free of charge. Some are advertiser supported, whereas others offer optional in-app purchase options to access extra levels or gain special power-ups, items, or added functionality within a game. Many games are paid apps, ranging in price from $.99 to $6.99 (although occasionally, you'll find a game priced a bit higher).

> **! CAUTION** Some games are initially free of charge and offer a wonderful game-play experience. However, to access certain gaming features, obtain specific in-game items, or reach otherwise locked levels, you'll need to make in-app purchases, which over time can get expensive. These in-app purchases are typically optional but greatly enhance your game-play experience.

In some cases, a free game offers just one or two sample levels or just a preview of the game play, but ultimately requires you to purchase or upgrade to the paid version of the game to experience it in its entirety.

As a parent, you may want to use the iPhone or iPad's Restrictions feature to block your kids from making in-app purchases altogether.

TIPS FOR FINDING GAMES YOU'LL LOVE

With literally tens of thousands of games to choose from, and more being introduced every day, there are several strategies you can use to quickly find games that'll appeal to you as you explore the App Store or Game Center.

TIP On the iPhone, to discover the hottest games sorted by genre, launch the App Store app and tap on the Categories icon that's displayed near the top-left corner of the screen. From the Categories screen, tap on the Games option. Then, from the Games screen, select a sub-category, such as Action, Adventure, Board Games, Card Games, Puzzle Games, or Role Playing Games. You can then browse through listings for popular games that fall into that genre. Next to the New, What's Hot and Paid headings, for example, tap on the See All option to see what's offered.

On the iPad, to discover what other people are playing and what's truly popular, visit the App Store and tap on the Charts icon at the bottom of the screen. Then, in the upper-left corner of the screen, tap on the All Categories button. From the pull-down menu, choose Games, and then select one of the 19 Games sub-categories (such as Action, Adventure, Casino, Puzzle, or Sports) to see listing for the top Paid, Free and Top Grossing games in that sub-category.

As you explore the App Store looking for games to purchase, download, and install, focus on the description of each game, and pay attention to its overall star-based rating as well as its detailed reviews. Chances are, a game with dozens or hundreds of four- or five-star reviews will be a top-quality game.

NOTE If you look at Angry Birds Free for the iPhone, it has more than 111,160 ratings total, and the majority of those ratings are five stars. The iPhone version of this mega-popular game is shown in Figure 16.9.

FIGURE 16.9

Shown here is the iPhone version of Angry Birds. Whether you play Angry Birds HD on the iPad or this edition, you'll find yourself facing many hours worth of challenges and entertainment.

In addition to focusing on the game ratings, pay attention to the sample screen-shots offered in each detailed game listing. This will give you a good idea of what the game looks like and the quality of its graphics.

Another reliable source for discovering the best iOS games is to read independent reviews from well-respected websites and publications.

> 🔍 **MORE INFO** To find reliable, independent iOS game reviews, check out GameSpot (www.gamespot.com/iphone/index.html), MacWorld (http://www.macworld.com/category/ios-apps/software-games), MacLife (www.maclife.com/articles/games), or IGN Entertainment (http://www.ign.com/games/iphone).

After you've acquired a handful of games, from the App Store, you can seek out game recommendations from the Genius for Apps. Based on your past downloads and purchases, the Genius feature (when it's turned on) will suggest other games you might be interested in.

To access the Genius feature within the App Store, launch the App Store app and tap on the Genius icon that's displayed near the bottom of the screen. Then, to get game recommendations, tap on the Categories button that's displayed near the top-left corner of the screen and select Games.

> ☑ **TIP**   Another example of a simplistic and adorable, one or multi-player game that's easy to learn but very difficult to master, suitable for people of all ages, and that offers a fast-paced challenge is Doodle Jump (shown in Figure 16.10). The goal is to help the main character continuously jump upwards and successfully land on stable and moving platforms. Doodle Jump offers a variety of fun and seasonal themes.

FIGURE 16.10

Doodle Jump is a fast-paced, but challenging game that involves perfect timing, hand-eye coordination, strategy, and a bit of luck.

55 iOS GAMES WORTH PLAYING

Just like video and computer games, iOS games are offered in many different genres and are designed to cater to very different audiences. One person might enjoy an interactive version of chess, checkers, the *New York Times* crossword puzzle or a Sudoku game, whereas someone else might prefer a high-action adventure game, a first-person shooter, a racing simulation, or an authentic re-creation of a Las Vegas–style poker game.

Based on past sales, ratings, and popularity, Table 16.1 offers a brief summary of 55 top-quality iPhone and/or iPad games that will help you get started using your iOS device as a powerful hand-held gaming system.

> ☑ **TIP** In some cases, separate iPhone-specific and iPad-specific versions of a particular game are offered at different prices. If separate versions of the game are available, make sure you choose the correct version for your iOS device.
>
> Remember, although all iPhone and hybrid games run on an iPad, iPad-specific games do not run on an iPhone or iPod touch.

Table 16.1   55 Popular iPhone and iPad Games

Game Title	Genre	Price*	Available for iPhone, iPod touch (or as a Hybrid App)	Available for iPad	Optional In-App Purchases Available
Angry Birds Free	Action-Based Puzzle Game	Free	X	X	X
Angry Birds Rio	Action-Based Puzzle Game	$.99	X	X	X
Angry Birds Seasons	Action/Puzzle	$2.99	X	X	X
Angry Birds: Space	Action-Based Puzzle Game	$.99	X	X	X
Bejeweled Blitz	Action-Based Puzzle Game	Free	X	X	X
Call of Duty: Black Ops Zombies	First-Person Shooter	$6.99	X	X	X
Chaos Rings for iPad	Role-Playing	$15.99		X	
Checkers Free	Board Game	Free	X	X	
Chess Free	Board Game	Free	X	X	
Civilization Revolution for iPad	Simulation/ Strategy	$6.99		X	
Command & Conquer Red Alert for iPad	Simulation/ Strategy	$4.99		X	
Cut the Rope Free	Action-Based Puzzle Game	Free	X	X	X
Doodle Jump	Action-Based Puzzle Game	$.99	X	X	X

continues

Table 16.1   55 Popular iPhone and iPad Games *(continued)*

Game Title	Genre	Price*	Available for iPhone, iPod touch (or as a Hybrid App)	Available for iPad	Optional In-App Purchases Available
Doom Classic	First-Person Shooter	$4.99	X	X	
Fibble	Action Game	$.99	X	X	X
FIFA Soccer 13 by EA Sports	Sports Simulation	$6.99	X	X	X
Final Fantasy Tactics: The War of the Lions	Role-Playing	$15.00–$17.99	X	X	
Flick Fishing Free	Arcade-Style Fishing Simulation	Free	X	X	X
Flight Control	Action-Based Puzzle Game	$.99	X	X	X
Fruit Ninja HD	Action-Based Puzzle Game	$2.99	X	X	X
Grand Theft Auto: Chinatown Wars HD	Driving Simulation & Adventure	$9.99		X	
Guitar Hero	Arcade-Style Action	$2.99	X	X	X
Lili	RPG/Adventure	$2.99	X	X	X
Madden NFL 12 by EA Sports	Sports Simulation	$4.99– $6.99	X	X	
Monopoly for iPad	Board Game	$9.99		X	
Ms. Pac-Man	Arcade-Style Action	$4.99	X	X	
NBA Jam by EA Sports	Arcade-Style Sports Simulation	$.99– $4.99	X	X	
NYTimes Crosswords	Puzzle	Subscription-Based	X	X	X
Order & Chaos Online	Multi-Player RPG	Free	X	X	X
Pac-Man	Arcade-Style Action	$4.99	X	X	
Plants vs. Zombies	Action-Based Puzzle Game	$2.99	X	X	

Game Title	Genre	Price*	Available for iPhone, iPod touch (or as a Hybrid App)	Available for iPad	Optional In-App Purchases Available
Pocket Planes	Action-Based Strategy Game	Free	X	X	X
Poker by Zynga	Card Game	Free	X	X	X
Scrabble	Board Game	$9.99	X	X	
SHIFT 2 Unleashed for iPad	Racing Simulation	$1.99– $4.99	X	X	X
Sid Meier's Pirates for iPad	Action-Based Simulation	$2.99– $4.99	X	X	
Smurfs' Village	Simulation	Free	X	X	X
Social Sudoku	Puzzle	$1.99	X	X	
Solitaire	Card Game	Free	X	X	
Sonic the Hedgehog 4: Episode II	Classic Sega Video Game Adaptation	$6.99	X	X	
Space Invaders	Arcade-Style Action	$4.99	X	X	
Starfront: Collision	Multi-Player Simulation / Strategy Game	$4.99	X	X	
Superbrothers: Sword & Sworcery EP	Action/ Adventure	$4.99	X	X	
Temple Run: Brave	Action/ Adventure	$.99		X	X
Tetris	Action-Based Puzzle Game	$2.99	X	X	
The Room	Puzzle/Mystery	$4.99		X	
The Sims FreePlay	Simulation	Free	X	X	X
Ticket To Ride	Strategy Game	$1.99 / $6.99	X	X	X
Tiger Woods PGA Tour 12 for iPad	Sports Simulation	$4.99		X	
Tiny Tower	Simulation	Free	X	X	X
Topia	Simulation	$.99	X	X	
UNO	Card Game	$.99	X	X	

continues

Table 16.1   55 Popular iPhone and iPad Games *(continued)*

Game Title	Genre	Price*	Available for iPhone, iPod touch (or as a Hybrid App)	Available for iPad	Optional In-App Purchases Available
Words with Friends	Word-Based Puzzle Game	$2.99	X	X	X
World of Goo	Strategy Game	$4.99	X	X	
Zen Bound 2 Universal	Puzzle	$2.99	X	X	

* Game prices are subject to change, and newer versions and/or sequels of popular games might be released. Free, scaled-down, or sampler versions of some games might also be available.

TIP   Apple has compiled a list of iPhone and iPad game suggestions for first-time gamers. This game listing is referred to as the Games Starter Kit.

To access the iPhone-Specific Games Starter Kit from the App Store, launch the App Store app from your iPhone, tap on the Featured icon, and then scroll down and look for the Games Starter Kit banner. Tap on it.

To access the iPad-specific Game Starter Kit from the App Store, launch the App Store app from your iPad, tap on the Featured icon, and then scroll down and tap on the banner labeled Games Starter Kit.

EXPERIENCE MULTIPLAYER GAMES WITH GAME CENTER

Your iOS device gives you the option to play multiplayer games in several ways, depending on how the game itself is designed. When it comes to competing head-on against other human players (as opposed to computer-controlled opponents), your options typically include these:

- Multiple people can play on the same iPhone or iPad by passing the device from one person to the next in between turns.
- A direct link can be established between two or more iOS devices with the same game installed.
- Through Apple's Game Center, you can play games online with one or more other people who are located anywhere in the world. This is a safe way to interact with other gamers whenever you're looking for a competitor.

> **☑ TIP** Most multiplayer games also have a one-player mode, which enables you to compete against computer-controlled opponents, for example.

Apple's Game Center is a free, online-based service that is a centralized hub for multiplayer games. You can access Game Center using a compatible game app or by launching the Game Center app directly from the Home Screen. To access Game Center, your iPhone, iPad, or iPod touch must have access to the Internet via a 3G/4G or Wi-Fi connection.

> **✐ NOTE** Game Center is an online-based social gaming network that's operated by Apple. It's specifically for iOS device and Mac OS X Mountain Lion users. The Game Center app comes preinstalled with iOS 6. You can set up an account free, using your Apple ID.

After Game Center is running, you can create an online profile for yourself (which can include your photo). To do this, tap on the Me icon at the bottom of the Game Center screen. You can also use Game Center to meet up online with friends.

The Game Center app can automatically search the iPhone field in your Contacts database, as well as your list of online Facebook friends, for others who are active on Game Center, and it allows you to send friend requests to those people. To do this, tap on the Friends icon at the bottom of the screen, and then tap on the Use My Contacts flag.

> **☑ TIP** You can also invite people you know to become your "friend" on Game Center, so you can easily challenge them on any Game Center–compatible game that you both have installed on your iOS device. You can also compete against Mac users who have a Game Center–compatible game running on their computer.
>
> To email a friend, tap on the Add Friends flag from the Friends screen of Game Center, and then in the To field of the email message template that appears, enter the email addresses for the people you want to invite.

When you install Game Center–compatible games on your iOS device, you will have the option to turn on Game Center functionality for that game. In addition to being able to invite people to compete against, you can post your game-related accomplishments online for all to see.

Tap on the Games icon that's displayed at the bottom of the Game Center screen, to see a listing of the Game Center–compatible games you currently have installed on your iOS devices, as well as your published game-related achievements for those game titles.

> **TIP**   Tap on the Games icon that's displayed at the bottom of the Game Center screen, and then tap on the Find Game Center Games flag to quickly locate games in the App Store that you might be interested in and that are Game Center (multiplayer) compatible.
>
> Tapping the Find Game Center Games flag within Game Center will cause a special area of the App Store to load on your iOS device. It displays multiplayer games that are compatible with Game Center and your particular device. The Game Center listings are divided by game genre (as shown in Figure 16.11). An Internet connection is required to use Game Center or to find Game Center-compatible games from the App Store.

FIGURE 16.11

From the Game Center area of the App Store (which is actually accessible from the Game Center app), you'll find a vast selection of popular, multiplayer games in all genres that are suitable for all ages.

After you have established one or more online "friends" within Game Center, use the Requests feature to send or respond to game invitations and challenges involving other players. Tap on the Requests icon, displayed at the bottom of the screen, to do this.

When you're using the Game Center app, whenever you see a game app icon displayed on the screen (on the Me or Games screens, for example), it means that the featured game associated with that icon is Game Center compatible. Tap on the displayed app icon to access the App Store to read a detailed description of that game, and then download, install, and play it.

> **TIP**   Looking for new online "friends" to compete against? In Game Center, tap on the Friends icon that's displayed near the bottom of the screen. Then, tap on the Recommendations banner to find a list of people you probably don't know, but who share your taste in games or who have comparable game skills (based on published scores).
>
> Tap on the Send Friend Request icon to initiate contact with that fellow gamer. When that person accepts your request, you can play multiplayer games with them.
>
> At the bottom of the Recommendations list, tap on Use My Contacts to search your Contacts database and find other people you know who are also registered players within Game Center.

OTHER ENTERTAINMENT ACTIVITIES

In addition to the tens of thousands of games available from the App Store, which are designed to keep you entertained for minutes or hours at a time, in the App Store you can also discover a wide range of entertainment-oriented apps that aren't necessarily games.

From the App Store, however, if you tap on the Categories option, you'll discover thousands of additional apps that fall into the Entertainment, Lifestyle, and Sports categories, for example, that can also provide countless hours' worth of entertainment, but that are not games.

Also in the App Store, you can find and download personal enrichment apps that can teach you about fine wine, how to cook, how to knit, or how to fix or build something. There are also apps designed to help you create a journal or digital diary, improve your overall health and fitness, manage your diet, or shop via an interactive (app- and web-based) catalog from your favorite store. You'll find these types of apps listed in the Lifestyle section of the App Store.

> **TIP** If you enjoy shopping online, three free "must have" apps that allow you to quickly find both popular and unique or unusual items, and save money at the same time, include: Amazon Mobile, FAB and Catalog Spree.
>
> Amazon Mobile allows you to browse and shop for any of the millions of items offered by Amazon, while FAB focuses on unique or unusual items. Catalog Spree makes hundreds of traditional mail order catalogs from well-known companies available in an interactive format, and allows you to browse and shop from these catalogs on your iPhone or iPad using a single app.
>
> Meanwhile, the free Groupon app allows you to find bargains from local companies for a wide range of products, as well as services and discounts at local restaurants.

> **NOTE** If you're looking to acquire new knowledge or experience personal enrichment classes, lectures and workshops, be sure to download and explore the free iTunes U app.
>
> Apple has teamed up with leading educators, academic institutions, museums, libraries and other philanthropic organizations to offer a vast and ever-growing collection of online-based classes, workshops, lectures and interactive programs that are all available from your iPhone or iPad for free. iTunes U offers programs and classes for people of all ages. iTunes U is one of the most interesting, expansive and yet under-utilized free content libraries available on the Internet.

EDUCATE AND ENTERTAIN YOUR KIDS

If you have kids and will allow them to use an iPhone, iPad, or iPod touch, there is a vast selection of kid-friendly games, educational apps, and activity-oriented apps suitable for young people. You'll also find many interactive storybook apps that will read to your kids, help them learn to read, and offer interactive elements on the various book pages.

To find some of these kid-friendly apps, access the Education category of the App Store, or look for games in the Kids sub-category. You can find interactive storybooks via iBooks by accessing the iBookstore and looking in the Children & Teens category.

TIP Before allowing your kids to use your iPhone or iPad, be sure to launch Settings, and from under the General option, tap on the Restrictions option. Using the Restrictions feature, you can quickly "childproof" your iOS device so that your kids can't surf the Web, make online purchases, or access specific apps or content. For example, you can restrict them from watching R-rated movies on the iPhone or iPad, or keep them from listening to music with explicit lyrics.

When you set up Restrictions on an iPhone or iPad, you'll need to create a separate passcode than the one you created if you activated the Passcode Lock feature of your device. Do not forget this passcode, or you might have to restore your iOS device from backup files created before the Restrictions feature was activated. If a backup doesn't exist, it might be necessary to erase all content and settings on your iPhone or iPad, and then manually reload the content (which is something you definitely want to avoid).

NOTE To help control your kids online spending through the iTunes Store, App Store, iBookstore and Newsstand, you can provide them with pre-paid iTunes Gift Cards, or you can use the iTunes Allowance feature to automatically deposit a pre-determined amount of money into their Apple ID account each month. To learn more about these options, visit www.apple.com/itunes/gifts.

17

USE THE MUSIC AND VIDEOS APPS

What do eight-track tapes, vinyl records, cassettes, and most recently CDs have in common? These are all outdated methods for storing music that have been replaced by digital music players, like Apple's iPods. The music in your personal library can now be kept in a purely digital format, transferred via the Internet, and listened to on a digital music player.

iOS 6 comes with the Music app preinstalled. This app serves as your digital music player and transforms your iPhone or iPad into a full-featured iPod. However, before playing your music, you first need to load digital music files into your iPhone or iPad. There are several ways to do this, including the following:

- Purchase digital music directly from the iTunes Store (using the iTunes app) on your iPhone or iPad. An Internet connection is required, and your purchases are billed to the credit or debit card that's linked to your Apple ID.

- You can purchase music using the iTunes software on your primary computer (used to connect to the iTunes Store), and then transfer music purchases and downloads to your iPhone or iPad using the iTunes Sync process or through iCloud.

- You can "rip" music from traditional CDs, and convert it to a digital format using your primary computer, and then transfer the digital music files to your iOS device. For this, the free iTunes software on your computer, or other third-party software, is required.

- You can upgrade your iCloud account by adding the optional iTunes Match feature, for $24.99 per year, and access your entire digital music library via iCloud, whether that music was purchased from the iTunes Store, ripped from your own CDs, or purchased/downloaded from another source. To learn more about iTunes Match, visit www.apple.com/itunes/itunes-match.

- You can shop for and download music from another source besides the iTunes Store, load that music into your primary computer, convert it to the proper format, and then transfer it to your iPhone or iPad using the iTunes Sync process.

> **NOTE** Apple's iTunes Store offers an ever-growing selection of more than 20 million songs available for purchase and download, including all the latest hits and new music from the biggest bands and recording artists, as well as up-and-coming and unsigned artists/bands. You'll also find classic songs and oldies from all music genres, including the entire Beatles music collection.

The Music app is used for playing digital music, audiobooks, and other audio content that you load into your iPhone or iPad. If you want to watch videos, TV show episodes, or movies that you've purchased and/or downloaded from the iTunes Store, you need to use the Videos app, which also comes preinstalled with iOS 6.

Meanwhile, to experience the free podcasts available from the iTunes Store, you need to download and install Apple's optional Podcast app, or to utilize the vast collection of educational and personal enrichment content available from Apple's iTunes U service, download and install the free iTunes U app.

Another option for watching video or listening to audio content (including music videos, TV show episodes, movies, radio stations, and so on) is to stream it directly from the Internet. For this, you typically need a Wi-Fi Internet connection (which is often faster than 3G/4G Internet connection, but has no monthly data limits). However, in some cases, a 3G/4G connection will work, but using it quickly uses up your monthly wireless data allocation from your wireless service provider.

> ☑️ **TIP**   When you stream content from the Internet, it gets transferred from the Internet directly to your iOS device. However, your iPhone or iPad does not save streamed content, just as your standalone television set doesn't record the shows you watch (unless you have a DVR or another recording device hooked up to it).
>
> Streaming content from the Internet requires a specialized app, which is provided by the source of the content. Later in this chapter you'll discover which apps to use to access specific on-demand television programming, movies, videos, radio stations, and other content that gets streamed (not downloaded) to your iPhone or iPad.

TIPS FOR USING THE MUSIC APP

The Music app displays the music in your digital music library that's currently stored on your device (as shown in Figure 17.1 on the iPad). It enables you to play one song at a time, listen to entire albums, or create personalized playlists that can provide hours' worth of music listening without your having to tinker with the app.

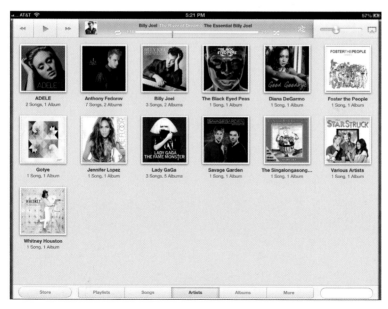

FIGURE 17.1

Shown here is the main Artists screen of Music app on the iPad. On the iPhone, the fame features and functionality are available from the Music app, but the menu layout is different due to the phone's smaller screen size.

If you have the Music app set up to work with iCloud, all of the music you've purchased from iTunes (in addition to what's stored on your iOS device) is displayed.
Songs that are accessible to you for download via iCloud have an iCloud icon
displayed next to their listings. Tap on the iCloud icon to download the song (or
album) from iCloud and store it on your iPhone or iPad.

> **NOTE** Storing music within the internal storage of your iPhone or iPad
> (as opposed to streaming music) takes up storage space within your iOS device,
> but it allows the music to be accessible anytime, without needing an Internet
> connection.

> **TIP** The Music app works seamlessly with Siri. Use your voice to com-
> mand Siri to play music from a specific artist, a specific playlist, or to play a specific
> song, just by speaking its title. This applies to music stored on your iPhone or iPad.
> For example, if you want to hear, *Rolling in the Deep* from Adele, and it's stored on
> your iOS device, activate Siri and say, "Play Rolling in the Deep." Or to play a Lady
> Gaga song, say "Play a song from Lady Gaga." See Chapter 5, "Using Siri and Dicta-
> tion to Interact with Your iOS Device," for more details about how to use Siri.

Thanks to iOS 6's multitasking capabilities, you can play music from the Music
app while using other apps on your iPhone or iPad. Once music is playing, you
can also place your iOS device into Sleep mode, and the music continues playing (unless you pause it first.) To play music, you don't need to launch the Music
app, however. Instead, you can use the Music Controls accessible directly from the
multitasking bar.

> **TIP** Music Controls are also accessible from the Lock Screen. To activate
> these Lock Screen controls, quickly press the Home button twice when viewing the
> Lock Screen. You can control the last Playlist or album (or audiobook), for example,
> that was loaded into the Music app (as shown in Figure 17.2).

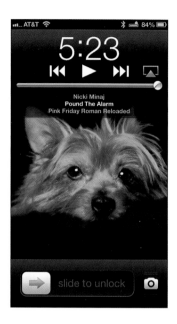

FIGURE 17.2

You can access the Music Controls from the iPhone or iPad's Lock Screen, and then play, pause, fast forward, rewind, move between music tracks, use the AirPlay feature, and/or adjust the music volume from the Lock Screen.

To access the Music Controls on the multitasking bar, when using any app on the iPhone or iPad (or viewing the Home screen), double-tap on the Home button. When the multitasking bar appears at the bottom of the screen, swipe your finger from left to right until you see the Music Controls (shown in Figure 17.3). Tap the Play icon to begin playing the pre-selected playlist, album or audiobook.

> **TIP** It's also possible to control the Music app from the controls found on the cord of the Apple EarPods or Apple's original ear buds, as well as on some other optional corded headphones.

To fully manage your digital music library, create playlists, and play songs or albums using the Music app, launch the app from the Home Screen. Displayed along the top of the screen are various icons for controlling the selected music (which is playing or about to be played).

FIGURE 17.3

You can control the music playing on your iPhone or iPad from the Music Controls, accessible from the multitasking bar, or directly from the Music app. From this iPhone screen, swipe your finger from left to right to access the separate volume slider.

TIP From Settings, it's possible to customize some of the Music app-related options available to you. To do this, launch Settings, and then select the Music option. In addition to turning on or off the iTunes Match service (if you've subscribed to it), and/or turning on or off the Home Sharing feature (which is one way to share your digital music library with your primary computer or Apple TV via a wireless network), you can tinker with the EQ or impose a maximum volume limit when listening to music (shown in Figure 17.4).

If you want your iPhone or iPad to only download music from iTunes and/or iCloud when you're connected to the Internet using a Wi-Fi connection (as opposed to a 3G/4G connection which uses up some of your monthly wireless data allocation), from Settings, select the iTunes & App Stores option. Then, adjust the virtual on/off switch associated with the Use Cellular Data option, and turn this feature off. When you do this, unless a Wi-Fi connection is present, no iCloud or iTunes Match functionality will be offered within the Music app. You can only listen to music that's stored on your iOS device or access content "in the cloud" via a Wi-Fi Internet connection.

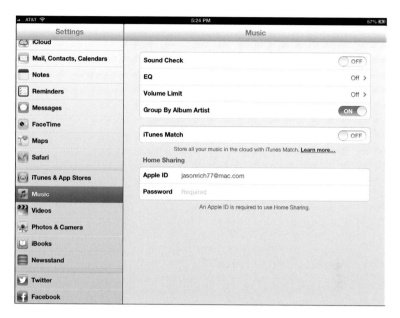

FIGURE 17.4
You can adjust Music app-related options from within Settings.

MUSIC APP CONTROLS ON THE iPHONE

When you launch the Music app on your iPhone and then tap on the Playlists, Artists, Songs or Albums button that are displayed along the bottom of the screen, the Store button is displayed in the upper-left corner of the screen. Tap on it to access the iTunes Store via the Internet and shop for new music. (The iTunes app automatically launches.)

At the bottom of the Music app's screen are five command buttons, labeled Playlists, Artists, Songs, Albums, and More (shown in Figure 17.5). Here's what each is used for:

■ **Playlists**—Create and manage personalized playlists within the Music app. A playlist is a list of songs that you manually compile from music that's in your music library. The feature allows you to create a "digital mix tape," featuring only the music you want, in the order you want it. You can create as many separate playlists as you'd like, so you can listen to music based on what you're doing (such as jogging or working) or your current mood.

Store Button — Now Playing Button

Music App Command Buttons

FIGURE 17.5

When you tap on the Songs button at the bottom of the Music app, you'll see an alphabetized listing of songs you own.

- **Artists**—View an alphabetized listing of all recording artists and music groups whose music you own. Tap on an artist's name to view the albums or individual songs you own from that artist, music group or band.
- **Songs**—View a complete (alphabetical) listing of all songs stored in your iOS device, sorted by song title.
- **Albums**—View a complete listing of all album or partial albums that represent music you own. A thumbnail of each album cover is displayed. Tap on an album listing to view the songs you own from that album.

> **TIP** If you rotate your iPhone to view the Music app in landscape mode, you can browse through your music by viewing album cover artwork using the Cover Flow menu (shown in Figure 17.6). Swipe your finger from left to right, or from right to left, across the screen in order to view album artwork. Tap on the album cover to view the song(s) you own from that album, and then tap on a song listing to play it.

FIGURE 17.6

The Cover Flow menu on the iPhone allows you to scroll through the music you own on your iPhone.

■ **More**—Beyond music purchased from the iTunes Store, you can listen to audiobooks, by tapping on the More option. Plus, you can view a listing of songs sorted by composers, compilations or music genre.

> **TIP** On the iPhone, you can change the menu buttons that are displayed along the bottom of the Music app's screen. Instead of displaying, from left to right, the Playlists, Artists, Songs, Albums an More buttons, you can swap out the Playlists, Artists, Songs or Albums button with an Audiobooks, Compilations, Composers and/or Genres buttons, plus change the positions of these menu buttons. To do this, launch the Music app, tap on the More button, and then tap on the Edit button that's displayed near the top-left corner of the screen.
>
> From the Configure screen that's displayed, one at a time, drag one of the command buttons shown at the top of the screen to the desired location along the menu bar that the Music app displays along the bottom of the screen. As you do this, keep in mind that the More button remains constant. Tap the Done icon when you're finished.
>
> Your new selection of command buttons will now be displayed at the bottom of the Music app screen.

CREATE A MUSIC APP PLAYLIST ON THE iPHONE

Playlists are personalized collections of songs that you can group together and then play at any time. Each playlist is given its own title, and can include as many songs from your personal music collection as you wish.

You can create separate playlists for working out, to enjoy while you drive, to listen to when you're depressed, or to dance to when you feel like cutting loose. There is no limit to the number of separate playlists you can create and store on your iOS device. Here's how to create a playlist:

> ☑ **TIP**   When listening to any playlist, you can play the songs in order or have the Music app randomize the song order (using the Shuffle command). A playlist can also be put into an infinite loop, so it continuously plays until you press Pause.

1. Launch the Music app, and tap on the Playlist button that's displayed near the bottom of the screen.

2. To create a new playlist, tap on the Add Playlist option. Several default play-list options, such as My Top Rated, Purchased Music, Recently Added, and Top 25 Most Played, will be available to you right away. You can edit these playlists, or create your own from scratch.

3. When prompted after tapping on the Add Playlist option, create a title for your new playlist, such as Workout Music or Favorite Pop Songs, and tap the Save button.

4. When the Songs screen appears, one at a time, tap on the blue-and-white plus sign icon that's associated with each song you want to add to your playlist. All songs currently stored on your iPhone (or available to you from iCloud) will be listed within the Songs screen. Tap the Done button to save your selections. (As you pick and choose songs, you can repeat the same song in your playlist multiple times, if you desire.)

5. The Playlist screen that appears next (shown in Figure 17.7) lists the name of your new playlist near the top of the screen. Three command buttons (labeled Edit, Clear and Delete) are displayed below the title, and below that, is the Shuffle option. As you move downwards on the screen, you'll see a list of the individual songs added to that playlist. Use the command Edit, Clear or Delete buttons to manage the newly created playlist.

Return To Playlists Listing Button

Edit, Clear and
Delete Buttons

Shuffle Option

Now Playing Button

iCloud Icon

Playlists Command Button

FIGURE 17.7

A sample playlist screen shown here on the iPhone 5.

Tap the Edit button to delete individual songs from the playlist or change
the order of the songs. To delete a song, tap on the red-and-white negative
sign icon. To move a song, place your finger on the Move icon displayed to
the right of a song's title (it looks like three horizontal lines) and drag is up
or down to reposition that song within the playlist's order. Tap the Done
button when you're finished editing your playlist.

Tap the Clear button to keep the master playlist file, but remove all the
songs from it. Or tap the Delete button to delete the playlist altogether
from your iOS device.

TIP Unless you tap on the Shuffle option, when you opt to listen to a
playlist, songs are played in the order displayed on the screen (that you selected).
When you tap the Shuffle command, songs from the playlist are played in a random order.

> **✏ NOTE** If you notice an iCloud icon displayed at the bottom of the playlist, this means one or more of the songs you've selected is stored on your iCloud account, but not on your iPhone (or iPad). Tap the iCloud icon to download that music from your iCloud account and add it to your playlist. (Since you own the music, you will not be charged to download it again.)

6. To listen to your newly created playlist, return to the main Playlist screen by tapping on the Playlists button at the bottom of the screen (if you're not already there), and tap on the playlist title of your choice. Next, tap on a song from that playlist and begin listening. To start the playlist from the beginning, tap on the first song listed. Tap on the Shuffle option to continue playing the playlist in a random order.

7. The Music app's Now Playing screen (shown in Figure 17.8) shows what song is currently playing. You'll also see commands to Play/Pause the music, as well as to rewind or fast forward. A volume slider, for adjusting the music's volume is also displayed.

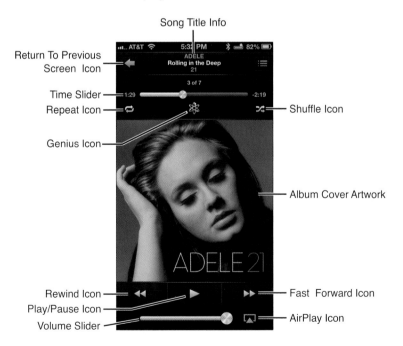

FIGURE 17.8

The Now Playing screen appears when music first starts playing using the Music app. Use the command icons on this screen to control the music that's playing.

If you press and hold the rewind or fast forward icon, you can move backward or advance within the song that's currently playing. However, if you tap on one of these two icons, you jump to the previous track or advance to the next track within your playlist, respectively. Using your finger, you can move the playhead indicator along the scrubber bar (where it shows the point in time the song is at) to a specific position within the song.

FIND YOUR WAY AROUND THE NOW PLAYING SCREEN

Displayed along the top of the screen is a left-pointing arrow icon that allows you to return to the previous screen you were viewing. In the upper-right corner of the screen is an icon that allows you to view a text-based listing that includes additional information about the song or album that's playing. Between these two icons, the song's title that's currently playing is displayed, along with the artist's name and the album name the song is associated with. (Refer back to Figure 17.8 to see an example of the Now Playing screen.)

Below the song title information is the song's time slider. Use your finger to move this slider right to advance within the song, or left to move back within the song manually. On the left of this slider, a timer shows how much of the song you've already listened to. On the right side of the slider is a timer that shows how much of the song is remaining.

Below the time slider are three additional command icons. The icon to the left allows you to place that song into a continuous play loop. The middle icon is the Genius icon. Tap on it to find songs that are similar to what you're currently listening to. Tap on the right-most shuffle icon to shuffle the order of the songs in the playlist or album you're listening to.

Displayed in the middle of the screen is the album artwork associated with the song that's playing. Directly underneath the album cover artwork are the Rewind, Play/Pause and Fast Forward icons, and below those, the volume slider is displayed.

If available, the AirPlay icon appears in the lower-right corner of the screen. This allows you to stream the music you're listening to from your iOS device to your home theater system or television speakers (via Apple TV) or to AirPlay compatible external speakers.

Keep in mind, once music is playing, you can control the volume from the on-screen volume slider, using the Volume Up or Volume Down buttons on the side of your iOS device, or using the controls found on the cord of your Apple ear buds or Apple EarPods.

Also while music is playing, you can exit out of the Now Playing screen and access other areas of the Music app, use another app altogether (thanks to the multitasking feature of your iPhone or iPad), or you can place your device into Sleep mode and continue listening to the music.

MUSIC APP CONTROLS ON iPAD

When you launch Music on your iPad (shown in Figure 17.9), the Store button appears in the lower-left corner of the screen. Tap it to access the iTunes Store via the Internet in order to shop for new music using the iTunes app.

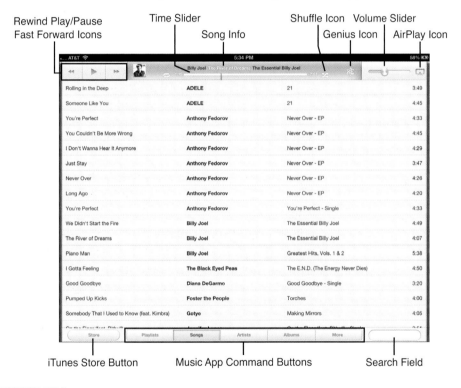

FIGURE 17.9

This is what the Music app looks like on the iPad when the Songs button is selected.

TIP   Have you ever been listening to the radio, watching TV, or riding in an elevator and want to know the name of a song that's playing so you can purchase it? Well, there's an app for that. Download the free Shazam app from the App Store. When you hear a song you want to identify, launch the app. It "listens" to what's playing, and then identifies the song for you, complete with its title and artist. It then launches iTunes giving you the option to purchase the song. This is one of the most popular, free iPhone/iPad apps of all time. (Another similar app is called SoundHound.)

Also near the bottom of the screen are five additional command buttons labeled Playlists, Songs, Artists, Albums, and More. See the section earlier in this chapter, called "Music App Controls On The iPhone" to discover how each of these command buttons is used.

In the upper-left corner of the Music app's screen on the iPad are the music control icons. These include the Rewind, Play/Pause, and Track Forward icons.

Near the top center of the screen are details about the song currently playing. Use the time slider to manually move forward or backward (fast-forward or rewind) within that song using your finger. Tap on the circular arrow-shaped icon displayed to the left of the slider to put whatever song, album or playlist you're listing to into endless repeat (loop) mode. The Shuffle icon that's displayed to the immediate right of the time slider is used to put the playlist you're listening to into Shuffle mode, so the songs play in a random order.

Displayed to the left and right sides of the time slider are timers. The timer on the left shows how much of a song you've already heard, while the timer on the right shows how much of the song remains.

Tap the Genius icon that's displayed to the right of the Shuffle icon to access the Music app's Genius feature and discover songs you might also enjoy, based on the song, album or playlist you're currently playing and your past iTunes downloads.

The smaller slider that's displayed near the upper-right corner of the screen is your onscreen volume control. Move it to the right to increase the volume or to the left to decrease it. You can also use the volume control buttons on the side of your iPad for this purpose, or, if applicable, the volume control buttons on the cord of your headset. If applicable, the AirPlay icon will be displayed near the top-right corner of the Music app screen.

TIP Quickly find any song stored on your iPhone or iPad by using a keyword search. In the Search field that's displayed near the lower-right corner of the screen, enter a song title (or a portion of a title), an artist's name, an album title, or any other keyword that's relevant to your music to find specific music content stored on your iOS device.

On the iPhone, the Search field appears at the top of the Artists, Songs, or Albums screen if you swipe your finger downward, starting from the middle of the screen.

On the iPad, the Search field is always displayed as part of the Music app, in the lower-right corner of the screen.

Tap on the Search field to make the virtual keyboard appear. Enter your keyword or search phrase, and then tap the Search key on the keyboard to see the results. Tap on the search result of your choice to select a specific song, album, or artist.

CREATE A MUSIC APP PLAYLIST ON THE iPAD

You can create personal playlists on your iPad and then sync them for use with the iTunes software on your computer(s), or use iCloud to sync your playlists so they're available to you on your other iOS devices. Here's how to create a custom playlist on an iPad:

1. Launch the Music app, and tap on the Playlist button that's displayed near the bottom of the screen.

2. To create a new playlist, tap on the New button that appears near the upper-right corner of the screen, below the volume slider. Several default playlist options, such as My Top Rated, Purchased, Recently Added, and Top 25 Most Played, are available to you right away. You can edit these playlists, or create your own from scratch.

3. When prompted after tapping the New icon, create a name for your new playlist, such as Workout Music or Favorite Pop Songs, and tap the Save icon. A New Playlist pop-up window appears with an empty Title field for you to fill in using the virtual keyboard.

4. When the Add Songs To The "[Insert Playlist Title]" Playlist" screen appears, one at a time, tap on the plus sign icon that's associated with each song that you want to add to your playlist, and then tap the Done button (shown in Figure 17.10) to save your selections. If you want to add all of the songs stored on your iPad, tap the Add All Songs button (displayed near the top of the screen, next to the Done icon).

5. The Playlist screen that appears next (shown in Figure 17.11) lists the name of your new playlist near the top-center of the screen, and then the individual songs within that newly-created playlist.

    To change the order of the songs while accessing this screen, tap on the Edit button, select a song, hold your finger on the Move icon (that contains three horizontal lines) that can be found to the right of each song title, and drag it upward or downward.

FIGURE 17.10

Choose the songs you want to add to your playlist, based on the listing of all songs stored on your iPad.

> **NOTE** Later, you can go back and edit a playlist by viewing the Playlist screen for that playlist and then tapping on the Edit button.

To delete a song from the playlist, tap on the red-and-white minus sign icon that's displayed to the left of each song title.

Tap on the Add Songs button (displayed near the upper-right corner of the screen, below the volume slider) to add additional songs to your playlist.

6. Tap the Done button, displayed in the upper-right corner of this Music app's screen (below the volume slider) to save your changes.

7. To listen to your newly created playlist, tap on any song title listed in that playlist to choose where you want to begin listening from.

8. Use the music control icons at the top of the screen to control the music you're now listening to.

FIGURE 17.11
The Playlist screen of the Music app allows you to play, edit or manage a selected playlist. It's shown here in Edit mode.

MORE MUSIC APP FEATURES

After music is playing on your iPhone or iPad, you can exit the Music app and use your iOS device for other purposes. The music will keep playing. It will automatically pause, however, if you receive an incoming call on your iPhone or an incoming FaceTime call on your iPhone or iPad.

After you purchase a song from iTunes, it gets download to the computer or device it was purchased from, but is also instantly made available to all of your iOS devices via iCloud. Thus, you can purchase music on your primary computer, but for no extra charge, also download it wirelessly to your iPhone, iPad, and/or iPod touch. Or you can purchase a song on your iPhone, yet have it available on all of your other computers and devices that are linked to your iCloud account.

> **NOTE** Refer to Chapter 6, "Sync and Share Files Using iCloud," for more information about how to use iCloud in conjunction with your iPhone and iPad.

As you're looking at any song listing or album graphic within the Music app (after tapping on the Songs, Artists or Albums button), you can delete that content from your iOS device. If it's a song listing, swipe your finger across that listing, from left to right. When the Delete button appears (as shown in Figure 17.12) , tap on it. If it's a thumbnail for an album cover, hold your finger on that graphic until an X icon appears in the upper-left corner of the thumbnail image. Tap on the X to delete the image and all related music content.

Keep in mind, when you delete a song or album from your iOS mobile device, that music remains in your iTunes library (and stored on iCloud), so you can re-download it at anytime, as long as your iPhone or iPad has Internet access.

Piano Man	Billy Joel	Greatest Hits, Vols. 1 & 2	5:38
I Gotta Feeling	The Black Eyed Peas	The E.N.D. (The Energy Never Dies)	4:50
Good Goodbye	Diana DeGarmo	Good Goodbye - Single	3:20
Pumped Up Kicks	Foster the People	Torches	Delete
Somebody That I Used to Know (feat. Kimbra)	Gotye	Making Mirrors	4:05
On the Floor (feat. Pitbull)	Jennifer Lopez	On the Floor (feat. Pitbull) - Single	3:51
Poker Face	Lady GaGa		3:36
You and I	Lady GaGa	Born This Way (Bonus Track Version)	
Alejandro	Lady GaGa	The Fame Monster (Deluxe Version)	4:35

FIGURE 17.12

You can delete one song at a time, or entire albums' worth of songs, from your iOS device. In this case, to delete the one song, swipe your finger from left to right across the listing, and then tap on the Delete button.

> **TIP** To introduce you to new songs, new bands, and up-and-coming artists, the iTunes Store regularly makes certain music available for free. This free music selection changes weekly. To access free music via the iTunes Store, launch the iTunes app from your iPhone or iPad. On the iPad, for example, tap on the Music icon at the bottom of the iTunes app's screen, tap the All Genres tab near the top center of the screen, and then scroll down to the Quick Links section at the bottom of the screen. Tap on the Free On iTunes option.
>
> If you visit any participating Starbucks Coffee location, you can also preview and download featured music for free using the coffee shop's advertiser-supported Wi-Fi hotspot. Free music is also available for download via the official Starbucks app.

After you've downloaded one or more singles (individual songs) from an artist or band's album, you can later purchase the rest of the album and get credit for the eligible song(s) you've already purchased by tapping on the Complete My Album option as you're shopping for music from the iTunes Store.

To use the Complete My Album feature, launch the iTunes app, tap on the Music icon (displayed at the bottom of the screen), and then access the listing for the Album you want to purchase. You can use the Search field to find the album quickly. If you already own songs from that Album, the Price icon automatically displays a lower price than the Regular Price, and it has a Complete My Album label next to it (as shown in Figure 17.13). The prorated price that's displayed for the Album is based on how many songs you already own from it.

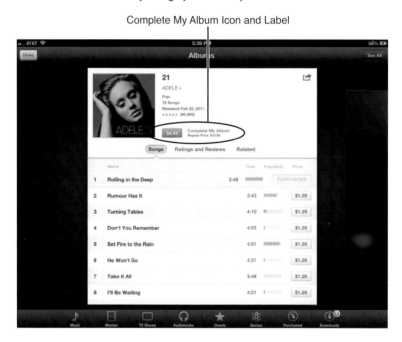

FIGURE 17.13

If you already own songs from a specific Album and want to later purchase the rest of the album, you can do this from the iTunes Store at a prorated price using the Complete My Album feature.

Apple wants you to shop for your music from the iTunes Store (via the iTunes app), for obvious reasons. However, you do have other options. From your primary computer, you can shop for (or otherwise download) music from other sources, and then transfer that content to your iPhone or iPad by importing the music files into the iTunes software on your primary computer, and then performing an iTunes Sync. Or you can upgrade to the iTunes Match service and gain access to your entire digital music library via iCloud.

Some other sources for legally buying and downloading music include the Amazon MP3 music store (www.amazonmp3.com), Napster (www.napster.com), eMusic (www.eMusic.com), and Rhapsody (www.rhapsody.com).

> **✓ TIP** Want to sing along with your favorite songs but don't know the lyrics? No problem! Purchase and download the Lyrics ID app ($.99) from the app store. It displays the song lyrics to the songs currently stored on your iPhone as the music is playing. There are also a handful of karaoke apps available from the App Store. Use the App Store's Search feature (with the keyword Karaoke) to find third-party apps, like The Singing Machine ($.99) and Karaoke Party ($5.99).
>
> The Shazam and SoundHound apps also have features built-in that can display a song's lyrics.

USE THE VIDEOS APP TO WATCH TV SHOWS, MOVIES, AND MORE

After you purchase and download TV show episodes, movies, or music videos from the iTunes Store, that video-based content can be enjoyed on your iPhone and/or iPad using the Videos app. It can also be viewed on your primary computer using the iTunes software and shared between devices via iCloud.

> **✓ TIP** Video content acquired from the iTunes Store can be watched on your iOS device or, if you have Apple TV, streamed from your iPhone or iPad to your home theater system. How to do this using iOS 6's AirPlay feature is covered in Chapter 21, "Use Airplay for Entertainment, Connectivity," posted online at www.quepublishing.com/title/9780789750969.

After you've downloaded or transferred iTunes Store video content to your iPhone or iPad, it will be accessible from the Videos app.

When you launch the Videos app on your iPhone or iPad, at the top center of the screen are between one and four tabs, based on the types of video content stored on your device (as shown in Figure 17.14). These tabs will be labeled TV Shows, Movies, and/or Music Videos. If you have movies rented from iTunes, as opposed to movies you own stored on your iOS device, a tab labeled Rentals is displayed in addition to or instead of a tab labeled Movies.

When you tap on the TV Shows, Movies, Rentals, or Music Videos tab, thumbnail graphics representing that video content is displayed. To begin playing a video, tap on its thumbnail graphic.

Rentals, TV Shows and Music Videos Tabs

FIGURE 17.14

The Videos app shows what video content you have stored on your device. Content is categorized based on whether it's a TV show episode, movie, or music video. Here, the TV Shows tab (near the top-center of the screen) is selected.

> **TIP** To delete video content from your iOS device, on the iPhone, swipe your finger from left to right across the listing, and then tap the Delete icon. On the iPad, tap on the Edit icon displayed in the upper-right corner of the screen. When X icons appear in the upper-left corner of each thumbnail, tap on the appropriate X icons to delete that corresponding video content from your device.

To shop for additional video content from the iTunes Store while using the Videos app, tap on the Store button that's displayed in the upper-left corner of the screen.

To play a video, tap on a thumbnail representing a TV show, movie, or music video that you want to watch. If you've downloaded a TV show, for example, a new screen will appear, listing all episodes from that TV series currently stored on your iOS device (as shown in Figure 17.15). Tap on the episode of your choice to begin playing it. You can also tap on the Play icon.

FIGURE 17.15

If you have downloaded multiple episodes of a TV series, they'll be grouped together for easy access and viewing.

For music videos or movies, a similar information screen pertaining to that content will be displayed. Tap on the Play icon to begin watching your movie or music video.

> **TIP** When playing video content, you can hold your iPhone or iPad in either portrait or landscape mode. However, the video window is significantly larger if you position your iOS device sideways and use landscape mode.
>
> If applicable, based on the video content you're watching, by tapping the icon displayed in the upper-right corner of the screen, you can instantly switch between full-screen mode and letterbox mode as your onscreen viewing option.

While video content is playing on your iPhone or iPad, it displays in full-screen mode. Tap anywhere on the screen to reveal the onscreen command icons used for controlling the video as you're watching it. These controls are identical on the iPhone and iPad (shown in Figure 17.16). When a video is playing, these controls disappear from the screen automatically after a few seconds. Tap anywhere on the screen to make them reappear.

FIGURE 17.16
The onscreen icons for controlling the video you're watching on your iOS device.

> **TIP** As you're watching a movie using the Video app, to the left of the on-screen controls you may see a text-bubble icon. Tap on this icon to adjust captions and/or switch between audio languages, if the video content you're watching supports these features. If not available, the text-bubble icon will not be visible.

Displayed in the upper left of the Videos app screen while you're watching video content is the Done icon. Tap on this to exit the video you're watching. Along the top-center of the screen is a time slider. On either end of this slider are timers. To the left is a timer that displays how much of the video you've already watched. On the right of the slider is a timer that displays how much time in the video remains.

> **TIP** To manually fast-forward or rewind while watching a video, place your finger on the dot icon that appears on the timer slider. Move it to the right to advance within the video, or move it to the left to rewind within the video.

Near the bottom center of the screen as you're watching video content are the Rewind and Fast Forward icons. Tap on the Rewind icon to move back by scene or chapter, or tap the Fast Forward icon to advance to the next scene or chapter in the video (just as you would while watching a DVD). Press and hold down the Rewind or Fast Forward icon to rewind or fast forward while viewing the on-screen content. For example, you can rewind or advance by a few seconds at a time.

Tap the Play icon to play the video. When the video is playing, the Play icon transforms into a Pause icon, used to pause the video.

NOTE If you pause a video and then exit the Videos app, you can pick up exactly where you left off watching the video when you re-launch the Videos app. This information is automatically saved.

Below these three icons is the volume control slider. Use it to manually adjust the volume of the audio. You can also use the volume control buttons located on the side of your iPhone or iPad, or, if applicable, the volume control buttons on the cord of your headset (such as the Apple EarPods).

TIP From the iTunes Store, you can purchase TV show episodes (or entire seasons from your favorite series), as well as full-length movies. In addition, you can rent certain movies.

When you rent movies from the iTunes Store, each rented movie remains on your device for 30 days before it automatically deletes itself, whether or not the content has been viewed. However, after you press Play in the Videos app and begin watching rented content, you have access to that video for 24 hours before it deletes itself. During that 24-hour period, you can watch and re-watch the movie as often as you'd like.

The first time you tap Play to watch a rented movie, you're prompted to confirm your choice. This starts the 24-hour clock and allows the rented movie to begin playing.

Unlike movies you purchase from iTunes (that you can load into all of your computers and/or iOS mobile devices that are linked to the same Apple ID account), rented movies can only be stored on one computer, Apple TV or iOS mobile device at a time, but you can transfer unwatched rented movies between devices.

MUSIC, TV SHOWS, MOVIES, AND MORE: THE COST OF iTUNES CONTENT

The costs associated with acquiring content from iTunes are in Table 17.1.

Table 17.1   The Cost of Content from Apple's iTunes Store

Content Type	Standard Definition	High Definition
Purchase Music Single (One Song)	$.69 to $1.29	N/A
Purchase Music Album	$7.99 to $15.99	N/A
Purchase Music Video	$1.99	N/A
Purchase TV Show Episode	$1.99	$2.99
Purchase Made-for-TV Movie	$3.99	$4.99
Purchase Entire Season of a TV Show	Price varies, based on TV series and number of episodes. It's always cheaper to purchase an entire season than to purchase all episodes in a season separately.	Price varies, based on TV series and number of episodes. It's always cheaper to purchase an entire season than to purchase all episodes in a season separately.
Purchase Movie	$.99 to $14.99	$.99 to $19.99
Rent Movie	$.99 to $3.99 (New releases start at $3.99, with library titles available for as little as $.99 per rental.)	$1.99 to $4.99 (New releases start at $4.99, with library titles available for as little as $1.99 per rental.)
Audiobooks	$.95 to $41.95 (Unabridged audiobooks of current bestsellers tend to be among the higher priced titles. These tend to range from $14.95 to $26.95.)	N/A
Ringtones	$1.29	N/A

> ☑ **TIP**   After you've purchased one or more songs from a full-length album (but not the whole album), you can later purchase that entire album at a discount from iTunes using the Complete My Album feature. How much of a discount you're given will depend on how much music from that album you already own.
>
> The iTunes Store also offers the Complete My Season feature that works with TV show seasons. If you purchase one or more single episodes of a TV series (from a

specific season), you can later return to the iTunes Store and purchase the rest of the episodes from that season at a reduced price (based on how many episodes from that season you already own). This feature works just like the Complete My Album feature, but relates to TV shows.

QUICKLY FIND TV EPISODES YOU WANT TO PURCHASE ON iTUNES

When shopping for TV show episodes to purchase and watch using the iTunes app, tap on the TV shows button that's displayed near the bottom of the screen. Shows are displayed by series name. So to see a list of episodes of *The Office*, for example, that are available, use the Search field to find *The Office*. The search will display the TV show by season number and by available episodes. For example, the listings will say *The Office* Season 2 or *The Office* Season 8.

Tap on the TV series artwork icon that's associated with the season from which you want to purchase episodes from to reveal a listing of individual episodes from that season, in chronological order, based on original airdate. The most recently aired episodes will be listed toward the bottom of the list, so scroll down.

At the top of the screen, you'll also have the option to purchase the entire season (as opposed to individual episodes) at a discounted rate, plus be able to choose between high definition (HD) or standard definition (SD) video quality.

To save money, purchase an entire season of your favorite show's current season. This is called a Season Pass. Then, when a new episode airs each week and becomes available from the iTunes Store (about 24 hours later), it can automatically be downloaded to your iOS device and made available to you via iCloud using a Wi-Fi Internet connection. You'll also receive a weekly email from Apple telling you when each new episode in your Season Pass is available.

When you shop for TV episodes from the iTunes Store (via the iTunes app), those files get downloaded and stored on your iPhone or iPad. They're commercial free and will be available to watch whenever you wish. They're also permanently accessible via your iCloud account to be downloaded to any computer, iOS device, or Apple TV device that's linked to the same iCloud account. Once an episode is download to your iPhone or iPad, an Internet connection is no longer needed to watch that episode.

NOTE   Keep in mind that, without commercials, a one-hour program appears within the iTunes Store (and within the Videos app) as being between 42 and 44 minutes long, while a half-hour program appears as being between 21 and 24 minutes long.

When you stream TV episodes from the Internet using a specialized app, such as Netflix, HBO Go, Xfinity (from Comcast), or ABC Player, for example, this programming does not get stored on your iOS device and is available only when your iPhone or iPad has a constant connection to the Internet while you're watching that content (and in many cases, a Wi-Fi connection is required).

STREAMING VIDEO ON YOUR iPAD

To stream video content to your iPhone or iPad from the Internet, you need to use a specialized app, based on where the content is originating from on the Internet.

Whenever you're streaming video content from the Internet, you can pause the video at any time. Depending on the app, you can also exit the app partway through a video and resume watching it from where you left off when you re-launch the app later.

> **! CAUTION** The capability to stream content from the Internet and experience it on your iPhone or iPad gives you on-demand access to a wide range of programming. However, streaming audio or video content requires a tremendous amount of data to be transferred to your iOS device. Therefore, if you use a 3G or 4G connection, your monthly wireless data allocation will quickly get used up. So, when you're streaming Internet content, it's best to use a Wi-Fi connection.
>
> Not only does a Wi-Fi connection often allow data to be transferred to your iPhone or iPad at faster speeds, there's also no limit as to how much data you can send or receive. Plus, when streaming video content, you can often view it at a higher resolution using a Wi-Fi connection.

The following sections describe some of the popular apps for streaming TV shows, movies, and other video content directly from the Internet. Keep in mind, many cable television service providers (such as Xfinity/Comcast and Time Warner), and satellite TV service providers, as well as individual television networks (ABC, NBC, CBS, The CW, USA Network, Lifetime, SyFy, etc., and even specific TV shows, often have their own proprietary apps available for streaming content from the Internet directly to your iPhone and/or iPad. There are also paid streaming services, such as Netflix and HuluPlus, that offer vast libraries of TV shows and movies available for streaming.

> **NOTE** As a general rule, free streamed programming from a television network app (from ABC, NBC, or CBS, for example) includes commercials. Programming from a premium cable network that you're already paying for through your cable TV service (such as HBO or Showtime), is commercial free, as is streamed TV shows or movies accessed through a paid service, such as Netflix or HuluPlus.

ABC PLAYER

The ABC Player is a free app from the ABC Television Network that allows you to watch full-length episodes of your favorite ABC-TV dramas, reality shows, sitcoms, game shows, and soap operas, for free. The episodes are streamed to your iPhone or iPad and can be watched using this app. The shows are advertiser supported, so you need to watch ads during the programs you stream.

> **NOTE** When you purchase TV show episodes from the iTunes Store, they are ad free.

The ABC Player app is separate from the free ABC News app, which allows you to watch news coverage from the network.

> **TIP** All the major TV networks offer free apps for streaming full-length episodes on an on-demand basis, seeing previews of upcoming shows, and for keeping track of your favorite shows. Using these apps, you can watch your favorite shows whenever you want. However, the selection of available episodes at any given time may be limited.

HBO GO

If you're already a paid subscriber to the HBO cable television network, you can download the free HBO Go app (shown in Figure 17.17) and watch every episode of every HBO original series on-demand, as well as an ever-changing lineup of movies, comedy specials, sports programs, and documentaries that are currently airing on HBO.

After you set up a free online account with your local cable or satellite television provider, sign in to the HBO Go app and select the programming you want to watch. Begin playing a TV episode or movie with the tap of a finger, or create a queue of shows to watch at your leisure. Movies and TV episodes can be paused and resumed later.

One great feature of the HBO Go app is that HBO sometimes releases episodes on this app one week before they air on television. Plus, you can access behind-the-scenes content of popular HBO series, like *Game of Thrones*.

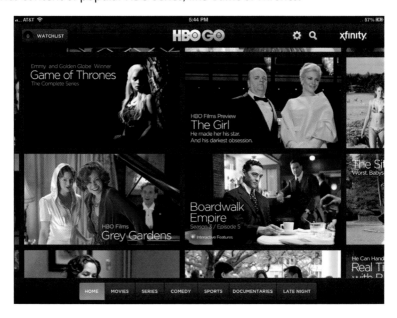

FIGURE 17.17
Using the HBO Go app, you can watch episodes from HBO's original TV series, as well as a new lineup of movies each month.

> **!CAUTION**   Most of the streaming video apps for the iPhone and iPad work only in the United States. If you try to access HBO Go from abroad, for example, the app will not work.

HULU PLUS

Full-length and commercial-free episodes from thousands of current and classic TV series (as well as an ever-growing library of movies) are available on your iOS device using the free Hulu Plus app. However, this service requires you to pay a flat monthly subscription fee ($7.99) to access and view it.

Hulu Plus members can access season passes to current TV shows airing on ABC, FOX, and NBC, for example, or pick and choose from thousands of episodes from classic TV series. A Wi-Fi connection is recommended, although the app does work with a 3G or 4G Internet connection.

The *Hulu Plus* app allows you to pause programs and resume them later, plus create a queue of shows to watch on your tablet.

> 🔍 **MORE INFO**   Visit www.hulu.com/plus to subscribe to the Hulu service and browse available programming.

INFINITY TV

If Infinity is your cable TV provider, use this app to watch a wide range of free, on-demand programming, including TV shows and movies. The free TWCable TV app from Time Warner Cable offers similar functionality. If you subscribe to another cable TV or satellite TV service, check the App Store to see whether a similar app is available.

MAX GO

This free app works just like the HBO Go app, but enables you to watch Cinemax programming on demand from your iOS device. The content is free, as long as you're already a paid Cinemax subscriber. This app offers you instant access to more than 400 movies per month, plus access to Cinemax's original TV programming.

> 📝 **NOTE**   There's also a free Showtime app, called Showtime Anytime, available for the iPhone and iPad (if you're a paid Showtime subscriber with AT&T U-verse or Verizon FiOS). This app offers on-demand programming from the Showtime network, including original TV series, like *Dexter*, as well as an ever-changing selection of movies. For Xfinity and Time Warner cable subscribers, on-demand Showtime programming is available from the Xfinity or TWC TV apps.

NETFLIX

Netflix is a subscription-based service that enables you to watch thousands of movies and TV show episodes via the Internet on your Internet-enabled television, on your computer screen, from a video game console (such as Xbox 360 or PlayStation 3), using Apple TV, using a DVR (such as TiVo), or directly on your iPhone or iPad (when you use the free Netflix app). The subscription fee for Netflix is a flat $7.99 per month for unlimited access.

You can watch as much streaming content as you'd like per month from any compatible computer or iOS mobile device. Simply browse the Netflix Instant Watch library, and tap on the Play button when you find the movie or TV show episode you want to watch. You can also create and manage an Instant Queue.

YOUTUBE

The YouTube app no longer comes preinstalled on your iPhone or iPad. However, an official YouTube app (free) is now available for the iPhone and iPad from the App Store. This app enables you to watch unlimited streaming videos produced and uploaded by everyday people, companies, television networks, and other organizations. In addition to millions of entertaining videos and video blogs, YouTube features free educational content and how-to videos. All YouTube content is free of charge to watch. Some of it is advertiser supported, however.

> **TIP** In addition to streaming videos, TV shows, and movies to watch on your iPhone or iPad, you can stream audio programming from AM, FM, and satellite-based radio stations and radio networks, as well as Internet-based radio stations. Some of the apps available for doing this are Pandora Radio, TuneIn Radio Pro, Spotify, and SiriusXM. A monthly fee applies to stream SiriusXM programming.

CUSTOMIZE YOUR READING EXPERIENCE WITH iBOOKS AND NEWSSTAND

When it comes to reading eBooks, Apple has a solution to meet every person's reading habits and taste. Thanks to the newly revamped version of iBooks (version 3), eBooks can easily be read on any iOS mobile device. However, if you find the screen too small to read your favorite books on the iPhone, you can utilize the larger 7.9-inch screen of the iPad mini and hold the tablet easily in one hand as you read. Many people, however, appreciate the larger 9.7-inch screen of the iPad 2 or 3rd/4th generation iPads.

Of course, if you have an iPhone and/or an iPad (or iPad mini), you can use iCloud to sync your eBook library and related bookmarks between devices automatically, so your books, even if you've acquired hundreds of them, are available to you regardless of which iOS mobile device you're using.

Anything having to do with shopping for, downloading, installing, and then reading eBooks on your iPhone or iPad is done using Apple's free iBooks app, which does not come preinstalled on your device. However, as soon as you begin using a new or newly upgraded iPhone or iPad, you're automatically prompted to download and install Apple's latest edition of the iBooks app.

> **☑ TIP** Keep in mind that you also have the option to download and use other third-party eBook reading apps with your iOS device. These apps, which include the Amazon Kindle and Barnes & Noble Nook apps, are discussed later in this chapter.

iBooks has two main purposes. First, it's used to access Apple's online-based iBookstore. From iBookstore, you can browse an ever-growing collection of eBook titles (including traditional book titles from bestselling authors and major publishers that have been adapted into eBook form). Although some eBooks are free, most must be paid for.

> **☑ TIP** As with all purchases from the iTunes Store, App Store, or Newsstand, all eBook purchases made from iBookstore get charged to the credit or debit card associated with your Apple ID. iBookstore and Newsstand purchases can also be paid for using prepaid iTunes gift cards.

After you've downloaded eBooks to your iOS device, the iBooks app is used to transform your mobile device into an eBook reader, which accurately reproduces the appearance of each page of a printed book on your device's screen. So reading an eBook is just like reading a traditional book in terms of the appearance of text, photos, or graphics that would otherwise appear on a printed page.

iBooks allows you to customize the appearance of a book's pages. For example, you can select a font that is appealing to your eyes, choose a font size that's comfortable to read, and even turn on or off a Sepia or Night theme that changes the background color to the screen (which some people find less taxing on their eyes).

iBooks offers many features that make reading eBooks on your iOS device a pleasure, several of which will be explained shortly. For example, when you stop reading and exit the iBooks app (by pressing the Home button), the app automatically saves the page you're on using a virtual bookmark and later reopens to that page when the iBooks app is restarted. It can sync your bookmarks and eBook library with iCloud and your other iOS mobile devices automatically.

CUSTOMIZE iBOOKS SETTINGS

To customize settings related to iBooks, launch Settings and tap on the iBooks option. From the iBooks menu screen, you can turn on or off Full Justification and/or Auto-Hyphenation, as well as the Both Margins Advance feature (which when turned on, allows you to tap the left or right margin of the screen to turn a page, instead of using a horizontal finger swipe).

To turn on the iCloud syncing functions for iBooks, turn on the virtual switches associated with Sync Bookmarks and Sync Collections. If you turn on the Show All Purchases option, on the Library screen (which will be discussed shortly), all of the eBooks you own are displayed, even if they're not currently stored on the device you're using. To download one of eBooks you own from iCloud, simply tap on the iCloud icon.

You only need to customize the settings associated with iBooks once, but you can return to Settings at anytime to adjust the customizable options as you see fit.

> **iOS 6 WHAT'S NEW** One new feature that iBooks 3.0 offers is the ability for publishers to update eBook content, and for your iOS device to download that content automatically (and for free). For this feature to work, turn on the virtual switch associated with the Online Content option.

> **NOTE** iBooks allows you to store and manage a vast library of eBooks on your iOS device, the size of which is limited only by the storage capacity of the device itself.
>
> Plus, all of your iBookstore purchases automatically get saved to your iCloud account. Thus, you can easily download eBook titles you've previously purchased via iCloud when you want to access a particular eBook that is not currently stored on your device. If you have the Show All Purchases option turned on (from within Settings), tap on the eBook's iCloud icon that appears within the Library screen to download the book. Otherwise, return to iBookstore and tap on the Purchased icon that's displayed at the bottom of the screen to download a previous eBook purchase.
>
> Thanks to iCloud, you can also begin reading a chapter of an eBook on your iPhone and then switch to reading that same book on your iPad, because even your virtual bookmarks get automatically saved and synced.

DOWNLOAD AND INSTALL iBOOKS ON YOUR iOS DEVICE

iBooks 3.0 is available for free from the App Store. From your iPhone or iPad that's connected to the Internet, launch the App Store app. Use the App Store's Search feature to find the iBooks app, or wait to be prompted to download it (along with some of Apple's other apps.) When the iBooks app listing appears in the App Store, tap on the Free button to download and automatically install it.

After the iBooks app is installed on your iPhone or iPad, launch the app from the device's Home Screen by tapping on its app icon.

> **TIP** Your iPhone or iPad needs Internet access to download and install the iBooks app, and then to browse or shop for eBooks via iBookstore. However, after one or more eBooks are loaded into your iOS device, the Internet is no longer required. Thus, you can read an eBook while on an airplane, for example, with your iPhone or iPad in Airplane Mode, as long as you preload the eBook(s) you want to read onto your device before your flight.

THE iBOOKS MAIN LIBRARY SCREEN

When you launch iBooks for the first time, the app's main Library screen is displayed. However, the Library screen, which looks like a virtual bookshelf, will be empty. From the Library screen, tap on the Store button to access Apple's iBookstore in order to browse and shop for eBooks. An Internet connection is required for this.

> **TIP** If you've already purchased eBooks from iBookstore from another computer or device, tap on the Books icon that's displayed near the top-center of the screen and then tap on the Purchased Books option to view a listing of all eBooks you own that are formatted to be read with iBooks. You can then tap on the iCloud icon for each book and download it to your iPhone. If you have the Sync Collections option from within Settings turned on, this happens automatically.
>
> On the iPad, to access your already purchased eBooks, if you have the Sync Collections option turned off, tap on the Collections button and then tap on the Purchased books option to display a listing of books you own on the Library screen. Tap on the iCloud icon for each book you want to download and read on the iPad (or iPad mini) you're using.

On the iPhone, the Store button is located in the upper-right corner of the Library screen. On the iPad, the Store button can be found in the upper-left corner of the Library screen.

> **NOTE** Throughout this chapter, the term *purchased* eBooks refers to eBook titles you already have purchased from iBookstore, as well as free eBooks you download through iBookstore. These are eBooks already stored within your iCloud account or that are displayed when you tap on the Purchased Books option or have the Sync Collections option within Settings turned on.

Typically, the Library screen displays all the eBook titles currently stored on your device (as shown in Figure 18.1). From this screen, you can manage your eBook library, access iBookstore, or access PDF files stored on your device.

FIGURE 18.1

Shown here is the Library screen on an iPad, with a collection of eBooks stored on the tablet. After tapping on the Collections button on the iPad, the Books option was selected. (The Sync Collections option from within Settings is turned on.)

After you've begun expanding your personal eBook library and have one or more eBook titles stored on your device, the cover art for each title is displayed on the Library screen. You can see an alternative view of the Library screen by tapping on one of the two formatting icons that are displayed near the upper-right corner of the screen.

To see an alternate listing view, tap the icon that's comprised of three horizontal lines (shown in Figure 18.2). To return to the default view, tap the icon showing four squares.

> **✓ TIP** From the bottom of the alternative Library viewing screen, tap on the Bookshelf, Titles, Authors or Categories tab (displayed near the bottom-center of the screen) to sort your eBook collection.

eBook Sort Tabs

FIGURE 18.2

Sort and then view your eBook collection using this alternative listing format, as opposed to viewing eBook covers on a virtual bookshelf. This feature now works on the iPhone and iPad.

MANAGING YOUR eBOOK COLLECTION FROM THE LIBRARY SCREEN

While looking at the Library screen, you can sort and manage your eBook collection. To do this on the iPhone, tap on what by default is labeled the Books button that's displayed near the top-center of the screen. On the iPad, tap on the Collections button that's displayed near the top-left corner of the screen.

By default, the Collections screen (iPhone) or window (iPad) is comprised of the Books, Purchased Books, PDFs and Favorites folders (also called Collections). However, by tapping on the New button, you can create additional folders (Collections) with custom names, and then place one or more eBooks into those folders. From the Library screen, tap the Edit button to delete or rearrange the order in which the folders are displayed.

Once folders are created, from the main Library screen, tap on the Edit button in order to select eBooks (by tapping on their covers). Then, tap on the Move button to move those eBooks from the main Library screen into a specific folder (Collection). Or, you can tap the Delete key to erase those eBooks from your iPhone or iPad. Tap the Done button when you're done organizing your eBook collection.

> **TIP** You can create separate eBook folders (Collections) for specific book series, authors, various subject matters, or based on whether the books are related to work, pleasure or personal enrichment, for example.

To free up internal storage space on your iPhone or iPad, it's possible to delete one or more eBooks that aren't currently being read. However, those eBooks will remain available to you via iCloud and can quickly be reloaded anytime (as long as an Internet connection is available). You can access iBookstore using a 3G, 4G, or Wi-Fi Internet connection.

> **NOTE** Although your iOS device needs to be connected to the Internet to access iCloud and reload an already purchased eBook title, no Internet connection is required to delete eBooks, to manage your eBook collection from the Library screen, or to read them.

BROWSE AND SHOP FOR eBOOKS VIA iBOOKSTORE

When you're ready to begin browsing the vast eBook selection offered by iBookstore, make sure your iPhone or iPad is connected to the Web, and then tap on the Store button. The interface and layout of iBookstore are similar to those of the App Store and Newsstand; however, what's offered here are exclusively eBooks.

> **TIP** You also have the option to shop for eBooks using the iTunes software on your primary computer. As soon as you make an eBook purchase, it will be added to your iCloud account, so you can then download it to your iOS device without having to perform an iTunes Sync. Remember, all purchases made from the App Store, iTunes Store, and iBookstore automatically get saved to your iCloud account and become accessible from any iOS device or computer that's also linked to your iCloud account.

Many of the eBooks offered from iBookstore are digital versions of traditionally printed books from bestselling authors and major publishers. However, as you browse iBookstore, you'll also find an ever-growing selection of self-published eBooks, which are written by up-and-coming or nonprofessional writers who are not affiliated with a major publishing house. Plus, you'll find self-published works by well-known authors, as well as books that were taken out of print but have been rereleased as eBooks. There are also eBooks available that are not available in printed form, including a growing selection of Enhanced eBooks created specifically for the iPads using Apple's free iBooks Author 2.0 software for the Mac.

You can browse through iBookstore's offerings by subject, book title, an author's name, by viewing bestseller lists, or using various other methods. When you access iBookstore, you see the main screen, which on the iPhone looks like what's shown in Figure 18.3.

Figure 18.4 shows the main iBookstore screen on an iPad. While browsing and shopping from iBookstore are basically the same on the iPhone and iPad, the main command icons vary slightly between an iPhone versus an iPad.

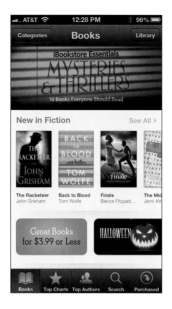

FIGURE 18.3

The iPhone version of the iBookstore. The Books button that's displayed at the bottom of the screen has been selected. From here, you can begin browsing for eBooks to purchase and download (or download for free in some cases).

FIGURE 18.4

When you browse iBookstore using an iPad, more content can be displayed on the screen at once. Shown here, the Books button that's displayed at the bottom of the screen has been selected.

iBOOKSTORE COMMANDS ON THE iPHONE

Displayed along the top of most iBookstore screens when accessing this online bookseller from an iPhone, you'll see a Categories button (displayed near the top-left corner of the screen) and a Library button (displayed near the top-right corner of the screen). Along the bottom of the screen are five additional command buttons. Here's a summary of how these features work:

 Categories—View eBooks by category, such as Arts & Entertainment, Business & Personal Finance, Fiction & Literature, Nonfiction, and Reference. There are 24 categories to choose from within iBookstore; they become accessible when you tap on the Categories button. Under some categories, you'll also discover sub-categories.

 Library—Tap this button to exit iBookstore and return to the Library screen of the iBooks app.

 Books—View a selection of what Apple decides are "featured" eBook titles currently available from iBookstore. Under each heading, such as New In Fiction or New In Nonfiction, you see a selection of eBook listings. Scroll horizontally through the listings below each heading, or tap on the corresponding See All option to view a separate screen that displays all eBook listings that fall under that heading.

 Top Charts—View Books or the *New York Times* Bestseller charts relating to paid and free eBooks available from iBookstore. The Books lists are compiled based on sales or downloads from iBookstore. Both the Books and the *New York Times* lists are updated regularly. Tap on the Books or NYTimes tab at the top of the screen to switch between chart sources.

> ✓ **TIP** Initially, when you tap on the Books tab (after tapping on the Top Charts icon at the bottom of the screen), each chart displayed is comprised of bestselling or popular eBooks from all categories. To narrow down the list and see charts for a specific category, tap on the Categories button, and then choose a category. The Paid Books and Free Books charts are compiled based on books from the selected category.

 Top Authors—This option displays an alphabetical listing of popular authors is displayed. You can narrow down your search by tapping on the Top Paid or Top Free tab that are displayed near the top-center of the screen. Or, to quickly find an author without having to scroll through a list, tap on the Search button.

Search—When you tap on this button, a blank search field is displayed at the top of the screen. Enter the book title, author name, subject, or any keyword associated with an eBook title or description that you're looking for. Then, tap the Search key on the virtual keyboard to initiate the search and view the results. A selection of eBook listings is displayed. Tap on a listing to display the Description screen for the selected eBook.

Purchased—This command icon allows you to access your iCloud account and load any previously purchased eBooks to your iPhone, regardless of which computer or iOS mobile device the eBooks were originally purchased from. Tap the All tab to view all of the eBook titles you own, or tap on the Not On This Phone tab to view eBooks you own that are not installed on the iPhone you're using. To download one of the eBooks listed, tap on the iCloud icon displayed to the right of its listing.

Use the Books, Top Charts, Top Authors, Search, or Purchased option to find, purchase (if applicable) and download eBooks. What you initially see are eBook listings that include the book's cover artwork, title and author. Tap on the eBook's cover to reveal a more detailed Description screen for a book.

iBOOKSTORE COMMANDS ON THE iPAD

When you shop for eBooks through iBookstore from your iPad, much more information is displayed on the screen than when viewing the same screens on the iPhone. When viewing most screens within iBookstore, displayed along the top of the screen are the Library button and five Categories tabs, along with the Search field. Displayed along the bottom of the iBookstore screen are five command icons. Here's a summary of how these features work:

Library—Tap this icon to exit iBookstore and return to the Library (Bookshelf) screen of iBooks.

Category Tabs—Displayed near the top-center of the screen are five Category tabs, labeled All Categories, Fiction, Nonfiction, Mysteries, and More. (Apple sometimes changes the category headings that are displayed here.) Tap on All Categories to view information about books from all categories within iBookstore, or narrow down your search by selecting a specific category. Tap on the More button to access a pull-down menu of categories (shown in Figure 18.5).

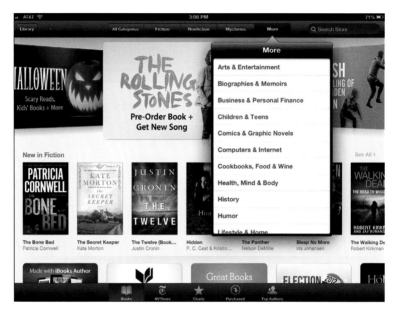

FIGURE 18.5

From the main iBookstore screen on the iPad, tap on the More tab to display a listing of categories. Tab on one of the categories to make searching for the type of eBook you're looking for easier.

 Books—Tap on this button that's displayed at the bottom of the iBookstore screen to access the New In Fiction, New In Nonfiction and other categories of books that Apple is currently featuring within its online-based bookstore. This screen features both eBook listings (displayed under specific headings), as well as graphic banners showcasing specific books, themes or special interest categories.

> **☑ TIP** After tapping on the Books button at the bottom of the screen, scroll downward to access the Quick Links section. Here are buttons for browsing eBooks that fall into in a handful of specialized themes or categories that change regularly.
>
> Below the Quick Links section is the Apple ID [You Username] button and the Redeem button. Tap on the Apple ID button to manage your Apple ID account, or tap on the Redeem button to redeem iTunes Gift Cards.

 NYTimes—Tap on this button to reveal two *New York Times* Bestsellers lists—one for Fiction (displayed on the left side of the screen) and one for Nonfiction (displayed on the right side of the screen), as shown in Figure 18.6.

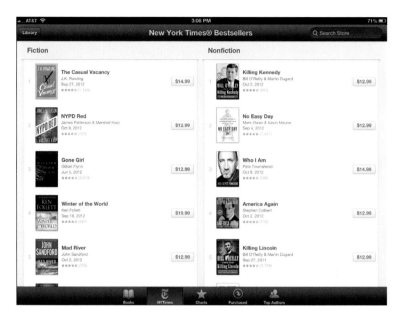

FIGURE 18.6
View New York Times Bestseller lists on your iPad.

Charts—Tap on this button to reveal two lists of the current most popular eBook titles among iBookstore customers. The Top Paid Books list is displayed on the left side of the screen, and the Top Free Books list is displayed on the right side of the screen. Initially, these lists are comprised of books from all categories. To narrow down your search, tap on the All Categories button (that's displayed near the top-left corner of the screen, and choose a specific category).

Purchased—This command icon allows you to access your iCloud account and load any previously purchased eBooks to your iPad, regardless of on which computer or iOS mobile device those eBooks were originally purchased from. Tap on the All tab to view all of the eBook titles you own, or tap on the Not On This iPad tab to view eBooks you own that are not installed on the iPad you're using. To download one of the eBooks listed, tap on the iCloud icon displayed to the right of its listing.

Top Authors—Tap on this button to search for eBooks by author. An alphabetical listing of popular authors is displayed on the left side of the screen. When you tap on an author's name, the eBooks they've written are displayed as listings on the right side of the screen. Narrow down your search by tapping on the Paid or Free tabs that are displayed near the top of the authors list. Or, to quickly find an author without having to scroll through a list, tap on the Search button.

HOW TO FIND A SPECIFIC eBOOK—FAST

Although you can use the various command buttons and spend hours browsing through eBook titles, just as you can spend an equal amount of time perusing the shelves of a traditional bookstore, here are some simple strategies for quickly finding a specific eBook title you're looking for.

As soon as iBookstore loads, use the Search field to enter the eBook title, author's name, subject, or keyword that's associated with what you're looking for. Entering a specific book title will reveal very specific search results. However, entering a keyword relating to a topic or subject matter will reveal a selection of eBook suggestions that somehow relate to that keyword.

> ☑ **TIP**   If you're interested in reading eBooks about digital photography, for example, but you don't know any specific book titles or authors who have written such books, simply enter the keywords "digital photography" into the Search field. A series of individual eBook listings that relate to digital photography are displayed in the main part of the iBookstore screen. Some of these are paid books, whereas others are free publications.

Tap on any listing to reveal a more detailed Description relating to a particular eBook. As you review a Description screen (iPhone) or window (iPad) for an eBook, look carefully at its ratings and its written reviews, especially if it's a paid eBook.

> ☑ **TIP**   One way to choose an eBook is by looking at what's popular, especially if you enjoy reading any type of fiction. The *New York Times* Bestsellers lists reveal which books are popular nationwide (that are also available from iBookstore in eBook form), and the separate Charts lists help you quickly determine which eBooks are the most popular among your fellow iPhone and iPad users.
>
> Keep in mind that not all *New York Times* Bestsellers listed in the printed newspaper are available in eBook format, or they might not be available from iBookstore. Thus, only those bestselling books available from iBookstore for your iPhone or iPad are listed in the *New York Times* Bestsellers lists.
>
> If you're looking for a steamy romance novel, for example, tap on the Charts button, tap on the Categories button, and then select the Romance option from the Categories listing.

> **NOTE** Also available from iBookstore are a selection of enhanced, full-color, interactive eBooks. For example, some popular children's books fall into this category, as do some cookbooks or textbooks and reference books. These enhanced eBooks include animations, interactive elements, "pop-up" graphics (which replace traditional pop-up book pages), and sound, plus they take full advantage of the iPhone or iPad's full-color, high-definition Multi-Touch display. All of these enhanced books are available from iBookstore.

LEARN ABOUT AN eBOOK FROM ITS DESCRIPTION

While browsing iBookstore, you will see individual eBook listings for titles that relate to what you are looking for. A typical eBook listing includes the eBook's cover artwork, its title and author.

While viewing eBook listings after tapping on the Books, NY Times, Charts, or Top Authors button, for example, tap on an eBook's title or cover artwork to access a more detailed Description. This is how you access the capability to download and read a free sample of the eBook, and/or purchase (if applicable) and download it.

> **TIP** To quickly purchase and download an eBook, tap on the price button displayed within its Description screen (iPhone) or window (iPad). When you tap on a price button, it changes to a Buy Book button. Tap this Buy Book button to confirm your purchase decision. You will then need to enter your Apple ID password to begin the download process.
>
> If you're downloading a free eBook, tap on the Free button that is displayed instead of a price button. Then, instead of a Buy Book button, a Get Book button appears. Tap on it, enter your Apple ID, and download the free eBook. Even though you need to enter your Apple ID, you will not be charged to download a free eBook. At the same time it's downloaded to your device, that free eBook will also be saved to your iCloud account.

It typically takes between 10 and 30 seconds to download a full-length eBook to your iPhone or iPad, depending on the speed of your Internet connection and the size of the eBook's digital file. As soon as it's downloaded and ready to read, the book's front cover artwork is displayed as part of the Library screen within the iBooks app.

UNDERSTANDING THE BOOK'S DESCRIPTION

An eBook's Description screen (iPhone) or window (iPad) is divided into several sections. On both an iPhone and iPad, displayed near the upper-left corner of a typical eBook Description, as shown in Figure 18.7, is the eBook's cover artwork. To the right of this is a text-based summary of the book, including its title, author, the book's publication date and publisher, its average star-based rating, the number of ratings it's received, and the book's length. (The page length of the printed edition of the book is displayed.)

The book's price button and Sample button are also displayed near the top of the Description screen/window.

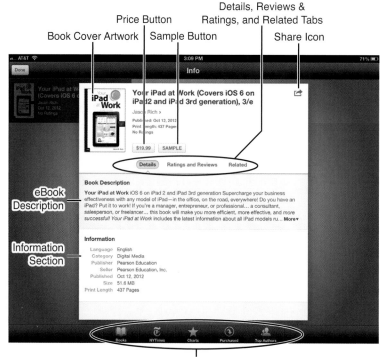

FIGURE 18.7

Read a detailed description of an eBook before making your purchase and/or downloading it.

> **TIP** From the iBookstore, to return to the main Library screen of iBooks, tap on the Library button that's displayed near the top of the screen.

If you look at the upper-right corner of an eBook Description screen or window, you'll see a Share icon. Tap on it to share information about the book with others via email, text/instant message, Twitter, or Facebook. You can also copy a link for the eBook into your iOS device's virtual clipboard, and then paste that information into another app.

> **TIP**   You can preview an eBook before paying for it. On each book's Description screen/window you'll discover a Sample button. Tap on it to download a free sample of that eBook. The length of the sample varies, and is determined by the eBook's publisher. It is usually between a few pages and a full chapter.

Below the price and Sample buttons are three options, labeled Details (the default selection), Ratings and Reviews, and Related. Tap on the Details option to view a detailed description or summary of the book, as well as the Information section. The Information section displays the Language, Category, Publisher, Seller, Publication Date, File Size and Print Length of the book (refer to Figure 18.7).

Tap on the Ratings and Reviews option (shown in Figure 18.8) to access the iBookstore Ratings chart, which showcases the book's average star-based rating, and how many ratings the book has received. Below the star-based ratings are more detailed, text-based reviews written by other iBookstore customers.

Also on the Ratings and Reviews screen/window, is the Facebook "Like" button. Tap on it to "like" the book and share details about it with your Facebook friends. This feature only works if you have Facebook integration turned on within your iPhone or iPad. From this same window/screen, you can also add your own star-based rating and/or tap on the Write A Review button to compose and publish your own review of that book which will then appear on iBookstore.

Tap on the Related option to view other books by that same author, or similar books that Apple recommends.

To exit an eBook Description screen on the iPhone, tap on the left-pointing arrow icon that says Books. It's displayed in the upper-left corner of the screen. Or, on the iPad, tap anywhere on the tablet's screen that is outside the Description window.

Remember, don't just pay attention to an eBook's average star-based rating. Also, pay attention to how many people have rated that eBook. After all, it's harder to get a good idea of a book's true quality if it has a five-star rating but has been rated by only a small number of people, versus a book with dozens or hundreds of five-star ratings.

Facebook "Like" Button

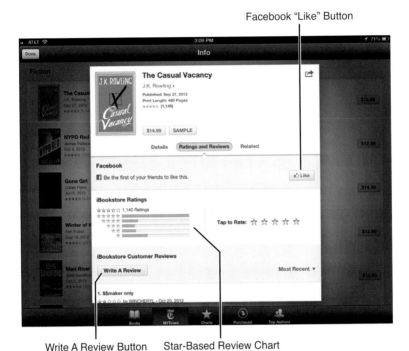

Write A Review Button   Star-Based Review Chart

FIGURE 18.8

From the Ratings and Reviews section of an eBook's Description screen/window, you can see the book's star-based ratings, more detailed reviews, "Like" the book on Facebook and/or create your own rating or review.

If the average star-based rating is inconclusive, take a look at the iBookstore Ratings chart. From this, you can see how many people have rated the eBook, as well as how many one-, two-, three-, four-, and five-star ratings it's received.

Still not sure whether an eBook is worth buying and/or downloading? Scroll down, below the customer ratings, and take a look at the more detailed text-based customer reviews. Here, people who have theoretically read the book have written their own (sometimes lengthy) reviews.

USING iCLOUD WITH iBOOKS

As you know by now, all of your iBookstore purchases are automatically stored within your iCloud account and become accessible from all of your iOS devices that are linked to that same account. This means that you can purchase an eBook on your iPad, for example, but also download and read it on your iPhone, without having to repurchase that title.

Adjust the customizable options from within Settings that relate to the iBooks app in order to turn on or off specific iCloud-related features and functions related to how eBooks are synced with iCloud. See the section, "Customize iBooks Settings," found earlier in this chapter.

HOW TO RELOAD A PREVIOUSLY PURCHASED eBOOK

Here's one way to manually load a previously purchased or downloaded eBook from iCloud (if you have the Sync Collections feature within Settings turned off):

1. Launch the iBooks app from the Home Screen.
2. From the Library screen, tap on the Store button.
3. Tap on the Purchased button that is displayed near the bottom of the iBookstore screen.
4. When the Purchased screen appears (shown in Figure 18.9), either use the Search field to type the title of the eBook you want to load, or scroll through the list of already purchased eBook titles that are not currently stored on your device.

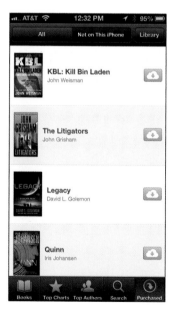

FIGURE 18.9

From the Purchased screen, select the previously purchased eBook title that you want to transfer from your iCloud account to your iOS device.

5. When the listing for the pre-purchased eBook you want to load is displayed, tap on the iCloud icon that's displayed to the right of that listing.

6. The selected eBook will be transferred from iCloud to your device. In a minute or so, it will be displayed on iBook's Library screen. A blue-and-white New label will appear across the book's cover, indicating that the eBook has just been added to your device and has not yet been accessed or read.

7. From the iBooks app's Library screen, tap on the eBook's cover to launch the eBook reader functionality of the app and begin reading your eBook.

> **(iOS 6) WHAT'S NEW** An alternate method for downloading previously purchased eBooks (from iBookstore) is to launch the iBooks app, tap on the Books button (iPhone) or Collections button (iPad), and then tap on the Purchased Books option, as long as your device is connected to the Internet. Then, from the Library screen, tap on any previously acquired book by tapping on the iCloud icon that's associated with it.

CUSTOMIZE YOUR eBOOK READING EXPERIENCE USING iBOOKS

From the Library screen of iBooks, tap on a book cover thumbnail to open an eBook and start reading it. While reading eBooks, hold the iPhone or iPad in portrait or landscape mode. As you're reading an eBook, tap anywhere on the screen to make the various command icons and buttons appear.

> **TIP** Tap on the Library button that's displayed near the upper-left corner of the screen to bookmark your location in that eBook and return to the iBooks Library (Bookshelf) screen.

On both the iPhone and the iPad, located to the right of the Library button is the Table of Contents icon. Tap on it to display an interactive table of contents for the eBook you're reading (as shown in Figure 18.10).

As you're looking at a table of contents, tap on any chapter number or chapter title to immediately jump to that location in the book. Or near the top-center of the Table of Contents screen, tap on the Bookmarks option to see a list of bookmarks you have previously set as you were reading that eBook.

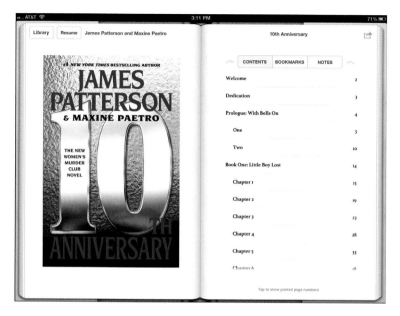

FIGURE 18.10
The Table of Contents screen for every eBook is interactive. Tap on the chapter number or chapter title to jump to the appropriate page.

> **TIP** Whenever you tap on the Library button while reading an eBook, or press the Home button to return to the device's Home Screen, your current location within the book is automatically bookmarked and saved. At any time, however, you have the option to manually add a virtual bookmark to as many pages in the eBook as you want. Then, by tapping on the Table of Contents icon, and then on the Bookmarks option, you can see a complete listing of manually placed virtual bookmarks in that eBook and return to any of those pages quickly.

To exit the Table of Contents screen and return to reading your eBook, tap on the Resume button that is displayed near the upper-left corner of the screen.

As you're reading an eBook, if you look in the upper-right portion of the screen, you'll see additional command icons. Tap on the "aA" icon to reveal a pop-up window (shown in Figure 18.11). It offers a screen brightness slider, as well as a small and large "A" button that are used to instantly decrease or increase the font size within the book you're reading. Tap on the Fonts button to change the the text font, or tap on the Theme button to change the Theme that's used to display the text and background color within the eBook you're reading.

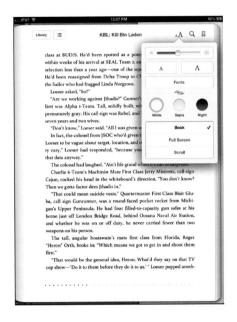

FIGURE 18.11

Tap on the "aA" icon to customize the appearance of the text within the eBook you're reading. In this example, the Themes button that initially appears within this menu window has been tapped in order to reveal the additional menu options.

Your Theme choices include Normal, Sepia or Night. Each displays the text and background in a different color combination. Choose the Theme that is best suited for the lighting available and that is visually pleasing to your personally.

iOS 6 WHAT'S NEW   When you tap on the Theme button, you can switch between White, Sepia or the Night theme by tapping on the circular icon for your selection. However, near the bottom of the window, you can also switch between normal Book viewing mode, Full Screen mode (iPad only) or the Scroll mode.

The Book viewing mode shows each page of the book you're reading, as well as icons on the top of the page, and page number information on the bottom. Full Screen mode (iPad only) gets rid of some of this on-screen "clutter," so you can just focus your eyes on the eBook's page.

The new Scroll mode allows you to scroll up or down within an eBook, as opposed to turning pages by swiping horizontally or tapping on the left or right margin of the screen.

Tap on the Search icon (which is shaped like a magnifying glass) to display a Search field. Use this feature to locate any keyword or search phrase that appears in the eBook you're currently reading.

> **TIP** Tap on the virtual bookmark icon to manually add a bookmark to the page you're on. You can then view a listing of your saved bookmarks by tapping on the Table of Contents icon and selecting the Bookmarks option.

As you're reading, to turn the page, swipe your finger from right to left (horizontally) across the screen to move one page forward, or swipe your finger from left to right to back up one page at a time.

Displayed near the bottom-center of the screen is the page number in the eBook you're currently reading, as well as the total number of pages in the eBook. The number of pages remaining in the current chapter is displayed to the right of the page number.

> **iOS 6 WHAT'S NEW** As you're reading an eBook, hold your finger on a single word. A group of six command tabs appears above that word. They're labeled Copy, Define, Highlight, Note, Search, and Share.
>
> At this point, use your finger to move the blue dots that appear to the left and right of the word in order to expand the selected text to a phrase, sentence, paragraph or an entire page, for example.
>
> Tap on the Copy tab to copy the selected text into iOS 6's virtual clipboard. You can then paste that text into another app or into a Note within iBooks.
>
> Tap on the Define tab to look up the definition of a selected word. Tap on the Highlight tab to highlight the selected text. It's possible to choose the color of your highlights, or underline the selected text by tapping on the yellow circle icon that's displayed above the word. Tap on the white circle (with a red line through it) to remove highlights, or tap on the Note icon to create a new Note. The Share icon also appears above the selected text after you tap on the Highlight option, as do the Copy, Define and Search options, if you tap on the right-pointing arrow.
>
> If you tap on the Note tab, a virtual sticky note appears on your device's screen, along with the virtual keyboard. Using the keyboard, type notes to yourself about what you're reading. When you're done typing, tap anywhere on the screen outside the sticky note box. A sticky note icon appears in the margin of the eBook. You can later tap on this icon to read your notes or annotations.

When you tap on the Highlight option, you're given the option to choose a high-light color. The last highlight color you selected determines the color of the sticky note that appears when you tap on the Note option. This allows you to easily color-code your highlights and/or notes.

Tap on the Search tab to enter any word or phrase and find it in the eBook. A search window will appear below the Search field. References to each occurrence of your keyword or search phrase will be displayed by chapter and page number. Tap on a reference to jump to that point in the book.

When you tap on the Share option, a Share menu will appear, giving you the option to email, text/instant message, tweet or send the selected text to your Facebook friends. From the Share menu, you can also copy text to the virtual clipboard and then paste it elsewhere.

READ PDF FILES WITH iBOOKS

The iBooks app can also be used to read PDF files you download or transfer to your iPhone or iPad. This can include a wide range of business-related documents, ranging in length from a single page to a book-length manuscript.

When you receive an email with a PDF file as an attachment, tap on the PDF thumbnail in that email so the file downloads to your iPhone or iPad. Next, tap and hold your finger on that same PDF thumbnail for a few seconds, until a menu window appears. The options in this window (as shown in Figure 18.12) are Quick Look, Open in iBooks, and, if applicable, Open In...[Compatible App].

The Open in iBooks command automatically launches the iBooks app and allows you to read the PDF document as if you're reading an eBook you downloaded from iBookstore.

NOTE If applicable, the Open In command enables you to open a PDF file using another third-party app. When you tap on this menu option, a list of compatible apps for viewing, printing, sharing, and/or annotating PDF files that are currently installed on your iPhone or iPad will be displayed. These apps might include PDF Reader, GoodReader, or PDFpen, for example.

When a PDF file opens in iBooks, you see command icons displayed along the top of the screen, as well as small thumbnails of the PDF document's pages displayed along the bottom of the screen.

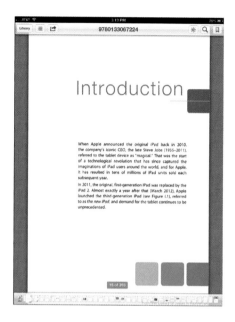

FIGURE 18.12
You can open and read a PDF file that is an attachment in an incoming email using the iBooks app.

Tap on the Library button that's is displayed near the upper-left corner of the screen to return to iBook's main Library screen. When you do this, however, the Bookshelf displays all the PDF files stored on your device—not eBooks downloaded from iBookstore.

To once again access your eBooks, tap on the PDFs button on the iPhone, or the Collections command icon on the iPad, and then select the Books option.

> **TIP** As you're viewing a PDF file from within iBooks, next to the Library icon is the Table of Contents icon. Tap on it to display larger thumbnails of each page in your PDF document, and then tap on any of the thumbnails to jump to that page. Or tap on the Resume icon to return to the main view of your PDF file.

To the immediate right of the Table of Contents icon (near the upper-left corner of the iBooks screen as you're reading a PDF file) is a Share icon that enables you to email or print the PDF document you're currently viewing. Near the upper-right corner of this screen are three additional command icons. The sun-shaped icon enables you to adjust the brightness of the screen. The magnifying glass–shaped icon enables you to search a PDF file for specific text in the document, and the Bookmark icon enables you to bookmark specific pages in the PDF file for later reference.

> **✔️ TIP** As you're viewing a PDF file using iBooks, you can zoom in on or out of the page using a reverse pinch or pinch finger motion on the touchscreen display, or by double-tapping on the area you want to zoom in or out on.

Also, as you're reading a PDF file, you can hold the device in either a vertical or a horizontal position. If you tap anywhere on the screen (except on a command icon or page thumbnail), the icons and thumbnails on the top and bottom of the screen disappear, giving you more onscreen real estate to view your PDF document. Tap near the top or bottom of the screen to make these icons and thumbnails reappear at any time.

CREATE YOUR OWN eBOOKS USING APPLE'S iBOOKS AUTHOR SOFTWARE

If you want to create your own content to be viewed using the iBooks app on the iPhone, iPad (or iPad mini), create a PDF document, and then load it into iBooks. However, if you want to create interactive and visually compelling eBooks for the iPad (or iPad mini), use Apple's free iBooks Author software for the Mac. (It's available from the Mac App Store.) To learn more about what this software can do, visit www.apple.com/ibooks-author.

ALTERNATIVE METHODS FOR READING YOUR eBOOKS

While Apple has worked out distribution deals with many major publishers and authors, the iBookstore does not offer an eBook edition of every book in publication.

> **✔️ TIP** In some cases, eBook titles will be available from Amazon.com or Barnes & Noble (BN.com), but not from iBookstore. Or if Amazon.com, BN.com, and iBookstore offer the same eBook title, the price for that eBook might be lower from one of these other online-based booksellers. So, if you're a price-conscious reader, it pays to shop around for the lowest eBook prices. Just because you're using an iPhone or iPad does not mean you must shop for eBooks exclusively from iBookstore.

Perhaps you owned a Kindle or Nook eBook reader before purchasing your iPhone or iPad and have already acquired a personal library of eBooks formatted for that device. Using the iBooks app, Kindle- or Nook-formatted eBooks are not accessible on your iOS device.

If you want to access your current Kindle eBook library from your iPhone or iPad, this is possible using the free Kindle app from the App Store. To purchase new Kindle-formatted eBook titles, you must visit Amazon.com using Safari or your primary computer. You cannot currently make in-app eBook purchases from within the Kindle app on your iOS device. However, after eBooks or digital publications are purchased from the Amazon.com website, your eBooks or digital newspapers/magazines will automatically download to your iPhone or iPad.

Likewise, you can shop for eBooks from BN.com, and then use the Nook app to access and read your Nook-formatted eBook library from your iPhone or iPad. In-app purchases from within the Nook app on your iPhone or iPad are not currently possible.

READ DIGITAL EDITIONS OF NEWSPAPERS AND MAGAZINES WITH THE NEWSSTAND APP

Many local, regional, and national newspapers, as well as popular consumer and industry-oriented magazines, are now available in digital form and accessible from your iPhone or iPad via the Newsstand app. This app comes preinstalled with iOS 6.

WORKING WITH THE NEWSSTAND APP

Not to be confused with the iBooks app (which is used for finding, purchasing, downloading, and reading eBooks), the Newsstand app is used to manage and access all of your digital newspaper and magazine single issues and subscriptions in one place. However, the iBooks and Newsstand apps have a similar user interface, so after you learn how to use one, you'll have no trouble using the other.

> **NOTE**   Many of the world's most popular newspapers, including *The New York Times, The Wall Street Journal, Barron's*, and *USA Today* are now published in digital form, as are popular business-oriented magazines, such as Entertainment Weekly, *TIME, Good Housekeeping, Mac/Life, O: The Oprah Magazine, National Geographic, US Weekly, Family Fun, The New Yorker, Wired, Sports Illustrated. GQ* and *PEOPLE Magazine.*
>
> In fact, starting in 2013, *Newsweek* will only be available as a digital publication and will no longer be sold on traditional newsstands or through subscriptions in print form.

After you launch Newsstand (shown in Figure 18.13), tap the Store button and browse through the ever-growing selection of digital newspapers and magazines that are available. With the tap of an icon, you can subscribe to any publication, or in most instances, purchase a single current or back issue.

FIGURE 18.13

The main Newsstand screen displays thumbnails for all newspaper and magazine issues currently stored on your iPhone or iPad.

All purchases you make are automatically billed to the credit or debit card you have on file with your Apple ID account, or you can pay using iTunes gift cards.

> **TIP**   To entice you to become a paid subscriber, some publishers offer free issues of their digital newspaper or magazine that you can download and read before actually paying for a subscription.
>
> Some publications give away the digital edition of their publication for free to paid subscribers of the print edition.

After you purchase a digital newspaper or magazine subscription (or a single issue of a publication), it appears on your Newsstand shelf within the Newsstand app. Tap the publication's cover thumbnail to access the available issue(s).

If you've subscribed to a digital publication, Newsstand automatically downloads the most current issue as soon as it's published (assuming your phone or tablet has a Wi-Fi Internet connection available), so when you wake your iPhone or iPad from Sleep Mode each morning, the latest edition of your favorite newspaper can be waiting for you.

> **TIP** To use a 3G or 4G wireless data network to automatically download digital publications, you must turn on this feature from within the Settings app. Launch Settings, select the iTunes & App Stores menu option, and then turn on the virtual switch associated with the Use Cellular Data option.
>
> Keep in mind, downloading digital publications using a cellular data network quickly uses up your monthly data allocation, and could ultimately result in additional charges if you're not on an unlimited data plan.
>
> Also from within Settings, tap on the Newsstand option to turn on the virtual switches associated with each specific newspaper or magazine subscription that's listed.
>
> Once you do this once, when using a Wi-Fi connection, your iPhone or iPad automatically downloads all new publication content when it becomes available, without you having to worry about using up your monthly wireless data allocation.

A Home Screen icon badge and/or the Notification Center screen/window notifies you immediately whenever a new issue of a digital publication is automatically downloaded to your iOS device and is ready for reading. When you access Newsstand, you also see a thumbnail of that publication's cover on the main Newsstand shelf screen.

While each digital publication requires its own proprietary app to read its content, the downloading and installation of those apps, as well as when they need to be launched, is all handled automatically from within the Newsstand app.

READING DIGITAL PUBLICATIONS

Every publisher utilizes the iPhone or iPad's vibrant Multi-Touch display in a different way in order to transform a traditionally printed newspaper or magazine into an engaging and interactive reading experience. Thus, each publication has its own user interface.

Figure 18.14 shows what a sample issue of a popular magazine looks like when being read in its digital form on the iPad.

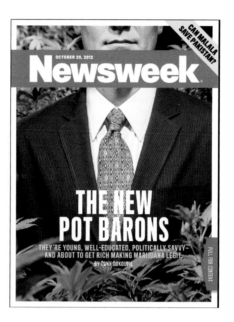

FIGURE 18.14

A sample digital magazine cover displayed via the Newsstand app on the iPad.

In most cases, a digital edition of a publication faithfully reproduces the printed edition and features the same content. However, sometimes the digital edition of a publication that's accessible from your iPhone or iPad also offers bonus content, such as active hyperlinks to websites, video clips, animated slide shows, or interactive elements not offered by the printed edition.

Reading a digital publication is very much like reading an eBook. Use a finger swipe motion to turn the pages, or to scroll up or down on a page. Tap the Table of Contents icon to view an interactive table of contents for each issue of the publication. When viewing some publication, you can also use a reverse pinch, pinch, or double-tap finger motion to zoom in or zoom out on specific content. Depending on the publisher, you might be able to access past issues of a publication at any given time in addition to the current issue. (An additional per-issue fee may apply.)

MANAGING YOUR NEWSPAPER AND MAGAZINE SUBSCRIPTIONS

If you opt to subscribe to a digital publication, you often need to select a duration for your subscription, such as one year. However, almost all digital subscriptions acquired through the Newsstand app are auto-renewing. Thus, when the subscription ends, unless you manually cancel it, Newsstand automatically renews your subscription and bills your credit or debit card accordingly.

To manage your recurring subscriptions, launch the Newsstand app and tap the Store button. From the Newsstand store, tap the Featured command button that's located near the bottom of the screen. Tap the Apple ID [Your Username] button. When prompted, enter your Apple ID password.

Next, from the Account Settings window that appears, tap the Manage button that's displayed under the Subscriptions heading. Displayed on the Subscriptions screen is a listing of all publications you've subscribed to. Tap any publication's listing to see the expiration date of your subscription, to cancel a subscription, or to renew your subscription.

IN THIS CHAPTER

- How to use Pages as a full-featured word processor
- How to use Numbers for "number crunching" and spreadsheet management
- How to create and showcase compelling digital slide presentations using Keynote

19

BE PRODUCTIVE USING PAGES, NUMBERS, AND KEYNOTE

For business users, three of the best designed, most versatile, and feature-packed apps available for the iPhone and iPad are Pages, Numbers, and Keynote, which together make up Apple's trio of iWork for iOS apps. Each app, however, is sold separately for $9.99.

Although each has its own purpose, Pages, Numbers, and Keynote all utilize the same basic user interface and menu structure. This design similarity between apps greatly reduces the learning curve for getting the most use out of them.

If you're not familiar with what each app in the iWork for iOS trio is designed for, here's a quick overview:

- Pages is a full-featured word processor. It is Microsoft Word (for PC and Mac) compatible, as well as fully compatible with the Pages software for the Mac.

- Numbers is an extremely powerful spreadsheet management tool that was designed specifically for the iPhone and iPad. However, its capabilities are similar to what's offered by Microsoft Excel running on a desktop computer. In fact, Numbers is compatible with Excel (for PC and Mac), as well as with the Numbers software for the Mac.

- Keynote is a versatile digital slide show presentation tool that enables you to create and showcase presentations. After you create a presentation, you can connect your iOS mobile device to an HD television set or LCD projector, for example, in order to share your presentation with a group. Or, you can take advantage of the full-color display built into your iPhone or iPad to convey information graphically (using animated digital slides) to one or two people at a time. Keynote is compatible with both Microsoft PowerPoint (for PC and Mac) and Keynote for the Mac.

In addition to enabling you to import Word, Excel, or PowerPoint documents or files into the appropriate app in order to view, edit, print, or share them, you also have the ability to create documents or files from scratch and export them into Word, Excel, or PowerPoint format, as well as PDF format, before transferring them to your primary computer or another device.

> **NOTE** If you also use the iWork for Mac software (Pages, Numbers, or Keynote), thanks to iCloud, files and documents sync and transfer easily between a Mac, iPhone, and/or iPad, without requiring that you change file formats during the import or export process. Pages, Numbers, and Keynote for the Mac are sold separately from the Mac App Store for $19.99 each.

One of the most useful features of the iWork for iOS apps is that you have several options for easily importing and exporting files and documents between the iPhone or iPad, and your Mac or PC (or another iOS device). For example, you can email files as attachments to or from the iPhone or iPad, or you can sync files using the iTunes Sync process. However, the easiest method of transferring files is to use iCloud or another compatible cloud-based file sharing service.

Unlike most other iPhone or iPad apps, Pages, Numbers, and Keynote can be seamlessly integrated with iCloud's "Documents & Data" option, so your files and documents always remain synchronized (wirelessly) with your primary computer and other iOS mobile devices.

Using this feature, if you make a change to a Pages document on your iPad, for example, within seconds, the revisions are transferred to iCloud and sent to all of the computers and other iOS mobile devices that are linked to the same iCloud account. The process happens in the background and is fully automated.

✓ TIP Because Pages, Numbers, and Keynote require significant data entry, consider using these apps with an optional external keyboard. In addition to making touch-typing easier, an external keyboard typically offers navigational arrow keys, which make moving around within a document or file more efficient. All three apps, however, make excellent use of the iPhone or iPad's virtual keyboard.

Data entry is also possible using the Dictation feature. Instead of typing, tap the Dictation key on the virtual keyboard, and when prompted, begin speaking for up to 30 seconds at a time. Then, have your iOS device transcribe what you say into text, and insert that text into the document or file you're working with. See Chapter 5, "Using Siri and Dictation to Interact with Your iOS Device," for more information on how to use the Dictation feature.

WORD PROCESSING WITH PAGES

When you launch Pages, Numbers, or Keynote, the main Library screen showcases thumbnails of the documents or files stored within that app (shown in Figure 19.1).

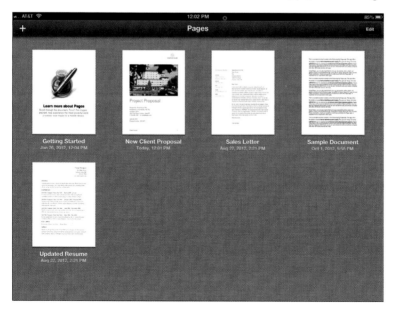

FIGURE 19.1

Shown here is the main Library screen of Pages. From here, you can manage, import, or export your document files. Similar functionality is offered by Numbers and Keynote.

From the Library screen, you can create a new document or file from scratch; rename a document; or import a document or file manually by tapping on the plus-sign icon. Or, you can tap on the Edit button to select and then share (export), copy, or delete a document or file from the app you're working with.

> **📝 NOTE** When exporting a Pages, Numbers, or Keynote document or file from your iPhone or iPad, you can keep it in its current format, or export it using the Microsoft Word, Excel, or PowerPoint format (depending on which app you're using). All three apps also allow files to be exported as PDF files.

To open a document or file, tap on its thumbnail while viewing the Library screen. When in the document editing mode of Pages (shown in Figure 19.2), at the top of the screen there are several command icons and buttons. Displayed near the top-left corner of the screen is the Documents button. Tap on Documents to return to the app's Library screen.

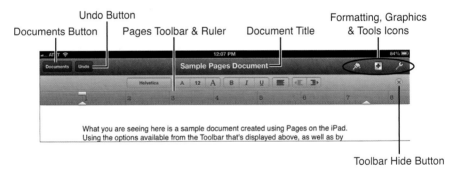

FIGURE 19.2

The main editing mode screen of Pages.

To the immediate right is the Undo button. It enables you to undo your most recent action(s) within the app. Displayed near the top-center of the Pages document editing screen is the active document's filename. Near the top-right corner of the screen are three command icons which provide access to sub-menus.

The Formatting icon (which looks like a paintbrush) is context sensitive. It adapts based on what type of content you're working within Pages. For example, if you're working with traditional text, tapping this icon reveals a pop-up window containing menu options for formatting that text. Near the top of this window are three command tabs. They're labeled Style, List, and Layout (shown in Figure 19.3).

FIGURE 19.3

The Formatting icon reveals a menu window with three command tabs and grants you access to a series of sub-menus.

When you tap on the Style tab, you can easily apply a font, type style (bold, italics, underlined, and so on), paragraph style, heading style, and/or add a bulleted or numbered list to a document. You can also create a header and footer.

Upon tapping on the List tab, you can adjust tabs and indents and format a bulleted or numbered list. You can control the size of the bullet or opt to use letters or numbers for creating an outline. Tap the Layout tab to create multiple columns within a documents and control line spacing.

USING GRAPHICS, CHARTS, AND SHAPES WITHIN PAGES

When you tap on the Graphics icon (it looks like a plus-sign, and is displayed near the top-right corner of the Pages editing mode screen), a menu window displays with four command tabs along the top. Each command tab reveals separate sub-menu options.

Tap the Media tab to import a photo that's stored on your iPhone or iPad into the document you're working with. Tap the Tables tab to create and format a table within the document. When you tap the Charts tab, two additional command tabs appear that enable you to create colorful 2D or 3D bar, line, area, or pie charts that can be fully customized. As you're looking at this menu, be sure to scroll up and down, as well as left and right, within the menu window in order to reveal all of your chart options.

Tap the Shapes tab to import and customize colorful shapes into your document. You can resize these shapes and place them over or under text, or you can make the text wrap around the shapes.

ACCESSING THE TOOLS MENU WITHIN PAGES

By tapping on the Tools icon, which is shaped like a wrench, and is displayed near the top-right corner of the Pages editing screen, the Tools menu is revealed (shown in Figure 19.4).

FIGURE 19.4

The Tools icon reveals a handful of submenu options for customizing documents in Pages. Similar functionality is offered when you access this menu in Numbers or Keynote.

The following options are available from the Tools menu:

- **Share and Print:** Reveals a submenu that enables you to email a document from within Pages, print a document wirelessly to a printer that's set up to work with your iPhone or iPad, or upload and share the document you're working on via WebDAV (which are cloud-based file sharing services that the iWork for iOS apps are all compatible with, in addition to iCloud).

> **TIP**   To export a document you're work with in Pages, PDF or Word format to another app that's installed on your iOS mobile device (such as Evernote or QuickOffice), tap on the Tools menu icon, select the Share and Print option, and then tap on the Open In Another App option. Select which format you want to export the document in, and then when prompted, choose a compatible app that's installed on your iOS mobile device.

- **Find:** Enables you to search for any keyword or phrase within the document you're using. When the Search field appears, tap the gear-shaped icon to access the Find, Find and Replace, Match Case, and Whole Words features.

Or, if multiple results are found for your search, tap the left- or right-pointing arrow keys to scroll through and display each result within the document.

■ **Document Setup:** Enables you to adjust the margins of the document you're working with, including the header and footer. For example, from the Document Setup screen you can add and format page numbers or line breaks.

■ **Settings:** Enables you to control the auto Spell Check feature built into Pages, as well as the Word Count feature. You can also turn on or off the Center Guides, Edge Guides, and Spacing Guides that can be displayed within a document. These guides are useful when sizing and placing photos, charts, or graphics into a document.

■ **Help:** Accesses the interactive help feature that's built into each iWork for iOS app.

> ✓ **TIP** Many of the document formatting commands available under the Style command tab are also available within the main toolbar that's displayed near the top of the main Pages editing screen (just above the ruler). However, to save on-screen real estate, you can remove the toolbar and ruler by tapping the "X" icon that's displayed to the extreme right of the toolbar. The "X" icon can be seen if you refer to Figure 19.2.

USING THE DOCUMENT NAVIGATOR FEATURE

If you're working with a multipage document, you can easily scan thumbnails of the entire document thanks to the Document Navigator (shown in Figure 19.5). As you're viewing, creating, or editing a document, hold your finger on the right margin of the document. An oversized magnifying glass icon displays along with a vertical slider. Drag your finger up or down to scan the entire document.

> ✓ **TIP** Using the Document Navigator, you can scroll down within a document by dragging your finger. When you release your finger, you can continue viewing or editing the page you scrolled to in the document.

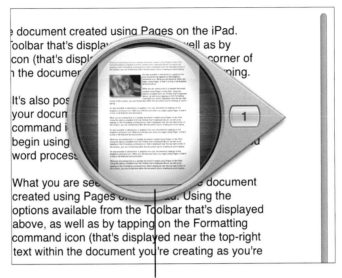

Document Navigator

FIGURE 19.5

The Document Navigator feature is exclusive to Pages. It makes it easier to scroll through a long document by looking at thumbnails of each page. You can also jump to a specific page within the document you're using.

WORKING IN FULL-SCREEN MODE

As you're proofreading a document, or if you're using an optional external keyboard for typing, position your iPhone or iPad in portrait mode in order to take advantage of the full-screen viewing mode offer by Pages. This mode allows you to fully utilize the on-screen real estate to view your document (shown in Figure 19.6).

> **NOTE** When typing using the iPhone or iPad's virtual keyboard, the individual keys appear larger on the screen when the iOS mobile device is positioned in landscape mode. The larger keys make it easier to touch-type. However, less of your document can be displayed on the screen at any given time.

In full-screen mode, most of the formatting buttons, the on-screen ruler, and the virtual keyboard temporarily disappear, giving you almost the entire screen to see and read your document.

To remove the on-screen keyboard, tap the hide keyboard key on the virtual keyboard. It's the key located at the bottom-right corner of the keyboard.

FIGURE 19.6

When you position your iPad in a portrait position and use the full-screen viewing mode, you can see an entire page on the screen at once.

To remove the formatting bar and on-screen ruler from the screen, tap the circular X icon that's displayed on the right side of the toolbar.

Swipe your finger on the screen to scroll up, down, left, or right while in full-screen mode. Tap and hold your finger anywhere on the screen (within the document) for a second or two to exit out of full-screen mode.

INSERT SPECIAL SYMBOLS OR CHARACTERS INTO YOUR DOCUMENTS

From within Settings, you can activate an additional virtual keyboard format that provides you with easy access to hundreds of special symbols, graphics and emoticons that you can incorporate into your Pages document, or when entering data into any other app (such as Messages, Keynote or Mail).

> **TIP** While using the regular virtual keyboard, if you press and hold down certain keys (a, e, i, o, u, c, or n), you can access alternate versions of those keys that include tildes and diacriticals.

To activate this additional keyboard layout, launch Settings and tap on the General option. Scroll down to the Keyboard option and tap on it. From the Keyboard menu screen, tap on the Keyboards option. Then, from the Keyboards menu screen, tap on the Add New Keyboard option. Scroll down on the Add New Keyboard list, and select the Emoji option by tapping on it. Exit out of Settings and return to Pages. (This process only needs to be done once.)

> **☑ TIP**   Instead of selecting the Emoji keyboard layout, you can choose from dozens of other language-specific keyboard layouts from the Add New Keyboard list. Some of these alternate keyboards make it easy to insert characters that are specific to that language into your text.

Now, anytime you activate the virtual keyboard on your iPhone or iPad, you'll discover a new key on the keyboard that's located between the "123" key (iPhone) / ".?123" key on the iPad, and the Dictation key (shown in Figure 19.7). This new key looks like a globe.

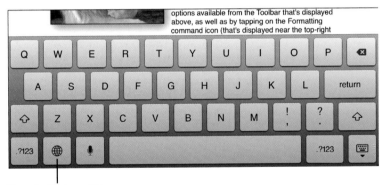

Alternate Keyboard Key

FIGURE 19.7

When you activate the Emoji keyboard, a new key (which looks like a globe) becomes accessible on the iPhone or iPad's virtual keyboard.

As you're using the iPhone or iPad's virtual keyboard, tap on the globe-shaped key to reveal the Emoji keyboard layout that contains hundreds of emoticons and symbols. Once this keyboard is visible (shown in Figure 19.8), tap on the keys on the very button of the keyboard to switch symbol pallets. Within each symbol pallet, you can then swipe your finger from right to left (or left to right) to view all of your options. Tap on a specific key to insert that symbol or graphic into whatever you're typing.

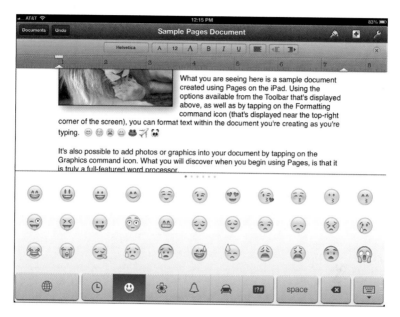

FIGURE 19.8

The alternate keyboard layout gives you access to hundreds of symbols and emoticons that you can insert into your document or into any text-based content you're inputting into your iPhone or iPad using the virtual keyboard.

To return to the normal QWERTY-style virtual keyboard, tap on the globe-shaped icon again.

> **TIP** Remember, the emoticons and symbols accessible from this secondary keyboard layout can be used with any app. This feature also works exceptionally well when composing text or instant messages using the Message app, for example.

> **TIP** To remove the globe key from the virtual keyboard, return to Settings and repeat the process described earlier in this section, but instead of selecting the Emoji keyboard layout, unselect it by tapping on it.

NUMBER CRUNCHING WITH THE NUMBERS APP

Whereas Pages is for word processing, the Numbers app is used for organizing, analyzing, and crunching numbers, and for creating powerful spreadsheets and beautifully rendered, full-color charts and tables that showcase numeric data graphically.

The latest version of Numbers offers the ability to create, display, and print customizable, 3D bar, line, area, and pie charts in full-color using spreadsheet data (shown in Figure 19.9). Plus, when it comes to navigating your way around a complex spreadsheet, the app offers a series of highly intuitive sliders, steppers and pop-up menus that makes it easier to work with your numeric data on the phone or tablet's screen.

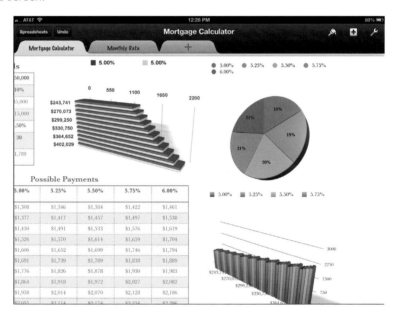

FIGURE 19.9

Create 3D charts from spreadsheet data that look amazing on the iPhone or iPad's display. Charts created in Numbers can be copied and pasted into Pages documents or Keynote presentations, or exported for use in other compatible apps.

When it comes to performing complex mathematical calculations, Numbers has it covered. Built into the app is a calculations engine that can handle more than 250 different functions. When the numbers have been crunched, you can decide exactly how you want to view them in either a spreadsheet, table, or graphical form, and you can customize every aspect of the format you choose.

Like all the iWork for iOS apps, Numbers is fully AirPrint compatible. Before print-ing, you can see an on-screen preview of exactly what a spreadsheet, chart, table or graph will look like. Then, you can format the printed page with headers, foot-ers, and page numbers.

If you're already familiar with the Pages app, the Numbers app (and the Keynote app) offer a very similar user interface and menu layout. Upon launching the Numbers app, you see the Library screen. From here, it's possible to create a new spreadsheet from scratch, rename an existing spreadsheet, open a spreadsheet file that's stored on your iPhone or iPad, or import a spreadsheet from iTunes, iDisk, or WebDAV. (Remember, iCloud file syncing can be automatic.)

By tapping the Edit button that's displayed on the Library screen, you can select a file and then share (export) it via email, iTunes or WebDAV; copy the file into another compatible app; make a copy of the file on the device you're using; or delete the file altogether from your iPhone or iPad.

To open a spreadsheet file, tap on its thumbnail on the app's Library screen. Just like within the Pages app, as you're viewing, creating, or editing a spreadsheet within Numbers, you see a handful of command icons displayed along the top of the screen.

Located near the top-left corner of the screen is the Spreadsheets button. Tap it to return to the Library screen within Numbers. Next to the Spreadsheets button is the Undo button. Tap on it to undo the last action (or last several actions) you per-formed within the app.

Displayed near the top-right corner of the Numbers screen are three command icons (which are similar to what's offered within Pages). These are the Formatting icon (which is shaped like a paintbrush), the Graphics icon (which is shaped like a plus-sign), and the Tools menu icon (which is shaped like a wrench).

THE FORMATTING ICON WITHIN NUMBERS

When you tap the Formatting icon, it reveals a pop-up menu window. However, the command tabs and menu options displayed within this window vary based on the type of data you currently have selected within the spreadsheet.

For example, if you have a headline or text highlighted, the command tabs that are displayed at the top of the menu window are Style, Text, and Arrange. Upon tapping on any of these command tabs, various formatting options are revealed. However, if you have a specific cell within a spreadsheet highlighted, the com-mand tabs displayed are Table, Headers, Cells, and Format, and the command options relate to the number-crunching features of the app.

Likewise, if you have a chart or graph selected when you tap the Formatting icon, you see an entirely different selection of submenus, which you can use for creating and editing 2D or 3D charts and graphics.

ACCESS THE GRAPHICS MENU WITHIN NUMBERS

When you want to import a photo or shape into your spreadsheet, or you want to create a table or chart from scratch, tap the Graphics icon. The pop-up window that appears displays four command tabs at the top: Media, Tables, Charts, and Shapes. Each of these command tabs reveals a separate submenu. Tap the Chart tab (shown in Figure 19.10) to select a chart style and color scheme that you can fully customize.

FIGURE 19.10

Choose between full-color 2D or 3D graphs when you tap on the Graphics menu icon and then the Charts tab.

ACCESS THE TOOLS MENU WITHIN NUMBERS

The Tools menu includes a Share and Print submenu option, along with Find, Settings, and Help features. The menu layout and what's offered here is very similar to what's offered within Pages.

> ✅ **TIP** When you opt to create a document from scratch in Pages, a spreadsheet from scratch in Numbers, or a presentation from scratch in Keynote, the app gives you a selection of templates to choose from. Numbers, for example, offers 16 different templates, including Blank, Checklist, Loan Comparison, Budget, Mortgage Calculator, Expense Report, Invoice, Employee Schedule, and Auto Log. Each template, within each app, is fully customizable.

WORKING WITH THE KEYNOTE APP

When it comes to creating, viewing, and giving presentations using the iPhone or iPad, one of the most powerful tools at your disposal is the Keynote app. Using Keynote, you can create a digital slide show presentation, complete with animated slides and eye-catching transitions. Or, you can import and utilize presentations created on a PC or Mac using Microsoft PowerPoint.

> ✅ **TIP** To give presentations to groups, you might want to check out the Keynote Remote app ($0.99). It enables you to wirelessly control a Keynote presentation running on your Mac, iPad, iPhone or iPod touch (that's connected to an LCD projector via a cable, for example) from another iPad, iPhone, or iPod touch in the room, as long as both devices are connected to the same wireless network.

Keynote enables you to create, animate, and display visually impressive 3D bar, line, area, and pie charts within your presentations, in addition to using text, shapes, graphic images (clip art), and/or photos to get your points across within each slide.

Keynote also includes a handful of visually impressive slide animations and animated slide transition effects.

> ❗ **CAUTION** When importing a PowerPoint presentation into Keynote, or exporting a Keynote presentation to PowerPoint, you may experience partial file incompatibility issues if the fonts, animations and/or slide transitions used within the presentation are not available on both the computer and iOS mobile device.
>
> During the import or export process, the Keynote app will attempt to compensate and automatically replace these elements with fonts, animations and slide transitions that are compatible, but you'll want to manually check to insure that the changes made are acceptable and didn't impact slide formatting. When import problems arise, for example, a Presentation Import Warnings screen is displayed (as shown in Figure 19.11)

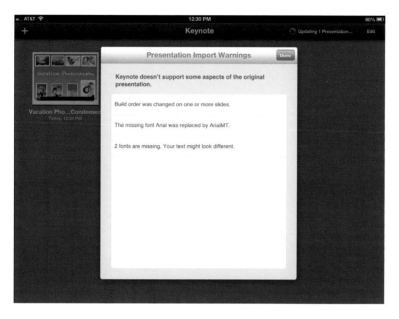

FIGURE 19.11

Sometimes, when you import or export a PowerPoint presentation into Keynote on the iPhone or iPad, some fonts, slide transitions and animations are not supported. The app attempts to automatically compensation for this, but makes you aware of the problem(s).

The functionality available from the Library screen of the app (when it's launched) allows you to create a new presentation from scratch; rename an existing presentation; import (Copy) a presentation from iTunes or WebDAV; email a presentation to someone else; export a presentation to iTunes or WebDAV; copy a presentation to another app; or make a copy of the presentation on your iPhone or iPad and save it with a new filename. You can also delete a presentation from your iOS mobile device.

It's from the Library screen that you can also load an existing Keynote or PowerPoint presentation in order to view or edit it. Tap any presentation thumbnail to load it from the iPhone or iPad's internal storage into the app.

> **NOTE** Just as with Pages and Numbers, iCloud integration is built into Keynote. After you initially set it up, the integration works automatically, in the background, to make sure all of your presentation files are synchronized between your iPhone, iPad, and the computers that are linked to the same iCloud account.
>
> While the Keynote app is available for the Mac (sold separately), you can also export your Keynote presentations into Microsoft PowerPoint format and then load them into PowerPoint that's running on a PC.

After you begin creating or editing a Keynote presentation, the now familiar command icons from the other iWork for iOS apps are displayed along the top of the Keynote screen.

Tap the Presentations button to return to the Library screen of the app. Use the Undo button (displayed to the immediate right of the Presentations button) to undo the last action you took using the app. The presentation's filename that you're working with is displayed near the top-center of the screen.

Near the upper-right corner of the Keynote screen are four command icons, including the Formatting, Graphics, Tools, and Play icons. As you can see in Figure 19.12, the thumbnails for each slide in your presentation are displayed along the left margin of the screen while you're creating or editing slides.

FIGURE 19.12

You can change the order of slides by using your finger to drag their thumbnails (displayed along the left margin of the screen) up or down.

THE FORMATTING TOOLS WITHIN KEYNOTE

When you tap the Formatting icon (the paintbrush) within Keynote, you see three command tabs: Style, Text, and Arrange. Each reveals a separate submenu used for formatting text within slides. For example, from the Style command tab, you can change the appearance of text, including font and background colors, borders, shadows, and other effects.

The Text command tab offers menu options for choosing a font, type size, typestyle, and justification, among other things. Tap the Arrange tab to access the Move to Back/Front feature to create layers within a slide. You can also adjust text alignment, adjust spacing, or add multiple columns to a slide.

However, if a graphic or photo is selected within a slide, the paintbrush icon reveals the Style and Arrange tabs, which offer commands used for customizing the appearance of graphics and photos.

THE GRAPHICS TOOLS WITHIN KEYNOTE

Just like in the other iWork for iOS apps, tapping the Graphics icon enables you to import photos or shapes into a slide, create or modify tables, or create colorful 2D or 3D charts, depending on which command tab you tap.

ACCESSING THE TOOLS MENU WITHIN KEYNOTE

From the Tools menu within Keynote, you can access the Share and Print, Find, Help features (which are similar to the what's found in Pages and Numbers).

The Tools pop-up window also reveals a Transitions and Builds submenu used to add animations to individual slides or to establish slide transition effects for the presentation (as shown in Figure 19.13). There's also a Presenter Notes feature that enables you to compose and later view notes to yourself as you're giving the presentation.

FIGURE 19.13

Keynote offers many built-in slide animations and transitions.

The Advanced menu option enables you to automatically number each slide in the presentation, add on-screen guidelines when formatting your slides, incorporate interactive hyperlinks into slides, set up a presentation type, turn on and off the Loop presentation or self-playing features, and turn on or off the Enable Remotes feature (also used when giving a presentation).

THE PLAY ICON WITHIN KEYNOTE

The Play icon (the right-pointing arrow) is used to transition the Keynote app from the slide creation and edit mode to the app's presentation mode. Tap it to display your presentation in full-screen mode. You can use the iPad's AirPlay feature (or optional cables) to showcase the presentation on an HD television, monitor, or LCD projector.

USING THE iWORK FOR iPAD APPS WITH iCLOUD

After you set up a free iCloud account (see Chapter 6, "Sync and Share Files Using iCloud"), you can set up Pages, Numbers, and Keynote to automatically sync documents and files with your other Mac and iOS devices via iCloud.

For each of the iWork for iOS apps, the iCloud functionality needs to be set up separately. However, after you've set it up, as long as your iPhone or iPad has access to the Internet, changes you make to a document or file are reflected almost instantly on your Mac and other iOS devices.

Like Contacts, Calendar, Reminders and Notes, Pages, Numbers, and Keynote are among the apps that offer automatic iCloud integration and file synchronization that works behind the scenes.

To set up Pages, Numbers, and Keynote on your iPad to work with iCloud, follow these steps:

1. After installing Pages, Numbers, and Keynote onto your iPhone or iPad, launch Settings.

2. Tap the iCloud option.

3. At the top of the iCloud screen, turn on iCloud functionality, and enter your Apple ID and password.

4. Also on the iCloud menu screen within Settings, tap the Documents & Data option.

5. When the Documents & Data screen is displayed, tap the virtual switch associated with the Documents & Data option to turn it on. If you want your iPhone or iPad to automatically sync your iWork for iOS documents and files

using a 3G or 4G cellular network (as opposed to Wi-Fi), turn on the virtual switch that's associated with the Use Cellular option. Otherwise, to only sync files and data when your iPhone or iPad is connected to the Internet using a Wi-Fi connection, leave the Use Cellular option in the default off position. (This applies only to the iPhone and iPads capable of accessing a 3G or 4G data network.)

6. If you have Pages installed on your iPhone or iPad, return to the main Settings menu and scroll down to the Pages option. Tap on it.

7. When the Pages menu screen appears within Settings (shown in Figure 19.14), tap the virtual switch that's associated with the Use iCloud feature to turn on the auto file syncing feature with iCloud that kicks in each time the Pages app is launched. Repeat steps 6 and 7 for the Numbers and Keynote apps, if applicable.

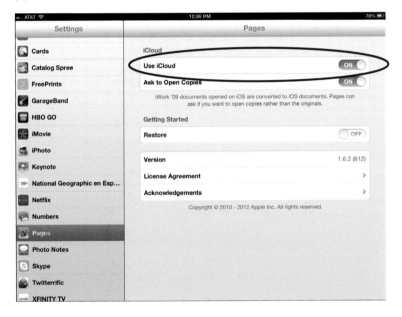

FIGURE 19.14
In addition to turning on the Documents & Data feature from the iCloud menu screen within Settings, you also need to turn on the iCloud feature for Pages, Numbers, or Keynote separately.

8. Repeat this process on each of your other iOS devices that you have Pages, Numbers, and Keynote installed on, including your iPhone, iPad and/or your iPod touch.

9. On your Mac, launch System Preferences.

10. From the System Preferences menu, click the iCloud icon (displayed under the Internet & Wireless heading).

11. When the iCloud window appears, make sure you sign into iCloud using the same account username and password as you used on your iPad (and other iOS devices).

12. On the right side of the iCloud window (on your Mac), add a check mark to the checkbox associated with the Documents & Data option.

13. Within the Pages, Numbers, and Keynote software running on your Mac, turn on the iCloud functionality for each program.

When you begin experiencing the word processing capabilities of Pages, the number-crunching functionality of Numbers, and the digital-slide creation and viewing tools offered by Keynote on your iPad, and combine these capabilities with the iPhone or iPad's long battery life and other functionality, you'll see why so many businesspeople are incorporating the iWork for iOS apps into their daily work lives, instead of carrying around a heavier and more cumbersome laptop computer (with a shorter battery life) and using word processing, spreadsheet and/or digital slide presentation software on it.

> **✓ TIP** Once you have your Pages, Numbers or Keynote documents and files being syncing with iCloud, from any computer or Internet-enabled mobile device, you can access your documents or files online by visiting www.iCloud.com, signing into this website using your Apple ID and password (or iCloud username and password), and then clicking on the iWork icon.
>
> Displayed at the top of the screen will be three command tabs, labeled Keynote, Pages and Number. Tap on any of these tabs to access any of your app-specific documents or files. Then, click on the thumbnail for the document or file you want to download and work with on the computer (or device) you're currently using.

Appendix A

TAKE ADVANTAGE OF THE PASSBOOK APP AND DISCOVER OTHER AWESOME THINGS YOUR iOS DEVICE CAN DO

One of the new apps Apple added to iOS 6 is called Passbook. It's an iPhone-only app that's designed to manage electronic airline boarding passes, movie, show and sporting event tickets, store rewards cards, and digital retail coupons—all from a single app.

For the Passbook app to function, it must be used in conjunction with one or more third-party apps. Plus, it's necessary to have your iPhone's Location Service functionality turned on for use with this app.

As of late-October, only a handful of companies were supporting Passbook functionality. Each company is using it in a slightly different way in order to interact with iPhone users who are their customers.

For example, American Airlines and United Airlines have added Passbook integration into their iPhone apps. Thus, once you load your electronic boarding pass into your phone, it will appear on your phone's display when you arrive at the airport and need to check in. Currently, this option is only available at certain airports, however.

Likewise, when you purchase movie tickets online using the Fandango Movies app, when you arrive at a participating theater, the electronic movie ticket will be displayed automatically on your iPhone's screen, and can be scanned by the box office or ticket taker.

The Live Nation and Ticketmaster apps also allow you to purchase tickets online for sporting events, concerts and live shows from your iPhone, and then store your electronic tickets within the app. A growing number of major venues now have the ability to scan your electronic ticket right from your iPhone's screen. (Just make sure your phone's battery doesn't die before you reach the venue.)

Companies like Starbuck allow you to build up rewards and pay for your food and beverage purchases using a digital edition of a Starbucks pre-paid card, which is stored within the official Starbucks app.

Meanwhile, Walgreens and Target are among the first companies to integrate Passbook functionality into their apps so you can access online coupons, refill prescriptions, or track earned rewards for purchases.

When you launch the Passbook app for the first time, make sure your iPhone has Internet access, and then tap on the App Store button that's displayed near the bottom of the screen. This launches the iTunes app and allows you to view and download free apps from companies with proprietary apps that offer Passbook integration.

> **NOTE** By the time you read this, Apple Stores will offer Passbook integration through the official Apple Store app. Among other things, this feature will allow you to quickly pay for in-store purchases using credit or debit card information that's linked with the app on your iPhone.

In the months and years to come, companies will innovate new ways to interact with their customers by taking advantage of Passbook functionality, combined with the iPhone's Location Services feature. However, this functionality and technology is still in its infancy.

THERE'S SO MUCH MORE YOUR iPHONE OR iPAD CAN DO

Much of this book has focused on ways to use your iPhone or iPad in conjunction with the apps that come preinstalled with iOS 6, as well as a wide range of third-party apps that can dramatically enhance the functionality of your iOS mobile device.

Keep in mind, however, a vast selection of optional accessories are currently available for your iPhone or iPad, that can be used in conjunction with apps to also greatly expand what's possible. Plus, through wireless connectivity (via a home network or the Internet), you can link your iPhone or iPad with other devices.

Here are just a few examples of what's possible:

- Using a wireless home network or the Internet, you can control the Nest thermostat in your home ($249.00, www.nest.com). This intelligent and programmable thermostat also learns from your living habits and automatically finds ways to save you money on your utility bills, while keeping your home at a comfortable temperature while you're there.

- Whether you're concerned about home security, or want to keep tabs on your kids, infant (and nanny/babysitter), or pets while you're away from your house, a handful of wireless baby monitor and security cameras are available that can be controlled from the iPhone or iPad via the Internet. As a result, you can see and hear what's going on in your home, in real-time, from your iOS device's screen. The SmartBaby monitor from Withings ($299.00, www.withings.com/en/babymonitor) and the iBaby Monitor from iBaby Labs ($199.95, http://ibabylabs.com/ibabymonitor) are two products available for this purpose.

- For kids, teens, and those who are young at heart, a handful of companies offer remote control cars, hovercrafts, helicopters, and other vehicles that can be controlled wirelessly via an iPhone or iPad. You'll find these toys at Brookstone stores (www.brookstone.com) and high-end toy stores.

- Hasbro Toys has taken the popular laser tag game and has given it a high-tech twist by building a housing for the iPhone 3GS, iPhone 4, iPhone 4S or iPod Touch into its Lazer Tag blasters (www.lazertag.com/en-us). By downloading free game apps to use with the blasters, the iOS device super imposes aliens and enemies over what can be viewed in the "real world" as you're playing Lazer Tag. The end-result in a really awesome, cutting-edge, single or multiplayer game that takes place in the real-world (inside or outside), but incorporates interactivity and augmented reality using the Lazer Tag blaster and iPhone/iPod touch. The price is $39.99 for a one blaster pack, or $74.99 for a two blaster pack.

- For getting work done while on-the-go, Brookstone has introduced a wide range of battery-powered accessories for the iPhone or iPad, including a portable scanner, portable projector, external keyboards, external battery packs and wireless (Bluetooth) speakers. Visit www.brookstone.com for information about this company's latest accessory offerings.

- If you're a musician, a wide range companies offer optional microphones, specialized apps, and proprietary adapters for connecting instruments directly to the phone or tablet, allowing you to create a professional-quality recording studio almost anywhere. iRig from IK Multimedia ($39.99, www.ikmultimedia.com) is one product that can be used to connect an instrument directly to your iOS mobile device. Beyond using the optional GarageBand app to record music, many other apps are available for serious musicians, that are designed for composing, recording, editing/mixing and performing music.

- If you're more comfortable handwriting on your iPhone or iPad's screen, as opposed to typing using the virtual keyboard, or dictating text using your voice, a growing number of apps support a stylus, and allow you to handwrite (or draw) on the screen. A basic stylus can be purchased for under $30.00. Visit www.stylusshop.com to see a sampling of what's available. However, for applications (such as drawing or photo editing) that require more precision, a more advanced, pressure-sensitive stylus, such as the Pogo Connect, is available ($79.95, www.tenonedesign.com/connect).

- Nike offers a selection of running shoes and a monitoring device, called the Nike+ FuelBand (http://nikeplus.nike.com/plus/products/fuelband), which is worn on your wrist. When used with your iPhone or iPad, these tools can help you stay fit and/or lose weight. Thanks to Nike+ technology, the running shoes and FuelBand device link wirelessly to your iOS mobile device, allowing you can track your progress and achieve your fitness or weight loss goals faster.

And that's just the beginning. Companies in many different industries have begun inventing unique iPhone or iPad accessories that transform the way we handle everyday tasks and/or that can provide your iOS mobile device with dramatically enhanced functionality.

While Apple may have just released the iPhone 5 and 3rd generation iPad, for example, the ways other companies are utilizing this technology in conjunction with proprietary accessories is only in its infancy. As English poet and playwright Robert Browning once said (back in the 1800s), "The best is yet to come!"

Index

O

P

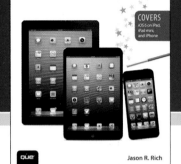

Your purchase of *iPad and iPhone Tips and Tricks (Covers iOS 6 on iPad, iPad mini, and iPhone)* includes access to a free online edition for 45 days through the **Safari Books Online** subscription service. Nearly every Que book is available online through **Safari Books Online**, along with thousands of books and videos from publishers such as Addison-Wesley Professional, Cisco Press, Exam Cram, IBM Press, O'Reilly Media, Prentice Hall, Sams, and VMware Press.

Safari Books Online is a digital library providing searchable, on-demand access to thousands of technology, digital media, and professional development books and videos from leading publishers. With one monthly or yearly subscription price, you get unlimited access to learning tools and information on topics including mobile app and software development, tips and tricks on using your favorite gadgets, networking, project management, graphic design, and much more.

Activate your FREE Online Edition at
informit.com/safarifree

STEP 1: Enter the coupon code: FITANXA.

STEP 2: New Safari users, complete the brief registration form.
Safari subscribers, just log in.

If you have difficulty registering on Safari or accessing the online edition,
please e-mail customer-service@safaribooksonline.com